Shades of the Planet

Shades of the Planet

AMERICAN LITERATURE AS WORLD LITERATURE

Edited by

Wai Chee Dimock and Lawrence Buell

PRINCETON UNIVERSITY PRESS

PRINCETON AND OXFORD

Copyright © 2007 by Princeton University Press
Published by Princeton University Press, 41 William Street,
Princeton, New Jersey 08540
In the United Kingdom: Princeton University Press, 3 Market Place,
Woodstock, Oxfordshire OX20 1SY

Library of Congress Cataloging-in-Publication Data

Shades of the planet: American literature as world literature / edited by Wai Chee Dimock
and Lawrence Buell.
 p. cm.
Includes bibliographical references and index.
Contents: Global and Babel : language and planet in American literature / Jonathan Arac —
The deterritorialization of American literature / Paul Giles — Unthinking manifest destiny :
Muslim modernities on three continents / Susan Stanford Friedman — Mr. Styron's planet /
Eric J. Sundquist — Planetary circles : Philip Roth, Emerson, Kundera / Ross Posnock —
World-bank drama / Joseph Roach — Global minoritarian culture / Homi K. Bhabha —
Atlantic to Pacific: James, Todorov, Blackmur, and intercontinental form / David Palumbo-
Liu — Ecoglobalist affects : The emergence of U.S. environmental imagination on a planetary
scale / Lawrence Buell —
At the borders of American crime fiction / Rachel Adams — African, Caribbean, American :
Black English as creole tongue / Wai Chee Dimock.
    ISBN-13: 978-0-691-12851-1 (cloth : acid-free paper)
    ISBN-10: 0-691-12851-0 (cloth : acid-free paper)
    ISBN-13: 978-0-691-12852-8 (pbk. : acid-free paper)
    ISBN-10: 0-691-12852-9 (pbk. : acid-free paper)
    1. American literature—History and criticism. 2. American literature—Foreign influences.
3. Boundaries in literature. 4. Globalization in literature. 5. Geography in literature.
6. Multiculturalism in literature. I. Dimock, Wai-chee, 1953– II. Buell, Lawrence.
PS157.A45 2007
810.9—dc22   2006046073

British Library Cataloging-in-Publication Data is available

This book has been composed in Goudy and KochAntiqua display

Printed on acid-free paper. ∞

press.princeton.edu

Printed in the United States of America

10 9 8 7 6 5 4 3 2 1

Contents

Shades of the Planet

Planet and America, Set and Subset

Wai Chee Dimock

WHAT EXACTLY IS "AMERICAN LITERATURE"? Is it a sovereign domain, self-sustained and self-governing, integral as a body of evidence? Or is it less autonomous than that, not altogether freestanding, but more like a municipality: a second-tier phenomenon, resting on a platform preceding it and encompassing it, and dependent on the latter for its infrastructure, its support network, its very existence as a subsidiary unit?

This jurisdictional language is meant to highlight American literature as a constituted domain and the variously imagined *ground* for its constitution. That ground, though methodologically crucial, is often left implicit. On what footing can the field call itself a field, and according to what integrating principle? What degree of self-determination can it lay claim to? And what does it have in common with the territorial jurisdiction whose name it bears, whose clear-cut borders contain an attribute we are tempted to call "American-ness"?

After the World Trade Center, and after Katrina, few of us are under the illusion that the United States is sovereign in any absolute sense. The nation seems to have come literally "unbundled" before our eyes, its fabric of life torn apart by extremist militant groups, and by physical forces of even greater scope, wrought by climate change and the intensified hurricane cycles. Territorial sovereignty, we suddenly realize, is no more than a legal fiction, a man-made fiction. This fiction is not honored by religious adherents who have a different vision of the world; nor is it honored by the spin of hurricanes accelerated by the thermodynamics of warming oceans.[1] In each case, the nation is revealed to be what it is: an epiphenomenon, literally a superficial construct, a set of erasable lines on the face of the earth. It is no match for that grounded entity called the planet, which can wipe out those lines at a moment's notice, using weapons of mass destruction more powerful than any homeland defense.

"Globalization" is the familiar term used to describe this unraveling of national sovereignty. This process, seemingly inevitable, has been diagnosed in almost antithetical ways. On the one hand, theorists from Michael Walzer to Jürgen Habermas see an enormous potential in the decline of the nation-state; for them, this jurisdictional form, historically monopolizing violence, and now increasingly outmoded, must give way to other forms of human association: a "global civil society," a "postnational constellation."[2] On the other hand, theorists such as Fredric Jameson caution against such optimism, pointing to the "McDonaldization" of the world, a regime of standardization and homogenization ushered in by the erosion of national borders, presided over by global capital and the "unchallenged primacy of the United States."[3]

What Katrina dramatizes, however, is a form of "globalization" different from either scenario. Not benign, it is at the same time not predicated on the primacy of any nation. Long accustomed to seeing itself as the de facto center of the world—the military superpower, the largest economy, and the moral arbiter to boot—the United States suddenly finds itself downgraded to something considerably less. "It's like being in a Third World country," Mitch Handler, a manager in Louisiana's biggest public hospital, said to the Associated Press about the plight of hurricane victims.[4] This Third-Worlding of a superpower came with a shock not only to Louisiana and Mississippi but to unbelieving eyes everywhere. Not the actor but the acted upon, the United States is simply the spot where catastrophe hits, the place on the map where large-scale forces, unleashed elsewhere, come home to roost. What does it mean for the United States to be on the receiving end of things?[5] The experience is novel, mind-shattering in many ways, and a numbing patriotism is not incompatible with a numbing shame. To the rest of the world, however, this massive systemic failure confirms their view of the United States not only as a miscreant abroad—a "rogue nation" both in its rejection of the Kyoto Protocol and in its conduct of the Iraq War—but as one equally inept at home, falling far below an acceptable standard of care for its own citizens.[6] Scale enlargement has stripped from this nation any dream of unchallenged primacy. If Europe has already been "provincialized"—has been revealed to be a smaller player in world history than previously imagined, as Dipesh Chakrabarty argues—the United States seems poised to follow suit.[7]

In this context, it seems important to rethink the adequacy of a nation-based paradigm. Is "American" an adjective that can stand on its own, uninflected, unentangled, and unconstrained? Can an autonomous field be built on its chronology and geography, equal to the task of phenomenal description and causal explanation? Janice Radway, in her presidential address to the American Studies Association in 1998, answers with a resounding "no," and proposes a name change for the association for just that reason. A field calling itself "American" imagines that there is something exceptional about the United States, manifesting itself as "a distinctive set of properties and themes in all things American, whether individuals, institutions, or cultural products."[8] This premise of exceptionalism translates into a methodology that privileges the nation above all else. The field can legitimize itself as a field only because the nation does the legitimizing. The disciplinary sovereignty of the former owes everything to the territorial sovereignty of the latter. Against this conflation of nation and field, Radway proposes a rigorous decoupling, a methodology predicated on the *noncoincidence* between the two. The nation has solid borders; the field, on the other hand, is fluid and amorphous, shaped and reshaped by emerging forces, by "intricate interdependencies" between "the near and far, the local and the distant."[9] In short, as a domain of inquiry, the "Americanist" field needs to be kept emphatically distinct from the nation. Its vitality resides in a carefully maintained and carefully theorized zone, a penumbra intervening between it and the conceptual foreclosure dictated by its name. That penumbra makes the field a continuum rather than a container:

> It suggests that far from being conceived on the model of a container—that is, as a particular kind of hollowed out object with evident edges or skin enclosing certain organically uniform contents—territories and geographies need to be reconceived as spatially-situated and intricately intertwined networks of social relationships that tie specific locales to particular histories.[10]

Radway's challenge to the "container" model turns the United States from a discrete entity into a porous network, with no tangible edges, its circumference being continually negotiated, its criss-crossing pathways continually modified by local input, local inflections. These dynamic exchanges suggest that the American field has never been unified, and will never be.[11] Still, though not unified, the nation remains central for Radway: it is a first-order phenomenon, a primary field of inquiry. If it is no longer a "hollowed out object" filled with contents unique to it and homogenized within it, it remains a *disciplinary* object second to none, conceptually front and center, and naturalizing itself as the methodological baseline, a set of founding coordinates, reproducing its boundaries in the very boundaries of the field.

What sort of distortion comes with this nation-centered mapping? And how best to rectify it? The essays collected here implicitly engage these questions, trying out various paradigms not U.S.-centric. Rather than taking the nation as the default position, the totality we automatically reach for, we come up with alternate geographies that deny it this totalizing function. Forging such geographies might be one of the most critical tasks now facing the field.[12] How best to fashion a domain of inquiry not replicating the terms of territorial sovereignty? What landscape would emerge then? And what would American literature look like when traced through these redrawn and realigned entities?

The language of set and subset is especially helpful here as a heuristic guide.[13] While that language can sometimes conjure up a hierarchical ordering of part to whole, its interest for us lies in a different direction: not in stratification, but in modularization. What it highlights is the strategic breakup of a continuum, the carving of it into secondary units, and the premises and consequences attending that process. For units are not given but made. They are not an objective fact in the world, but an artifact, a postulate, aggregated as such for some particular purpose. Their lengths and widths, the size of their grouping, their criteria of selection, the platforms they rest on—all of these can be differently specified. Each specifying throws into relief a different kind of entity: mapped on a different scale, performing a different function, implementing a different set of membership criteria. And looming over all of these is the long-standing, still evolving, and always to be theorized relation between each unit and the larger continuum. A language of set and subset, in short, allows us to "modularize" the world into smaller entities: able to stand provisionally and do analytic work, but not self-contained, not fully sovereign, resting continually and nontrivially on a platform more robust and more extensive.

"American literature" is best understood as a subset in this sense. The field does stand to be classified apart, as a nameable and adducible unit. It is taxonomically useful as an entity. At the same time, that taxonomic usefulness should not lure us into thinking that this entity is natural, that its shape and size will hold all the way up and all the way down, staying intact regardless of circumstance, not varying with specifying frames. On the contrary, what we nominate as "American literature" is simply an effect of that nomination, which is to say, it is epiphenomenal, domain-specific, binding only at one register and extending no farther than that register. Once it is transposed, its membership will change also, going up or down with the ascending or descending scales of aggregation.[14] And, across those scales, at every level of redescription, it can be folded back into a larger continuum from which it has only been momentarily set apart.

In *Gödel, Escher, Bach* (1979), Douglas Hofstadter discusses these ascending and descending scales and their intricate enfolding as "recursive structures and processes," to be found not only in mathematics, the visual arts, and music, but also in domains still more elementary: the grammar of languages, the geometry of the branches of trees, even particle physics. What all of these have in common is the phenomenon of "nesting": a generative process that modulates continually from the outside to the inside, from the background to the foreground, with several units, differently scaled, reciprocally cradling one another and overlapping with one another, creating an ever wider circumference as well as an ever greater recessional depth. Rather than proceeding as a straight line, recursive structures and processes give us a reversible landscape that can be either convex or concave, either bulging out or burrowing in, sometimes pivoted on the smallest embedded unit and sometimes radiating out to take in the largest embedding circumference. Hofstadter calls this reversible hierarchy a *heterarchy*. "The whole world is built out of recursion," he says.[15] This entanglement between inner and outer limits allows entities to snowball, with each feedback loop generating an "increasing complexity of behavior," so much so that "suitably recursive systems might be strong enough to break out of any predetermined patterns," modifying the input to such an extent that the outcome becomes utterly unpredictable. Such unpredictability, Hofstadter adds, "probably lies at the heart of intelligence."[16]

We explore the intelligence of American literature in just this light, as the unpredictable outcome stemming from the interplay between encapsulation and its undoing: between the modularity of the subset and an infinite number of larger aggregates that might count as its embedding "set." What are some of these aggregates? They are uncharted and uncataloged for the most part. One thing is clear, though. In order for American literature to be nested in them, these aggregates would have to rest on a platform broader and more robustly empirical than the relatively arbitrary and demonstrably ephemeral borders of the nation. They require alternate geographies, alternate histories. At their most capacious, they take their measure from the durations and extensions of the human species itself, folding in American literature as one fold among others, to be unfolded and refolded into our collective fabric.

Gayatri Chakravorty Spivak and Paul Gilroy have proposed the term "planet" as one aggregate that might do this work of enfolding. In *Death of a Discipline* (2003), Spivak argues that "planetarity" is a term worth exploring precisely because it is an unknown quantum, barely intimated, not yet adequate to the meaning we would like it to bear, and stirring for just that reason. It stands as a horizon impossible to define, and hospitable in that impossibility. Its very sketchiness makes it a "catachresis for inscribing collective responsibility," for that sketchiness preserves a space for phenomena as yet emerging, not quite in sight.[17] In *After Empire* (2004), Paul Gilroy also invokes the "planet" in this loose-fitting sense. The concept can be helpful only in the optative mood, as a generative principle fueled by its less than actualized status. For its heuristic value lies in its not having come into being: it is a habitat still waiting for its inhabitants, waiting for a humanity that has yet to be born, yet to be wrested from a seemingly boundless racism.[18]

What are the consequences of invoking the planet, in its actualized and unactualized dimensions, as a research program? What practical difficulties might arise? What professional training is required? And what sort of creatures would literary scholars have to become to be practitioners of this new craft? It is helpful here to turn to another presidential address, delivered by Philip Curtin to the American Historical Association in 1983, one that eerily speaks to the current situation. Entitled "Depth, Span, and Relevance," this presidential address zeroes in on the very question of professional training. "The discipline of history has broadened in the postwar decades, but historians have not," Curtin observes. "We teach the history of Africa and Asia, but specialists in American history know no more about the history of Africa than their predecessors did in the 1940s."[19] Nor is Africa alone terra incognito in the minds of scholars. Europe, it seems, is also a dark continent: "Americanists know less European history than they did thirty years ago."[20] Expertise so narrowly defined has serious consequences for the field as a whole. Americanists seem to have forgotten "that one of the prime values of a liberal education is breadth, not narrow specialization. Even before the explosion of new kinds of historical knowledge, historical competence required a balance between deep mastery of a particular field and a span of knowledge over other fields of history. Depth was necessary to discover and validate the evidence. Span was necessary to know what kind of evidence to look for—and to make some sense of it, once discovered."[21]

The elimination of "span" as a scholarly requirement undermines the work of Americanists in the most basic way. For one thing, it arbitrarily restricts the database, limiting it to a national archive. This foreclosing of evidence makes the modularity of the field deceptively absolute: it is a distorting lens in some cases, a fatal pair of blinkers in others. Jerry Fodor, one of the leading cognitive scientists of the twentieth century, and best known for his work on the "modularity of mind," nonetheless sees fit to warn us against what he sees as a "characteristic pathology" of modular thinking:

> It is worth emphasizing a sense in which modular processing is *ipso facto* irrational. After all, by definition modular processing means arriving at conclusions by attending to arbitrarily less than all of the evidence that is relevant and/or by considering arbitrarily fewer than all of the hypotheses that might reasonably be true. . . . Informational encapsulation is economical; it buys speed and the reduction of the computational load by, in effect, delimiting *a priori* the data base and the space of candidate solutions that get surveyed in the course of problem solving. But the price of economy is warrant. The more encapsulated the cognitive mechanism that mediates the fixation of your beliefs, the worse is your evidence for the beliefs that you have.[22]

To take just one example of such undue encapsulation, slavery, so often studied only within the geography and chronology of the United States, becomes a virtually unrecognizable phenomenon when it is taken outside these space and time coordinates. Curtin's own classic study, *The Rise and Fall of the Plantation Complex* (1990), dramatizes the conceptual broadening that comes with this broadening of the evidentiary ground, giving us a history that does indeed try to collect data from the long human sojourn on the planet.

By "plantation complex," Curtin refers to "an economic and political order centering on slave plantations in the New World tropics."[23] The phenomenon cannot be confined to the United States, since "many of the trade goods to buy African slaves came from India, and silver to buy these same Indian goods came from mainland South America." Though slavery did evolve to become a distinctly American institution, its tributary and circulatory networks were exogenous, extending to Africa, Europe, as well as Asia. This geographical spread must, in turn, be complemented by a long history, for the "origins of this economic complex lay much further back in time. Its earliest clear forerunner was the group of plantations that began growing sugarcane in the eastern Mediterranean at the time of the European crusades into the Levant. These plantations, like their successors, produced mainly for a distant market in Europe, thus becoming the center for a widespread commercial network."[24]

The space and time coordinates needed to understand slavery are five continents and some thirteen hundred years. Curtin's first chapter—"The Mediterranean Origins"—begins with "the rise of Islam after about 700 A.D."[25] The rise of this Afro-Eurasian civilization means that "the old intercommunicating zone of the Indian Ocean came into much closer contact with the southern Mediterranean. As a result, a whole range of new crops from the Asian tropics began to be grown in the Mediterranean basin." Among these, one that would soon rise to world-historical importance was sugarcane: "Europe's contact with sugarcane began at the time of the Crusades, Europe's first intense contact with the Muslim world. It was an impressive discovery for people whose only source of sugar was honey."[26]

That impressiveness was not only a matter of taste, for sugar also had a unique economic value. "Once concentrated, cane sugar products had a high value-to-bulk ratio. This meant that they could be transported for long distances, especially by relatively cheap water transport, and still sold at a profit. Economically, therefore, sugar could enter long-distance trade over far greater distances than wheat, rice, or other starchy staples in common use." With the discovery of sugar, the star ingredient of a world economy was found. Once the Europeans seized control of the Muslim-owned sugar production already flourishing in the Levant, the stage was set for a "plantation complex" with its four requisite features: slave labor on the plantations; maritime trade routes; European capitalization; and long-distance markets. Cotton and coffee would later be added as variations on this theme, but sugar was its first prototype. These fourfold ingredients would be reworked and retooled as they migrated from the Mediterranean to the Atlantic, to the Pacific, and back to the Indian Ocean, linking Asia, Europe, Africa, and the two Americas as circulatory networks on a terraqueous globe. This is as encompassing a "set" as one can hope for. Slavery in the United States is very much its subset, caught up in this large-scale world history. Curtin writes: "The North American segment of the plantation complex is hard to understand if it is merely seen in the context of U.S. history. The origins of the plantation complex antedate Columbus's voyages, and it lasted elsewhere long after its end in the United States."[27]

Given this large-scale history, the *prenational* emerges, along with the *postnational*, as two domains of evidence that cannot simply be written off the temporal map, falling as they do on either side of the nation, bearing a diacritical relation to it. This transnational axis dissolves the field's autonomized chronology, meshing it with a continuum still evolving, and stretching as indefinitely into the past as it does into the future. There are many levels of aggregation here—many "sets"—to which U.S. history might be reintegrated as a subset. These aggregates, by their very nature, require alternate geographies—a span of five continents, no less—a world atlas of which the national map is inextricably a part. These are the longitudes and latitudes needed in order to examine U.S. history as a "nested" phenomenon, cradled by the history of the world. It is a staggering research program, beyond the competence of most of us. Curtin writes: "Historians of the medieval Mediterranean, of Africa, of Latin America, of Europe, and of the United States all deal with parts or aspects of the complex, but they rarely try to see it as a whole."[28]

What is true of history is equally true of literature. The planet stands here too as a cradle—a set that describes and redescribes its subsets—and one that puts an impossible burden on the Americanist trying to come to terms with its daunting amplitude. The essays gathered here face up to that burden and try to parse it on two fronts. On the one hand, we see the unactualized (and perhaps unactualizable) dimensions of the planet as a justification for modular analysis, though without undue encapsulation. The trick is to come up with well-defined projects that are, at the same time, entry points to a broad continuum. On the other hand, the interest of that broad continuum is such that we also see it as a cognitive horizon in its own right, a challenge to all of us to rethink the institutional landscape of the university: the division of the academic fields, the professional training required of each, and the claims and limits of American literature as a field of knowledge, as yet to be theorized, not to be automatically equated with the nation.

We begin with "Global and Babel," Jonathan Arac's attempt to drive a wedge between nation and field by way of the multitudes of tongues. The languages of American literature are a subset of the languages of the world; they take their cue not from their membership in a nation, but from their membership in a universe of tongues. For Arac, this transational "set" realigns American English, and realigns as well the protocol for language requirements in graduate training. Drawing on the work of Edward Said and Gayatri Spivak, he argues for a remapping of the disciplinary boundaries of three fields—American studies, area studies, and comparative literature—both as a template for a new practice of close reading and as an ambitious ground plan for curricular reform. How many languages should a doctoral student in American literature be required to learn, and which ones in particular? Arac comes up with an intriguing number and one highly unlikely candidate, while arguing at the same time that the emphasis of language instruction should fall less on mastering a "high cultural accent" and more on a degree of familiarity with the street vernacular, "flawed and irrevocably marked by one's own English."[29] Rather than mastering the world as the master language, American English is in fact foreign sounding to most human populations. It is helpful for our own education to acknowledge that fact in reverse.

For Arac, foreign words embedded in American literature turn this body of material from a modular unit into part of a continuum, folded into a transnational babel. This enfolding of the outside and the inside is crucial to all the essays in this collection. In the hands of Paul Giles, it emerges as a methodological argument directed against our tendency to integrate the field on the basis of the nation's territorial integrity. In "The Deterritorialization of American Literature," Giles points out that the geographical borders of the discipline are not a given, and not a constant. They must be seen against a history of their operating environments, against "other kinds of geographical projection, of the kinds found in cartography and other forms of mapping," and, even more crucially, against various social, political, and economic forces with a vested interest in stipulating (or not stipulating) those borders. Beginning with the early years of the republic, and tracing a series of transformations extending through the presidency of Jimmy Carter, Giles argues that the identification of American literature "with the current geographical boundaries of the United States is a formulation that should be seen as confined to relatively limited and specific time in history," roughly from 1865 to 1980. American literature as a spatially determinate set is a thing of the past. For Giles, deterritorialization is both salutary and necessary in order to integrate the field into a larger research program.

The articulate shapes of that research program are, of course, very much an open question. Some of its lineaments can already be traced, however, in Susan Stanford Friedman's essay, "Unthinking Manifest Destiny: Muslim Modernities on Three Continents," the most thoroughgoing in this volume, one that puts the maximum distance between the boundaries of the field and the boundaries of the nation. Shanghai and Hong Kong, Baghdad and Basra are cities that Americanists need to know about, for they are not extraneous, but an enfolded part of the American landscape. With this in mind, Friedman revisits the long histories of Chinese and Arabic civilizations, against which the brief chronology of the United States can only be seen as a humble subset. Once this subset is recognized for what it is—not self-contained, and not blessed with any provable advantage over other subsets—modernity in general, and American literature in particular, will be seen to be "polycentric," with multiple horizons, alive with the possibility that the future of the world (like its past) might be more vitally developed in other regions on the planet. Feminism, quintessential child of modernity, is a case in point. Friedman analyzes the writings of Fatima Mernissi and Azar Nafisi as feminism with a difference: indigenized, indebted to Scheherazade, enmeshed in Islamic politics, and, for all these reasons, reflecting more of the vexed contours of the world than its Western counterpart.

Friedman's essay marks the outer limits of a paradigm that rejects the nation and embraces the world as its evidentiary ground. From this explosive performance, we turn to two essays weighted toward material more recognizable as "American," nested, however, in a geography and a chronology far exceeding the bounds of that adjective. Both take Eastern Europe as a test case. This is a part of the world quite different from the France and Germany and Italy traditionally conjured up by the word "Europe," a locality whose deep entanglement with American literature is just beginning to be recognized. In "Mr. Styron's Planet," Eric J. Sundquist asks what it means for William Styron, in *Sophie's Choice*, to imagine a "sinister zone of likeness" between Poland under the Nazis and the slaveholding American South. In making his heroine a Polish Catholic anti-Semite and embroiling her in a pornographic melodrama, Styron stages a Holocaust without Jews, claiming that its driving force is not anti-Semitism but totalitarianism, productive of a vast system of "slave labor" more reprehensible than a system of genocide. In this way, *Sophie's Choice* picks up where *The Confessions of Nat Turner* leaves off. This de-Judaization does not stand alone, Sundquist argues, nor is it at the center of its own universe. Rather, it is a subset, a sideshow, of a piece with the sanitized account of the Holocaust in postwar Poland, with the *Historikerstreit* (the debate in Germany in the 1980s about the uniqueness of Nazi crimes), and with the Christian triumphalism promulgated at Auschwitz by Pope John Paul II. These are facts that have a bearing on American literature, facts that Americanists need to know. Our understanding of *Sophie's Choice* would have been infinitely poorer without this scrupulous reconstruction of a larger set of evidence.

That larger set of evidence is also the animating force in Ross Posnock's essay, "Planetary Circles: Philip Roth, Emerson, Kundera." Likewise centered on Eastern Europe, this essay in many ways reverses the flow of Sundquist's argument. While Sundquist sees "de-Judaization" as an affront and a denial of history, Posnock sees it as a tribute, a broadening of the web of filiations extended to authors hitherto identified only by their ethnicity. Philip Roth, he argues, is better seen as a cosmopolitan rather than Jewish-American writer: one who for thirteen years lived half the year in London, and who played a crucial part in the translation and publication of Eastern European authors, forming close friendships with several of them, including Kundera and Havel. The Americanist field, as Posnock envisions it, is necessarily intercontinental, with America flowing into Europe and Europe flowing into America. The presence of Kundera and Havel gives us not only a new Roth, but also a new Emerson, a new Melville, and a new clustering within the "world republic of letters," as described by Pascale Casanova.[30] American literature is very much a subset of this republic, "simply the first circle," Posnock says, around which a series of larger circles can be drawn.

Joseph Roach injects a cautionary note. The drawing of larger and yet larger circles for our discipline can be less than benign, he suggests; indeed, it is an act of self-aggrandizing not unlike the global transactions of capitalism. Operating under conditions of inequality, it might lead to a World Bank model of aggregation. Rather than taking American phenomena as a subset of the phenomena of the world, this Word Bank model globalizes the world by instituting a vertical hierarchy, imposing itself as the most encompassing of sets, and through a continual transfer of local resources to corporate structures, devours the rest of the world as its tributaries. The incorporation of two Australian performances—*Bran Nue Dae*, widely known as the "first Aboriginal musical," and *Ningali*, a subsequent solo performance by Josie Ningali Lawford—into the Broadway musical *Oklahoma!* dramatizes this insidious logic. Aggregation of this sort strips away the protective barrier put up by local governments, taking what it will and where it will, giving new currency to indigenous legacies, but always by engulfing them and subordinating them.

It is a frightening scenario. Still, it is probably not the only scenario at play as we bring the circumference of the globe to bear on the circumference of the nation. The complex tension between these two can also be the genetic ground for a different kind of aggregate: not from the top down, as in the World Bank model, but from the bottom up, what Arjun Appadurai calls "grassroots globalization."[31] Grassroots activities of this sort suggest that the most vital cross-border filiations might be below the threshold, operating at a *subnational* level.[32] This is the focus for Homi K. Bhabha. Using W.E.B. Du Bois as a point of depature, Bhabha calls attention to a "global minoritarian culture," one that does not necessarily add up to a racial or ethnic minority within a single nation. That not-adding-up allows a different aggregate to emerge—what Bhabha calls a "partial community"—rendered partial by its off-center relation to the national government, and by its far-reaching and locally mediated kinship with other distant minority groups. This is a subset of humanity that cannot be integrated into a sovereign whole, a subset always partly external to any nation-based set. Its resilience lies precisely in that reversed hierarchy.

Nor is this an isolated instance. Indeed, reversed hierarchy might turn out to be the rule rather than the exception in most localities porous to a global flow of culture, but not so porous as to stop existing as *localities*. Put another way, we can also say that the subset, in requiring more specifying than the set, will in most instances *overflow* that supposedly larger container. David Palumbo-Liu explores that paradox in "Atlantic to Pacific: James, Todorov, Blackmur, and Intercontinental Form," a study of the signatures of the local, operating below the threshold both of the nation-state and of a transnational regime. Beginning with the sense of spatial disorientation starkly recounted in Henry James's "The Jolly Corner," Palumbo-Liu uses this as a generative matrix, linking the formal experiments of James as an expatriate American in Britain to the reinvention of poetics by Tzvetan Todorov as an expatriate Bulgarian in France, and to a series of lectures delivered by R. P. Blackmur in Japan in 1956, at the Nagano Summer Seminar in American Literature. These dislocations are more than just variations on a theme; they are variations that cannot be recuperated as a theme. Palumbo-Liu sees them as "ghosts" of a sort that resist homogenization: ghosts that stalk not only the linguistic forms of

James, Todorov, and Blackmur, but also the architectural forms of, say, Paris in the 1960s, or the "International Style" in postwar Japan.

Haunting, for Palumbo-Liu, stands as a shorthand for the untotalizable sum between part and whole, between set and subset. It is a perennial witness to a reversible hierarchy. That reversible hierarchy appears in an even more striking guise in environmental thinking, a paradox that Lawrence Buell explores. Buell begins with the observation that the oldest form of globalism is environmental rather than economic or political. To think "environmentally" is to think against the grain of a nation-based paradigm. And yet, environmentalism is more than just a cognitive style; it is, perhaps even vitally, an affective style, animated by an attachment to particular localities, a feel for the near-at-hand, and haunted by the fragility and finiteness of mountains, streams, plants, and living creatures. Buell calls these emotional bonds "ecoglobalist affects," and traces their presence throughout the length of American literature, from Mary Rowlandson to Leslie Silko and Karen Tei Yamashita. While environmental *thinking* invokes the large-scale as its analytic coordinates—climate change, toxic fallouts, nuclear proliferation, phenomena that lie outside the purview of any single nation—environmental *feeling* tends to attach itself to the near rather than the far, the tangible rather than the disembodied. Here too the subset, in its intensities, might turn out to overflow the set. Buell, for that reason, acknowledges the force of place-centered ethics, more locale-based than nation-based, as a complement and offset to the more abstract, planetary scales of identification.

The importance of affect in environmental writing highlights the function of *genre* as a point of transit—a kind of switch mechanism—in the reversible hierarchy between the local and the global. Genre is, in fact, the analytic pivot for Rachel Adams as she studies local innovations emerging in the shadow of global players in one particularly volatile part of the world: the U.S.-Mexico border. The genre in question is the crime novel. Initially aligned with the mean streets of Los Angeles and New York, of late it has drifted significantly to other cultural terrains: Ciudad Juárez, El Paso, Tijuana. This internationalization of the genre provides an excellent test case for measuring the strengths of the local against the power of the global. Drawing on the work of Walter Mignolo, Adams argues that the crime novel embodies a special form of knowledge, "border gnosis,"[33] that it has as much to tell us about the impact of NAFTA as it does about the grassroots filiations of bilingual, bicultural, and binational communities. Rolando Hinojosa, Paco Ignacio Taibo II, and Alicia Gaspar de Alba use various conventions of detective fiction to highlight not only the arbitrary nature of territorial regimes but also the sustained efforts of local groups to collaborate across linguistic and national boundaries. Just as the subset of crime fiction can no longer be fitted into a nation-based set, neither can any vibrant understanding of community.

This reversible hierarchy between subset and set also animates the last essay in this collection, one that explores the "nesting" of the transnational in the subnational by tracing the planetary circuits embedded in one of the most baseline of activities: the use of language. In "African, Caribbean, American: Black English as Creole Tongue," Wai Chee Dimock looks at this street vernacular as a linguistic form bearing the imprint of many geographies, many chronologies. Though clearly local, it is nonetheless the effect of an African diaspora, enriched by a host of European languages along the way. Drawing on the research of Lorenzo Dow Turner, Robert Hall, William Stewart, and William Labov, Dimock argues that the apparent ungrammaticalness of Black English will appear in a new light when it is seen as a subset in a linguistic continuum, comprising such West African languages as Wolof, Ewe, Fon, Mende, and Ibo. Basic syntax requires at least three continents in order to make sense. With the help of these large-scale coordinates, inflected always by the small-scale signatures of local groups, this volume circles back to Jonathan Arac's opening plea for curricular reform, with language instruction playing a crucial part, as an empirical link between American studies, area studies, and comparative literature. What is intimated here is the field as a multilingual and intercontinental domain. Its features are just becoming legible, and we invoke it in that spirit: as a cipher, a cradle, a horizon yet to be realized.

NOTES

1. The correlation between intensified hurricane cycles and warmer ocean temperatures was first reported in the July 31, 2005, online edition of the journal *Nature* by Kerry Emanuel, professor of meteorology in MIT's Department of Earth, Atmospheric, and Planetary Sciences. See the release from the MIT News Office, http://web.mit.edu/newsoffice/2005/hurricanes.html. See also "Is Global Warming Fueling Katrina?" *Time*, August 29, 2005; "Katrina's Real Name," *Boston Globe*, August 30, 2005; "Katrina Reignites Global Warming Debate," *USA Today*, September 1, 2005.

2. *Toward a Global Civil Society*, ed. Michael Walzer (Providence, R.I.: Berghahn Books, 1995); Jürgen Habermas, *The Postnational Constellation*, trans. Max Pensky (Cambridge: MIT Press, 2001). For other important works that argue along these lines, see David Held, *Democracy and the Global Order: From the Modern State to Cosmopolitan Governance* (Stanford, Calif.: Stanford University Press, 1995); Mary Kaldor, *Global Civil Society* (Cambridge: Polity, 2003); Étienne Balibar, *We, the People of Europe? Reflections on Transnational Citizenship* (Princeton: Princeton University Press, 2004); Anne-Marie Slaughter, *A New World Order* (Princeton: Princeton University Press, 2004).

3. Fredric Jameson, "Notes on Globalization as a Philosophical Issue," in *The Cultures of Globalization*, ed. Fredric Jameson and Masao Miyoshi (Durham, N.C.: Duke University Press, 1998), 54–77, quotation from 64. For critiques of global capital, see John Gray, *False Dawn: The Delusion of Global Capitalism* (New York: New Press, 1998); and Joseph Stiglitz, *Globalization and Its Discontents* (New York: Norton, 2003). For

McDonaldization, see George Ritzer, *The McDonaldization of Society* (London: Sage, 1992); *Global America?* ed. Ulrich Beck, Natan Sznaider and Rainer Winter (Liverpool: Liverpool University Press, 2003); and, for a qualifying argument, *Golden Arches East: McDonald's in East Asia*, ed. James L. Watson (Stanford, Calif.: Stanford University Press, 1997).

4. See http://www.cnn.com/2005/WEATHER/08/31/Katrina.people/.

5. This development puts a wrinkle not only in Jameson's argument but also in the arguments about "empire" set forth by Michael Hardt, Antonio Negri, and Niall Ferguson. See Michael Hardt and Antonio Negri, *Empire* (Cambridge: Harvard University Press, 2000); Niall Ferguson, *Colossus: The Price of America's Empire* (New York: Penguin, 2004).

6. For the United States as a rogue nation, see Clyde Prestowitz, *Rogue Nation: American Unilateralism and the Failure of Good Intentions* (New York: Basic Books, 2003); Peter Scowen, *Rogue Nation: The America the Rest of the World Knows* (Toronto: McClelland and Stewart, 2003).

7. Dipesh Chakrabarty, *Provincializing Europe* (Princeton: Princeton University Press, 2000).

8. Janice Radway, "What's in a Name? Presidential Address to the American Studies Association, November 20, 1998," *American Quarterly* 51 (March 1999): 1–32, quotation from 4.

9. Ibid., 10, 15.

10. Ibid., 15.

11. For important collections that affirm the multicultural nature of the United States, see, for instance, *The Ethnic Canon: Histories, Institutions, and Interventions*, ed. David Palumbo-Liu (Minneapolis: University of Minnesota Press, 1995); *Mapping Multiculturalism*, ed. Avery F. Gordon and Christopher Newfield (Minneapolis: University of Minnesota Press, 1996); *Global/Local: Cultural Production and the Transnational Imaginary*, ed. Rob Wilson and Wimal Dissanayake (Durham, N.C.: Duke University Press, 1996); *Streams of Cultural Capital*, ed. David Palumbo-Liu and Hans Ulrich Gumbrecht (Stanford, Calif.: Stanford University Press, 1997); *The Politics of Culture in the Shadow of Capital*, ed. Lisa Lowe and David Lloyd (Durham, N.C.: Duke University Press, 1997); *Postnational American Studies*, ed. John Carlos Rowe (Berkeley: University of California Press, 2000).

12. See, for instance, Sheila Hones and Julia Leyda, "Geographies of American Studies," *American Quarterly* 57 (December 2005): 1019–32; and Donald E. Pease, "The Extraterritoriality of the Literature for Our Planet," *ESQ* 50 (2004): 177–221. For a discussion of the carving of spaces in Africa that bears on American studies, see Achille Mbembe, "At the Edge of the World: Boundaries, Territoriality, and Sovereignty in Africa," in *Globalization*, ed. Arjun Appadurai (Durham, N.C.: Duke University Press, 2003), 22–51.

13. Set theory is a highly technical mathematical field, considered by some to be the foundation of mathematics. Much of the literature is difficult for humanists to understand. I have found the following helpful: Abraham Fraenkel, *Foundations of Set Theory* (Amsterdam: Elsevier Science Publishers, 1984); E. Kamke, *Theory of Sets*, trans. Frederick Bagemihl (New York: Dover, 1950); Michael Potter, *Set Theory and Its Philosophy* (New York: Oxford University Press, 2004). For a bracingly partisan account, see David Lewis, *Parts of Classes* (Cambridge, Mass.: Blackwell, 1991).

14. For a more detailed discussion, see my "Scales of Aggregation: Prenational, Subnational, Transnational," *American Literary History* 18 (Summer 2006): 217–27.

15. Douglas Hofstadter, *Gödel, Escher, Bach: The Eternal Golden Braid* (New York: Vintage, 1979), 127–52, quotation from 142.

16. Ibid., 152.

17. Giyatri Chakravorty Spivak, "Planetarity," in *Death of a Discipline* (New York: Columbia University Press, 2003), 71–102, quotation from 102. In this context, also see my essay, "Literature for the Planet," *PMLA* 116 (2001): 173–88.

18. Paul Gilroy, *After Empire* (Abingdon, UK: Routledge, 2004). Spivak and Gilroy reverse Mary Louise Pratt's understanding of "planetary consciousness," which she aligns with an imperialist vision. See Pratt, *Imperial Eyes: Travel Writing and Transculturation* (New York: Routledge, 1992).

19. Philip Curtin, "Depth, Span, and Relevance," Presidential Address to the American Historical Association, San Francisco, December 18–30, 1983. Reprinted in *American Historical Review* 89 (February 1984): 1–9, quotation from 1.

20. Ibid., 1.

21. Ibid., 2.

22. Jerry A. Fodor, "Modules, Frames, Fridgeons, Sleeping Dogs, and the Music of the Spheres," in *Modularity in Knowledge Representation and Natural-Language Understanding*, ed. Jay L. Garfield (Cambridge: MIT Press, 1987), 25–36, quotation from 25. Fodor's well-known argument in favor of modularity is set forth in *The Modularity of Mind* (Cambridge: MIT Press, 1983).

23. Philip Curtin, *The Rise and Fall of the Plantation Complex: Essays in Atlantic History* (New York: Cambridge University Press, 1990), ix.

24. Ibid., ix.

25. Ibid., 3. This unexpected incorporation of the rise of Islam into the discussion of slavery is characteristic of world history as a subfield of history. William McNeill and Marshal Hodgson, two other leading practitioners, likewise put Islam at the center of their accounts of world history. See Marshall Hodgson, *Rethinking World History: Essays on Europe, Islam, and World History* (Chicago: University of Chicago Press, 1993); William McNeill, *The Rise of the West* (Chicago: University of Chicago Press, 1963).

26. Curtin, *Rise and Fall of the Plantation Complex*, 4.

27. Ibid., 4, x.

28. Ibid., x. Curtin's other works are equally intimidating in their range. See, for instance, his *Cross-Cultural Trade in World History* (New York: Cambridge University Press, 1984); *The World and the West* (New York: Cambridge University Press, 2000).

29. Arac's thinking about the institutional meaning of vernacular speech has evolved over the years. See, for instance, his "Whitman and the Problem of the Vernacular," in *Breaking Bounds: Whitman and American Cultural Studies*, ed. Betsy Erkkila and Jay Grossman (New York: Oxford University Press, 1996), 44–61; and *"Huckleberry Finn" as Idol and Target: The Function of Criticism in Our Time* (Madison: University of Wisconsin Press, 1997), 203–6.

30. Pascale Casanova, *The World Republic of Letters*, trans. M. B. DeBevoise (Cambridge: Harvard University Press, 2004). For Casanova, this is not an entirely benign development, with peripheral innovation flourishing under the aegis of first-world domination.

31. Arjun Appadurai, "Grassroots Globalization and the Research Imagination," in *Globalization*, 1–21. In an earlier essay, Stuart Hall has also called attention to globalization from the bottom up. See Hall, "The Local and the Global: Globalization and Ethnicity," in *Culture, Globalization, and the World System*, ed. Anthony D. King (Minneapolis: University of Minnesota Press, 1997), 1–29.

32. Thomas Bender has likewise argued that "[r]ather than shifting our focus from the nation to some other social/territorial unit, we would do well to imagine a spectrum of social scales, both larger and smaller than the nation and not excluding the nation." See Bender, Introduction, to *Rethinking American History in a Global Age*, ed. Thomas Bender (Berkeley: University of California Press, 2002), 1–21, quotation from 8.

33. Walter Mignolo, *Local Histories/Global Designs: Coloniality, Subaltern Knowledge, and Border-Thinking* (Princeton: Princeton University Press, 2000), 11.

PART ONE

The Field, the Nation, the World

CHAPTER 1

Global and Babel: Language and Planet in American Literature

Jonathan Arac

OUR CURRENT CONCERN with the planet has important precedents. Nearly fifty years ago, the German émigré philosopher Hannah Arendt was moved, and moved to thought, by Sputnik. Her remarkable and enduring book *The Human Condition* begins: "In 1957, an earth-born object made by man was launched into the universe, where for some weeks it circled the earth."[1] Reflecting on this accomplishment within the whole course of human history, Arendt feared that it signaled a "repudiation of the earth who was the Mother of all living things under the sky."[2] Turning from the idiom of archaic mythology to the language of Western philosophy, she continued, "The earth is the very quintessence of the human condition."

This resolutely planetary perspective led Arendt at once to questions of language, for, she argued, insofar as human beings "live and move and act in this world," the world of the earth, humans "can experience meaningfulness only because they can talk with and make sense to each other."[3] Human language makes possible the lives we live with each other, which means that "speech is what makes man a political being," and therefore that "whenever the relevance of speech is at stake, matters become political by definition."[4] Arendt followed out this logic in dialogue with the heritage of Greek thinking, but in Hebrew tradition, the myth of Babel uses language to account for the diversity of human nations, and consequent political failures to "make sense to each other."[5] One thread of human cultural history "after Babel" twists together two contrary elements, our yearning to regain unity and our pleasure in diverse plurality; and each of these, in turn, carries its negative shadow, the fear of uniformity, the dread of chaos. In literary studies the relations between human life on earth and the multiplicity of human speech have been renewed in Gayatri Chakravorty Spivak's *Death of a Discipline*, which raises the question of "planetarity" to reframe the scholar's obligation to know a sufficient variety of languages. In Spivak's usage, the planetary grounds the problem of alterity, the need to acknowledge that we must all live together, yet we are not as others are.

Inspired by such thinking, this essay attempts to develop lines of thought concerning language more hopeful than the critique I had proposed in "Anglo-

Globalism?" which reflects on the implications for literary study of the possible global hegemony of the English language.[6] The first section below, "World Literature and Its Alternatives," turns to the planet. It explores the potential of world literature as a way of thinking that may evade the limits of Anglo-globalism. It places the study of American literature in dialogue with the internationalism of area studies and comparative literature. Despite its short-comings, such internationalism does work that is salutary for challenging the nationalist and monolingual enclosure toward which American studies has tended. The first section is oriented toward institutions of learning and disci-plinary formations. The second section, "Global and Babel," is oriented to-ward reading literary texts and the resources of criticism that enable such analysis, especially the work of Edward Said. This section emphasizes the in-ternal differences that in some cases fracture American English and that arise from the place of the United States in a larger world. Finally, in a brief coda the essay returns to dialogue with a renewed comparative literature, arguing for an American studies that acknowledges the necessity of working in lan-guages other than English. The goal is a critical, cosmopolitan, polyglot way of working with the literature of the United States.

WORLD LITERATURE AND ITS ALTERNATIVES

World literature marks the crossover between *modernization*, which is the term most associated with the history of area studies as an organization of knowl-edge, and *comparative literature*, which is the discipline that has named the multinational study of literatures. In its standard American practice since the Second World War, comparative literature formed a restricted plurality; it long did its work through conjoining national units, and it long sought to cultivate in its students the high mastery of the literary languages of several different national cultures. Modernization, in contrast, disrupts established restric-tions—it frees energies, it liberalizes traditions.[7] So, then, to cross comparative literature and modernization, to raise the question of world literature, seems in the lens of language to point in two extreme and incompatible directions: not only the proliferation of Babel, but also the uniformity of global English.

These hopes—whether of variety or unity—and these fears—whether of dispersal or homogeneity—are replayed in the realm of the American nation-state and in the discipline of American studies. The hallowed slogan of *e pluribus unum* comes up against the rainbow multicultures that have for some decades been reclaiming their political rights and discursive territory. Ameri-can studies is the lost twin of area studies—each is an interdisciplinary inquiry put into operation over fifty years ago and putatively defined by the uniqueness of a culture.[8] I write as an Americanist who has always hoped to think as a comparatist.[9]

From its beginnings, since Goethe coined the term in 1827,[10] world literature has helped activate the crisis that troubles area studies. Listen to the *Communist Manifesto*:

> The bourgeoisie has through its exploitation of the world market given a cosmopolitan character to production and consumption in every country. . . . All old-established national industries have been destroyed or are daily being destroyed. They are dislodged by new industries . . . that no longer work up indigenous raw material, but raw materials drawn from the remotest zones; industries whose products are consumed, not only at home, but in every quarter of the globe. In place of the old wants, satisfied by the productions of the country, we find new wants, requiring for their satisfaction the products of distant lands and climes. In place of the old local and national seclusion and self-sufficiency, we have intercourse in every direction, universal interdependence of nations. And as in material, so also in intellectual production. The intellectual creations of individual nations become common property . . . and from the numerous national and local literatures, there arises a world literature.[11]

So much of the business of this passage is condensed in the single word translated "intercourse": German *Verkehr*. A standard dictionary lists the meanings for this word in sequence as: traffic, transportation, communication, commerce, intercourse in its sexual as well as other senses, and communion. It is all but communism (in German, *Kommunismus*), for which Marx and Engels required recourse to a Latin, rather than Germanic, derivation, perhaps to signal the movement's internationalism. The related verb, *verkehren*, means to turn over, with the usual off-key sense carried by the prefix *ver-*, so to put it colloquially, to screw up. *Die verkehrte Welt* is the world turned upside down, which in the metahistory of Marx and Engels is just what the bourgeoisie does by means of its *Verkehr*.

The twentieth century from early on demonstrated the real weight of what might seem, in reading, an ungrounded simile in the *Manifesto*: "As in material, so also in intellectual production." What has proved decisive is not the theory of base and superstructure (on which this claim seems to rest) but the eruption of the culture industry, from Hollywood and radio and recordings and advertising to the present. Because this apparatus indeed produces new wants that require material fulfillment, it is no longer possible to dismiss the superstructure as epiphenomenal, and so cultural considerations such as those of world literature are not simply interesting but are perhaps consequential. "Common property" in the intellectual world, we have found, may not simply prefigure communism, but it certainly does trouble capitalism, as witnessed in the controversies and legal action provoked by Napster and other forms of file-sharing or so-called digital piracy.

Marx and Engels wrote of the "national and local"; nations and locales are not the same as areas, but what encompasses the whole planet overrides area boundaries as well as national and local borders. The very modernization that motivates area studies is also its undoing. Moreover, the formulation of world literature that Marx and Engels invoked comes from the writings of Goethe, an author more closely identified with an area, the teutonophone zone, than with any nation-state. In Goethe's time (1749–1832), no political entity existed that could be called *Germany*, and we may imagine this a significant reason for the appeal of the "world" to Goethe, as over against the national state cultures of England and France.[12]

A century after the *Manifesto*, some fifty years ago, in the aftermath of the Second World War, in a spirit comparable to that which underlay the foundation of the United Nations, the great German émigré scholar Erich Auerbach wrote on philology and world literature, but his perspective proved marginal.[13] It was the time of the Cold War, and against the unbounding force that Marx and Engels had celebrated, however ambivalently, the age was theorized by "containment" in realms beyond that of the anti-Communist geopolitics proposed by George Kennan. Literary studies emphasized the "well wrought urn" of individual, self-enclosed poems as studied by new criticism; the new intellectual formation of American Studies defined itself through an exceptionalist enclosure; and even comparative literature defined itself as crossing the limits of national units otherwise well bounded. To an outsider, it seems that area studies suffered a similar empowering reduction.

As area studies is now concerned with the need to cross borders, or perhaps to respond to the fact of borders having been crossed, world literature has emerged again as an active focus for discussion among literary scholars.[14] Among these, some of the most compelling are Franco Moretti, Pascale Casanova, David Damrosch, and Wai Chee Dimock; the perspective of Gayatri Chakravorty Spivak offers a crosscurrent, to which I shall return in my coda. All of these powerful theorists and critics agree that whatever world literature is, it is not best understood as a corpus or canon or list of works.

In "Conjectures on World Literature," Franco Moretti draws on Max Weber's methodology for the sociology of culture to define world literature as a possible object of knowledge, which must be constructed by an act of synoptic synthesis on the basis of the innumerable studies done by scholars of the national literatures.[15] World literature, then, is the general, and the national is the specific. Moretti elaborates a model derived from "core and periphery" in Immanuel Wallerstein's comparative historical sociology of the "world system." Equally sociological, in the vein of Bourdieu, Casanova's *La république mondiale des lettres* is even more committed to the "global reality" of "literary space."[16]

In contrast to the spatial model that undergirds Moretti's and Casanova's arguments, David Damrosch, in *What Is World Literature?* and Wai Chee Dimock, in recent essays entitled "Deep Time" and "Literature for the Planet," both work with a model that I associate more with Walter Benjamin than with Max Weber. Rather than institutional in emphasis, their concerns are dyadic (whether work to work, or work to reader). The connections they establish are more arbitrary—that is to say both willed and contingent—than rule bound. Above all, they delineate a complex temporality by which world literature arises from the interaction of what we might call different time zones.[17] In distinguishing their work from Moretti's (to a lesser degree Casanova's), I am trying to articulate a distinction that is both subtle and implicit. One slogan for this might come from Dimock: "deep time is denationalized space."

In the United States all forms of comparative and international study always carry an implicit critique of the continental insularity that marks this country. In this respect comparative literature and area studies are at one. This implicit critique persists even when the scholarship is in the service of national political interests, and it is of course more intense when the scholarship is explicitly detached from any such concerns. Wai Chee Dimock is Americanist by training, unlike Moretti, Damrosch, and Spivak, all of whom are disciplinarily comparatists, so her challenge to American cultural provinciality in the name of world literature and deep time is all the more striking. In a gesture that is even more challenging after September 11 and now the war in Iraq, she invokes the geographical and chronological sweep of Islam to model the denationalized deep time she explicates and values.

The United States is notoriously Anglophone monolingual.[18] This despite Harvard's remarkable Longfellow Project, initiated in 1994 by Mark Shell and Werner Sollors, a comparatist from Quebec and an Americanist from Germany. This project has recovered a thick body of texts in many languages produced within the geographical limits of what is now the United States.[19] Historically, it has been a crucial role shared by comparative literature with area studies to supplement Anglophone monolingualism. What do the new proponents of world literature offer here? It is a striking feature of Moretti's project that despite his own work in several European languages, the actual collective project that he envisages seems to require the universal solvent of English to accomplish its synoptic generalizations. This was the point of my "Anglo-globalism." But a legitimate concern about the imperial role of English hides an equally salient and perhaps even more disturbing set of facts. David Damrosch reports from Lawrence Venuti's *Scandals of Translation* a remarkable statistic and symptom: in 1987 in Brazil there were published over fifteen hundred works translated from English, while in the same year only fourteen Brazilian works were translated into English.[20] So by a ratio of one hundred to one, English may be more world-significant for its disseminal powers than its powers of appropriation. This point is even more obvious if we think of movies, TV, and the music industry.

Damrosch and Dimock both—each differently—highlight translation and multilinguality as key features of the accounts they offer. As Dimock notes of

Islam, "spread through at least three languages—Persian, Arabic, Turkish—it acquired the status of a 'civilization' primarily through the mixing of these tongues. . . . Islam came to much of the world translated and hybridized."[21] We face a problem of scale. World literature requires both the largest scale and the finest detail. Such hybrid mixtures demand attentive study of texts at their microlinguistic level. Yet Moretti's project for world literature abjures close reading. My exploration of "babel" in the next section shows, I hope, the value of working at both scales.

In the early 1990s, I was a member of the committee charged with addressing standards and practices in the discipline of Comparative Literature. I proposed a view on the role of language in comparative literature that was lost in the final document.[22] I suggested that comparatists should seek less to master a perfected high cultural accent and less to work up reading skills for exams, though of course these both have their place; instead, we should devote new effort to helping students learn the use and value of an imperfect everyday speech—that is, the capacity to speak on the street and respond with some skill to the modes of popular culture in a given language zone, even if one's grammar and vocabulary were both flawed and irrevocably marked by one's own English. This perspective sustains the hope for new language studies in the coda to this essay, and it was the comparatist precursor to the "babel" that I shall now discuss from an Americanist perspective.

GLOBAL AND BABEL

In accepting the challenge posed by joining language, the planet, and American literature, one drops into messy border country. As my discussion of world literature has demonstrated, the planetary conjures political, social, and economic concerns at some odds with what we usually mean by the literary, and the planetary no less overruns everyday limits of the American. My working dyad proposes a dynamic interaction: Let *global* name a movement of expansion that one imagines may homogenize the world, as in global English; and let *babel* name a movement of influx that diversifies our land, as in multiculturalism.[23] Is it just the difference between America taking the world and taking from the world? In literature, think of two great novels set in the early twentieth century: it is the difference between the global *Golden Bowl* by Henry James (1904) and the babel of *Call It Sleep* by Henry Roth (1934).[24] The verbal texture of James's page remains the same whether Prince Amerigo and Charlotte Stant are speaking together in English or Italian, while Roth distinguishes within his English between David Schearl's speaking in English and in Yiddish.

I acknowledge the near reversal between my use of Babel and the original biblical story, in which babel names a failed expression of human totality, and diaspora follows from the failure. I should also offer a few further preliminary clarifications. My pair of global and babel is not equivalent to Bakhtin's dubious contrast between the univocality of poetry and the polyphony of prose. My babel is not Bakhtin's "heteroglossia"; nor is it simply the local, for my emphasis falls on what has come from elsewhere, rather than what might seem indigenous. The interaction between these perspectives is not uniquely or quintessentially American, but my analysis is specific, for it depends on the coexistence within the United States of an imperial mission that leaves national borders behind ("global") together with borders that are (relatively, and as I write, all too uncertainly) open to ideas and persons from without.

My two perspectives appear in a moment from Emerson on Plato, an essay that grows from the relations between "the one, and the two," "oneness and otherness," and for Emerson these pairs also figure Asia and Europe:[25]

> Our strength is transitional, alternating; or, shall I say, a thread of two strands. The sea-shore, sea seen from shore, shore seen from sea . . . the experience of poetic creativeness, which is not found in staying at home, nor yet in traveling, but in transitions from one to the other, which must therefore be adroitly managed to present as much transitional surface as possible.

Emerson's figure of the sea-shore, the border seen from both sides, yokes expansion and influx. This passage also activates another, cryptic, dimension of my title, for in despite of etymology, which says they have nothing to do with each other, I had meant to suggest by my biblical term of *babel* also our ordinary language sense of *babble*, to pour out sound without meaning. This homophony captures the problem of scale mentioned above: the large scale, the tall tale, of babel often manifests itself in microruptures of verbal texture, where language turns to babble.

Northrop Frye, that most synoptic and encyclopedic, if not exactly planetary, of theorists, has suggested as the two primitive radicals from which poetry is generated *babble* and *doodle*—that is, ear and eye, sound and pattern.[26] Emerson here offers a seascape, a pattern illustrating the interplay of one and other, but his vision devolves into pure sonority: to insert the term *see* between the elements of *sea-shore*, thus prying the compound open perspectivally, breaks it down into babbling repetition ("Sea seen from shore, shore seen from sea"). The chiasmus here does not punctuate an antithesis but rather holds up a mirror—more of the same, from sea to shining sea.

Emerson fixes on a transition that I take as that between America globalizing and the globe Americanizing. Thoreau offers a very different path to planetaritude, delving into the earth rather than surveying its surface, yet like Emerson he also produces an interplay between design and detail, clear schemata and thick knots of sound. As spring comes to Walden, the sun brings the frozen earth to life, and Thoreau is delighted "to observe the forms which thawing sand and clay assume in flowing down the sides of a steep cut on the railroad."[27] The grotesquerie of these shapes seems organic, mimicking the leaves of plants and even the organs of a body. Thoreau feels as if he is in the "laboratory of the Artist who made the world," and thereby "nearer to the vitals of the globe":

> This sandy overflow is something such a foliaceous mass as the vitals of the animal body. You find thus in the very sands an anticipation of the vegetable leaf. No wonder that the earth expresses itself outwardly in leaves, it so labors with the idea inwardly. . . . The overhanging leaf here sees its prototype. (566)

Having set this visual schema, the passage turns to sound. Thoreau deploys the etymological resources of Indo-European philology, one of the great intellectual achievements made possible for the West by its imperial outreach.[28] Its analytic techniques allow him to break down into sound elements the key terms of the schema, above all *globe* and *leaf*:

> *Internally*, whether in the globe or animal body, it is a moist thick *lobe*, a word especially applicable to the liver and lungs and the *leaves* of fat (λείβω, *labor*, *lapsus*, to flow or slip downward, a lapsing; λοβος, *globus*, lobe, globe; also lap, flap . . .), *externally* a dry thin *leaf*, even as the *f* and *v* are a pressed and dried *b*. The radicals of lobe are *lb*. . . . In globe *glb*, the guttural *g* adds to the meaning the capacity of the throat.

Thoreau concludes, "The very globe continually transcends and translates itself, and becomes winged in its orbit." Thoreau's globalism at home provides the most morally reassuring babble.

I cannot go farther without mourning the loss to planetary American literature that we have suffered in the death of Edward W. Said. Over twenty-five years ago in *Orientalism* he developed the notion of "imaginative geography" to characterize the practices by which human beings give shape and meaning to the planet they inhabit by delimiting it: drawing bounds and attributing qualities differentially inside and outside those bounds.[29] This practice, and its analysis, was already familiar in American Studies in such figures as Frederick Jackson Turner's frontier, Perry Miller's errand into the wilderness, and Henry Nash Smith's virgin land. Said gave it a theoretical clarity and an orientation toward the world beyond the borders of the United States that together helped to enable not only postcolonial studies, but also the transformation within American studies that brings us the topic of this volume. Moreover, Said not only contributed to the study of our subject, he also in his career exemplified it. In the world of politics and letters, he was one of the few American scholars to achieve worldwide influence, recognition, and translation.

For my own work on Mark Twain and Ralph Ellison, a decade ago, I found important resources in Said's *Culture and Imperialism* (1993).[30] Read in the light of Said's concerns, Ellison's critical internationalism becomes far more evident than when one follows the highly Americanistic emphases by which

Ellison characterized his own work and by which he has been interpreted.[31] Consider the following extraordinary sentence from Ellison:

> In the nineteenth century, during the moment of greatest middle-class stability—a stability found actually only at the center, and there only relatively, in England and not in the colonies, in Paris rather than in Africa, for there the baser instincts, the violence and greed could destroy and exploit non-European societies in the name of humanism and culture, beauty and liberty, fraternity and equality while protecting the humanity of those at home—the novel reached its first high point of formal self-consciousness.[32]

Alongside this global vigilance, let me briefly register the babel in one of the most famous moments in *Invisible Man*. The narrator has come north to Harlem, and an encounter with a street vendor of yams awakens memories of the South he has left behind. Tautology turns into babel in a way we now would associate with Derrida, by the agency of a written letter that is not exactly audible: In a bold, bald pun, as the narrator eats a root he feels his roots, "I yam what I am."[33] This is undoubtedly what Bakhtin called heteroglossia, insofar as it sets against each other radically different social registers of language: the church voice of the Lord to Moses from the burning bush and the street song of Popeye the Sailor Man are joined in an African American context. This is also what I call babel, for the root and its name are not simply Southern, they are African: "The story goes that Portuguese slave traders, watching Africans digging up some roots, asked what they were called. Failing to understand the question aright, the Africans replied that it was 'something to eat', *nyami* in Guinea. This became *inhame* in Portuguese and then *igname* in French and yam in English."[34] The babble of echolalia scales up to the babel of African diaspora. The etymology of Ellison's yam renews our sense of the nurturing earth, yet the history of slaving is connected to the character's personal elation and the reader's literary pleasure.

Said's work enables us to think openly, rather than defensively, about the imperialism that inescapably girds the planetary reach of Whitman's democratic idealism. Recall a poem such as "A Broadway Pageant," written to celebrate the New York street parade honoring the first diplomatic representatives to visit the United States from Japan. The poem ends on the Spanish word "Libertad," assimilated by Whitman to name one of his highest values, the meaning he sees in this event, in which, "Comrade Americanos! to us, then at last the Orient comes."[35] For in Whitman's vision, this event includes not only "the envoys nor the tann'd Japanee from his island," but also:

> Lithe and silent the Hindoo appears, the Asiatic continent itself appears,
>   the past, the dead,
> The murky night-morning of wonder and fable inscrutable.
> . . . .
> Geography, the world, is in it.

Sea-shore, sand spill, and yam growth, my previously cited figurations of the planet, are here abstracted by Whitman in a term that names our study of the earth, "geography."[36]

Said's work has another current, and controversial, relation to our topic. In recent congressional testimony concerning the terms on which universities receive Title VI area studies funds for the teaching of foreign languages, his work was denounced for antipatriotism, as if he were an enemy of America rather than someone who for decades sought to persuade the Arab world that it needed to study the United States, from which it has much to learn.[37] To recognize the dogmatically partisan distortion in these public arguments, consider how Said discusses *Moby-Dick*:

> [Ishmael's] hyperbolic statements about the American quest for world sovereignty are playful and should be read mainly in an aesthetic context. Yet no one, no American or non-American who has read this superb novel has ever doubted that in such passages . . . Melville has very accurately caught something of the imperial motif that runs consistently through United States history and culture. Far from simple and reductive, the discourse of American specialness which Melville so powerfully delivers in the majestically energetic diction of *Moby-Dick* begins with the Puritan "errand into the wilderness." . . . Melville's contribution is that he delivers the salutary effect as well as the destructiveness of the American world presence, and he also demonstrates its self-mesmerizing assumptions about its providential significance.[38]

In taking its distance from the "providential," Said's argument here practices what he called "secular criticism."[39] This does not just mean antireligious; for Said it means also worldly, that is, partaking of the complexity, the good and ill, of human life, rather than transcending into perfection. He stands against idealizations of the aesthetic, but his terms of praise for *Moby-Dick* make clear that he is himself committed to the aesthetic in its secular modes.

Said's work offers a precious resource for our cultivation of the literary in American literature, and it does so all the more because his work cannot be understood to have scanted the planet. Said never stopped teaching literature, and his later writings argued that in order to foster the future study of literature, we must show that it coexists with the study of the world at large. In the historical study of literature, Said focused especially on the power with which a writer may endow his or her work, and the power in turn that a later reader or writer may bring to that earlier powerhouse. In *Culture and Imperialism*, Said had warned against the "rhetoric of blame" that dismisses past works because they do not espouse the moral or political positions that we do.[40] He proposed "contrapuntal" reading as richer, because it makes connections between the work of culture and the larger world of human actions, without requiring that the human past correspond to our wishes.[41] Contrapuntal reading may offer one resource for joining the small scale of language texture to the large scale of planetary history, as in Ellison's yam. Yet the contrapuntal project provokes a worry: if one links the realm of aesthetic pleasure to the world of historical pain, what assures that the pain will not overwhelm the pleasure?[42] I think some of the last things Said published before his death point us well beyond this problem.

Shortly before Said's death, there appeared his introduction to the fiftieth anniversary edition of Erich Auerbach's *Mimesis* in English.[43] My reflections on *global* and *babel* have learned from Auerbach's fundamental thesis that the great realistic literature of the West achieves its power by a stylistic technique that violates the norms of classical rhetoric through mixing levels of style, including such features as idiom, grammar, and rhythm. With a somewhat different emphasis, Said takes from Auerbach the methodological emphasis on the critic's situatedness in a time different from the time that he or she is studying—what Said calls Auerbach's "Nietzschean audacity" in affirming a perspectivism and the necessary relativism that comes with it.[44]

This perspectivism shapes a passage from the last book Said published in his lifetime, in which he explained his own perspective as a historical and humanistic scholar toward Freud, and he illustrated the issues with regard to Conrad's *Heart of Darkness*. Conrad's work may seem Eurocentric, Said argued, but it has provoked later writers from the Third World; its power calls forth their power:

> Later history reopens and challenges what seems to have been the finality of an earlier figure of thought, bringing it into contact with cultural, political, and episte-mological formations undreamed of by—albeit affiliated by historical circumstances with—its author.

This is one form of what Said means by the contrapuntal; as he goes on to assert, "The often surprising dynamics of human history can . . . dramatize the latencies in a prior figure or form that suddenly illuminate the present." Said continues:

> In the grip of Conrad's Africa, you are driven by its sheer stifling horror to work through it, to push beyond it as history itself transforms even the most unyielding stasis into process. . . . And of course with Conrad, as with all such extraordinary minds, the felt tension between what is intolerably there and a symmetrical compul-sion to escape from it is what is most profoundly at stake. . . . Texts that are inertly of their time stay there: those which brush up unstintingly against historical con-straints are the ones we keep with us, generation after generation.[45]

In characterizing the past that stays past, the texts inertly of their time that stay there, Said reworks a Gospel phrasing, recited by Marx in the *Eighteenth Brumaire*, "Let the dead bury their dead."

This passage argues that the encounter with history resuscitates the work rather than endangering it. The dynamism of "personal effort"—the human actions that make history, first the writer's and then the reader's—breaks open the dead husk of the past and releases its energies for future uses.[46]

Said's essay on *Moby-Dick* asserts of Melville that his work, like Conrad's "felt tension," as we have just seen it, is "at odds with itself."[47] This is what it is to be great but, like all human beings, time-bound at the moment in which one lives. We might focus our understanding of Said's humanism by contrasting it with Coleridge's in the *Biographia Literaria*. Both seek to bring "the whole soul of man into activity," but for Coleridge this coincides with the "balance or reconciliation of opposite or discordant qualities" rather than the state of discrepancy that Said values.[48] Said prefers a sublime disruption.[49] My project here is cognate to his in seeking the incursions of babble that signal a larger world.

One of Said's last essays published in his lifetime is entitled "Living in Arabic." It offers an analogy germane to these thoughts. The essay highlights the feature of Arabic that is most unfamiliar to many speakers of English— the practice of diglossia among its educated speakers. *Diglossic*, although etymologically the same as *bilingual* ("two tongues"), has quite a different meaning: it refers not to using two different languages but to using two different varieties of the same language in some regulated, systematic way. So standard Arabic is still in touch with Koranic tradition and is shared by educated speakers across the Arab world, while there are many local colloquial varieties, which are effectively mutually unintelligible. (This is different yet from Chinese, in which truly distinct if related languages are conjoined by a writing system alone.) This relation between standard and colloquial is a version of global and babel, the One and the two. The diglossia Said describes seems to me not unfamiliar among many educated African Americans, who are equally capable in high standard English and in what is called Black English Vernacular.

Said's essay also offers briefer reflections on bilingualism, naming it as a topic urgently requiring further exploration. This returns to a line of thought he had broached thirty years earlier: "the formal and psychological question of the interdependence of literary and sociological approaches in dealing with how English is at once a national and a world language (for some writers a first and for others a second language)."[50] At the time, this question seemed to derive from his intensive study of Conrad (for whom English was actually a third or fourth language); now it may be linked also to Said's renewed study of Arabic. Said proposed a value in the frustration that he sometimes found in the limits of his bilinguality. He registered "the dynamic state of both languages, their perfect inequality."[51] This "perfect inequality" between languages may be transposed to define the relation between different historical moments, each fully human and yet quite distinct, requiring different specific resources for their comprehension—and the difference is precisely the dynamism that mobilizes history. No one knows a language without having learned it, yet all human beings are capable of acquiring all languages. This is the utopia of philological humanism, and Said has shown through the example of his career that this legacy from Auerbach's time still offers resources to help us understand and live with others in a world that Western humanism never imagined or desired.

In pressing Said's concern with language, I return again to the relation between global and babel. Faulkner's *Absalom, Absalom!* has been importantly and influentially characterized in planetary terms by Hortense Spillers as "choreograph[ing] Canada, the Caribbean, Africa, Europe, and the United States."[52] In its use of New Orleans, it pointedly departs from one of its major precursor texts, *The Grandissimes* (1880), by George W. Cable, which gives a great deal to Faulkner's plotting, but very little to his language. Cable, in representing the city as just incorporated into the United States by Jefferson's purchase, offers a linguistic environment that conveys that foreignness through thick, challenging dialect.[53] In contrast, while Faulkner's different narrators do not all sound alike, and brief moments from the country speech of Wash Jones repeatedly punctuate the text, set against the high talk that variously marks all the other major voices, nonetheless he does not sink his readers into the babbling marshes of thick dialect. It's quite another babel that we encounter in "I became all polymath love's androgynous advocate."[54]

Yet the story of Sutpen's design, and its collapse, is framed by the unrepresented sounds of incomprehensible languages. At the ending of the novel's narrative, in 1910, the last that remains of Sutpen's family and its hopes is Jim Bond, the idiot whose howling may be heard nights; and in 1833, the beginning of the process, as played out in Mississippi, featured Sutpen on horseback with his twenty "wild" (8) slaves, with whom he spoke in a language unknown to its Mississippi auditors, who imagined it sui generis. It was actually Haitian Creole. The Creole comes from the past, and at least a few of those present know it; the howling comes from the future, and no one yet knows what it says. Babel is more thematized than enacted, yet the novel is framed by alterity.

Reflecting on the story of Sutpen's learning both French and Creole on Haiti, Quentin Compson's grandfather developed a perspective like what we began with in Arendt. Insofar as human beings live with each other and not in individual solitude, language is what makes this possible: "that meager and fragile thread . . . by which the little surface corners and edges of men's secret and solitary lives may be joined for an instant now and then before sinking back into the darkness."[55]

These reflections on joining as a response against darkness follow a fifty-line sentence that conjures the island of Haiti, which is represented both as dark and isolated yet also as itself a scene of multiple conjunctions, "where high mortality was concomitant with the money and the sheen on the dollars was not from gold but from blood." Faulkner carefully places imperialist clichés of racialized cultural difference within the realm of fable, of the things people say. This "little island" marks

> the halfway point between what we call the jungle and what we call civilization, halfway between the dark inscrutable continent from which the black blood, the black bones and flesh and thinking and remembering and hopes and desires, was ravished by violence, and the cold known land to which it was doomed, the civilized land and people which had expelled some of its own blood and thinking and desires that had become too crass to be faced and borne longer, and set it homeless and desperate in the lonely ocean.

Faulkner's island reworks *Heart of Darkness* in imaginative geography very different from Emerson's sea-shore or Thoreau's bubbling globe. Yet enacted in the plot-shape of Sutpen's design collapsing into incomprehensible babble is something like the pattern noted in Thoreau, moving from clear schemata to thick knots of sound.

We confront here the problem of scale—Faulkner's big novel, Thoreau's little paragraph—which poses a problem for scholarship, for critical writing, and for education alike. The close analysis of language presents different problems from the analysis of large formal contours, not simply in that different reading skills are required, but also regarding the question of how one writes what one has learned. In the study of literature in the United States, the institutional standard of what it means to read language closely remains the new-critical explication of a lyric poem, in which the critic writes at far greater length than the poet had done. The problem is that one may write a twenty-page essay on a sonnet, but not write a twenty-thousand-page book on *Moby-Dick*.

The *Literary History of the United States* came to seem antiquated rather soon after its 1948 publication, because it failed to incorporate the skills of close reading into its historiographic practice.[56] In contrast, Erich Auerbach's *Mimesis* (1946) endures because it bases its history on close readings, yet only at the cost of coverage, through extreme selectivity in works chosen. Attempting to combine the old model of historical completeness with the full interpretation of individual works, Paul de Man in *Allegories of Reading* (1979) professed defeat and chose reading over history.[57] It seems to me that Moretti's project for world literature implicitly, and at an unnecessary cost, like de Man takes the new-critical integral interpretation as defining close reading. As I have begun to suggest by example in this essay, and have tried to develop at greater reach in other work,[58] one may do much to combine large and small scale if one acknowledges the impossibility of completeness and therefore faces the necessity of inventing devices by which to do one's best. Similarly, I think Moretti's project for world literature gives up too quickly upon recognizing that there are too many languages for anyone to learn them all. In conclusion, I sketch alternatives more hopeful for our educational responsibilities.

CODA

In *Death of a Discipline*, Gayatri Chakravorty Spivak seeks a transformative rebirth for comparative literature. Faced with the poverty of languages in established comparative literature—in the United States, nothing beyond French, German, Spanish, Italian, and Latin can be considered widely studied—she seeks pedagogical symbiosis with area studies: in return for the many languages they can teach, she proposes that literature can teach the skills of reading necessary to make area studies truly critical. She calls on the new comparative literature to require that students develop real capability in some language of the global South, the subaltern cultures of the world. The promise in Spivak's scholarly imperative may be gauged through such remarkable new work as Brian Edwards's *Morocco Bound*, which brings Arabic materials into its American Studies orbit, and Aamir Mufti's *Enlightenment in the Colony*, which constructs a genealogy in which German, English, and Urdu materials all receive close reading.[59]

To Spivak's thought, I would add a wrinkle. Let such new language learning become a means of collective solidarity among students. Trying to develop a productive curricular relation between the large-scale and the small, I envisage as a part of the first year curriculum of doctoral programs in comparative literature a seminar that would teach about world languages and cultures (the large) in a way that could yield the following result: by the end of the course, the students will choose together one less-studied language (the small), previously known to none of them, and the next semester they will together begin to study that language, developing the intellectual and pedagogical resources necessary to foster this project.

As I suggested in the first section of this essay, the goal is not high-culture mastery but contemporary street competence, and the global media resources of film and song may well form important resources. This work should be student-driven and yet a credited, and required, part of the course of study. The development of the introductory course on world languages is a daunting future task for scholarly collaboration, and I leave details to the foundations I hope may be moved to help fund such enterprises, but the large idea is that for each student cohort, their shared new language should remain a collective project even as the students are also completing their doctorates in their chosen fields, not necessarily related to the language. Of course there should be time abroad, and there should be dialogue with area study specialists in other disciplines who study the given culture. The upshot cannot fail both to transform what it means to be a comparatist and also to provide the United States with cadres of highly skilled and unusually oriented experts in some little-studied languages and cultures. In contrast to either the tedium or the babel that we now fear, the world literature that might begin to emerge from such scholars would be quite an alternative.

Likewise, one might imagine that doctoral studies in American literature should require all its students to know three languages, two of them extremely well: English, Spanish, and a third that is either non-Indo-European or of the global South. This agenda will not lack for language study resources. The ground seems fully prepared for innovative programs such as I envision here. I have examined language offerings at twenty-six universities, a list made up by combining top-ranked doctoral programs in English, top-ranked departments for U.S. literature before and after 1865, and the five departments that produced the greatest number of new doctorates in American literature. Half of these universities offer seventeen or more (up to forty-two) currently spoken languages that are either non-Indo-European or of the global South, and even at the ten universities offering the fewest such languages, at least eight (up to twelve) are available for study. The following thirteen languages are offered at more than half of the institutions (in order of frequency): Chinese, Japanese, Arabic, Hebrew, Russian (all five at all twenty-six), Portuguese, Korean, Hindi, Persian, Kiswahili, Turkish, Vietnamese, Thai. The total number of such languages offered across the twenty-six universities is sixty-one.[60] If we take seriously the arguments for American literary planetaritude developed by the contributors to this volume, and accept the force of what Shell and Sollors and their collaborators have produced through the Longfellow Project, then this modest proposal might also transform what it means to be an Americanist.

Notes

Many thanks to those whose invitations spurred my writing that has gone into this essay: Paul Bové, Lawrence Buell, Vilashini Cooppan, Wai Chee Dimock, Betsy Erkkila, and Michael Holquist; and special thanks to Susan Z. Andrade for searching conversation and commentary on versions in progress.

1. Hannah Arendt, *The Human Condition* (Chicago: University of Chicago Press, 1958), 1.

2. Ibid., 2, for this and the quotation in the following sentence.

3. Ibid., 4.

4. Ibid., 3.

5. See the neglected, flawed, and inspiring *After Babel: Aspects of Language and Translation* by George Steiner (London: Oxford University Press, 1975).

6. Jonathan Arac, "Anglo-Globalism?" *New Left Review*, n.s, no. 16 (July/August 2002): 35–45.

7. I emphasize the disruptive tendency of modernization, but for a critique of area studies as itself restrictively limited by national and disciplinary borders, see the introduction by Masao Miyoshi and Harry Harootunian to their edited volume, *Learning Places: The Afterlives of Area Studies* (Durham, N.C.: Duke University Press, 2002), esp. 8.

8. Paul A. Bové defines a fundamental difference between the two: area studies has served policy functions for the American nation state in the realm of *Realpolitik*, while

American studies has enhanced hegemony in the realm of culture. See "Can American Studies Be Area Studies?" in Miyoshi and Harootunian, eds., *Learning Places*, 206–30.

9. For perspective on area studies and comparative literature complementary to mine, but different because contrasting these to cultural studies and ethnic studies, rather than to American studies at large, see Gayatri Chakravorty Spivak, *Death of a Discipline* (New York: Columbia University Press, 2003), chap. 1, esp. pp. 3–9.

10. See, for instance, the selection from Goethe's scattered comments on the term in Johann Wolfgang von Goethe, *Essays on Art and Literature*, ed. John Gearey, trans. Ellen von Nardroff and Ernest H. von Nardroff (Princeton: Princeton University Press, 1994), 224–28.

11. Karl Marx and Friedrich Engels, *Manifesto of the Communist Party* (1848), in Lewis S. Feuer, ed., *Marx and Engels: Basic Writings on Politics and Philosophy* (Garden City, N.Y.: Doubleday, 1959), 11. For the German I use *Manifest der Kommunistischen Partei*, in Kurt Rossmann, ed., *Deutsche Geschichts-Philosophie: von Lessing bis Jaspers* (Bremen: Carl Schünemann Verlag, 1959), 247–48. For the deepest discussion of world literature in this passage, see Martin Puchner, *Poetry of the Revolution: Marx, Manifestos, and the Avant Gardes* (Princeton: Princeton University Press, 2006), 48–66.

12. On this line of thought see further David Damrosch, *What Is World Literature?* (Princeton: Princeton University Press, 2003), 6–13, esp. 8.

13. Erich Auerbach, "Philology and *Weltliteratur*" (1952), trans. Edward W. and Maire Said, *Centennial Review* 13 (1969): 1–17; see discussion in Arac, "Anglo-Globalism," 41–42.

14. I allude specifically to the multiyear, multisited initiative by the Ford Foundation, "Crossing Borders—Revitalizing Area Studies," which supported a conference at Yale's Center for International and Area Studies in November, 2002, at which I first presented some of this material.

15. Franco Moretti, "Conjectures on World Literature," *New Left Review*, n.s., 1 (2000): 54–68.

16. Pascale Casanova, *La république mondiale des lettres* (Paris: Seuil, 1999), 16. My translation.

17. I refer to Walter Benjamin, "Theses on the Philosophy of History," in *Illuminations*, trans. Harry Zohn (New York: Schocken, 1969); he argues that "to articulate the past historically" means to "seize hold of a memory as it flashes up at a moment of danger" (255).

18. For an important counterview of the plurality within American English, see Ronald Bush's Inaugural Lecture, as the first Oxford University Professor of American Literature, *American Voice/American Voices* (Oxford: Oxford University Press, 1999).

19. See Mark Shell and Werner Sollors, eds., *The Multilingual Anthology of American Literature: A Reader of Original Texts with English Translations* (New York: New York University Press, 2000). See also the essays in Werner Sollors, ed., *Multilingual America: Transnationalism, Ethnicity, and the Languages of American Literature* (New York: New York University Press, 1998).

20. Damrosch, *What Is World Literature?* 113.

21. Wai Chee Dimock, "Deep Time: American Literature and World History," *American Literary History* (2001). This and Dimock's other essay to which I refer are

now incorporated in Wai Chee Dimock, *Through Other Continents: American Literature Across Deep Time* (Princeton: Princeton University Press, 2006). For important critical engagement with Dimock, see Donald E. Pease, "The Extraterritoriality of the Literature for Our Planet," *ESQ* 50, nos. 1–3 (2004), esp. 179–91.

22. See Charles Bernheimer, ed., *Comparative Literature in an Age of Multiculturalism* (Baltimore: Johns Hopkins University Press, 1995).

23. See especially Marc Shell, ed., *American Babel: Literatures of the United States from Abnaki to Zuni* (Cambridge: Harvard University Press, 2002), and now also Evelyn Nien-Ming Ch'ien, *Weird English* (Cambridge: Harvard University Press, 2004).

24. For a critical reading in detail, see my "Compelling Language in *Call It Sleep*: The Tongs Set Free," forthcoming in a volume edited by Gayatri Chakravorty Spivak, tentatively entitled *What Is It to Read? A Dialogue with Jacques Derrida*.

25. Ralph Waldo Emerson, "Plato; or the Philosopher" (1850), in *Essays and Lectures*, ed. Joel Porte (New York: Library of America, 1983), 637. The following quotation comes from the same text, 641.

26. Northrop Frye, *Anatomy of Criticism* (Princeton: Princeton University Press, 1957), 275.

27. Henry David Thoreau, *Walden* (1854; reprint, New York: Library of America, 1985), 565. The following quotations come from 566–67.

28. See Edward W. Said, *Orientalism* (New York: Pantheon, 1978), 98, for a start on this topic, which is one of the book's major themes.

29. Ibid., 54–55.

30. Jonathan Arac, *"Huckleberry Finn" as Idol and Target: The Functions of Criticism in Our Time* (Madison: University of Wisconsin Press, 1997), 203–6.

31. I have argued further for Ellison's cosmopolitan perspective in "Toward a Critical Genealogy of the U.S. Discourse of Identity: *Invisible Man* after Fifty Years," *boundary 2* 30, no. 2 (2003), esp. 201–2.

32. Ralph Ellison, "Society, Morality and the Novel" (1957), in *Collected Essays*, ed. John F. Callahan (New York: Modern Library, 1995), 700.

33. Ralph Ellison, *Invisible Man* (1952; reprint, New York: Random House, 1992), 260.

34. Alan Davidson, *The Oxford Companion to Food* (New York: Oxford University Press, 1999), 856. Dictionaries support this account, offering cognate terms in Wolof and Bambara.

35. Walt Whitman, *Poetry and Prose*, ed. Justin Kaplan (New York: Library of America, 1982). The poem runs from p. 383 to p. 387.

36. For more on the complications of Whitman's language, see my "Whitman and Problems of the Vernacular," in *Breaking Bounds: Whitman and American Cultural Studies*, ed. Betsy Erkkila and Jay Grossman (New York: Oxford University Press, 1996).

37. See the testimony by Stanley Kurtz (listed as a Research Fellow, Hoover Institution, and Contributing Editor, *National Review Online*) before the House Select Subcommittee on Education, June 19, 2003. Available online at: http://edworkforce.house.gov/hearings/108th/sed/titlevi61903/kurtz.htm. For a brief print account, see Sara Roy, "Short Cuts," in *London Review of Books* 26, no. 7 (April 1, 2004).

38. Edward W. Said, "Introduction to *Moby-Dick*" (1991), in *Reflections on Exile and Other Essays* (Cambridge: Harvard University Press, 2002), 364.

39. Edward W. Said, "Introduction: Secular Criticism," in *The World, the Text, and the Critic* (Cambridge: Harvard University Press, 1983), 1–30.

40. Edward W. Said, *Culture and Imperialism* (New York: Knopf, 1993), esp. 96.

41. For fuller explanation of "contrapuntal," a term drawn from the discourse of music, see my discussion in *"Huckleberry Finn" as Idol and Target*, esp. 204.

42. See my contribution to "Edward Said's *Culture and Imperialism*: A Symposium," *Social Text*, no. 40 (Fall 1994): 14.

43. This introduction also appears as a chapter in the first of Said's posthumous books. See Edward W. Said, *Humanism and Democratic Criticism* (New York: Columbia University Press, 2004), 85–118.

44. Said, "Introduction" to *Mimesis*, xxvi.

45. Edward W. Said, *Freud and the Non-European* (London: Verso, 2003), 25–27.

46. On "effort," see Said, "Introduction" to *Mimesis*, xxxii, and also, Auerbach, "Introduction: Purpose and Method," in *Literary Language and Its Public in Late Latin Antiquity and in the Middle Ages*, trans. Ralph Manheim (Princeton: Princeton University Press, 1965), 18.

47. Said, "Introduction to *Moby-Dick*," 358.

48. Samuel Taylor Coleridge, *Biographia Literaria*, ed. James Engell and Walter Jackson Bate, volume 7 of *Collected Works*, ed. Kathleen Coburn (Princeton: Princeton University Press, 1983), 2:15–16.

49. On the challenge posed by the sublime to Coleridge's goal of harmony, so fundamental to the established pedagogical aesthetics of Anglophone literary study in the twentieth century, see Jonathan Arac, *Critical Genealogies: Historical Situations for Postmodern Literary Studies* (New York: Columbia University Press, 1987), 139–40.

50. Edward W. Said, *Beginnings: Intention and Method* (New York: Basic, 1975), 380.

51. Edward W. Said, "Living in Arabic," *Raritan* (Spring 2002): 235.

52. Hortense J. Spillers, *Black, White, and in Color: Essays on American Literature and Culture* (Chicago: University of Chicago Press, 2003), 327.

53. For the best discussion, see Gavin Jones, "George Washington Cable and the Creole Language of Louisiana," in *Strange Talk: The Politics of Dialect Literature in Gilded Age America* (Berkeley and Los Angeles: University of California Press, 1999), 115–33.

54. William Faulkner, *Absalom, Absalom!* (1936: reprint, New York: Modern Library, 1951), 146.

55. Ibid., 251. The following quotations come from 250–51.

56. Robert E. Spiller et al., eds. *Literary History of the United States*, 3 vols. (New York: Macmillan, 1948). See Jonathan Arac, "Problems of Nationalism in American Literary Historiography," in *REAL—Yearbook of Research in English and American Literature*, vol. 11 (Tübingen: Gunter Narr Verlag, 1995), 15–27.

57. See Jonathan Arac, "Paul de Man's Ambivalence: Rereading 'Literary History and Literary Modernity,' " in *Time and the Literary*, ed. Jay Clayton et al. (New York: Routledge, 2002), 121–44.

58. See especially, Jonathan Arac, *The Emergence of American Literary Narrative, 1820–1860* (Cambridge: Harvard University Press, 2005).

59. Brian Edwards, *Morocco Bound: Disorienting America's Maghreb, from Casablanca to the Marrakech Express* (Durham, N.C.: Duke University Press, 2005); Aamir Mufti, *Enlightenment in the Colony: The Jewish Question and Dilemmas in Postcolonial Culture*

(Princeton: Princeton University Press, forthcoming). Within American ethnic studies note also several outstanding books that work across languages: Matthew Frye Jacobson, *Special Sorrows: The Diasporic Imagination of Irish, Polish, and Jewish Immigrants in the United States* (Cambridge: Harvard University Press, 1995), with an archive including Polish and Yiddish sources; Brent Edwards, *The Practice of Diaspora: Literature, Translation, and the Rise of Black Internationalism* (Cambridge: Harvard University Press, 2003), which triangulates African American writing with Paris and Africa; and Hana Wirth-Nesher, *Call It English: The Languages of Jewish American Literature* (Princeton: Princeton University Press, 2006), which analyzes the traces of Yiddish and Hebrew in English-language writing.

60. Many thanks to the excellent assistance provided by Elaine Vitone. Since our research was confined to Web sites, it is quite possible that we have understated by failing to find some resources that actually exist. I am grateful to the University of Pittsburgh for supporting our research while I was a visiting faculty member in fall term, 2005.

CHAPTER 2

The Deterritorialization of American Literature

Paul Giles

THE THEME OF THIS ESSAY IS the relationship between American literature and physical space. My concern will be not only with fictional works that are organized, explicitly or implicitly, around particular conceptions of place, but also with how these texts are informed by other kinds of geographical projection, of the kinds found in cartography and other forms of mapping. My thesis will be that the relationship between American literature and geography, so far from being something that can be taken as natural, involves contested terrain, terrain which has been subject over the centuries to many different kinds of mutation and controversy. I will argue these instabilities have too frequently been overlooked in the ways the subject of American literature has been codified and institutionalized, especially over the past hundred years. David Harvey wrote in 1989 about the desirability of reconstructing a matrix of "historical-geographical materialism" within which cultural conditions can be analyzed, and to reconsider American literature in the context of geographical materialism is to think through the variegated forms of its imaginary relations to the real dimensions of space.[1] More specifically, I will contend that the association of America, and by extension the subject of American literature, with the current geographical boundaries of the United States is a formulation that should be seen as confined to a relatively limited and specific time in history, roughly the period between the end of the American Civil War in 1865 and the presidency of Jimmy Carter, which ended in 1980. In the early years of the republic, I shall suggest, the more amorphous territorial framework of the United States engendered parallel uncertainties about the status and authority of American discourse, whereas since 1980 the effects of globalization have impelled us to reexamine the premises of U.S. national identity in a quite different light.

There are two significant theoretical considerations to address before proceeding with this argument. The first is the problem of periodization. It is important to acknowledge how any boundary that historians draw, in time or in space, must inevitably be arbitrary in some way, but it is also important not to lose sight of the valuable cultural work that a retrospective process of chronological remapping can perform. As Fredric Jameson observed in his classic essay "Periodizing the 60s," the value of this kind of historicization lies in the way it can bring to light structural analogies between apparently disparate events within particular eras. This has the beneficial effect of moving narratives of the past away from both anecdotal self-indulgence and sentimental forms of nostalgia through a contrary insistence that, in Jameson's words, "History is necessity," that the past "had to happen the way it did, and that its opportunities and failures were inextricably intertwined, marked by the objective constraints and openings of a determinate historical situation."[2] In this regard, Arjun Appadurai has similarly described the identification of "isomorphic" correspondences between disparate points on a grid as a way of bringing into illuminating juxtaposition events that might otherwise have been considered entirely unrelated, thereby bringing to light correspondences that would otherwise have remained hidden.[3]

The second theoretical caveat emerges from Paul Ricouer's observation, in *Time and Narrative*, of how cultural historians have no choice other than to read time backward, as what Ricoeur calls "retrodiction" rather than prediction. This method inevitably involves projecting from effect to cause, rather than the other way around. This means not only that all history is narrative, but also that we reconfigure such narratives in the light of what Ricoeur calls a "redistribution of horizons," changing our view of the past in accordance with revised expectations about the present and the future.[4] This in turn lends all historical remapping a reflexive dimension, since scholars necessarily find themselves imitating the formula that Edgar Allan Poe ascribed to the writing of detective stories, starting at the conclusion and then retracing forward what had already been traced backward. This kind of structural double bind has manifested itself recently in the manifold attempts to change the genealogy of American literary history, to revise beginnings rather than ends: Cyrus Patell, to take just one recent example, discovers the precursors to multicultural twenty-first-century America in the Dutch ethnic legacy of cosmopolitan New York, rather than in the time-honored Puritan origins of New England.[5] The teleology we impose upon the past, in other words, is embedded necessarily in concerns of the present.

This recognition of the inevitably perspectival slant of institutional narratives, however, can also serve beneficially to demystify the old institutional narratives associated with American Studies. At the beginning of the twenty-first century, it becomes increasingly apparent that twentieth-century narratives of American cultural history, framed as they were by assumptions about the country's national destiny, became accustomed to looking out for phenomena that seemed to anticipate the national power of the United States, a power that had only been consolidated in hegemonic terms relatively recently. The very category of the "early republic" is itself an anachronistic term, of course, implying there was a later republic into which these anterior events naturally led. This is why, for example, the Puritan poet Edward Taylor was often celebrated in the last century as a harbinger of the tortuous romantic spirit of Emily Dickinson, in the same way that Anne Bradstreet was hailed as an honorary ancestor by post-1945 writers such as John Berryman, who prized her confessional aspects, and Adrienne Rich, who emphasized her sturdy spirit of feminist independence.[6] All of these misprisions involve a creative and interesting use of the past, but in a historical sense they are manifestly misleading, since they tend to gloss over Taylor's Calvinist silences and Bradstreet's courtly, Renaissance conservatism in the interests of aligning them with a national narrative that is projected backward so as to validate American national culture of a later time.

There is, however, little to suggest such a sense of national triumphalism appeared a fait accompli to Americans themselves in the first half of the nineteenth century, when their structures of governance and tentative moves toward political cohesion were based on what many at the time considered to be the dubious theoretical hypothesis of federal union. In the first sixty years of U.S. history, in the aftermath of the colonial period, the country's sense of national identity was as uncertain, as provisional, as its cartography. Matthew Lotter's map of Philadelphia in 1777 symptomatically illustrates the gaping discrepancy between a tiny rational grid at the heart of the city center and the sprawling, amorphous terrain in the unmapped, unregulated countryside of surrounding Pennsylvania.[7] The western part of the present-day United States was even more inchoate: to look at a historical map of Latin America in 1830 is to see the territories of Mexico extending up through present-day California, Arizona, and New Mexico, with the shape of the nation itself appearing very different from the "sea to shining sea" model with which we are familiar today.[8] The point here, quite simply, is that when Ralph Waldo Emerson writes in 1844 about America being a "poem in our eyes," it is precisely that, a hypothetical or imaginative conception, or at least one that has not yet achieved any firm sense of territorial grounding or enclosure.[9] Walt Whitman's national poetry in the 1850s similarly has a tentative, optative dimension, something that is frequently overlooked because of the blustering and hortatory tone of his verse. All of the political investments in notions of Manifest Destiny in the 1840s and 1850s, the drive to expand westward and to claim the land in the name of the Stars and Stripes, speak to a desire to, as it were, fill in the blank spaces on the map, to subjugate the continent in a cartographic as well as a military sense. Indeed, the frequent U.S. wars at this time—with the British in 1812 culminating in the Battle of New Orleans, with the Mexicans in the 1840s over Texas and the Southwest territories, and with Native Americans over the question of Indian removal— all of these speak to an impulse to redescribe the map of the nation. This is one reason maps themselves were so popular in American education in the early nineteenth century, as Martin Brückner has shown, and why geography came to be considered a basic, compulsory subject in American schools; the textbook *Geography Made Easy*, produced by the "father of American geography" Jedediah Morse in 1784, had gone through twenty-two editions by 1820, and geographical writing at this time was, in Bruce Harvey's words, a "patriotic genre."[10] The reciting of place names became as familiar in American educational contexts at this time as the learning by rote of spelling or multiplication tables in other countries, and it testified to the pioneering attempt imaginatively to appropriate what was, of course, a dauntingly large and unsettled continent.

To talk of early-nineteenth-century American culture in relation to deterritorialization, then, is to suggest that its way of identifying itself as something different did not necessarily involve simply a mimetic reflection of locality. The writings of Ralph Waldo Emerson have traditionally been thought of as a source for the national identity of American literature because of his principled emphasis on what he calls in "Nature" (1836) an "original relation to the universe."[11] But there is, in fact, very little description of the natural world in this or any other part of Emerson's writing, and the way he marks his originality is not through mimesis but through intertextuality, through taking icons and ideas from classical European culture and spinning them round in a new way. The exuberantly weightless quality of Emerson's prose thus derives from the way he remaps nineteenth-century American culture in relation to the classical monuments of the past. Just as Handel's biblical oratorios of a hundred years earlier rehouse epic mythologies of the past within a radically disjunct neoclassical environment, a form of "sacred parody" that flaunts ebulliently the gap between past and present, so Emerson presents himself in a deliberately belated fashion as the intellectual heir of Plato and Montaigne, someone whose project involves the vertiginous transformation of one culture into another.[12] It is perhaps unfortunate that Emerson was designated by the twentieth-century critical tradition of American Romanticism most closely associated with Harold Bloom as the institutional progenitor of American literature—the ultimate source of Transcendentalism, Pragmatism, William James, Wallace Stevens, and so on—without an equivalent emphasis on what Emerson describes in his essay "Experience" (1844) as the inherently intertextual quality of perception: "Life is a train of moods like a string of beads," he writes, "and, as we pass through them, they prove to be many-colored lenses which paint the world their own hue, and each shows only what lies in its focus." "Experience," with its emphasis on what Emerson calls the attainment of a soul's "due sphericity," exemplifies ways in which, for a person living in the United States in the 1840s, her home appeared to be positioned in a paradoxical situation somewhere between the empirical and the abstract, between place and placelessness.[13] It is one of the burdens of Emerson's writing that location itself is always relative and arbitrary, that Goethe is his neighbor as much as the man in the next street, that, as he remarks in his 1844 essay "The Poet," banks and tariffs are "dull to dull people" but in fact rest on "the same foundations of wonder as the town of

Troy, and the temple of Delphi."[14] To read Emerson in intertextual terms, in other words, is to deterritorialize him, to extract him from the limiting circumference of antebellum New England and to think about ways in which he attempts deliberately to reconceptualize Enlightenment universalism within an alternative New World environment.

In the 1850s, geography itself increasingly became part of the rhetoric of Manifest Destiny in the United States. The American Geographic Society was established in 1851, three years before Arnold Guyot, the most influential American geographer of his era, took up the chair at Princeton he was to occupy for the next thirty years. Emerson himself owned the 1851 edition of Guyot's *The Earth and Man*, in which the author's project was to develop a theory of hemispheric evolution as providential and thus as entirely consonant with the exceptionalist qualities of U.S. national identity. The "vital principle" of geography, asserted Guyot, was the "mutual exchange of relations" between "inorganic nature" and "organized beings," so that the physical world should not be seen merely as an inert or inanimate object, but as a phenomenon "organised for the development of man." According to "the decrees of Providence," he claimed, "nature and history, the earth and man, stand in the closest relations to each other, and form only one grand harmony." Guyot's conception of hemispheric symmetry was of a piece with his narrative of westward historical progression, the notion that the center of civilization, which had originated in Asia, was now passing from Europe to North America. Guyot further verified the cultural superiority of North to South America by presenting this hemispheric antithesis as analogous to that which appertained in Europe: "The contrast between the North, mitigated in the temperate regions of the mother country, is reproduced in the New World, more strongly marked, and on a grander scale, between North America, with its temperate climate, its Protestant and progressive people, and South America, with its tropical climate, its Catholic and stationary population."[15] It is not difficult to see why this version of geographical providence would have appealed especially to Emerson in the 1850s, after the war with Mexico, the annexation of Texas, the evacuation of the British from the Pacific Northwest, and the American incorporation of the Oregon Territory. In a journal entry of 1853, Emerson notes how "Columbus was the first to discover the equatorial current in the ocean," and he cites with approbation a passage from *The Earth and Man*, where Guyot declares it "beyond a doubt . . . that the waters of the ocean, move with the heavens; that is, in the direction of the apparent course of the sun and stars, from east to west."[16]

What crucially changed the cultural and political landscape of the United States was, of course, the Civil War, which after its conclusion in 1865 consolidated the geography of the nation by ensuring it would henceforth be integrated into one political territory. It is not surprising that scholars, particularly in the United States, have kept returning compulsively to the Civil War as a turning point of national destiny because, despite all of the internecine regional and racial conflicts it highlighted, the outcome of the war also facilitated the emergence of the United States as the world's leading economic power in the second half of the nineteenth century. It was then that the country began to take the continental shape that we know today: California was admitted to the union in 1850, Oregon in 1859, Kansas in 1861, Nevada 1864, Nebraska 1867, Colorado 1876, the Dakotas, Montana and, Washington in 1889, Idaho in 1890, and so on. The joining together of the North and the South, in other words, ran in parallel with the joining together of the East and the West; America was metamorphosed from a series of local economies into an imposing continental edifice. Given the simultaneous growth in communications and technology at this time, the expansion westward of the railways, the development of the telegraph, and so on, it becomes easy to see how the United States could understand itself as a coherent political and economic entity by the year 1900 in a way that simply had not been possible when Emerson wrote "Nature" in 1836.[17]

This vision of the United States as a culturally and politically unified entity had, of course, been anticipated during the Civil War by Abraham Lincoln. In his Gettysburg address, Lincoln invoked a self-replicating, circular representative structure of "government of the people, by the people, for the people," as though the model of the country were predicated upon a mythic form of egalitarian democracy, something that was certainly very far from the minds of the Founding Fathers eighty years earlier. Not coincidentally, it was around Lincoln's time that *the United States* began to take on the form of a singular noun, rather than the plural noun that had been conventionally used in the first half of the nineteenth century, with this shift from plural to singular exemplifying again the consolidation of the nation into a state of indivisible unity. It was also around the turn of the twentieth century that the notion of the land as bearing inherent national values came to be invested with a sacred aura. Florida and New Orleans, for instance, were bartered and traded quite happily in the early nineteenth century, but after the Civil War the idea of the United States as a national space was mystified in such a way that no politician would dare henceforth to think of paying off the national debt by, say, simply selling off the Florida Keys or southern California to the highest bidder.[18] America's purchase of Alaska from Russia for $7.2 million in 1867 was, in this sense, the last commercial transaction of its kind.

Much of the critical language in this era of burgeoning U.S. nationalism tended to involve a justification of American difference, of the particular qualities of American scenes and locations, such as we see in the novels of Theodore Dreiser, William Dean Howells, and others. This was also the era of the mythology surrounding Ellis Island, through which immigrants were to be socially assimilated and homogenized into American citizens. The high-water mark of immigration to the United States was 1.3 million in 1907, the year before Israel Zangwill produced his play *The Melting Pot*, which reproduced the mythology of America as a land of immigrants even in critiquing its efficacy. This kind of double vision, constructing and deconstructing an image of America as promised land simultaneously, was characteristic of the way American Modernism tended to be wrapped into a rhetoric of nativist utopia, a rhetoric that served as the foundational basis and underlying grid for all of the texts' subsequent vacillations and ironies.[19] Although Randolph Bourne's essay "Trans-National America," published in 1916, starts off in its first sentence by proclaiming "the failure of the melting pot" in the face of "diverse nationalistic feelings" among the American immigrant population during the First World War, the penultimate paragraph of Bourne's essay looks forward prophetically to a new version of the United States predicated upon a greater tolerance of ethnic diversity, what Bourne calls "a future America, on which all can unite, which pulls us irresistibly toward it, as we understand each other more warmly."[20]

American literature of the late nineteenth and early twentieth centuries thus tends not only to be saturated in locality but also to understand that locality as a guarantee of its own authenticity and its patriotic allegiance, something articulated most explicitly by the polemical essays of Howells in defense of the methods of realism. This is the realm of what Philip Fisher has called "hard facts," where the relationship between the local and the national becomes self-allegorizing, in the sense that the value of particular places, Willa Cather's Nebraska or Robert Frost's New England or William Carlos Williams's New Jersey, is validated not by their specific local characteristics or phenomenological qualities but from their synecdochic embodiment of a national impulse, their sense of being, as Williams put it, "in the American grain."[21] Tom Lutz's work on literary cosmopolitanism has emphasized the extent to which regional writing in late-nineteenth- and early-twentieth-century America was mediated by an external perspective that sought to integrate region and nation as the geographical corollaries of each other, as patriotic manifestations of what Howells called "our decentralized literature." John Dewey's 1920 essay "Americanism and Localism" paradoxically declared "locality" to be "the only universal" aspect of American national identity, while Carrie Tirado Bramen, in *The Uses of Variety*, has described how an emphasis on diversity, both ethnic and regional, became an "inviolable sign of national exceptionalism" for twentieth-century American culture.[22] Tracing this discourse of material and spatial abundance back to William James's writings on pluralism in 1909, Bramen shows how, so far from opposing identitarian politics, James became the precursor of latter-day theorists such as Cornel West who, even now, imagine a commitment to diversity to be emblematic of the way in which an open U.S. culture differentiates itself from the more repressive, restrictive systems of other countries.

This move to integrate and reconcile local variation within a larger national matrix was perpetuated in the early twentieth century through the rationalized industrial methods perfected by Henry Ford and others, which were based around a factory system where the national model was reproduced in every state of the union. The defining issue in John Dos Passos's novel *USA*, published in 1938, is how by this time national similarities have become more important than regional differences, how an industrial model of mass production and consumption has permeated every corner of the United States. (The title of the first volume of this trilogy, *The 42ⁿᵈ Parallel*, is taken pointedly from the geographical line of latitude that extends east to west across the U.S.) All of this generated tremendous political cohesion and economic wealth for the country in the middle part of the twentieth century, enabling it to intervene decisively in the Second World War and to establish itself iconically, particularly in Europe, as an emblematic land of the free, a Cold War alternative to both the brutality of Fascism and the poverty of Communism. It was of course in the aftermath of the Second World War that the American Studies Association was founded in the United States, in 1951. Most of the American studies programs in Europe also originated around this time, trading off the idea of America as an exemplary and exceptional nation, a beacon both of material regeneration, through its laissez-faire economic system, and also of cultural modernity. Such modernity was thought to emerge through a stylistic emphasis on colloquial informality, typified in the 1950s by jazz and other forms of popular culture, as well as in the incisive vernacular of Saul Bellow and the beat writers, all of which seemed to imply a welcome escape from the ossified class structures and social hierarchies of Europe. In a cover story of 1941, Henry Luce, editor-in-chief of *Time* magazine, famously described the twentieth century as the American century. As Neil Smith has observed, such a prophecy on Luce's part necessarily involved an assumption of "geographical amnesia," a putative triumph over the coordinates of physical space, the replacement of an imperial design based on territorial possession by one driven instead by a liberal internationalism, through which American economic and cultural ideas would penetrate overseas markets.[23]

What I want to suggest, though, is that the United States has now moved in significant ways beyond this national phase and that since about 1980 the country has entered what we might call a transnational era, one more centered around the position of the United States within global networks of exchange. In attempting to give some form of historical specificity to transnationalism, I'm drawing on the idea of deterritorialization first broached in 1972 by the French theorists Gilles Deleuze and Félix Guattari, in their psychoanalytical work *Anti-Oedipus*, to describe the flows of desire that traverse the boundaries of distinct, separate territories:

> The decoding of flows and the deterritorialization of the socius thus constitutes the most characteristic and the most important tendency of capitalism. It continually

draws near to its limit, which is a genuinely schizophrenic limit. . . . [C]apitalism, through its process of production, produces an awesome schizophrenic accumulation of energy or charge, against which it brings all its vast powers of repression to bear. . . . Far from seeing in the State the principle of a territorialization that would inscribe people according to their residence, we should see in the principle of residence the effect of a movement of deterritorialization that divides the earth as an object and subjects men to the new imperial inscription, to the new full body, to the new socius. . . . The State can no longer be content to overcode territorial elements that are already coded, it must invent specific codes for flows that are increasingly deterritorialized.[24]

The term "deterritorialization" has subsequently been used in a broader cultural and political context by critics such as Caren Kaplan, who has related it to the experience of women and ethnic minorities in "becoming minor," or living on the edge, and by Appadurai, who has discussed it more specifically in relation to the processes of globalization:

the world in which we now live—in which modernity is decisively at large [involves] a theory of rupture that takes media and migration as its two major, and interconnected, diacritics and explores their joint effect on the work of the imagination as a constitutive feature of modern subjectivity. . . . [M]y approach to the break caused by the joint force of electronic mediation and mass migration is explicitly transnational—even postnational. . . . [I]t moves away dramatically from the architecture of classical modernization theory, which one might call fundamentally realist insofar as it assumes the salience, both methodological and ethical, of the nation-state. . . . Until recently . . . imagination and fantasy were antidotes to the finitude of social experience. In the past two decades, as the deterritorialization of persons, images, and ideas has taken on a new force, this weight has imperceptibly shifted.[25]

Speaking in 2004, a senior diplomatic figure in the U.S. Embassy in London expressed the view that the crucial political shift within his own professional lifetime was not the transition in 2000 from Bill Clinton to George W. Bush, but the country's move in 1980 from Jimmy Carter to Ronald Reagan. All such dividing lines in history are of course arbitrary and approximate, as noted earlier, but this one might be more plausible than most, because it was in the 1970s and 1980s that the economic infrastructure of the United States began to change decisively. Richard Nixon anticipated this shift toward a global economy in August 1971 when he announced that the United States would no longer redeem currency for gold, thereby effectively abandoning the gold standard and ushering in an era of fluctuating exchange rates. David Harvey dates the decline of "the Fordist regime" from 1973, the same year that money became "de-materialized," as a fully floating system of currency conversion was adopted so that money no longer had "a formal or tangible link to precious metals."[26] With the loss of the mechanism that effectively regulated the growth rate of the country's money supply, the United States, like other na-

tion-states, found itself increasingly drawn into the marketplace of global exchange, something given greater momentum by the free-market philosophies
of President Reagan in the 1980s, and in the 1990s by the dramatic growth
in information technology that made it increasingly possible to transfer capital
around the globe at a moment's notice. These developments were replicated
slightly later in other parts of the world: in Britain, for instance, Margaret
Thatcher became prime minister of Britain in 1979, bringing to an abrupt end
the postwar years of liberal social consensus in that country, but the key symbolic event in Europe was the fall of the Berlin Wall in 1989, which not only
effectively ended the Cold War but also fatally undermined the social and
economic cohesion of what had been postwar Europe's most successful corporate state, West Germany. Michael Denning sees the fall of the Berlin Wall
as heralding the crucial break between what he calls the age of three worlds,
demarcated according to the discrete geopolitical zones that dominated area
studies in the Cold War era between 1945 and 1989, and the subsequent
era of globalization. Denning makes the point that it was pressure from the
International Monetary Fund and the transfer of finance capital across national borders that crucially destabilized at this time the autonomy of self-
enclosed political regimes of all kinds, Manley's social democratic Jamaica as
well as De Klerk's South Africa.[27]

It is important to emphasize how these forces of deterritorialization have
also operated powerfully to disturb and dislocate the national identity of the
United States itself, in particular the relationship between its domestic space
and the rest of the world. In *Empire*, produced not coincidentally at the height
of the neoliberal boom in 1999, Michael Hardt and Antonio Negri describe
international capitalism as "a *decentered* and *deterritorializing* apparatus of rule
that progressively incorporates the entire global realm within its open, expanding frontiers," and they suggest this was a "new imperial form of sovereignty," one not to be identified with any particular "nation-state." But such a
version of imperialism would appear to be oddly reminiscent of a disembodied
transcendentalism, wherein finance capital, rather than Emerson's transparent
eyeball, has become the force field whose center is everywhere and its circumference nowhere: in the words of Hardt and Negri, "Empire presents a superficial world, the virtual center of which can be accessed immediately from any
point across the surface."[28] By rendering spatial geography redundant, Hardt
and Negri implicitly mimic the rhetoric of empire in the way they render
territorial formations obsolete; according to Neil Smith, their "recognition of
empire remains clouded by the lost geography ideologies that should be its
target."[29] Within the world of geographical materialism, however, the actual
experience of deterritorialization manifests itself as much more jagged and
fractious, bound up with tensions and inconsistencies that cannot be subsumed merely within global systems or regimes of capital accumulation.

One fictional representation of this fraught state can be found in the novel *Primary Colors* by Joe Klein, published as an anonymous account of Bill Clinton's election campaign in 1992. The presidential candidate, called there "Jack Stanton," addresses a group of workers in Portsmouth, New Hampshire, and tells them he's not going to delude them into thinking he can protect their jobs for life in a new situation where transnational corporations can swiftly pull investment in and out of the country in a way that would never have occurred to Henry Ford sixty years earlier:

> "So let me tell you this: No politician can bring these shipyard jobs back. Or make your union strong again. No politician can make it be the way it used to be. Because we're living in a new world now, a world without borders—economically, that is. Guy can push a button in New York and move a billion dollars to Tokyo before you blink an eye. We've got a world market now. And that's good for some. In the end, you've gotta believe it's good for America. . . . I'll fight and worry and sweat and bleed to get the money to make education a lifetime thing in this country, to give you the support you need to move on up. But you've got to do the heavy lifting your own selves. I can't do it for you, and I know it's not gonna be easy."[30]

Stanton, or Clinton, deliberately positions himself here in relation to the flexible conditions of the global marketplace, the realm of outsourcing and transnationalization, where American corporate interests can be served just as easily, often more easily, by relocating service or production industries to Mexico or Asia, where wages are lower and costs are cheaper, rather than through domestic investment. What this has meant is that the stable patterns of middle-class prosperity and security that characterized the earlier Henry Ford era have all but evaporated; corporate profits have of course increased rapidly, but their growth is not related directly to or shared by large sections of the working population, as it tended to be in the mid-twentieth century, when corporations such as Ford usually took a benevolent, patriarchal interest in the welfare of their employees.

The relationship between American culture and globalization is a vast topic that touches upon telecommunications, media, and the expansion of transnational corporations; the main point to be made here is simply that it happened. For example, the hamburger chain McDonald's only opened its first two foreign outlets, in Canada and Puerto Rico, in 1967, but by 1999 overseas sales for McDonald's had actually overtaken domestic sales, and today a majority of their outlets, approximately seventeen thousand out of thirty thousand, are located outside the territorial boundaries of the United States.[31] Indeed, the relationship between geographical location and cultural identity has changed so radically in the wake of recent changes in communications technologies that Linda Basch has argued the traditional distinction between migrants and immigrants no longer holds good. She points, for example, to the Grenadian constituency in New York who remain socially, politically, and often economically part of their ancestral domain; in fact, of Grenada's population of ninety thousand only thirty thousand of them actually live there, and this has led to a new construct of what Basch calls a "deterritorialized" nation-state within which people can remain active electronically in their old countries. Such two-way relationships have increasingly been legally formalized: since the late 1980s, for example, the Philippine state has continued to collect income tax on all Filipino citizens residing abroad on a special overseas visa issued by the government. This has meant also that the U.S. Congress has found itself increasingly under direct pressure from Filipino voters in the United States to get involved directly in Filipino domestic politics, with the consequence that the traditional distinctions between domestic and foreign have come to appear increasingly unclear. Nor should this Filipino example be seen as especially anomalous; in *The Transnational Villagers* (2001), Peggy Levitt offers a case study of how migrants from Miraflores, a town in the Dominican Republic, to Jamaica Plain, a neighborhood of Boston, participate in the social, political, and economic lives of their homelands and their host society simultaneously.[32] The transnational village, in Levitt's sense, functions not through spatial proximity but through cheap telecommunications and airfares, and to conceive of a nation-state that stretches beyond its traditional geographical boundaries is also to imagine, by a reverse projection, an American state whose territory is no longer automatically synonymous with the interests of U.S. citizens.

None of this is intended to present neoliberalism or globalization as a simple fait accompli, nor to suggest that local or national politics have no part to play in the organization and redistribution of resources. What it is to argue, in relation to the study of American literature and culture, is that since about 1980 the rules of engagement have changed so significantly that old area studies nostrums about exceptionalist forms of national politics and culture, pieties about American diversity or whatever, have become almost irrelevant. In terms of ways in which this move toward a transnational infrastructure has manifested itself in American literature, some of the most illuminating instances occur in the works of writers such as Douglas Coupland and William Gibson—one brought up in Vancouver, Canada, but who writes about the Pacific Northwest as a transnational region; the other born in South Carolina, but resident in Vancouver since 1972—whose representations of American digital culture are organized obliquely around parallel computer universes. There is an extended treatment of the theme of deterritorialization in Gibson's novel *Pattern Recognition* (2003), whose heroine works for a public relations company called Blue Ant, described in the book as "more post-geographic than multinational." As she shuttles across national boundaries, Gibson's heroine thinks back to her father, who for twenty-five years had been "an evaluator and improver of security for American embassies worldwide" and whose watchword had always been "secure the perimeter." However, the old Cold

Warrior is lost in Manhattan on the morning of 9/11, with his wife saying "that when the second plane hit, Win's chagrin, his personal and professional mortification at this having happened, at the perimeter having been breached so easily . . . would have been such that he might simply have ceased, in protest, to exist."[33]

Gibson's novel highlights the way in which 9/11 has become for the United States the most visible and haunting symbol of the new permeability of its borders, its vulnerability to outside elements. In this sense, it is no surprise how the enormous stress on "homeland security" in the administration of George W. Bush should operate as a reaction against this widespread sense of dislocation and trauma. To turn a home into a "homeland" is, by definition, to move from a zone in which domestic comforts and protection could be taken for granted to one in which they had to be anxiously and self-consciously guarded; in that sense, the very phrase "homeland security" is almost a contradiction in terms, since it evokes the very insecurity it is itself designed to assuage. As Jean Baudrillard has said, terrorism might be seen as an almost inevitable counterpart to the development of liberal market economies, since its enabling structures are almost identical, based as they are around the exploitation of computer and aeronautic technologies, rapid capital transfers, the wide dissemination of scientific and other kinds of information, and the all-encompassing power of a global media: above all, terrorism trades off a culture of spectacle.[34] Whereas for most Americans the Second World War and the subsequent Cold War took place in alien locations, the distant world of European battlefields or the shadowy realm of spies coming in from the cold, the most uncomfortable thing about 9/11 was the way it demonstrated how borders separating the domestic from the foreign can no longer be so easily policed or, indeed, even identified. Such permeability became conflated in the minds of many Americans both with a threat to Christian fundamentalist values and with the loss of job security for large numbers of people in what Edward Soja has called a "postfordist" economic landscape, one driven by internationally mobile capital and technology, rather than by labor and more traditional forms of production.[35] The powerful impact of 9/11 might thus best be understood not in terms of how it appeared as an entirely unexpected event, a bolt from the blue, but, on the contrary, how it resonated as a symbolic culmination of the various kinds of deterritorializing forces that had been gathering pace since the Reagan years.

Considered in the light of these transnational pressures, the back-formation of nationalist reaction in twenty-first-century U.S. politics becomes less surprising. To regard the loss of a liberal, democratic idea of America as some kind of betrayal of inherent national values is simply to conflate the mythic version of exceptionalism that sustained American Studies in the mid-twentieth century with a just and accurate representation of the country as a whole. Moreover, to refer twenty-first-century politics back simply to the framework of an internecine conflict within the United States between conservatives and liberals—"a cold civil war," as Hortense Spillers called it in 2004—is to misunderstand how this situation has been brought about in large part by the way foreign bodies are interfacing uncomfortably with U.S. national interests.[36] To imagine the current situation in the U.S. simply as another civil war is to redefine it in domestic, nineteenth-century terms as a Manichaean conflict between emancipation and slavery, enlightenment and oppression; it ignores the more significant ways in which both the red and the blue states have become mutually self-defining in the way they square up against each other dialectically, comprising a protective circle within which each recognizes the other as the enemy. In this sense, the idea of a new civil war becomes a curiously comforting notion, one that assumes your antagonist is an old, familiar foe rather than one that is new and harder to recognize. There is also a danger within the liberal academy of superciliously dismissing the conservative agenda as simply intellectually backward, though the obstreperous rejection of deracination and cosmopolitanism as elitist conceits in the aggressively demotic poetry of Robert Pinsky suggests how anxieties about cultural, economic, and religious displacement are by no means confined merely to tub-thumping evangelicals.[37]

The larger framework here relates to the diminution rather than the agglomeration of U.S. power. Political theorist Immanuel Wallerstein has concluded that the relative decline of American hegemonic power over the next fifty years is inevitable, not because of any particular policies pursued or not pursued by U.S. presidents, but because of more structural reasons, in particular the increasing modulation of domestic economies within a transnational axis of geopolitical space. The amorphous processes associated with globalization will affect the United States politically as well as economically: as Niall Ferguson has pointed out, any nation is less powerful politically if it has a thousand nuclear weapons when every other nation has one than if it has one and other nations none at all. One of the policies being pursued by George W. Bush's administration, a policy surely doomed to long-term failure, is to freeze nuclear "proliferation," as they call it, at a stage most favorable to the United States.[38] This is a familiar enough ploy within the annals of imperial history, going back to the ancient Romans, who attempted strenuously to prevent potential enemies from getting their hands on all kinds of dangerous weapons. But given the way that the Internet has speeded up global exchanges of information, so that scientific knowledge is no longer locked within Cold War vaults but dispersed among many different centers, such an ambition of exceptionalist superiority and isolationism, geared toward preserving American world domination, would appear to have no chance at all of long-term success. Nor is it at all likely that, for all of its politically calculated rhetoric about the "axis of evil," the U.S. government itself is unaware of how this balance of power is slowly shifting. Indeed, one of President Bush's own advisory bodies, the National Intelligence Council, produced in December 2004 a report entitled *Mapping the Global Future*, which describes globalization as "an overarching 'mega-trend,' a force so ubiquitous that it will substantially shape all the other major trends in the world of 2020," so that "how we mentally map the world in 2020 will change radically." The report goes on to predict openly that although the United States will continue to be "the most important single country across all the dimensions of power," by 2020 it will also see "its relative power position eroded."[39]

In this light, one of the most interesting aspects of contemporary American literature is how it represents ways in which these pressures of deterritorialization are being internalized and understood affectively. John Updike, for instance, made his name in the 1960s and 1970s by chronicling the fortunes of Harry Angstrom in the Rabbit series of novels, and especially for the way he drew analogies between the fate of his main character and the contemporary condition of the United States. Thus, *Rabbit, Run* (1960) comments on the impulse toward romantic freedom among the beat writers of the late 1950s, *Rabbit Redux* (1971) sardonically observes the Apollo moon landings and the swinging sixties, and so on. Part of the structural difficulty with this Rabbit sequence, though, as many critics have observed, is that the parallels between the life of a white Pennsylvania automobile worker and the fate of the country as a whole seem ultimately to become forced and exclusionary.[40] Updike's Rabbit novels are attuned specifically to the nationalist ethos of a post–World War II era when white middle-class America was assumed to represent the fate of the country at large, and when the national radio and television networks, which function as a kind of chorus in Updike's novels, imagined themselves to be speaking on behalf of a unified people. However, in *Seek My Face* (2002) there is a specific meditation on what Updike's narrator calls "the fading Protestant hegemony" and on the erasure of the national security that formerly went along with a clearly defined sense of American identity. Ensconced at the age of seventy-nine in her house in Vermont, the painter Hope Chafetz thinks of how "owning this house restored her to certain simplicities of childhood, when houses and yards demarcated territories of safety and drew upon deep wells, mysterious cisterns brimming with communal reserves." She also watches the evening news on television and sees in place of the regular NBC newscaster, Tom Brokaw, what she calls "a perfectly stunning young woman, light topaz eyes as far apart as a kitten's," whose "name wasn't even Greek, it was more like Turkish, a quick twist of syllables like an English word spelled backwards. The old American stock is being overgrown," she thinks: "High time, of course: no reason to grieve."[41] The elegiac tone in this novel is related not only to Hope's personal sense of aging but also to her recognition of how the old American order itself is passing, how the traditional iconography of national identity now appears to be as insecure as the superannuated charms of Christian theology, whose demise, in typical Updike fashion, is also lovingly chronicled in this book.

Another kind of map is provided by Leslie Marmon Silko as a preface to her 1991 novel *Almanac of the Dead*, a narrative that ambitiously rewrites the history of America from the standpoint of Native American communities. Centered on Tucson, Arizona, this "five hundred year map" extends from the Laguna Pueblo Reservation in the north to Mexico City in the south, and it represents the current U.S.-Mexico border as incidental to the flow of human and cultural traffic across this land over the centuries. The novel itself, like the cartographic image that precedes it, encompasses a perspective of deliberate inversion that involves redrawing the map of the United States in space as well as time. Silko's novel deliberately eschews the chronologies of U.S. history to establish for the Arizona region an entirely different kind of cultural vantage point, seeing the American Southwest in the context of Aztec civilizations and the Apache wars, thereby rendering the familiar national narrative of the United States contingent and reversible. This in turn works as a corollary to the chronology of "the people's history" in the last section of this book, which foregrounds slave history and deliberately overlooks the celebrated landmarks of established U.S. history.[42] Silko herself has described the U.S. government as an illegitimate enterprise founded on land stolen from Native American peoples, though *Almanac of the Dead* represents American culture more in terms of a complex legacy of mixed ancestries, a hybrid concoction of Spanish and other indigenous cultures interlinked with the apparatus of the global village. Elsewhere, Silko has written of the shift in emphasis after 1980 by agencies of the U.S. government from the "Iron Curtain" to "Border Patrol," as the Immigration and Naturalization Service sought to prevent free travel not only across but also within U.S. borders, especially in the American Southwest, and to construct the kind of defensive mechanisms against a perceived threat of mass migration and "illegal aliens" that anticipated the current fetish of "homeland security."[43] Indeed, Native American culture offers an interesting microcosm and symbol of the current fate of U.S. culture, since the concept of deterritorialization was forcibly applied to Native American people in the early nineteenth century, when Andrew Jackson, president of the United States between 1829 and 1837, urged the nation to accept the loss of Indian tribes as inevitable. In *The Pioneers* (1823), James Fenimore Cooper represents the breakup of the ice on Lake Otsego as an organic analogue to the historical dispossession of Native American peoples, a process that the author thereby tries to naturalize.[44] Indeed, one might say that the loss of territorial security that was visited upon Native Americans in the nineteenth century has now become, in different ways and under different circumstances, something that is afflicting U.S. culture as a whole.

My general hypothesis, then, is that the nationalist phase of American literature and culture extended from 1865 until about 1980, and that the current transnational phase actually has more in common with the so-called early national period, between 1780 and 1860, when national boundaries and habits were much less formed and settled. The geography scholar Robert David Sack has linked the idea of territory above all to themes of power, protection, and political control, control that is sometimes projected onto the territorial formation itself, as in the familiar notion of something being "the law of the land." He has also written of how the notion of territory has frequently been endowed with an idea of mythical content, as in the way the ancient division of the Chinese Empire into four quarters was fondly imagined to be a mirror of cosmic order.[45] Such forms of sublimation involve what Deleuze and Guattari called a process of "reterritorialization," where the appropriation of territory is designed to occlude its own material flux, an approach that manifests itself, often in circuitous ways, even in contemporary readings of American literature.[46] For instance, in *Landscape and Ideology in American Renaissance Literature* (2003), Robert E. Abrams invokes the idea of what he calls "*negative* geography" in order to explain the resistance of Thoreau and others to rationalistic cartographies, cartographies that Abrams understands as alien impositions from the European world on a pristine American scene. In this reading, the escape from abstract geographical mapping into what Abrams calls "a sense of indefinite existential promise" becomes an implicit guarantee of an American literary nationalism that justifies itself by its escape from "the hallucinatory authority of centralized, panoptic vision" and defines itself instead by its relationship to the unmapped sublime.[47] Abrams thus critically recapitulates the classic Transcendentalist move whereby the erasure of specific locations in history and geography becomes the sign of the writer's separatist self-reliance and American authenticity. To place culture and geography in this kind of mutually exclusive relationship is, of course, to overlook ways in which their narratives are inextricably intertwined. In this sense, Abrams's version of "negative geography" operates much like a traditional form of dehistoricization, a transliteration of material conditions into a version of mythic idealism within which time and space are frozen out. Geographical materialism, by contrast, would seek to restore these spatial dynamics to American literature.

In an era of global warming and various forms of transnational circulation, when issues of the environment cannot be reduced simply to local or national specificities, such a dissolution of space into "negative geography" must surely appear merely parochial. One of the conceptual problems with the study of U.S. literature and culture has always been its tendency toward a relatively narrow theoretical matrix, its distinct preference for familiar nationalistic terms of reference enjoying a supposedly "natural" affinity with the native soil, a self-perpetuating loop through which American writers were critically validated for being identifiably American. By contrast, the conceptual displacement of U.S. territorial autonomy has opened up intriguing new possibilities for the international study of America's place within the world today, and there are two European theorists of transnationalism whose work might usefully, if provocatively, be read against the grain of the American polis. The first is the German philosopher Jürgen Habermas, whose book of essays *The Postnational Constellation* (2001) is one of the best investigations so far of the challenges posed by the contemporary world to social democratic models of community based around the secure foundations of a welfare state. Habermas goes on in this book to consider ways in which forms of representative democracy might be reconfigured within a new era of digital technology and genetic engineering, switching the arguments away from a religious fundamentalist focus by offering interesting observations on whether human cloning might be considered a new version of political slavery. He also raises important questions of how individual choice might be preserved within a postliberal environment, where, pace Thomas Jefferson, freedom can no longer be seen as a natural or inherent right linked organically to any particular national soil.[48] Habermas's rigorously secular philosophy forms a valuable transnational counterpoint to current American debates about multiculturalism and diversity, debates that too frequently assume an implicitly nationalistic and metaphysical dimension, shadowed as they are by the old patriotic ghost of *e pluribus unum*.

Another European theorist of transnationalism who might be said to open up crevices in the monolithic U.S. domain is French political thinker Etienne Balibar. Balibar's *We, the People of Europe? Reflections on Transnational Citizenship* (2004) discusses ways in which nations have traditionally attempted to guard their borders so as to preserve the integrity of their public sphere and have consequently defined themselves primarily through various mechanisms of exclusion, although he also points out how, in the twenty-first century, these borders are no longer "entirely situated at the outer limit of territories" but are—through international media, finance, and so on—dispersed everywhere within them, so that "border areas . . . are not marginal to the constitution of a public sphere but rather are at the center."[49] The central concern of Balibar's book is the changing political system in Europe and its slow evolution into something more like a federal union, but, by Ricoeur's logic of "retrodiction" that I invoked earlier, it's entirely possible these altered conditions in Europe will force us to reexamine the literature and culture of the nineteenth- and twentieth-century United States in a new light. Prophecy is always a risky business, but it would appear likely that over the next fifty years Europe will gradually evolve into a more integrated political state within which English will emerge as the dominant language, even though, as David Crystal suggests, this use of English as a lingua franca will exist alongside a range of other European languages historically embedded in particular national cultures.[50] What this will produce is a model of political union where multinationalism and multilingualism are the norm, and this may well induce scholars in the twenty-first century to take another look at American literary history of earlier eras, when the official rhetoric of melting-pot assimilation and monolingualism tended simply to gloss over aspects of U.S. culture that did not conform to these hegemonic ideals. Rather than seeing Europe as positioned in the kind of conceptual opposition to America that characterized the exceptionalist impulse of American Studies in the twentieth century, this transnational matrix will force scholars to think of Europe and the United States in terms of more complex relations of analogical convergence and divergence. Just as scholars today look back with a touch of condescension on the 1950s generation that equated American literature exclusively with books written by white males, so scholars in 2050 may look back in equal bemusement upon the generation of scholars around the turn of the millennium that understood American literature to be synonymous with literature written in English.

Deterritorialization as the term was used by Deleuze and Guattari had a quite specific psychoanalytical meaning, but the term can be extrapolated to make some suggestive observations about ways in which subjects of all kinds, both individual and national, find themselves compelled to relate to what Appadurai calls the "theory of rupture that takes media and migration as its two major, and interconnected, diacritics."[51] This is why I would see some of the recent work on American empire, which has become prominent recently within the world of American studies, as problematical. The concept of "United States imperialism" seems often to extrapolate a view of American influence abroad from the realist epistemologies associated with the nationalist era at home, thereby simply extending the familiar domain of U.S. nationalism around the globe. Its locus classicus is the Theodore Roosevelt paradigm of the strenuous frontier life, which certainly helped to galvanize American territorial excursions during the Spanish-American wars of the 1890s; but it is far from clear that the expansionist dimensions of U.S. imperialism at the turn of the twentieth century can be translated smoothly into the ubiquitous border conditions of a hundred years later.[52] David Harvey has written of the dialectic between a territorial and a capitalist logic of power within the "new imperialism," and of how "[i]n practice the two logics frequently tug against each other, sometimes to the point of outright antagonism."[53] This is the internal contradiction of twenty-first-century empire that the idea of deterritorialization effectively mediates. Rather than merely conflating America and empire and understanding U.S. power to be a "colossus," in Niall Ferguson's imperious phrase, there is an important sense in which we should read the United States itself as one of the objects of globalization, rather than as merely its malign agent, so that all of the insecurities associated with transnationalism are lived out experientially within the nation's own borders as well.

By restoring a matrix of historical and geographical materialism to the United States at the beginning of the twenty-first century, we come to understand how the idea of American culture has always been bound up inextricably with particular configurations of space, configurations that have changed their shape many times over the past two hundred years. From a critical point of view, deterritorialization, like transnationalism, is a doubled-up, recursive term that seeks to bracket off or contradict the trope associated with a prior metanarrative: territory, nation, or homeland. It speaks to a paradoxical situation where affective loyalties, local affiliations, and subliminal legacies are ironically traversed by larger vectors of political and economic disenfranchisement, vectors that threaten to push the nation further and further away from the representative center of its own imagined community. To speak of American literary culture under the rubric of deterritorialization is thus not simply to encumber it with the monolithic categories of globalization or imperialism but, rather, to think of it as a socially constructed, historically variable, and experientially edgy phenomenon, whose valence lies in the tantalizing dialectic between an illusion of presence and the continual prospect of displacement.

Notes

1. David Harvey, *The Condition of Postmodernity: An Enquiry into the Origins of Cultural Change* (Oxford: Blackwell, 1989), 359.

2. Fredric Jameson, "Periodizing the 60s," in *The 60s without Apology*, ed. Sohnya Sayres, Anders Stephanson, Stanley Aronowitz, and Fredric Jameson (Minneapolis: University of Minnesota Press—Social Text, 1984), 178.

3. Arjun Appadurai, *Modernity at Large: Cultural Dimensions of Globalization* (Minneapolis: University of Minnesota Press, 1996), 182.

4. Paul Ricoeur, *Time and Narrative*, vol. 1, trans. Kathleen McLaughlin and David Pellauer (Chicago: University of Chicago Press, 1984), 135; and *Time and Narrative*, vol. 3, trans. Kathleen Blamey and David Pellauer (Chicago: University of Chicago Press, 1988), 173.

5. Edgar Allan Poe, "The Philosophy of Composition" (1846), in *Essays and Reviews* (New York: Library of America, 1984), 13; Cyrus Patell, "A New Capital for American Literary History," paper presented at the Modern Language Association Annual Convention, Philadelphia, December 30, 2004.

6. For critiques of this teleology in relation to "early American literature," see R. C. De Prospo, "Marginalizing Early American Literature," *New Literary History* 23 (1992): 233–65; and William C. Spengemann, *A New World of Words: Redefining Early American Literature* (New Haven: Yale University Press, 1994).

7. William Boelhower, "Inventing America: A Model of Cartographic Semiosis," *Word and Image* 4, no. 2 (April–June 1988): 495.

8. On the instability of U.S. nationalism in the West in the early nineteenth century, see David Waldstreicher, *In the Midst of Perpetual Fêtes: The Making of American Nationalism, 1776–1820* (Williamsburg, Va. and Chapel Hill: Omohundro Institute of Early American History and Culture and University of North Carolina Press, 1997).

9. Ralph Waldo Emerson, "The Poet," in *Essays: Second Series*, vol. 3 of *Collected Works*, ed. Alfred R. Ferguson and Jean Ferguson Carr (Cambridge: Harvard University Press, 1983), 22.

10. Martin Brückner, "Lessons in Geography: Maps, Spellers, and Other Grammars of Nationalism in the Early Republic," *American Quarterly* 51 (1999): 311–43; Bruce A. Harvey, *American Geographics: U.S. National Narratives and the Representation of the Non-European World, 1830–1865* (Stanford, Calif.: Stanford University Press, 2001), 28.

11. Ralph Waldo Emerson, "Nature," in *Nature, Addresses, and Lectures*, vol. 1 of *Collected Works*, ed. Robert E. Spiller and Alfred R. Ferguson (Cambridge: Harvard University Press, 1971), 7.

12. Ronald Paulson, *Hogarth's Harlot: Sacred Parody in Enlightenment England* (Baltimore: Johns Hopkins University Press, 2003), 214–22.

13. Ralph Waldo Emerson, "Experience," in *Essays: Second Series*, 30, 46.

14. Emerson, "The Poet," 21–22.

15. Arnold Guyot, *The Earth and Man: Lectures on Comparative Physical Geography, in Its Relation to the History of Mankind*, trans. C. C. Felton (London, 1850), 17, 19, 294–95, 28–29, 284.

16. Ralph Waldo Emerson, *The Journals and Miscellaneous Notebooks, vol. 13, 1852–1855*, ed. Ralph H. Orth and Alfred R. Ferguson (Cambridge: Harvard University Press, 1977), 5, 169.

17. On the cultural and economic development of the United States in the late nineteenth century, see Alan Trachtenberg, *The Incorporation of America: Culture and Society in the Gilded Age* (New York: Hill and Wang, 1982).

18. Benedict Anderson, "National Citizenship, Private Property, and Domestic Migration: Witches' Brew?" paper presented at University of Oxford, October 13, 2004.

19. On the complementary aspects of racial identity and textual irony in American modernist narratives such as *The Great Gatsby*, see Walter Benn Michaels, *Our America: Nativism, Modernism, and Pluralism* (Durham, N.C.: Duke University Press, 1995), 41–42.

20. Randolph Bourne, "Trans-National America," in *War and the Intellectuals: Collected Essays, 1915–1919*, ed. Carl Resek (New York: Harper and Row, 1964), 107, 123.

21. Philip Fisher, *Hard Facts: Setting and Form in the American Novel* (New York: Oxford University Press, 1985); William Carlos Williams, *In the American Grain* (New York: Boni, 1925).

22. Tom Lutz, *Cosmopolitan Vistas: American Regionalism and Literary Value* (Ithaca: Cornell University Press, 2004), 38; John Dewey, "Americanism and Localism," in *The Middle Works, 1899–1924, vol. 12, 1920*, ed. Jo Ann Boydston (Carbondale: Southern Illinois University Press, 1982), 15; Carrie Tirado Bramen, *The Uses of Variety: Modern Americanism and the Quest for National Distinctiveness* (Cambridge: Harvard University Press, 2000), 1.

23. Neil Smith, *American Empire: Roosevelt's Geographer and the Prelude to Globalization* (Berkeley and Los Angeles: University of California Press, 2003), 17, 460.

24. Gilles Deleuze and Félix Guattari, *Anti-Oedipus: Capitalism and Schizophrenia*, trans. Robert Hurley, Mark Seem, and Helen R. Lane (1972; reprint, London: Athlone Press, 1984), 34, 195, 218.

25. Caren Kaplan, "Deterritorializations: The Rewriting of Home and Exile in Western Feminist Discourse," in *The Nature and Context of Minority Discourse*, ed. Abdul R. JanMohamed and David Lloyd (New York: Oxford University Press, 1990), 357–68; Appadurai, *Modernity at Large*, 3, 9, 53.

26. Niall Ferguson, *Colossus: The Rise and Fall of the American Empire* (London: Allen Lane, 2004), 102; Harvey, *Condition of Postmodernity*, 140, 297.

27. Michael Denning, *Culture in the Age of Three Worlds* (London: Verso, 2004), 24–26, 46.

28. Michael Hardt and Antonio Negri, *Empire* (Cambridge: Harvard University Press, 2000), xii, xiii–xiv, 58.

29. Smith, *American Empire*, 458.

30. Anonymous [Joe Klein], *Primary Colors* (London: Chatto and Windus, 1996), 161–62.

31. Ferguson, *Colossus*, 18.

32. Linda Basch, Nina Glick Schiller, and Cristina Szanton Blanc, *Nations Unbound: Transnational Projects, Postcolonial Predicaments, and Deterritorialized Nation-States* (Amsterdam: Gordon and Breach, 1994), 226–27, 258–69; Peggy Levitt, *The Transnational Villagers* (Berkeley and Los Angeles: University of California Press, 2001).

33. William Gibson, *Pattern Recognition* (London: Viking Penguin, 2003), 6, 44, 351.

34. Jean Baudrillard, "L'Esprit du Terrorisme," trans. Michel Valentin, *South Atlantic Quarterly* 101 (2002): 409.

35. Edward W. Soja, *Postmodern Geographies: The Reassertion of Space in Critical Social Theory* (London: Verso, 1989), 3.

36. Hortense Jeanette Spillers, "African Americanist Criticism and the State in the Age of Terror," paper presented at the Modern Language Association Annual Convention, Philadelphia, December 28, 2004.

37. Bruce Robbins, "The Village of the Liberal Managerial Class," in Vinay Dharwadker, ed., *Cosmopolitan Geographies: New Locations in Literature and Culture* (New York: Routledge, 2001), 15. In particular, Pinsky has taken exception to Martha Nussbaum's essay "Patriotism and Cosmopolitanism," which argues for recognition of the rights of noncitizens. See Joshua Cohen, ed., *For Love of Country: Debating the Limits of Patriotism* (Boston: Beacon Press, 1996), 87–88.

38. Immanuel Wallerstein, *The Decline of American Power* (New York: New Press, 2003), 207–8, 287; Ferguson, *Colossus*, 299.

39. *Mapping the Global Future: Report of the National Intelligence Council's 2020 Project* (Washington, D.C.: Government Printing Office, 2004), 10–11.

40. See, for example, Jay Prosser, "Under the Skin of John Updike: *Self-Consciousness* and the Racial Unconscious," *PMLA* 116 (2001): 579–80.

41. John Updike, *Seek My Face* (London: Hamish Hamilton, 2002), 70–71, 81, 11.

42. Leslie Marmon Silko, *Almanac of the Dead* (1991; report, New York: Penguin, 1992), 14–15, 742–46.

43. Leslie Marmon Silko, "The Border Patrol State" (1994), in *Yellow Woman and a Beauty of the Spirit: Essays on Native American Life Today* (New York: Simon and Schuster, 1996), 115–23.

44. David C. Lipscomb, "'Water Leaves No Trail': Mapping Away the Vanishing American in Cooper's Leatherstocking Tales," in Helena Michie and Ronald R. Thomas, ed., *Nineteenth-Century Geographies: The Transformation of Space from the Victorian Age to the American Century* (New Brunswick, N.J.: Rutgers University Press, 2003), 55–71.

45. Robert David Sack, *Human Territoriality: Its Theory and History* (Cambridge: Cambridge University Press, 1986), 1, 33, 77.

46. Deleuze and Guattari, *Anti-Oedipus*, 258.

47. Robert E. Abrams, *Landscape and Ideology in American Renaissance Literature: Topographies of Skepticism* (Cambridge: Cambridge University Press, 2004), 2, 12, 78.

48. Jürgen Habermas, *The Postnational Constellation: Political Essays*, trans. Max Pensky (1998; reprint, Cambridge: MIT Press, 2001), 58–112, 163–72.

49. Etienne Balibar, *We, the People of Europe? Reflections on Transnational Citizenship* (Princeton: Princeton University Press, 2004), 1–2.

50. David Crystal, *English as a Global Language*, 2nd ed. (Cambridge: Cambridge University Press, 2003), 5–7.

51. Appadurai, *Modernity at Large*, 3.

52. See, in particular, Amy Kaplan and Donald E. Pease, ed., *Cultures of United States Imperialism* (Durham, N.C.: Duke University Press, 1993); and Amy Kaplan, *The Anarchy of Empire in the Making of U.S. Culture* (Cambridge: Harvard University Press, 2002). For a discussion of the different stages of U.S. imperialism, contrasting "the acquisitive, classically colonial wars of 1898" with the "peculiarly anti-geographical ideology of post-nineteenth-century Americanism," see Smith, *American Empire*, 5, xiii.

53. David Harvey, *The New Imperialism* (Oxford: Oxford University Press, 2003), 29.

CHAPTER 3

Unthinking Manifest Destiny: Muslim Modernities on Three Continents

Susan Stanford Friedman

> Be careful that by modernization you don't mean Westernization.
> —Stephen K. Sanderson and Thomas B. Hall,
> *Civilizations and World Systems*[1]

> If the question of modernity and democracy can be historically
> and theoretically disentangled from the question of Western
> desires and designs for domination, and if its diverse cultural
> roots can be unearthed, then we can begin to talk of a new
> global modernity that celebrates and underscores difference
> rather than forced assimilation.
> —Abbas Milani, *Lost Wisdom: Rethinking Modernity in Iran*[2]

A planetary consciousness about American literary cultures requires thinking beyond the temporal and spatial boundaries of a nation that justified its expansion ever westward with the notion of its manifest destiny to rule the North American continent.[3] To break the conventional discursive borders of the United States, I plan to go far afield in space and time through a series of comparative juxtapositions loosely affiliated in a web of interconnected modernities. Detours are the way to get where I want to go: first, unthinking America's current imperial assumption of its global destiny; then examining how Muslim modernities in Asia, Africa, and the United States[4] unravel this new global manifest destiny, especially with gender as the flashpoint of conflict. The city of Baghdad—the current arena of America's "manifest destiny"—is the essay's leitmotif, the thread that draws the different parts of the far-flung web together. Two memoirs that have circulated widely in the United States—Fatima Mernissi's *Dreams of Trespass: Tales of a Harem Girlhood* (1994) and Azar Nafisi's *Reading Lolita in Tehran* (2003)—will provides test cases for examining Muslim modernities on three continents and how they help to redraw the boundaries of American literary studies.[5]

MODERNIZATION AS WESTERNIZATION?

I'll begin with a story, my first detour. I was in Shanghai, in July of 2001, sitting at a round banquet table with some faculty members and graduate students from Fudan University and talking about recent changes in Shanghai. Since 1992, the city has experienced what is probably the most rapid urban transformation in history. With the exception of the historic Bund area at the riverfront and one of the old foreign concession areas left standing for tourists, Shanghai has been entirely demolished. Everywhere are now tall buildings— tall buildings for business, tall buildings for living, tall buildings for schools, and markets, and shops. The number of highways crisscrossing the city, with elaborate ramping systems and elevated roads, outpaces even Los Angeles, and a new high speed monorail—the fastest train in the world—dashes high above the highways in a blur of twinkling neon lights, looking like a people mover out of a science fiction movie.

Suddenly, one of the graduate students—a tall, thin reed of a woman with an intense expression—burst into impassioned speech, her voice cracking with tears. She said that China was losing its soul to rampant commercializa- tion. She said, "Westernization" was leading to "money-means-all." It wasn't Starbucks and McDonald's that she worried about. What angered her was that Westernization had torn down all Shanghai's neighborhoods. And there was more: She said that she loved the music of Beethoven and Brahms, but she couldn't understand Chinese music. She said Plato and Aristotle and Hobbes and Locke were important to study. But where in her political science courses was there study of any Chinese political philosophers? Why couldn't China modernize the way Japan had—building the world's second most powerful economy but holding on to its difference, especially its cultural identity as distinct from the rest of the world? I looked around the table of stunned faces. No one said a word.

I decided I would try to defuse the situation by sharing some of my own culture shock in Shanghai—my sense of a city built like a space station— especially Pudong, Shanghai's new skyline across the river that had been fields a mere ten years ago. Shanghai made Manhattan feel provincial, caught in a time warp one hundred years out of date—with its streets of Korean and Italian grocers, its coffeeshops and bakeries and pizzerias, its little neighborhoods and parks, and men playing checkers in Washington Square Park. I said to her that I hadn't seen anything in "the West" like Shanghai. It seemed like a futuristic city, like nothing in the United States, like nothing in Europe, espe- cially Europe in which the past seems always to be around the next corner, in every preserved building, like the ancient columns that poke up amongst the trees and traffic of modern Rome. I told her what returning to Hong Kong

Figure 3.1. Pudong, Shanghai. Photo by Pin-chia Feng.

had been like, to the neighborhood I had lived in thirty years ago. Most of Hong Kong's open markets were gone. Driving down the main streets, I didn't see any stores where people could buy food, although I have been told that little stores still exist in the side streets. I visited some prized public housing, a tall complex whose interiors contained what used to be in the open: wet markets now on the first floor, dry on the second, and community organizations on the third. On the nearby mainland, the green paddy fields of rice just outside the city were still there, but sprouting up all over were scores of huge apartment buildings, connected by roads through the green fields, with no other kinds of buildings in sight. From my view inside one of the apartments, I could see scores of other apartments. Each building houses some five thousand people. Each contains its own school, restaurants, community organizations, swimming pool, and gymnasiums. Vertical villages in the sky.[6]

Nothing like it in "the West," I told the graduate student in Shanghai. Nothing. Why call this new way of living I was seeing in Shanghai and Hong Kong "Westernization"? She couldn't answer and didn't believe me anyway. It is true, I told her, that skyscrapers first appeared in the West, but now, the three tallest buildings in the world are in Taiwan and Malaysia. And Paris still won't sanction a single skyscraper. No effect. I then tried a new line of questions. People who study the culture of everyday life have said, I reminded her, that one of the most profound changes of the past thirty-five years has been the way people listen to music—now, walking around with earphones, tuned

Figure 3.2. Vesuvio Bakery, New York City. Photo © Greg Gawlowski.

into a private world of beat and lyric. At one time, music was largely a communal experience, and now people can opt for privacy. Where did this "modern" form of musical experience come from? I asked her. "The West," she replied. No, I said. The Walkman came from Japan. The Sony Corporation has led the world in the creation and marketing of electronics for everyday use. The new age of globalization is unthinkable without the innovations of Asia, I said. The formation of today's "modernity" cannot be reduced to the formulaic phrase, "the Westernization of the non-Western world."

She was not convinced. She did not believe that innovation in modernization could come from anywhere but the West. Cut off from China's history by its own modernization campaigns in the twentieth century and the ravages of the Cultural Revolution, she knew little of China's dominance of the world-system prior to 1500. And so I tried yet another tack, telling her about my recent visit to Quanzhou, a city in Fujian Province south of Shanghai, once the beginning of the Silk Road of the Sea and the world's largest port city for hundreds of years, at its height during the Song and Mongol Yuan Dynasties (1127–1367). She had never heard of Quanzhou and only half believed my tales of what I had learned. I had just walked on the Luoyang Bridge, a stone bridge from the eighth century whose floating technology was the first in history to span the sea. I had visited the skeleton of an innovative Chinese ship, 114 feet long by 32 feet wide, from the Song Dynasty period (ca. 1127–1279) and learned that large ships sailed from this port to West Asia and East Africa. Marco Polo is said to have left China from Quanzhou, and a huge, wall-size scroll shows a harbor with hundreds of masts and a variety of ships from all over the world. With amazement, I had walked through the substantial remains of the Great Mosque of Quanzhou, built from 1009 to 1310, and marveled at the way today's modern, bustling city of millions has adapted the characteristic Muslim arch as its signature architecture.

I later learned that in the mid-fourteenth century the first emperor of the Ming Dynasty (1368–1644) burned the ships in Quanzhou's harbor, anticipating the isolationist policy of his grandson (Zhu Zhanji) to ensure the purity of Chinese culture by ending his father's (Zhu Gaozhi's) grandiose armada of some sixty-two ships, each some 400 feet long and 170 feet across, that traded as far away as the great Swahili kingdoms of the Malindi and the Pate.[7] Quanzhou's multiculturalism apparently posed a special threat to the first Ming emperor, Zhu Yuanzhang. As a Han Chinese, he felt threatened by Quanzhou's multicultural, commercial population, a mixture of Chinese Arabs, Jews, Christians, Buddhists, and Taoists. The Chinese Arab community was especially large, going back to missionary-traders sent by Mohammed in 618 and to the vast trading empire of the Abbasid Dynasty (750–1258), centered in Baghdad.[8]

None of what I said changed the mind of the passionate graduate student from Shanghai. "The West," a place she had never been, remained on her horizon as a monolithic place to be desired and despised, longed for and feared. She remained convinced that Shanghai's modernization was an imitation of the West, especially of the United States, thus participating in a metonymic chain of fixed associations: urbanization = modernization = Westernization = Americanization. This chain is what I call the new manifest destiny of the United States—moving the sense of America's special right-to-power from a continental to a transcontinental or planetary landscape.

FROM EUROCENTRIC DIFFUSIONISM TO POLYCENTRIC MODERNITIES

A second detour allows us to explore the way that the equation of modernization with Westernization and then Americanization exhibits what geographer J. M. Blaut calls "Eurocentric diffusionism," a belief system that developed in the West with the rise of colonialism.[9] In what he characterizes as "the colonizer's view of the world" that has come to dominate Western thought across the disciplines and the political spectrum,

> Europeans are seen as the "makers of history." Europe eternally advances, progresses, modernizes. The rest of the world advances more sluggishly, or stagnates: it is "traditional society." Therefore, the world has a permanent geographical center and a permanent periphery: an Inside and an Outside. Inside leads, Outside lags. Inside innovates, Outside imitates. (1)

Figure 3.3. Great Mosque, Quanzhou, China. Built 1009–1310. Photo by Susan Stanford Friedman.

Functioning as an ideology of Western superiority, this view typically involves a belief in both Eurocentric diffusionism and exceptionalism. The former assumes that Europe is the source of modernizing innovations and the rest of the world receives them. The latter assumes that Europe's rise to world dominance after 1500 was due to Europe's internal and autonomous qualities—whether these were economic, political, cultural, religious, or some combination thereof. This belief system served to justify European dominance throughout the colonial period, producing such notions as the "white man's burden" or the West's "civilizing mission" toward the rest of the world. With the demise of European colonialism in Asia, Africa, and the Americas, Eurocentric diffusionism has continued to evolve, taking on new forms in modernization theory, development studies, and the world-systems approach pioneered by Immanuel Wallerstein, who divides the post-1500 "capitalist world-system" into the center (the West), its peripheries, and its semiperipheries. Like the colonial version, the post-1950 version of Eurocentric diffusionism assumes that the West invented modernity, and the Rest imitates the West—belatedly, derivatively, inadequately, and depending on one's political viewpoint, either fortunately or unfortunately. The basic plot line, however, has remained remarkably consistent. The West innovates; the Rest lags behind and imitates.[10]

The United States is there and yet not there in this story of global evolution. "Eurocentrism" has no corresponding term like "Americentrism" to signal an epistemological "centrism" accompanying American global power in the post–World War II and post–Cold War worlds. As in most critiques of Eurocentrism, Blaut's sole reference to the position of the United States within the West is parenthetical: "colonialism was the basic process after 1492, which led to the selective rise of Europe, the modernization or development of Europe (and outlying Europeanized culture areas like the United States), and the underdevelopment of Asia, Africa, and Latin America" (2). Subsuming the United States under the European umbrella is to misunderstand the complex global forces that have shaped the United States since its precolonial and colonial beginnings to the present—particularly the formative roles played by indigenous populations and the immigrations of Africans, Asians, and Latin Americans by force, necessity, and choice. American notions of its manifest destiny—in both earlier continental and more recent transcontinental forms—are the particular form Eurocentric diffusionism takes in the United States.

Both Eurocentric and "Americentric" diffusionism depend upon forgetting that "the West" is itself a social construct that reflects its own ethnocentrisms and that obscures the indeterminacy of its boundaries and the radical heterogeneities and stratifications *within* its circumference. The concept of "the West" originating during the rise of Western imperialism posited its beginnings in the Mesopotamian "cradle of civilization," between the Tigris and Euphrates Rivers in what is now Iraq, and charted a path of northwestward movement from the ancient Near East of the Hebrews, through Greece, then Rome, into France, and then to modern England. Blaut calls this view "a kind of westbound Orient Express" through a "tunnel of time. . . . History is a matter of looking back or down in this European tunnel of time and trying to decide what happened where, when, and why. . . . Outside its walls everything seems to be rockbound, timeless, changeless tradition" (4–5). What Blaut leaves out, I believe, is the continued westward drift of the "Orient Express"— at least in the national imaginary of the United States, with the United States taking the place of Britain in this mythology of modernity's march in time. It has become the manifest destiny of America to embody and promote modernization on the world stage of the late twentieth and early twenty-first centuries. Whether it's George W. Bush's plan to export democracy abroad (while undermining it at home), the current fear of America's "McDonaldization" of the world,[11] or the angst of the graduate student in Shanghai, the narrative of modernization as globalization, Westernization, and finally Americanization remains very powerful in today's increasingly interlocked world.

There is a difference, however, between the *cri de coeur* of the angst-ridden Shanghai graduate student and an American assumption of its global destiny—the important difference of standpoint. Historical accuracies aside, the student's lament expresses a psychical reality that reflects the inequalities of geopolitical power and often afflicts those outside the West who have internalized the West's belief system about its own superiority, its invention of modernity, and its mission to spread modernity around the globe. Postcolonial theorists have variously addressed this experiential dimension of global relations— from Frantz Fanon's diagnosis of the psychopathology of colonialism to Homi Bhabha's notion of "colonial mimicry" in *The Location of Culture* to Partha Chatterjee's exploration of the colonial subject's ambivalence toward Western modernity. As Chatterjee writes, "Ours is the modernity of the once-colonized. The same historical process that has taught us the value of modernity has also made us the victims of modernity. Our attitude to modernity, therefore, cannot but be deeply ambiguous."[12] Although Bhabha's concept of colonial mimicry emphasizes how the colonized's imitation of the colonizer denaturalizes the assumption of Western superiority, still, his approach puts the colonized in the position of the imitator, not the originator of modernity. As Dipesh Chakrabarty writes (citing Meaghan Morris), "'The modern' will then continue to be understood . . . 'as a *known history*, something which has *already happened elsewhere*, and which is to be reproduced mechanically or otherwise, with a local context.' This can only leave us with a task of reproducing . . . 'the project of positive unoriginality.' "[13]

The experience of modernity outside the West as "belated," "derivative," or "imitative" leaves the West in place as the site of innovation and suggests that the Rest can be at best a diluted, pale, or secondary version of the "original" modernity. R. Radhakrishnan calls this "the ignominy of derivativeness" and seeks a new way of thinking about modernity that does not privilege the West.[14] He asks, "[W]hy does Europe have to be the floating signifier [of modernity] in this entire process of the utopianization of the political-cultural imagination? Why not Asia, why not Africa?" (787). Why, he wonders, does the postcolonial alone come to represent "derivativeness?" "If it is indeed the case that there is nothing that is not derivative, why should postcoloniality alone be made to carry derivativeness as a stigma?" (788). In the attempt to go beyond merely problematizing Western modernity (as he sees Edward Said and Amitov Ghosh doing), he suggests an approach based on the notion of "polycentric modernities": "Through the processes of critical and relevant significations it would indeed be possible to think up alternative, alterior, heterogeneous, hybrid, and polycentric modernities. Either that, or a thorough and definitive break with the modern altogether, whatever and however that may mean" (788).

Rather than abandon the concept of modernity, we need to rethink it radically. First, we need to recognize the historical inaccuracies of Eurocentric definitions by revisiting the *longue durée* of history on a global landscape. Advocates for the notion of European exceptionalism are typically Europeanists who know little about the rest of the world, especially in the periods preceding the rise of the West after 1500. Modernity studies needs to be more fully comparative, drawing on the different knowledge bases produced by world historians, world-system social theorists, and specialists in non-Western parts of the world. André Gunder Frank, for example, has documented how far behind Europe was in 1500 in comparison to China, India, and the Muslim Empire in technological and economic terms. The rise of the West after 1500, he argues, was enabled first from its borrowings from other cultures and second by the sudden influx of gold and silver based on its conquests in the Americas. This capital allowed Europe to compete in the global market for the first time.[15] Blaut adds the significance of the transatlantic slave trade and the depopulation of Africa through theft and of the Americas through catastrophic disease (179–213). Janet Abu-Lughod challenges the assertions of Wallerstein and others that the West invented capitalism by examining the extensive trade practices over land and sea routes that interwove Europe and Asia as the basis for Europe's rise.[16] Addressing cultural aspects of modernity, Abbas Milani argues that Iranian writers a thousand years ago "developed the rudiments of a democratic theory, a rational historiography and cosmology, a kind of embryonic empiricism," and norms for "simple, precise, and parsimonious prose" (19). Jack Weatherford explores the critical advances enabled by the vast Mongol Empire in the thirteenth and fourteenth centuries, one that brought to Europe the technologies that were vital to its rise to dominance: gunpowder and cannon, moveable type in alphabetic form, and improved navigational technology based on advanced Arab, Indian, and Chinese mathematics.[17] In critiquing his own influential 1963, *The Rise of the West*, William H. McNeill reflects that this early work is filled with "residual Eurocentrism" as it "looks at Eurasia from a naively Western viewpoint," one that was a "rationalization of American hegemony," "history from the point of view of the winners," and a subconscious reflection of the United States's "post-war imperial mood"—in short, of the new American manifest destiny produced by its success at war.[18] What this body of work collectively shows is that the modern West is also "derivative," depending for its rise, like other dominant civilizations, on global factors and the long-standing transcontinental exchange of goods, technology, peoples, and cultures.

The second task required for rethinking modernity is to eliminate the circular definitions that characterize modernity as a universal project based on the particular modernity of Europe and the United States against which all other modernities are measured.[19] Anthony Giddens, to take one example of such circularity, answers his own question, "Is Modernity a Western Project?" by saying "yes," having already defined modernity by its European example: the break from the past (feudalism) that led to the nation-state and its bureaucracies, industrial capitalism, and the bourgeois subject.[20] We need a broader concept of modernity that can be both precise enough to be useful and yet capacious enough to encompass the divergent articulations of modernity in various local settings. Elsewhere, I have examined the epistemological and political difficulties of creating such an umbrella definition and then provisionally proposed that modernity involves a vortex of factors that coalesce to produce sharp ruptures from the past.[21] The velocity, acceleration, and dynamism of shattering change across a wide spectrum of societal institutions are key components of modernity, in my view—change that interweaves the cultural, economic, political, religious, familial, sexual, aesthetic, technological, and so forth, and can move in both utopic and dystopic directions. Moreover, modernity is often associated with the intensification of intercultural contact zones, whether produced through conquest, vast migrations of people (voluntary or forced), or relatively peaceful commercial traffic and technological or cultural exchange. Indeed, heightened hybridizations, jarring juxtapositions, increasingly porous borders both characterize modernity and help bring it into being. Edouard Glissant calls this phenomenon "a poetics of relation" based on "the immeasurable intermixing of cultures."[22] The speed and scope of widespread transformation often leads to what Marshall Berman calls (citing Marx) the sensation that "all that is solid melts into air," and what I have termed "the phenomenology of the new and the now."[23] Modernity has a self-reflexive, experiential dimension that includes a gamut of sensations from displacement, despair, and nostalgia to exhilaration, hope, and embrace of the new—a range that depends in part on the configurations of power and the utopic versus dystopic directions of change.

Understood as an umbrella term, modernity has a complex and contradictory relationship to its seeming opposites, "tradition" or "history." Modernity and tradition are relational concepts that modernity produces to cut itself off from the past, to distinguish the "now" from the "then." In some sense, modernity invents tradition as a claim to a future not determined by the past. Modernity's dislocating break with the past also engenders a radical reaction in the opposite direction. As a result, periods of modernity often contain tremendous battles between "modernizers" and "traditionalists," those who promote the modern and those who want to restore an imagined and often idealized past; rather than an inexorable march forward, modernity often involves radical oscillations between modernizing and traditionalizing forces. In this sense, past-oriented traditionalism is as much a feature of modernity as modernization. Moveover, modernity also produces what Paul de Man calls (citing Nietzsche) "a ruthless forgetting" of the past: "Modernity exists in the form of a desire to wipe out whatever came earlier."[24] The past that is repressed, that will not be remembered, comes back to haunt and trouble the present. Buried within the radical ruptures from the past are hidden continuities—all the things that refuse to change or can't change, often having to do with the uneven distributions of power and violent histories.

Broadening the provisional definition in these ways presumes a pluralization of modernity, the third task needed for rethinking modernity. As Dilip Parameshwar Gaonkar puts it, "modernity is not one, but many." He challenges what he calls the "acultural theory" of modernity, which posits "the inexorable march of modernity [that] will end up making all cultures look alike." He promotes instead what he calls a "cultural theory," one that "holds that modernity always unfolds within a specific culture or civilizational context."[25] Gaonkar is one among a growing chorus of theorists and historians who are calling for a new discourse about modernity, one based on an acknowledgment of "multiple modernities," "early modernities," "alternate modernities," "polycentric modernities," or "conjunctural modernities"—to cite some of the current terms in use.[26] This approach typically assumes that each manifestation of modernity is distinctive and yet affiliated through global linkages to other modernities or societal formations. Sanjay Subrahmanyam terms this concept of global linkages "conjunctural." Countering Wallerstein's metaphor of modernity as the "virus" of capitalism spreading from the exploitative West to the Rest, Subrahmanyam writes that "modernity is a global and *conjunctural* phenomenon, not a virus that spreads from one place to another. It is located in a series of historical processes that brought relatively isolated societies into contact."[27]

Multiple modernities, in short, involve global weblike formations, with many multidirectional links, affiliations, and often brutal inequities of power. They are not mosaics, each modernity separate and isolated from all others, evolving autonomously and equally. And yet they are not the same either, as each reflects the particular indigenizations of its own location. Such hybridization involves the transformative agencies of the local as people interact with the global—what James Clifford calls "localizing strategies."[28] Shmuel Eisenstadt and Wolfgang Schluchter call this process "creative appropriation." For them, "a globalization of cultural networks and channels of communication" result in "multiple modernities," not a convergence toward a "uniform modern world," as Marx and Weber claimed.[29] Charles Taylor favors the term "creative adaptation" to emphasize how ideas and practices coming from elsewhere are translated into local terms, a process that produces "alternate modernities" rather than global homogenization.[30] I prefer the term "indigenization" to highlight the way cultural practices from somewhere else become indigenous or native through transformative agencies in any given location. This association of modernity with indigeneity appears to fly in the face of the conventional association of the term with the traditional or the primitive. But because I regard tradition as the invention of modernity, as part of modernity's fashioning of its rupture with the past, I like the contradictions that the term *indigenization* suggests. It reminds us that modernity involves a presentist forgetting of origins, a claiming of cultural practices as so much one's own that the history of their travels is often lost.[31]

BAGHDAD AND BASRA IN THE GOLDEN AGE: A CASE STUDY OF TRAVELING CULTURES

To unthink American manifest destiny and rethink modernity, let's take a third detour, back to the Muslim Empire's golden age, when Baghdad was termed the City of Peace by the second caliph of the Abassid Dynasty (749–1248). Founded by the first Abassid caliph, Baghdad was a great metropolitan culture capital with commercial and cultural ties stretching across the African continent, far west to Spain, and far east to India, Southeast Asia, and China—arguably one among a number of modernities, including preeminently T'ang Dynasty China.[32] Under the Abbasid Dynasty based in Baghdad, the arts and sciences flourished, creating new knowledge and technologies that drew on a wide array of classical Greek and Roman texts and religious and secular works from many cultures, including Jewish and Christian ones. As the center of tremendous wealth and power, Baghdad was what André Gunder Frank calls a great "turntable" or "fulcral" city, a "crossroads" serving as a hub for the globe's other great cities and complex network of land and sea trade.[33] During the early Abbasid Dynasty, Arab and Persian navigational advances led to the opening of a direct sea route from the Persian Gulf to China, including the great port city of Quanzhou, with its large Muslim community. Since the Chinese themselves had little interest in long ocean voyages during this period, the Muslim traders quickly became the leading merchant middlemen, bringing ivory, pearls, incense, and spices to China (and ports along the way) and picking up Chinese silk, paper, ink, tea, and ceramics as prized luxury items in the Abbasid court centered in Baghdad. The Silk Road over the Asian land mass had been in existence since the beginning of the first millennium. But the relatively sudden advances that made longer seagoing voyages possible in the ninth century gave a particularly prominent role to the merchants of the vast Islamic empire.

Basra, Baghdad's great port city of the Abbasid period, is featured in a brilliant exhibit entitled "Iraq and China: Ceramics, Trade, and Innovation" at the Arthur M. Sackler Gallery in Washington, D.C., a show curated by Jessica Hallett in 2005. With the medium of ceramics, the exhibit tells a story of traveling cultures that perfectly embodies the qualities of indigenization as a specific form of interculturality and modernity. The Iraqi potters of Basra were not a particularly powerful center for ceramics until their own techniques for tin-glaze ceramics met up with the technologies for T'ang Dynasty white stoneware and porcelain from China. As the Sackler Gallery exhibit brochure puts it, "With unusual swiftness and without apparent precedent, the humble character of Near Eastern pottery changed radically during the rule of the powerful Abbasid Empire (750–1258). In less than forty years, Iraqi potters transformed common earthenware into a vehicle for complex multicolored designs."[34] The T'ang potters had developed exquisitely thrown ceramics with a pearly white glaze that was unlike anything in the Abbasid world. The Basra potters lacked the white clay, wheel skills, and firing technology of the more advanced Chinese potters and were unable to attain the transluscence or purity of T'ang porcelain or stoneware. But they improvised by combining their indigenous clays and unique tin-glazing technologies to produce a cloudy-white surface that approximated the hard white ceramics of the Chinese.[35]

The Basra potters' indigenization of T'ang ceramics involved even more radical improvisations, however. They applied bold designs in their signature glaze, an intense cobalt blue used only in Iraq, to the already-fired white surface and fired the vessels again. This blue made a striking contrast with the milky-white surface, and the Basra potters often signed their distinctive blue-and-white pieces thrown in shapes borrowed from China. They also experimented with brightly colored glazes applied to the white surface, and they improvised further with the luster glaze that Iraqi potters had been the first to apply to earthenware pottery. Luster glazes create a shiny, metallic surface produced by the mixture of silver and copper, a technology that was difficult, costly, and highly prized for its rich ambers, blues, and greens and for the golden sheen that some combinations produced. Lusterware itself represents an indigenization of foreign techniques, since the Iraqi potters adapted the process from the Egyptians, who had used the mixture of silver and copper on glass.[36] The Basra designs, especially in the beginning, were often strikingly abstract, full of seemingly improvisational "optical excitement" and a "wild appearance," according to Alan Caiger-Smith. He calls these early designs "modern," "ingenious," "extravagant and sometimes dra-

Figure 3.4. Bowl, white-glazed earthenware with design in cobalt blue and green. Iraq (Basra), ninth century. Freer Gallery of Art, Smithsonian Institution, Washington, D.C. F2000.2.

matic" in their stylizations of shapes taken from local leaves, flowers, and vines. Later, the potters created more representational forms—especially animals in motion in the vibrant blues, greens, and brown glazes that stood out so sharply off the white surface.[37]

These innovations, accomplished in the short space of about forty years, revolutionized ceramic art in the centuries that followed. First, they became a major new luxury item for Arab merchants to trade. Second, the Basra inventions were themselves indigenized as the process of traveling cultures evolved. But because the Iraqi luster technology was a closely guarded trade secret passed down orally by master potters, new improvisations developed slowly. With the decline of the Abbasids by the tenth century, the center of Islamic power moved to Cairo, and the Iraqi potters took their trade secrets to Egypt, where their influence continued to grow as their wares spread throughout the Mediterranean, to Persia, and eventually as far east as China. The intricately designed lusterware of Islamic Spain descends from Iraqi luster ceramics, as does Renaissance Italian majolica, known for its historical and religious subjects carefully drawn on the white surface of the tin glaze. The luster technology moved eastward as well, indigenized in Persia to produce the famous Kashan lusterware, often considered the most skilled and best designed of luster pottery. The traders brought the Iraqi ceramics as far east as China too. By the fourteenth century, it was the cobalt blue glaze that most interested the Chinese potters of the Yuan Dynasty. The Basra cobalt blue glaze was reborn in the famous blue-and-white porcelain of Ming Dynasty China, a much-coveted item for trade that made its way back to Europe, eventually inspiring the blue-and-white Delft pottery of the Netherlands, Portugal's *azulejo* tiles, and the Spode Blue Willow-on-white of eighteenth-century England, the most copied china pattern of all times.[38]

The point of this story of Iraq-China ceramics is that the global travels of aesthetic cultural practices like ceramics involve the local articulation of ideas from elsewhere, a form of mediation in which local agencies transform the influences from outside until they become nativized in the vernacular of indigenous tradition. The point is also that these origins from elsewhere are often forgotten, particularly as a given practice comes to symbolize the distinctive character of a given culture, people, or nation. Finally, the point is to underline one of the many instances in which the cultures of "the West" are "derivative" (to echo Radhakrishnan), though not uniquely so, since the story of Iraq-China ceramics demonstrates how all cultures combine derivation with innovation on a global landscape of interculturality.

Scheherazade's Sisters: Modern Juxtapositions, Reinventions of Tradition

The tin-glaze and lusterware pottery of Basra was one of the many luxury items that filled the palaces of the Abbasid caliphs of Baghdad, especially the huge palace complex of Samarra, not far from Baghdad. Samarra was the favorite residence of the most illustrious of the Abbasids, Harun al-Rashid, who figures centrally in *The Thousand and One Nights*, the great collection of Persian, Indian, and Arab oral tales compiled and first written down during the Abbasid Dynasty, starting around 1000.[39] In contrast to the warlike and nationalist epic tradition of *The Iliad* and *The Aeneid*, *The Thousand and One Nights* emphasizes trade, its tales more often than not featuring merchants and travelers, bazaars and caravans throughout the empire. As the empire's hub, Baghdad is the great metropole of *The Thousand and One Nights*, the fulcral city linking the wanderings of its many protagonists.

Scheherazade, the central figure of the book's frame narrative, links the Baghdad of the Muslim Empire with the Baghdad of today, the Muslim world more generally, the presence of the United States in the Middle East, and the circulation of Muslim writing in the United States. Personifying the golden age love of learning, Scheherazade "had read the books of literature, philosophy and medicine. She knew poetry by heart, and studied historical reports, and was acquainted with the sayings of men and the maxims of sages and kings. She was intelligent, knowledgeable, wise and refined."[40] The story of Scheherazade emphasizes the power of words and wit over swords. The king, furious at his wife's adultery, condemns the perfidy of women and in revenge takes a virgin as wife every night, killing her in the morning. Scheherazade, the learned daughter of a court official, is determined to stop the carnage and marries the king with a plan in mind to save herself and other Muslim women. Nightly she tells him stories, not quite finishing the tale by morning, promising to finish each of the "thousand and one tales" only if he allows her to live through the next day. Her cleverness with narrative suspense and riddles keeps her alive and undermines his tyranny. In the end, the king realizes the error of his ways and promises peace to her and her Muslim sisters. "O Scheherazade," he says, "you made me doubt my kingly power . . . and made me regret my past violence towards women and my killing of young girls."[41]

Scheherazade's victory with artful words has made her a heroic figure for Arab and Islamic feminists as Muslim women have striven to achieve a suitable modernity of their own in the twentieth and twenty-first centuries, even as they disagree on how to achieve it.[42] Farzaneh Milani calls Shirin Ebadi, the Iranian human rights lawyer who won the 2003 Nobel Peace Prize, a modern day Scheherazade whose voice "is a beacon of hope and temperance."[43] In this period, Scheherazade has been an emblem of an indigenous modernity for those seeking to modernize Muslim culture, particularly in the Arab states and in Iran. Her gender has been a key element of her appeal, but she has also signified more broadly the freedom and power of speech, as well as the dimensions of golden age Islam that valued the intellectual quest for knowledge and speculation. She is a figure of Islam's early modernity, one that vied with the powerful traditionalists from the beginning of the Abbasid dynasty. Recovered in the twentieth and twenty-first centuries, she signifies a countermodernity, undeniably feminist, but distinctly Muslim, not Western.

In April of 1999, Scheherazade drew three prominent Muslim feminists together for a program entitled "Shahrazad Then and Now" at the Freer Gallery in Washington, D.C.: Mahnaz Afkhami, Azar Nafisi, and Fatima

Mernissi, as Barbara Crossette reports in "Muslim Women Hear the Call of a Storyteller," a *New York Times* article featuring interviews with the three women about Scheherazade's significance for Muslim women today. In exile from Iran since 1978, Afkhami told Crossette that Scheherazade's significance today shows that "Muslim women have largely stopped being reactive to Western feminism" and instead find the roots of their feminism in their own cultures:

> I see that the salvation of our part of the world lies in our being able to recreate our culture and our beliefs in ways that are conducive to the life we must live. . . . Muslim women are not giving up their faith; they're not giving up their traditions or their culture, but they are re-imagining them in ways that let them build on that and get strength and nourishment from it. The prototype is Scheherazade . . . who made her world as she talked about it. (Crossette, B7)[44]

After leaving Iran in 1997, Nafisi told Crossette, "I became obsessed with Scheherazade" (B7). But this preoccupation with Scheherzade had begun before she left Iran and was associated with her efforts "to teach and write literature and be the kind of woman I wanted to be without compromising" (B7). As Crossette reports, Nafisi had begun in Iran "an intensive extracurricular study of a multivolume version of Scheherazade's stories" with the seven women who came to her house for a secret course in literature after she had withdrawn from university teaching—the course that forms the core structuring device of her memoir, *Reading Lolita in Tehran* (B7). In "Imagination as Subversion" (1997), Nafisi presents an extended analysis of Scheherazade's frame story, finding in it a message that addresses her attempt to link the life of the imagination with freedom:

> What can one do when reality seems like trap, when society offers no private or public spaces within which individuals can control and shape their lives? One answer can be provided by Shahrzad: many of one's rights in reality depend upon one's creation of those rights, on one's creation of free spaces in one's imagination, and upon the courage to fight for those rights and spaces. This is not easy. It is easier to abdicate, to become mere victims . . . [instead of being] like Shahrzad, who is waiting at unexpected corners of reality, redirecting life, subverting power, renaming relations.[45]

Mernissi, a Moroccan sociologist, likewise told Crossette that Scheherazade has been important for her teaching: "I'm starting to use her as a way to build self-confidence. . . . This woman gained the right to live by using the right words. It's fantastic material for talking about the extremely tragic problems society has. And it teaches how to fight violence with words" (B7). Mernissi further informed Crossette that Scheherazade's current importance goes back to the 1920s "as a number of Muslim countries began to modernize and secularize. . . . [B]ig names in the Arab world spoke of Scheherazade as an example for intellectuals fighting for their rights. She was a fighter for the right of free expression" (B7). Scheherazade appears pervasively in Mernissi's writing, especially in her memoir *Dreams of Trespass* and *Scheherazade Goes West* (2001), a comparative study of Scheherazade and harems in the Muslim world and the Western imagination.

While Scheherazade brought Afkhami, Nafisi, and Mernissi together in Washington, D.C., in 1999, they represent divergent approaches to feminism, Muslim identity, and Islam.[46] Known for her transnational advocacy of women's rights as human rights, Afkhami has served on the boards of numerous international organizations and commissions and been president of the Sisterhood Is Global Institute and the Women's Partnership for Rights international nongovernmental organization (NGO). In her mapping of debates about Muslim women and Islamic feminism, Valentine M. Moghadam notes that Afkhami told her in 1999, "I call myself a Muslim and a feminist. I'm not an Islamic feminist—that's a contradiction in terms" (1152). But in *Faith and Freedom: Women's Human Rights in the Muslim World*, Afkhami acknowledges that Muslim feminists like Mernissi are reinterpreting Islamic texts "in the light of the humane and egalitarian spirit of Islam as distinct from its rendition by its male guardians."[47]

Mernissi regards Islamic feminism as a return to the modern, rational, and egalitarian elements present in Islam from the beginning, elements distorted by fundamentalist Islam. She is a professor of sociology at the University of Mohammed V in Rabat, Morocco, and the author of over two dozen books in Arabic, French, and English on gender, Islam, and the Muslim world. She suggests in *Islam and Democracy* that the oppression of women arose not from Mohammed or the Qu'ran but from the *Hadith*, reports of the words and deeds of Mohammed compiled by later clerics, many of whom were misogynistic (like the Church Fathers of Christianity, I would add).[48] In *Scheherazade Goes West*, Mernissi further identifies herself as a Sufi who learned the liberalizing principles and practices of Sufism from her illiterate grandmother Yasima, whom she characterizes as a living example of the oral tradition that Scheherazade represents (2). According to Mernissi, Sufism is the mystical branch of Islam that claims Mohammed's daughter Fatima as its source, and interprets the Qu'ran symbolically, emphasizing direct spiritual experience of Allah. Often under attack as not Islam by orthodox and established Islamic sects, Sufism has also been associated for centuries with the religious practices and storytelling traditions of "common" people outside the clerical order. More recently, Sufism has also been linked with modernizing Islamic intellectuals and elites.[49] As a learned storyteller, Scheherazade combines elements of Sufism and the practice of *ijtihad*, a system of independent thought and reason that developed during the Abbasid period.[50]

Fleeing the continuing domination of fundamentalist clerics in Iran in 1997, Nafisi has not aligned herself with feminist reformers of Islam or Sufism, instead centering her advocacy in the secular realm of literature and aesthetics. She refers to "Islamic feminism" as "a contradictory notion, attempting to reconcile the concept of women's rights with the tenets of Islam" (*Reading Lolita*, 262). As she recounts in her memoir, Nafisi studied English literature in the United States and Britain and eagerly returned home to Iran to teach at the time of the 1979 revolution. As one of the many university intellectuals who supported the ouster of the hated Shah, she found herself quickly alienated by the Islamic "morality squads" who imposed a traditionalist Islam on the populace. She was expelled from her teaching post at the University of Tehran for refusing to wear the mandatory headscarf, and she resigned from her position at the University of Allameh Tabatabai, a somewhat more liberal university in Tehran where she taught from 1987 to 1995 (with a term at Oxford University in 1994). She then secretly taught a small group of women in her house for two years before emigrating to the United States in 1997. She is currently listed as the Director of the Dialogue Project, Professorial Lecturer, and Visiting Fellow at the Paul H. Nitze School for Advanced International Studies (SAIS) at Johns Hopkins University.[51] For some, such as John Carlos Rowe, her association with SAIS, her grant from the conservative Smith Richardson Foundation, and her acknowledgments in *Reading Lolita* to "Paul [Wolfowitz]" and Bernard Lewis have aligned her with the neoconservatives for whom the West represents modernity while the Muslim world represents backward traditionalism in need of Western enlightenment.[52] Whatever her affiliations, Nafisi's politics are not so easy to label, in my view. Opposing those who call her feminism "Western," she says, for example, "I have a history to go back to. I don't need to go back to Mary Wollstonecraft or all these Western feminists of the eighteenth and nineteenth centuries here. I have my own models."[53]

As different as Afkhami, Mernissi, and Nafisi are in relation to Muslim women and Islam, their shared attachment to Scheherazade signifies the different ways they occupy what Shanaz Khan calls the "third space" of negotiation between the poles of Orientalism on the one hand and Islamism on the other.[54] While invocations to Scheherazade are common as a sign of the desire to form a distinctive Muslim modernity, a wide spectrum of views exists on what modernity should mean in a Muslim context and how that modernity does or should relate to Western modernity. In *Feminism and Islamic Fundamentalism*, Haideh Moghissi notes that the flashpoint of these debates has often been the status of women, gender relations, and practices such as the veil, the harem or purdah, polygamy, honor killings, stoning for adultery, and the age of nine allowed for marriage in *Shari'a* (72–73, 78–97, 132–33). As European imperialism replaced the Ottoman Empire in the heterogeneous cultures of the Middle East in the late nineteenth and early twentieth centuries, the veil and the harem were often invoked, embodying the Eurocentric binaries of West/Oriental Other, modern/traditional, progressive/backward, democratic/

despotic and thus rationalizing European hegemony as beneficial to women. As in India and other colonized sites, incipient nationalist movements reacted ambivalently, on the one hand resisting the humiliations of colonialism and on the other indigenizing many aspects of Western modernity.[55]

As both secularists and religious reformers, women figured prominently in these movements, and the unveiling of women, desegregation of the sexes, education of girls, and laws on the rights of women often went hand in hand with nationalist or pan-Arab resistance to Western hegemony, a history that Nafisi herself (among many Muslim feminists) invokes as a tradition of Middle Eastern feminist activism.[56] As the new Islamic nation-states failed to extend the promises of modernity to Muslim populations, however, Islamic fundamentalist movements arose to argue for the "re-Islamization" of Muslim societies and the outright rejection of Western modernity as un-Islamic. In some countries women lost the rights they had acquired as new laws justified by the tradition of *Shari'a* were instituted to restrict their access to public space and control their bodies. Many Muslim women in the Middle East—and in the more populous Muslim populations in South and Southeast Asia—have fought back against fundamentalist Islam, some within the framework of Islam, others outside it.

For doing so, Muslim women have often been denounced as Westernized, decadent, and traitors to their faith, their nations, and the anti-imperialist struggle against first Europe and then, especially since 1979, the United States, the Great Satan of the Islamic Republic of Iran, the Taliban, and al-Qaeda. Consequently, negotiating between Western and indigenous modernities has been difficult, fraught, and yet essential. For many, Scheherazade has enabled this negotiation by countering the overwhelming power of Eurocentric diffusionist narratives of modernity. For Mernissi and Nafisi in particular, Scheherazade is a figure rooted in their own non-Western heritage who represents a Muslim modernity for all, including women, to be won with words, not violence; with imagination and reason, not fundamentalist traditionalism. In Scheherazade's promise to the king that her storytelling "will take him to far away lands to observe foreign ways, so he could get closer to the strangeness within himself" (Mernissi, *Dreams of Tresspass*, 15), she also represents an openness to traveling modernities, including traveling feminisms, from elsewhere.

The Memoirs of Mernissi and Nafisi: Indigenous and Indigenizing Modernities

The power of words, imagination, dreams, and storytelling—Scheherazade's particular strengths—are thematically and performatively evident in Mernissi's *Dreams of Trespass* and Nafisi's *Reading Lolita in Tehran*. Both memoirs are highly literary, sharing certain conventions of the genre such as the I-narrator's reflexive self-fashioning, selective re-creation of the past, and fictionalizing representational strategies. Moreover, like historical narrative in general and autobiography more specifically, both texts contain an underlying heuristic purpose in telling the story of the past as a way of addressing concerns of the present and the future. Both indirectly explain and justify how the writer came to be the person she is and the positions she takes on issues of debate about modernity, tradition, the West, and gender. While both reject fundamentalist Islam, they do so differently, signaled in part by the different ways in which Scheherazade is deployed. While Mernissi's memoir emphasizes the indigenous roots of Muslim women's rebellion, Nafisi's memoir suggests that women's resistance depends heavily upon an indigenization of forbidden Western modernity. Mernissi's text thus counters the Orientalist view that Muslim women need to be liberated by Western modernity while Nafisi's text appears to confirm this view. And yet, Nafisi's text also attests to Iran's indigenous modernity while Mernissi's acknowledges Morocco's selective indigenization of Western modernity. As such, both texts contribute to the theorization of multiple, polycentric, and traveling modernities and thus help break the myth of America's manifest destiny to save oppressed Muslim women from backwardness.

Written in English, translated into twenty-two languages, and widely read in the United States, where Mernissi frequently lectures, *Dreams of Trespass* covers the years of her early childhood (about 1940–49) in Fez while Morocco was still a French protectorate and the nationalist movement was just beginning to make headway. The geopolitical forces at work in colonial rule and postcolonial emergence of the new, "modern" nation-state pervade her account of everyday life within the family, a well-to-do urban extended family living in an urban harem. The memoir opens with her memories of the two "frontiers" of her early childhood: "the *hudud*, or sacred frontier" between women and the world and between Muslim and Christians: "Right on our threshold, you could see women of the harem contesting and fighting with Ahmed the doorkeeper as the foreign armies from the North kept arriving all over the city" (1). "Dreams of trespass," the memoir's organizing motif, interweave what Mernissi regards as two aspects of Moroccan modernity: the freedom of women from the harem and the freedom of Morocco from foreign, Christian rule. Morocco negotiated its independence by 1956, when Mernissi was sixteen, and by the time she was a young adult in the 1960s, the institution of the harem had essentially vanished in Morocco. *Dreams of Trespass* re-creates a world that had disappeared by the time Mernissi wrote about it. Implicitly, the memoir asks, what made the modern world the writer now inhabits and how did this new world come into being? Mernissi finds the roots for transformation predominantly *within* the harem itself, *within* the nation, *within*

Moroccan and Muslim culture, but also to some extent as these interacted with the West.

The first two chapters of *Dreams of Trespass* establish the memoir's pendulum structure, one that swings back and forth from the child Fatima learning about all the restrictions of women's lives in the harem to her observing the various ways they resist their confinement and dream of freedom. Chapter 1, "My Harem Frontiers," introduces the meaning of *hudud* and *harem*, focusing on how the young child learned the rules and prohibitions embodied in the spatial architecture of the harem and its threshold between inside and outside. "Education is to know the *hudud*, the sacred frontiers," Fatima learns from "Lalla Tam, the headmistress at the Koranic school where I was sent at age three to join my ten cousins. My teacher had a long, menacing whip, and I totally agreed with her about everything: the frontier, the Christians, education. To be a Muslim was to respect the *hudud*. And for a child, to respect the *hudud* was to obey" (3). The photo that precedes chapter 1 is a picture taken from outside of a padlocked door framed by a characteristic Muslim arch: the spatial configuration that locks women in and preserves the world beyond the door for men.

Chapter 2, "Scheherazade, the King, and the Words," opens with a picture of a woman's bed in silk and brocade, a lacy curtain half hiding the room, and the light pouring through the window, which is crowded with plants reaching for the sun. Like the locked doorway, this interior female space is an architectural representation of gender relations, in this case the domestic space of intimacy to which women are confined. Paradoxically, this space is both claustrophobic but also the site of women's storytelling, for which Scheherazade, whose own tale is elaborately narrated in the chapter, is the prototype. Scheherazade is also linked to another aspect of this space: *hanan*, "a Moroccan emotional quality" that Mernissi defines as "a free-flowing, easygoing, unconditionally available tenderness" (17). Scheherazade's living avatar is Aunt Habiba, the woman abandoned by her husband who is the memoir's supreme storyteller, "the high priestess of imagination" (115). "The main thing for the powerless is to have a dream," Aunt Habiba teaches little Fatima (114). "When you happen to be trapped powerless behind walls, stuck in a dead-end harem," she would say, "you dream of escape. And magic flourishes when you spell out that dream and make the frontiers vanish. Dreams can change your life, and eventually the world. Liberation starts with images dancing in your little head, and you can translate those images in words" (115). Aunt Habiba's storytelling is the living oral tradition out of which Scheherazade's *A Thousand and One Nights* came.

The unfolding chapters of the memoir follow Fatima's education into the ways of *hudud* and *hanan*, oscillating from one to the other and the opposition between them. About *hudud*, Fatima learns that the walls of the harem are only the external manifestation of "the harem within," the rules and prohibitions that are learned gradually over time.[57] Her grandmother Yasima, one of many co-wives in a rural harem without walls, teaches Fatima that the word *harem* is "a slight variation of the word *haram*, the forbidden, the proscribed," the "invisible rules" of culture that have been internalized through socialization (61–62). In the face of the forbidden, the women engage in the female arts of storytelling, playacting, singing, dancing, and embroidering—all forms of creativity that give expression to the desire of the nontraditionalist women to escape. Mernissi elaborates on a disagreement among the women over embroidery styles to embody their different views toward modernity. Fatima's mother expresses her longings for freedom by doing "modern" (*'asri*) designs in her embroidery, while Lalla Mani does "traditional" *taqlidi* embroidery, with its tiny, tedious stitches. Lalla Mani chastises Fatima's mother for creating a wild bird with the free-form, flowing *'asri* stitches and colors, claiming that "[t]o do anything new was *bid'a*, a criminal violation of our sacred tradition" (207).

The wild bird embroidery is "modern" in a double sense: first, it resists the traditionalist commitment to imitation by fostering innovation; and second, it draws on an earlier modernity within Muslim history and culture. The bird in her mother's embroidery is an illustration from "The Tale of Birds and Beasts," one of Scheherazade's stories that Aunt Habiba would often tell as an antiharem allegory on how "[t]o be alive is to move around, to search for better places, to scavenge the planet looking for more hospitable islands" (209). In support of contemporary change, Aunt Habiba returns to golden age Islam, to the oral tradition rather than the Qu'ran or *Hadith*, and to the love of learning and speculation fostered particularly by the most famous of the Abbasid caliphs, Harun al-Rashid, the ruler who features centrally in *A Thousand and One Nights*. The women in his harem, Aunt Habiba tells Fatima, "were very educated women, swallowing history and religious books as fast as they could, in order to entertain him. Men of that time did not appreciate the company of illiterate, uneducated women, and you had no chance of capturing the Caliph's attention if you could not dazzle him with your knowledge of science, history, and geography, not to mention jurisprudence" (154). Aunt Habiba also encourages Fatima to embrace *tanaqod* (contradiction) and use *'aql*—reason, Allah's "most precious gift"—to work through the complexities. Aunt Habiba invokes without naming the practice of *ijtihad*, independent thought and reason, developed during the Abbasid period; in so doing, she embodies Mernissi's belief that fundamentalist Islam betrays the tolerant and knowledge-loving Islam that struggled against the opposing literalist camps throughout the Abbasid period and thereafter.

One of the contradictions *Dreams of Trespass* embraces is the dual source of Moroccan modernity in the 1940s. On the one hand, the spirit of Scheherazade and the Abbasid dynasty that produced her pervades the association of women's desire for freedom and education with modernity—an *Arab* modernity rooted in early Islamic culture. On the other hand, the modernity of the colonizers, specifically the French, also beckons. The nationalist party in Morocco, Mernissi informs us, adapted aspects of French modernity as a way of strengthening their resistance to colonialism. At the center of this project was the education of girls, the gradual elimination of the harem, and a nuclear family structure. Fatima was ecstatic to move from the traditionalist Koranic school held within the harem to a "modern school" where boys and girls studied a varied curriculum together (197–201). This aspect of Western modernity indigenized to become a linchpin in the Moroccan nationalist movement. Fatima is encouraged to dress up and sing like Princess Aisha, who accompanied her father, King Mohammed V, around the country and made speeches about women's liberation (199–200).[58] As part of their nationalist modernization, the men in Fatima's family even encourage their wives to adopt French cosmetics and perfumes. The women's refusal allegorizes yet another contradiction of the text. As much as most of the women in the family harem hate the institutions of their confinement, they refuse to swallow French women's modernity whole, so to speak. They want the education and the freedom of the streets, but they also want to retain their own "beauty secrets," their own rituals for the cleansing and adornment of the body. The memoir ends with Fatima's initiation into the women's beauty secrets in the public baths—the *hamman*—from which her male cousin Samir is excluded as the children enter puberty (219–42).

Within the larger feminist project of the memoir, this initiation emphasizes the values of *hanan* and the special creativity of women nurtured in the harem. The harem is—in the end—a site of tremendous contradiction. On the one hand, Fatima's illiterate mother is furious when the men refuse her request to attend school; she tells her daughter, "You *are* going to transform this world, aren't you? You are going to create a planet without walls and without frontiers" (201). But on the other hand, the roots of Mernissi's feminism lie indigenously within the harem, within the restrictions against which the women rebelled, within the space where she learned how to remake the world with words, like Scheherazade. *Dreams of Trespass* is nostalgic for the harem at the same time that it narrates the necessity for its demise. What Mernissi's act of memory does is create a sense of tradition that can inform the writer's modernity, that can insist upon its own distinctiveness from Western modernity at the same time that it borrows from it, a blend linguistically emphasized by the continual introduction of Arabic words into the lyrical flow of the English. She aims to do exactly what Afkhami advocates for Muslim feminists: "recreate our culture and our beliefs in ways that are conducive to the life we must live."

Where *Dreams of Trespass* emphasizes the indigenous roots of Mernissi's Muslim modernity and feminism, *Reading Lolita in Tehran* stresses Nafisi's indigenizing acts of creative appropriation of a forbidden Western modernity as a

form of resistance to the Islamic Republic of Iran. The "foreign"—in the form
of novels from the West—are "emissaries of that forbidden world" that enable
Iranian rebellion against the fundamentalist state (30). Aspects of everyday
life that the regime associates with Western decadence—lipstick, makeup,
nail polish, colorful clothes, music, dance, eating ice cream in public, and the
like—are hidden from the morality police by black chadors, headscarves, and
gloves, but donned in secret and practiced in the privacy of homes.[59] This
contrast between *Dreams of Trespass* and *Reading Lolita in Tehran* attests to the
different historical conditions they record and out of which they emerged.
Mernissi lives and writes freely in a Muslim country with a government determined to repress Islamic fundamentalist political movements. Written in English for a post–Gulf War audience in the West, *Dreams of Trespass* re-creates
a transitional moment in Moroccan history, just before independence from
colonialism and significant changes in women's status. Written in the United
States and published in a post-9/11 era, *Reading Lolita in Tehran* burns Nafisi's
bridges back to Iran by recounting life in an authoritarian theocracy under
censorship as women are systematically stripped of the rights they had recently
acquired.[60] But like *Dreams of Trespass*, *Reading Lolita in Tehran* is centered on
stories of women's resistance to the restrictions on their bodies and their minds
by Islamic traditionalists. They share a belief in the power of the imagination
embodied in Scheherazade.

Like *A Thousand and One Nights*, *Reading Lolita in Tehran* has a frame narrative: an account of teaching seven women students from 1995 to 1997 in her
house. The memoir begins and ends with reference to this class, how it began,
how it ended, and its epilogue. But in fact, the class is a pretext of sorts for a
hybrid text that covers much more territory of time and space, from the 1970s
through the 1990s. As a modern-day Scheherazade, Nafisi tells "a thousand
and one tales," seamlessly weaving together stories of the seven women students, dialogue with many other people, pedagogical narrative and treatise
drawing on all her teaching experiences in Tehran since 1979, accounts of
reading as resistance, short exegeses of literature she taught, and riveting sagas
of her life during the revolution, the Iran-Iraq war, and their aftermath. The
memoir ends with Nafisi's claustrophobic nightmares, her wrenching decision
to leave Iran, and an epilogue, which lets us know that most of her students
have ended up leaving as well. Thus, covertly, the memoir functions heuristi-
cally to explain and justify her own and her students' exile to the West.

Scheherazade bookends the memoir, appearing briefly at the beginning and
end. Near the beginning, Nafisi briefly mentions that the secret class in her
house "read Persian classical literature, such as the tales of our own lady of
fiction, Scheherazade, from *A Thousand and One Nights*, along with Western
classics" (6). They focused especially on the frame narrative of Scheherazade,
which Nafisi fleetingly analyzes for its portrayal of three possible roles for
women: the adulterous queen, the silent victim-virgins, and the resourceful

storyteller Scheherazade (19–20). Banned by the revolutionary regime, it served as fitting introduction to the Western classics she taught. Nafisi structures the memoir with chapters on selected works and authors and her experiences teaching them: "Lolita," to her secret class; "Gatsby," at the University of Tehran during the revolution; "James," at Allameh Tabatabai University during the war; and "Austen," to her secret class. As the end of "Austen," the mysterious friend she calls her "magician" gives her an English edition of *A Thousand and One Nights* (311, 313), thus closing the memoir with an allusion to the indigenous text whose spirit informs her own. Like Scheherazade, Nafisi opposes tyranny with words and storytelling.

Like Mernissi, Nafisi explores Muslim spatial practice as it relates to the female body: fear of it, need to contain it, belief that its purity upholds the honor of the whole family. For both, the confined space where women congregate is a female space for storytelling and talk, for laughter and tears, for the comforts of food and tea or coffee. In Mernissi's text, this space is the terrace forbidden to men, or the second floor, where the women have their rooms. In Nafisi's text, this space is predominantly a "room"—a "room of their own" where she meets with her seven students, a room that indigenizes Woolf's "a room of one's own." It is "a place of transgression," "our sanctuary, our self-contained universe," a place to dream and imagine, a place from which to contemplate their "beloved Elburz Mountains" outside the window (8, 6). It is also a world that exists within the binary of outside/inside, as in Mernissi's harem and the world beyond the doorkeeper Ahmed. But rather than long for the world outside, as the women do in Mernissi's harem, the women in Nafisi's text long for the safety of the room where they are free of the morality police and can take off their black chadors to become individuals in a wide array of colors and styles of dress reflecting a spectrum from religious to secular.

Also in contrast to Mernissi, dreams, the imagination, and fictionality itself are dual—forces for both freedom and tyranny, modernity and revolutionary traditionalism. Inside the room is the women's fictionalizing, where they use their imaginations to create an alternative to the harsh reality of the morality squads. Outside the room, the world is itself a fiction produced in the imagination of the Islamic traditionalists. Nafisi explains:

> An absurd fictionality ruled our lives. We tried to live in the open spaces, in the chinks created between that room, which had become our protective cocoon, and the censor's world of witches and goblins outside. Which of these two worlds was more real, and to which did we really belong? We no longer knew the answers. Perhaps one way of finding out the truth was to do what we did: to try to imaginatively articulate these two worlds and, through that process, give shape to our vision and identity. (26)

The double potential of fictionality for liberation and tyranny is illuminated in startling ways through the meanings that novels like *Lolita, The Great*

Gatsby, and *Pride and Prejudice* acquire as they are read and indigenized in the context of revolutionary Iran. As Nafisi says in her opening section, "This, then, is the story of *Lolita* in Tehran, how *Lolita* gave a different color to Tehran and how Tehran helped redefine Nabokov's novel, turning it into this *Lolita*, our *Lolita*" (6). Although she resists a reductionist allegory of Humbert = the Ayatollah, Lolita = resistance (35), the feminist reading that she and her students devise identifies their plight in the Islamic Republic with that of the captured Lolita, betrayed by Humbert, abused in body and soul in the service of his fantasy of her nature, and to some degree complicit in their own capture. Like Lolita,

> we had become the figment of someone else's dreams. A stern ayatollah, a self-proclaimed philosopher-king, had come to rule our land. He had come in the name of a past, a past that, he claimed, had been stolen from him. And he now wanted to re-create us in the image of that illusory past. Was it any consolation, and did we even wish to remember, that what he did to us was what we allowed him to do? (28)

This reading of *Lolita* turns upside down the readings that prevail in the West, ones that view the novel either approvingly or critically as an aesthetic allegory of the artist and erotic fantasy. Nafisi and her students read the novel in relation to a non-Western nation, particularly its women, caught in the snares of a puritanical revolutionary movement for which the purity of its women is the mark of its resistance to Western modernity and power. So eager to resist the hateful regime of the "Westernizing" Shah, many women, including Nafisi, had been swept up in the dream of revolution and had donned their chadors as a sign of resistance to the Shah and to American imperialism. In rejecting the Shah's modernity, they had lost their own. Tehran's *Lolita* has been indigenized, swallowed up, taken into the belly and digested to become a radically different novel in its new context. This nativization is a good example of what Edward Said has theorized in "Traveling Theory Reconsidered" (1994), which amends his earlier essay "Traveling Theory" (1983). Whereas he had earlier thought that transplanted ideas are rather pale imitations of the original, he later came to recognize that sometimes—his example is Fanon's transplantation of Hegel—the intertext is more forceful and radical than its origin text.[61]

Read in the early days of the revolution at the University of Tehran, *The Great Gatsby* also takes on a newly radical meaning in its transplanted soil. Condemned by her fundamentalist students for teaching a decadent Western novel, Nafisi agrees to put the novel on trial and finds that she is the only one who will publicly defend it. In its defense she tells the students how the novel exposes the illusions at the heart of the American dream, but she also finds in the novel a parallel to Iran in the illusions of antimodern revolutionaries. "What we in Iran had in common with Fitzgerald," she writes, "was this dream that became our obsession and took over our reality" (144). She reflects on "how similar our own fate was becoming to Gatsby's. He wanted to fulfill his dream by repeating the past, and in the end he discovered that the past was dead, the present a sham, and there was no future. Was this not similar to our revolution, which had come in the name of our collective past and had wrecked our lives in the name of a dream?" (144). The interplay of tradition and modernity in *The Great Gatsby* is indigenized some fifty years later in revolutionary Iran, where the play of illusions becomes the dance of death in the daily executions that decimate even the ranks of the young who had hated the West and the "Westernization" associated with the Shah. Where for Mernissi, dreams, fantasy, and the imagination are entirely positive centers of resistance to tyranny, for Nafisi they can produce not only creative rebellion but also the fictions upon which tyranny depends. To counter such tyranny, she and her students travel through fiction to Islam's "other" in the West, fulfilling Scheherazade's promise to the king that her storytelling "will take him to far away lands to observe foreign ways, so he could get closer to the strangeness within himself."

For Niafisi, Iran is a country in a massive cultural and political war over modernity, a battle in which people find infinite ways in their everyday lives to resist the institutional power of the fundamentalist, theocratic state—with her secret class reading Western classics safe within the privacy of a home standing in metonymically for this spirit of resistance. In a 2003 interview, she observes, "Basically, fundamentalism is a modern phenomenon" in which religion is "used as an ideology, as a system of control" to maintain clerical power. In their hatred of Western imperialism, liberals and leftists in Iran had initially supported Ayatollah Khomeini and then felt "betrayed" by the revolution. In this climate, she explains, aspects of Western modernity banned by the regime became irresistible.[62]

However, Nafisi's emphasis on the deployment of Western culture as a form of private resistance to the authoritarian fundamentalist state in Iran confirms—whether Nafisi means to or not—the powerful diffusionist narrative of America's global destiny to bring a democratic modernity to a backward, tradition-bound Muslim world. *Reading Lolita in Tehran* can all too easily be assimilated into this narrative and may explain the book's unanticipated blockbuster success in the United States.[63] The book remained on *The New York Times* bestseller list for over two years; the "Questions for Discussion" in the paperback edition attest to the book's popularity with educated reading publics, book clubs, and classrooms. In focusing particularly on the Iranian regime's treatment of women, the book aligns with the American government's use of women's status within Islamic countries as a rallying cry and justification for U.S. interventions. As Mitra Rastegar points out in her exhaustive study of the memoir's reviews in the West, readers in the West have found confirmation in *Reading Lolita* for long-standing Orientalist views of Muslim culture that justify Western intervention into the Middle East as the introduction of modern Enlightenment humanism into the traditional, despostic, and backward culture of Islam—often in the name of women's liberation.[64]

Unlike Mernissi's memoir, *Reading Lolita in Tehran* backgrounds indigenous aspects of Persian culture and history as sources of a Muslim alternative modernity. Although brief references to Scheherazade and *A Thousand and One Nights* bookend *Reading Lolita in Tehran*, the obsession with Scheherazade that Nafisi confessed to Crossette in 1997 is hardly visible to an American reading public not familiar with Scheherazade's story. Nafisi steps seamlessly into Scheherazade's shoes as the modern storyteller, but this identification is only implicit and is most likely unclear to American audiences.

How might *Reading Lolita in Tehran* been a different reading experience for Americans if Nafisi had begun with a full account of her secret class's first reading assignment: the story of Scheherazade? What if the superb reading Nafisi gives of Scheherazade's frame narrative in her essay "Imagination as Subversion" had been woven into the opening section of *Reading Lolita in Tehran*? In a few instances of autobiographical narration, Nafisi mentions that during the war years she joined a reading group to study Persian classics and wrote articles on "modern Persian fiction" for a literary magazine (171–73). What if these experiences had formed a more substantial part of her narrative? In "The Veiled Threat" Nafisi discusses the history of Iranian modernizers by invoking the story of a mid-nineteenth-century poet, Tahareh, the first woman in Iran to unveil publicly and demand that "religion be modernized," actions that led to her brutal murder. What if she had woven this story into *Reading Lolita in Tehran*? Or, how would the effect of the book on American audiences been different if she had included the rebellious Iranian woman poet Forugh Farrokhzad (d. 1967), who has become a cultural icon in contemporary Iran, according to Farzaneh Milani, who reports on seeing a play based on her life in Tehran in 2005? The political climate of Iran today is a "complex mixture," Milani writes, "of protest and accommodation, of resistance and acquiescence, of tradition and modernity," with women both highly oppressed and also "a vibrant force for change."[65] To American audiences ignorant of Iran's literary output—classic and modern—*Reading Lolita in Tehran* can easily reinforce that ignorance in its focus on Iranian engagements with Western literature alone. Moreover, Nafisi leaves out of her memoir the Islamic and secular feminist movements of the 1990s within Iran that led to the restitution of some of the rights women had lost after the revolution. As Moghadam reports, a "lively and widely read women's press" made "the question of women" highly visible and much debated in Iran, leading to significant legislative changes and contributing to the rise of the reform movement of the late 1990s (1155–62). Although Nafisi's other essays and interviews allude to this feminist activism in Iran, *Reading Lolita in Tehran* never mentions it, thereby instilling the view that feminism is Western in origin, a view that Nafisi elsewhere directly disputes.

There is a danger, however, in simply condemning Nafisi for pandering to the West and deemphasizing in her book (though not in her essays and interviews) the indigenous roots of Iranian modernity. To do so misses the complexities of her text and the deep identification it shows with Iranians' creative resilience, the contradictions of living within an authoritarian regime, and the hybridity of modernity itself. Moreover, such a critique of Nafisi plays unwittingly into the hands of those within the Muslim world who claim that the freedoms associated with Western modernity, especially for women, are incompatible with Islam. As Abbas Milani points out, many Islamists are eager to support "the myth that modernity is European in nature, and came to Iran only with colonialism," a myth that allows them to suppress the history of indigenous Muslim modernities and justify the imposition of *Shari'a* as a return to "true" Islam (11). Haideh Moghissi furthermore argues that the postmodern critique of modernity in the West can end up in a strange alliance with the Islamist position. "To reject modernity in the Middle East without offering a more humane and egalitarian alternative," she writes, "is to validate fundamentalism . . . as the only hope appropriate for the Islamic world. . . . At a tremendous cost to women in the Islamic world, concepts of universality, equality, modernity and human rights are lost" (56, 47).[66] Even the discourse of multiple modernities has been appropriated by conservatives justifying authoritarian regimes in the Middle East, as well as in Singapore and China. Not all Islamists describe themselves as "traditionalists"; some advocate a distinctive Islamic modernity for which the women's and human rights promoted by the West are not suited. The current president of Iran, Mahmoud Ahmadinejad, for example, is a conservative Islamist, but in his inaugural address of 2005 he vowed to make Iran "a modern, advanced, powerful and Islamic model" for the world.[67] For Moghissi, such views typically argue for the repatriarchalization of Muslim societies and lead her to assert that "fundamentalists are against the ideas and ideals of modernity but not against the products of modernization, which they appreciate and use to establish their premodern social and political order" (71). The discourse of modernity within the Muslim world is highly contested, a political football kicked around to justify a full spectrum of political views. Reading Nafisi's book critically in the United States requires some sensitivity on how attacks can be deployed elsewhere.

Read in tandem, Mernissi's *Dreams of Trespass* and Nafisi's *Reading Lolita in Tehran* provide an excellent test case for Moghissi's notion of a blended Muslim modernity as well as Afkhami's assertion that "Muslim women have largely stopped being reactive to Western feminism." Both feature Scheherazade and thus indirectly assert a modernity linked with a feminism that is indigenous to Muslim culture. But they would also reject the view that Muslim feminism is completely distinct and separate from other feminisms, including Western

ones. In short, both would regard feminism as both indigenous and indigenizing, as both local and from elsewhere, as both transplanted and traveling.[68]
However, *Dreams of Trespass* and *Reading Lolita in Tehran* handle the balance
between the two differently, especially in the way each relates to its presumed
audiences in the West, most specifically in the United States. Almost in spite
of itself and Nafisi's avowed "obsession with Scheherazade," *Reading Lolita in
Tehran* fulfills the narrative compulsion of American manifest destiny, while
Dreams of Trespass directly challenges it. On the other hand, Nafisi's exposure
of the dangers of all illusionism holds a lesson for the United States as well:
What illusions feed America's current governmental crusade to save the "civilized" world? Moreover, Nafisi's book finds hope in cross-continental dialogues
and in the agencies of indigenizing appropriations of ideas from elsewhere on
a polycentric global landscape.

Conclusion

Why read Shanghai's modernization, the ceramics of the Abbasid Dynasty,
Scheherazade, *Dreams of Trespass*, and *Reading Lolita in Tehran* as instances of
"the planet and American literature"? Can doing so avoid an imperial assimilation of the globe into the sphere of American manifest destiny? I think so,
though I am keenly aware of the dangers, especially the threat that English as a
global language in conjunction with American global power poses to regional
languages and cultures. To break down the walls of national and nationalist
literary studies, we need to recognize how the worldwide web of interconnec-
tion is nothing new, but has been throughout history a central component of
all local formations, most particularly "modern" ones. To dissolve powerful
narratives of Eurocentric diffusionism and American manifest destiny, we
need to follow the threads of connection around the world, to recognize how
"the West" and the United States in particular were and are continuing to be
formed through transcontinental contact zones and migrations—peaceful and
violent alike.

The webs linking past and present, America and Muslim cultures on three
continents bear more reflection: *not* because it is America's global destiny to
bring modernity to Islam and the Arab world, but rather because the destinies
of the United States and Muslim countries are linked in sites of fierce struggle
between modernity and tradition, though the particulars in each location dif-
fer. On all continents, women—especially their bodies—are the flashpoint of
contestation about modernity. The rhetoric of the Bush administration to
bring freedom to women in the Muslim world falsely claims modernity as the
invention of the West while it obscures the administration's insistence on
a theocratically based fundamentalism at home. Everywhere on the globe,
feminism is the fly in the ointment, insisting on women's full human rights.

As a component of modernity, feminism is a polycentric phenomenon, both indigenous and indigenizing all over the globe in widely divergent cultures. Scheherazade comes to America through writers like Nafisi, the immigrant in exile, and Mernissi, the traveler whose books circulate far beyond their Moroccan origin. We would do well in the United States to listen to "the call of the storyteller." She might help us to unthink America's manifest destiny in the new global age. In her transcontinental reach, she might also help us rethink the boundaries of American literary studies.

As I write in June of 2005, Baghdad is burning, Baghdad is burning. Daily, the body parts fly, spattering the streets with blood. Baghdad is a city in flames, "bombed into the stone age" during the first Gulf War, bombed again during the "shock and awe" campaign of the second, and riven with the violence of an insurgency that is both sectarian and anti-American. As Baghdad's port city, Basra was the entry point for the American invasion in the spring of 2003—Basra, Iraq's second largest city, home to secular Muslims who are claiming the rights of an autonomous region; Basra, the golden gate for Baghdad's golden age transcontinental trade, knowledge, arts, and culture. They are part of America's story.

NOTES

For their informative critiques, suggestions, and encouragement, I am particularly grateful to Farzaneh Milani, Bahareh Lampert, Wai Chee Dimock, John Carlos Rowe, Jessica Hallett, and Mitra Rastegar; for her indefatigable assistance, I am indebted to Megan Massino.

1. Stephen K. Sanderson and Thomas D. Hall, "World System Approaches to World-Historical Change," in *Civilizations and World Systems: Studying World-Historical Change*, ed. Stephen K. Sanderson (London: Sage, 1995), 234; Sanderson and Hall cite Mathew Melko.

2. Abbas Milani, *Lost Wisdom: Rethinking Modernity in Iran* (Washington, D.C.: Mage Publishers, 2004), 20; hereafter quotations will be identified in the text.

3. My title borrows from Ella Shohat and Robert Stam's *Unthinking Eurocentrism: Multiculturalism and the Media* (London: Routledge, 1994), and I am indebted to their critique of Eurocentrism and their advocacy of a "polycentric" approach to "global thinking."

4. Most Muslims live in South and Southeast Asia, more than in the rest of the world combined; in this essay, I address mainly Persian and Arab Muslim cultures.

5. Fatima Mernissi, *Dreams of Trespass: Tales of a Harem Girlhood* (Cambridge: Perseus Books, 1994); Azar Nafisi, *Reading Lolita in Tehran: A Memoir in Books* (New York: Random House, 2003). Hereafter, quotations will be identified in the text.

6. A friend from Korea, Jong-Im Lee, tells me that this housing trend in Hong Kong is also characteristic of Korea.

7. The admiral of this huge fleet of *baochuan* (treasure ships), manned by some thirty thousand men, was a Muslim from Central Asia, Zheng He, an extraordinary visionary

and skilled navigator and trader who made seven voyages westward with his fleet, from 1405 to 1433; with him was Ma Huan, a fellow Muslim who wrote a detailed account of their journeys and the cultures they encountered, *The Overall Survey of the Ocean's Shores*. See Frank Viviano, "China's Great Armada," *National Geographic* 208, no. 1 (July 2005): 28–53.

8. Quanzhou's tourist information first acquainted me with the city's history. See also the following websites: www.mzfh.com/Mac/Quanzhou/aboutq.html; www.pbs.org/wgbh/nova/sultan/archeology.html; archnet.org/library/sites/one-site.tcl?site_id=9143. See notes 14–17 below for citations on world trade before 1500. Historians agree that the Ming Dynasty's policy of isolationism after the 1440s contributed greatly to China's decline and the rise of Europe on the global market.

9. J. M. Blaut, *The Colonizer's Model of the World: Geographical Diffusionism and Eurocentric History* (New York: Guilford Press, 1993); hereafter quotations will be identified in the text. See also Samir Amin, *Eurocentrism*, trans. Russell Moore (New York: Monthly Review Press, 1989); Shohat and Stam, *Unthinking Eurocentrism*; Victor Roudometof and Roland Robertson, "Globalization, World-System Theory, and the Comparative Study of Civilizations," in Sanderson, *Civilizations and World Systems*, 273–98; Victor Roudometof, "Globalization or Modernity?" *Comparative Civilizations Review*, no. 30 (Rolla: University of Missouri, Rolla, 1994): 18–45.

10. For some recent examples of Eurocentric diffusionism in current social theory across the political spectrum, see for example Anthony Giddens, *The Consequences of Modernity* (Stanford: Stanford University Press, 1990), esp. 1–10, 174–76; Samuel P. Huntington, *The Clash of World Civilizations and the Remaking of World Order* (New York: Simon and Schuster, 1996); Stuart Hall and Bram Gieben, *Formations of Modernity* (Cambridge: Polity Press, 1992), esp. 1–16; and Immanuel Wallerstein, "Eurocentrism and Its Avatars: The Dilemmas of Social Science," *New Left Review*, no. 226 (November/December 1997): 93–108.

11. See George Ritzer, *The McDonaldization of Society: An Investigation into the Changing Characters of Contemporary Social Life* (London: Sage, 1992) and the critique of this fear of global homogenization in *Golden Arches East: McDonald's in East Asia*, ed. James L. Watson (Stanford: Stanford University Press, 1997), a collection that documents the extensive Asianization of McDonald's in East Asia.

12. See Frantz Fanon, *Black Skin, White Masks: The Experiences of a Black Man in a White World*, trans. Charles Lam Markmann (1952; reprint, New York: Grove Press, 1967); Homi K. Bhabha, *The Location of Culture* (London: Routledge, 1994); Partha Chatterjee, "Talking about Our Modernity in Two Languages," in *A Possible India: Essays in Political Criticism* (Oxford: Oxford University Press, 1997), 281.

13. Dipesh Chakrabarty, *Provincializing Europe: Postcolonial Thought and Historical Difference* (Princeton: Princeton University Press, 2000), 39.

14. R. Radhakrishnan, "Derivative Discourses and the Problem of Signification," *European Legacy* 7, no. 6 (2002): 783–95; hereafter quotations will be identified in the text.

15. André Gunder Frank, *ReORIENT: Global Economy in the Asian Age* (Berkeley: University of California Press, 1998). See also Sanderson, *Civilizations and World Systems*.

16. Janet Abu-Lughod, *Before European Hegemony: The World System*, A.D. *1250–1350* (New York: Oxford University Press, 1989).

17. Jack Weatherford, *Genghis Khan and the Making of the Modern World* (New York: Three Rivers Press, 2004).

18. William H. McNeill, "*The Rise of the West* after Twenty-Five Years," in Sanderson, *Civilizations and World Systems*, 304–6.

19. On the circularity of prevailing definitions of modernity, see Susan Stanford Friedman, "Definitional Excursions: The Meanings of Modern/Modernity/Modernism," *Modernism/Modernity* 8, no. 3 (September 2001): 493–513.

20. Anthony Giddens, "Is Modernity a Western Project?" in *The Consequences of Modernity*, 174–78. Giddens argues that globalization is "a diffusion of Western institutions across the world, in which other cultures are crushed" and that "Modernity is universalizing" and "distinctively Western" (175). For cogent critiques of Giddens and similar views, see Roudometof and Robertson, "Globalization, World System Theory"; Roudometof, "Globalization or Modernity."

21. Friedman, "Definitional Excursions" and "Traveling Modernities," in *Transnational Modernism*, a book in progress.

22. Edouard Glissant, *Poetics of Relation* (1990), trans. Betsy Wing (Ann Arbor: University of Michigan Press, 1997), 138.

23. Marshall Berman, *All That Is Solid Melts into Air: The Experience of Modernity*, 2nd ed. (New York: Penguin Books, 1988); Friedman, "Traveling Modernities."

24. Paul de Man, "Literary History and Literary Modernity," in *Blindness and Insight* (Minneapolis: University of Minnesota Press, 1983), 147–48.

25. Dilip Parameshwar Gaonkar, ed., *Alternative Modernities* (Durham, N.C.: Duke University Press, 2001), 17.

26. See for example Radhakrishnan, "Derivative Discourses"; Gaonkar, *Alternative Modernities*; Abbas Milani, *Lost Wisdom*; Friedman, "Definitional Excursions"; Shmuel N. Eisenstadt and Wolfgang Schluchter, eds., Special Issue on Early Modernities, *Daedalus* 127, no. 3 (Summer 1998); S. N. Eisenstadt, ed., Special Issue on Multiple Modernities, *Daedalus* 129, no. 1 (Winter 2000); Sanjay Subrahmanyam, "Hearing Voices: Vignettes of Early Modernity in South Asia, 1400–1750," *Daedalus* 127, no. 3 (1998): 75–104.

27. Subrahmanyam, "Hearing Voices," 99–100; for virus imagery, see Wallerstein's "Eurocentrism and Its Avatars."

28. James Clifford, "Traveling Cultures" (1992), in *Routes: Travel and Translation in the Late Twentieth Century* (Cambridge: Harvard University Press, 1997), 19. I am greatly indebted to this seminal essay, as well as to the essay by Edward Said to which Clifford's title alludes, "Traveling Theory," in *The World, the Text, and the Critic* (Cambridge: Harvard University Press, 1983), 226–48.

29. Eisenstadt and Schluchter, Special Issue on Early Modernities, 5.

30. Charles Taylor, "Two Theories of Modernity," in Gaonkar, *Alternative Modernities*, 172–96.

31. For more extended discussion of indigenization, see Friedman, "Traveling Modernities."

32. For Baghdad during the Abbasid Dynasty, see Hugh Kennedy, *When Baghdad Ruled the Muslim World: The Rise and Fall of Islam's Greatest Dynasty* (Cambridge, Mass.:

Da Capo Books, 2004); Albert Hourani, *A History of the Arab Peoples* (Cambridge: Harvard University Press, 1991), esp. 33–36, 189–205; Fatima Mernissi, *Islam and Democracy: Fear of the Modern World*, trans. Mary Jo Lakeland, 2d ed. (1992; New York: Basic Books, 2001), 6–7, 34–37.

33. André Gunder Frank, "The Modern World System Revisited: Rereading Braudel and Wallerstein," in Sanderson, *Civilizations and World Systems*, 166.

34. "Iraq and China: Ceramics, Trade, and Innovation" (Washington, D.C.: Smithsonian Institution, 2005), 1. See also Jessica Hallett's article drawn from her dissertation and forthcoming book on the Iraq/China ceramics trade: "Iraq and China; Trade and Innovation in the Early Abbasid Period," *TAOCI*, no. 4, *Chine-Méditerranée: Routes et échanges de la céramique avant le XVIe siècle* (December 2005): 21–29.

35. Hallett, "Iraq and China," 21; she cites evidence that communication between Basra and Chinese potters led to the adaptation of some Chinese wheel and shaping technologies (25). See also Alan Caiger-Smith, *Tin-Glaze Pottery in Europe and the Islamic World: The Tradition of 1,000 Years in Maiolica, Faience, and Delftware* (London: Faber and Faber, 1973) and *Lustre Pottery: Technique, Tradition and Innovation in Islam and the Western World* (London: Faber and Faber, 1985).

36. See Caiger-Smith, *Lustre Pottery*, esp. 24–26, and Oliver Watson, *Persian Lustre Ware* (London: Faber and Faber, 1985).

37. Caiger-Smith, *Lustre Pottery*, 21–25; *Tin-Glaze Pottery*, 24, 25, 27.

38. "Iraq and China"; Caiger-Smith, *Tin-Glaze Pottery*, 28; *Lustre Pottery*, 51–154; and on the history of Spode's Willow earthenware, nmnm.essortment.com/ bluewillowspo_rnfq.htm.

39. See Caiger-Smith, *Lustre Pottery*, 27, and *Tin-Glaze Pottery*, 23. For the history of *A Thousand and One Nights*, see Hourani, *A History of the Arab Peoples*, 196; Joseph Campbell, "The Editor's Introduction," in *Arabian Nights*, ed. Joseph Campbell (New York: Viking Press, 1952), 1–35.

40. I quote from the Hussain Haddawy translation from the fourteenth-century Syrian manuscript (Norton, 1990), cited in Barbara Crossette, "Muslim Women Hear the Call of a Storyteller," *New York Times*, February 6, 1999, B7; hereafter quotations from Crossette will be identified in the text. See also p. 47 of the Campbell edition of *Arabian Nights*.

41. As translated by Fatima Mernissi, *Scheherazade Goes West: Different Cultures, Different Harems* (New York: Washington Square Press, 2001), 49.

42. My title for this section borrows from Assia Djebar's *A Sister to Scheherazade*, trans. Dorothy S. Blair (Portsmith, N.H.: Heinemann, 1987); Farzaneh Milani's "Shaherzad's Daughters: The Storytellers," in *Veils and Words: The Emerging Voices of Iranian Women Writers* (Syracuse, N.Y.: Syracuse University Press, 1991), 177–230; and the influential anthology of Egyptian women's writing, *The Night after the 1001 Nights*, ed. Yusuf al-Sharuni (Cairo: al-Hay'a al-Misriya al-'Amma lil-Kitab, 1975).

43. Farzaneh Milani, "Silencing a Modern Scheherazade," *Christian Science Monitor*, November 17, 2004, 9.

44. In her mapping of the debate about Islam and feminism, Valentine M. Moghadam associates Afkhami with the secular wing of Muslim feminism and quotes a personal interview in 1999 in which Afkhami told her, "I call myself a Muslim and a

feminist. I'm not an Islamic feminist—that's a contradiction in terms" ("Islamic Feminism and Its Discontents: Toward a Resolution of a Debate," *Signs* 27, no. 4 [Summer, 2002]: 1152; hereafter identified in the text).

45. Azar Nafisi, "Imagination as Subversion: Narrative as a Tool of Civic Awareness," in *Muslim Women and the Politics of Participation*, eds. Mahnaz Afkhami and Erika Friedl (Syracuse, N.Y.: Syracuse University Press, 1997), 70–71.

46. For different characterizations of the debate, see Valentine M. Moghadam, who sympathizes with efforts of Islamic feminists in "Islamic Feminism and Its Discontents: Toward a Resolution of a Debate," *Signs* 27, no. 4 (Summer 2002): 1135–71 (hereafter identified in the text), and Haideh Moghissi, who takes the secular side in *Feminism and Islamic Fundamentalism: The Limits of Postmodern Analysis* (London: Zed Books, 1999), 32–48, 78–97, 125–48 (hereafter identified in the text). Moghissi points out that the terms *Muslim* and *feminism* are themselves subject to ambiguity and debate: *Muslim* sometimes connotes religious belief and practice and at other times signifies a shared collective identity, history, and culture (138); *feminism* is not the term that advocates for women in the Middle East typically use because of its association with Western feminists (126). Moghissi uses "Muslim" as an identity category, insisting on the heterogeneity of Muslims, and "feminism" because of shared principles of women's advocacy worldwide. On Arab feminism and Islam, see also Miriam Cooke, *Women Claim Islam: Creating Islamic Feminism through Literature* (London: Routledge, 2001).

47. Mahnaz Afkhami, Introduction, *Faith and Freedom: Women's Human Rights in the Muslim World* (Syracuse, NY: Syracuse University Press, 1995), 6. Afkhami was minister of State for Women's Affairs in Iran prior to the Islamic revolution.

48. Mernissi, *Islam and Democracy*, esp. 13–84. See Cooke's discussion of Mernissi's political thought (*Women Claim Islam*, 70–74) and of many Arab women writers who regard Islam and feminism as compatible, in contrast to Moghissi, who appears to agree with the Muslim secularists that " 'Islamic feminism' may be an oxymoron" (134), although she hedges on aligning herself completely with this view (141–42).

49. On Sufism, see *The Oxford Dictionary of Islam*, ed. John L. Esposito (Oxford: Oxford University Press, 2003), 302–3. For a history of Sufism's evolution and different manifestations, from ascetic mysticism to animist cults and populist forms to association with Islamic reformers, see Fazlur Rahman, *Islam* (London: Weidenfeld and Nicolson, 1966), 128–66. During the Abbasid Dynasty, Sufism was centered especially in Baghdad (Rahman, *Islam*, 150). On Sufism's heterodox religious syncretism, blending aspects of Christianity (especially Gnosticism), Manicheanism, Hinduism, and Judaism, see Rahman, *Islam*, 133–34; Reza Aslan, *No God but God: The Origins, Evolution, and Future of Islam* (New York: Random House, 2006), 199–219, esp. 199.

50. Esposito notes that *ijtihad* is a term in Islamic jurisprudence meaning "independent reasoning" and that "Islamic reformers call for a revitalization of ijtihad in the modern world" (*Oxford Dictionary of Islam*, 134). See also Irshad Manji's, *The Trouble with Islam Today* (New York: St. Martin's Griffin, 2005), by a Canadian Muslim lesbian whose reform call for Islam centers in a revival of the independence and skepticism associated with *ijtihad* (50–70). Both Manji and Mernissi, in *Islam and Democracy* (32–41), stress that the battle between the fundamentalist and humanistic factions within Islam has been continual since the beginning.

51. SAIS website: http://www.sais-jhu.edu/.

52. John Carlos Rowe, "Reading *Lolita in Tehran* in Idaho," unpublished manuscript; I am grateful to him for showing me this essay. Farzaneh Milani pointed out to me that the "Paul" thanked in Nafisi's acknowledgments (346) was Paul Wolfowitz. In a 2006 interview with Nafisi, Edward Luce notes her surprise at "the overtly political uses to which some American conservatives sought to put her." Nafisi told him: "I came to America as a political innocent. . . . After I arrived here I used to accept every invitation to speak about Iran without realizing that it greatly mattered whom you were seated next to on the podium and which organization had invited you. To me these things weren't relevant. I got burned many times. Now I am much more careful." Edward Luce, "Great Literature Transcends Time and Place," *Financial Times*, April 29–30, 2006.

53. "Roundtable: Three Women, Two Worlds, One Issue," *SAIS Review* 20 (Summer–Fall 2000): 36.

54. Shanaz Khan, "Muslim Women: Negotiations in the Third Space," *Signs* 23, no. 2 (Winter 1998): 463–94.

55. Iran's brief Enlightenment under the Sufi king Mohammed Shah (1934–48) promoted rationalism, religious toleration for Jews and Christians, education of girls, and less power for clerics; it ended with the death of the king and the reassertion of clerical power (Moghissi, *Feminism and Islamic Fundamentalism*, 57).

56. In "The Veiled Threat: The Iranian Theocracy's Fear of Females," Nafisi tells the history of this leadership and activism by both religious and secular Muslim women for the past one hundred years and centers her hope for Iran's future in women's resistance (*New Republic*, February 22, 1999). See also Moghissi, *Feminism and Islamic Fundamentalism*, 38–42, 125–48; Afkhami and Friedl, *Muslim Women*; and Shahrzad Mojab, "Islamic Feminism," *Fireweed* 47 (Winter 1995): 18–25.

57. In *Scheherazade Goes West*, Mernissi not only contrasts Western fantasies of Muslim harems, but she also argues that the West has its own "harem within." While Muslim societies control the feared power of female sexuality through prohibitions on space and bodily display, Western culture, she argues, exercises a parallel control through women's internalized hatred of their bodies and their obsessive anxieties about weight and standards of beauty to which few can measure up (208–19).

58. In *Islam and Democracy*, Mernissi's analysis of Moroccan responses to colonial modernity is more complex and less sanguine. Since Western modernity was associated with colonial brutality in the eyes of Muslim nationalists, many aspects were simply rejected and efforts to modernize were often made without sufficient breaking from the past (45–50).

59. For rebellion enacted by Iranians (especially women) in the culture of everyday life, see Nafisi, "The Veiled Threat"; Farzaneh Milani, "Lipstick Politics in Iran," *New York Times*, August 19, 1999; Farzaneh Milani, "Dance as Dissent," *Ms. Magazine*, Spring 2004, 29; Christopher de Bellaigue, "Stalled in Iran," *New York Review of Books*, June 24, 2004.

60. Nafisi directly alludes to this reversal of direction (261) and without naming her, tells the story of Afkhami, who was Minister for Women's Affairs under the Shah, was abroad at his downfall, and has remained in exile; she notes that the only other woman cabinet minister, who had been her high school principal, was put in a sack

and executed (261–62). In "The Veiled Threat," Nafisi identifies this woman as Dr. Farokhroo Parsa and retells the story.

61. Edward W. Said, "Traveling Theory Reconsidered," in *Reflections on Exile and Other Essays* (Cambridge: Cambridge University Press, 1994), 436–52.

62. "The Fiction of Life: An Interview with Azar Nafisi," *Atlantic Monthly* on-line magazine (May 2003): 1–2.

63. For Nafisi's surprise, see Susan Domowitz, "Azar Nafisi: A Life of Connecting Cultures, Challenging Extremism," Department of State Washington File (August 25, 2003). Just five months after its publication, *Reading Lolita* was already being translated into twelve languages, including Chinese and Korean.

64. Mitra Rastegar, "Reading Nafisi in the West: Authenticity, Orientalism and 'Liberating' Iranian Women," forthcoming in *Women's Studies Quarterly*. I am grateful to Rastegar for sharing her essay with me. For a related criticism of *Reading Lolita*, see Rowe, "Reading *Lolita in Tehran* in Idaho."

65. Farzaneh Milani, "A Poet Who Pointed the Way to a New Iran," *Washington Post*, March 12, 2005, A19. See also Milani's chapter on Tahereh in *Veils and Words*, 77–99.

66. Nafisi's attack on "postmodern feminism" in the *SAIS Review* "Roundtable" makes a similar point; in their eagerness to critique the West, she notes, "postmodern feminists deny us . . . the right to change. So, if women like Shirin and I do not condone female genital mutilation and polygamy, they say we are not Iranian or Pakistani or Indonesian but Western and privileged" (35). Nafisi's critique of postmodern feminism may, as Rowe suggests, reflect her alliance with neoconservatives and unfairly characterize some feminist theory, but like Abbas Milani and Moghissi, Nafisi is also defending the indigenous roots of Iranian modernity and insisting on the right to abandon oppressive aspects of Islamic tradition.

67. Kathy Gannon, "New President Aims for Powerful Iran," *Wisconsin State Journal*, June 26, 2005, A11. For a sampling of this debate about modernity by mainly conservative Muslims, see Joseph E. B. Lumbard, ed., *Islam, Fundamentalism, and the Betrayal of Tradition: Essays by Western Muslim Scholars* (Bloomington: Indiana University Press, 2004). See also Saree Makdisi, "'Postcolonial' Literature in a Neocolonial World: Modern Arabic Culture and the End of Modernity," *boundary 2* 22, no. 1 (1995): 85–115; Makdisi argues that the "Nahda" movement (nineteenth-century Arab modernizers) were not critical enough of Western modernity in advocating nation-states instead of a pan-Arab and/or Greater Syria that he favors as an alternative modernity. Makdisi ignores the heterogeneity of Muslims and does not take into account gender at all, but his discussion of Arab modernity as "now," rather than yet to be achieved, has merit.

68. I explain this concept of traveling and localized feminism at length in *Mappings: Feminism and the Cultural Geographies of Encounter* (Princeton: Princeton University Press, 1998), esp. 3–14.

PART TWO

Eastern Europe as Test Case

CHAPTER 4

Mr. Styron's Planet

Eric J. Sundquist

> This is a man speaking out of an overwhelming obsession: he is
> obscene because he wants to be saved.
> —Philip Roth, "On *Portnoy's Complaint*"

Recalling years later that the compositional beginnings of *Sophie's Choice* in
the late 1960s coincided with a brief friendship with Hannah Arendt, during
which they commiserated over their "mutual martyrdom"—she having been
denounced for *Eichmann in Jerusalem* and he for *The Confessions of Nat
Turner*—William Styron attributed to Arendt the conviction, satisfying to
him, that an artist may trespass into worlds not known personally in order to
create "his own authenticity." What matters most is "imaginative conviction
and boldness, a passion to invade alien territory and render an account of
one's discoveries."[1] In his appeal to Arendt, Styron found justification for writing about the volatile subject of American slave resistance in the voice of one
of its heroes, as well as cover for his new novel then taking shape. In the latter
case, he managed to bring the Holocaust into mainstream American fiction
without outraging Jews nearly as much as he had outraged blacks by his depiction of "the tragic Negro firebrand Nat Turner."[2] In choosing as the heroine
of his Holocaust novel a Polish Catholic anti-Semite who survives Auschwitz
only to be dragged by a deranged American Jew into a relationship of chaotic
sadomasochism ending in their double suicide, however, Styron took risks that
far surpassed those he took with American slavery.

Styron's invasion of "alien territory" in *Sophie's Choice* may be understood
in several dimensions. His contestation of the prevalent view that Jews were
"unique" victims of the Holocaust marked Styron as a bold inquirer into the
problem of comparability in the new age of genocide, a concept dating from
the immediate aftermath of the war—the term "genocide" was coined by Ra-
phael Lemkin in 1944 and inscribed into the United Nations Genocide Convention in 1948[3]—and becoming year by year more conspicuous as an actual
or potential global phenomenon. By the time *Sophie's Choice* was published
in 1979, the carnage produced by the Khmer Rouge in Cambodia had come
to light, and the years ahead would be punctuated by instances of genocide
vividly summoned up by name alone—Bosnia, Rwanda, Darfur—as though

the Holocaust, rather than standing as a warning for all time against such mass atrocity, had instead spawned a new mode of warfare. Although Styron's perspective went backward, not forward, in this way, too, he broached a topic that would become increasingly familiar, and increasingly vexed, by the end of the century—namely, the relationship between the Holocaust and black slavery. In setting his Holocaust novel conceptually against the lingering problem of his Nat Turner novel, Styron undertook to see the defining catastrophic events of modernity, the Middle Passage and Auschwitz, to speak epithetically, in intimate relation and thereby open a sweeping inquiry into the making of nations and the destruction of peoples.

Writing at a time when the imaginative literature of the Holocaust was far from mature, Styron was likewise daring in appropriating so painful a topic to American usage. Translated and transcribed autobiographical witness was becoming relatively common, of course, but American fiction to date had tended toward the heroic (*The Wall*), the oblique (*The Pawnbroker, The Fixer*), or the factitious (*The Painted Bird*). The most inventive American novelistic treatment of the postwar decades, Leslie Epstein's *King of the Jews*, appeared the same year as *Sophie's Choice*, while the two stories that make up *The Shawl*, by Cynthia Ozick, appeared within a matter of years, the three works serving, in quite different ways, to establish the lasting contribution of American writers to one of the most important genres of world literature in the late twentieth century—and one destined to grow more salient as the age of genocide reached into the twenty-first century. Because he wrote against both archival and ideological constraints that obscured his interpretation of the Nazi Judeocide, however, and because those constraints were congenial to his preconceptions about the very meaning of the Holocaust, Styron produced a "historical" novel that was not worldly but parochial. What is more, by infusing his Holocaust novel with a disturbing, obsessive eroticism, Styron entered on the dangerous ground where atrocity and pornography meet. Whereas he proposed an epic engagement of the midcentury clash between liberalism and totalitarianism, America and Europe, eros and thanatos, he once again turned history into an arena of authorial fantasy. *Sophie's Choice* is therefore a challenging foray into territory little explored, while it is also an object lesson in the hazards of dramatizing cataclysmic global events on the solipsistic stage of one man's passions.

Anti-Semitism without Jews

Stung by attacks on his mistaken assumption that Nat Turner had virtually no history, even in black culture, before his novel gave him life, Styron, in the character of his autobiographical narrator Stingo, reports that he prepared for Sophie's novel through the "torture" of absorbing "as much as I could find of the literature of *l'univers concentrationnaire*."[4] But Styron's Nat Turner problem lay not in inadequate historicism. His depiction of slavery and slave-holding was evocative, and he recognized that the scriptural properties of Turner's 1831 "confession," an enigmatic but purposeful jeremiad, transcended Thomas Gray's attempt to contain it within a legalistic framework and put democratic revolution on a religious plane that was not at odds with slave culture but instead one of its signal expressions.[5] Rather, in deriving Turner's rampage from the sublimated desire to violate white women—in particular, Margaret Whitehead, apparently the only person the historical Turner killed—Styron subordinated a heroic motive to one plausible but anachronistic, confusing the "rape complex"[6] of the Jim Crow South with the ethos of the plantation and entangling his own imagined acts of violation with those of his hero.

A similar objection can be leveled at *Sophie's Choice*. Finding the fictional space of the South used up, writes Alvin Rosenfeld, Styron staged a Holocaust in "white-face, de-Judaizing Auschwitz" and making Sophie Zawistowska's ravaged body "the erotic centerpiece of a New Southern Gothic Novel," while joining together in Nathan Landau the white man's fears about "black potency" and the Christian's fears about "Jewish diabolism."[7] Like her failed seduction of Auschwitz commandant Rudolf Höss, Sophie's sexual bondage to Nathan stands in stark and unresolved contrast to the picaresque subplot of Stingo's futile offer of his virginity—what he refers to as his "inwardly abiding Golgotha"—to sultry Southern girlfriends and "cock-teasing" Jewish American princesses.[8] It is no coincidence, however, that this melodramatic Christological phrase recalls the "passion" of Styron's Nat Turner at the moment of his execution, released in death from his crucifying libido, a scene perfectly replicated by Stingo, having taken Nathan's place, in the ending of *Sophie's Choice*. We will return to this aspect of the novel, but the scandal of *Sophie's Choice* lies not in Styron's once more putting his psychosexual fantasies center stage and corroborating tendentious historiography with the testimony of fictional characters, but instead in building his story around a set of analogical substitutions that distort the meaning of the Holocaust.

The problem is adumbrated during Sophie's confession of complicity in her father's anti-Semitic pamphleteering when Stingo breaks in to expound upon the "sinister zone of likeness" between Poland and the American South. Imagine feudal and agrarian Poland as a land where "carpetbaggers swarmed not for a decade or so but for millennia," Stingo suggests, a proud land humiliated, with a passion for horses, military titles, and the domination of women. In defeat, both lands experienced a "frenzied nationalism"; in both the abiding question of race created "at the same instant cruelty and compassion, bigotry and understanding," a set of contradictory compulsions that led Southerners to cherish blacks as family members while enslaving them as a people, and led Poles both to save Jews and to persecute them with "undeviating savagery."[9] Here, however, the superficial similarity ends. Unlike Germany, the North did not invade the South in order to drive out its inhabitants, let alone enslave or slaughter them; unlike Poland, the Confederacy went to war not to resist the imposition of a racist ideology but to preserve one, even if Southerners, unlike those Poles who were complicit in the destruction of the Jews, would hardly have welcomed the mass murder of the black population.

Both the allure and the radical instability of Styron's analogy are expressed in a provocative metaphor that recurs throughout *Sophie's Choice*. Like the South, says Stingo, Poland in its experience of racism has been plagued by "centuries-long, all-encompassing nightmare spells of schizophrenia."[10] Best thought of in its colloquial sense of "split personality,"[11] schizophrenia in Styron's usage provides an especially apt way into a novel in which characters and narrators, as well as nations, peoples, and historical events, are frequently said to stand in analogical relation to one another. For the same reason, as we will see, it quickly calls to mind Primo Levi's "gray zone" of complicity between Auschwitz victim and Nazi perpetrator, the zone of moral erosion in which resistance to evil at length gives way to participation in evil.[12] The madman Nathan Landau is the novel's most conspicuous personification of such erosion, but the zones of psychic likeness inhabited by Styron's characters both encompass and depend upon other zones of likeness in *Sophie's Choice*: Jews and other victims of the Nazi genocide; the Holocaust and slavery; and, finally, witnessing victims and witnessing perpetrators, among them Styron's autobiographical narrator, in whose voyeurism and self-regard all such analogous zones come to rest.

When it appeared, *Sophie's Choice* was inevitably read within a context of public interest created by the television miniseries *Holocaust*, which aired the week before Passover in April 1978 and coincident with the thirty-fifth anniversary of the Warsaw Ghetto uprising. A highly publicized media event, *Holocaust* capitalized upon the vogue for ethnic nationhood stimulated by the 1976 miniseries *Roots* and, despite a few dissenting reviews, was favorably received by some 120 million viewers.[13] Two weeks later, President Jimmy Carter announced the appointment of a presidential commission to evaluate plans for the United States Holocaust Memorial Museum, which put a conclusive end to any lingering American "silence" about the genocide of the Jews. Not surprisingly, Styron criticized *Holocaust* as a melodrama of "skillfully rigged but hollow theatrics" that minimized both the suffering of non-Jews and the magnitude of the Nazis' "slave enterprise."[14] If the miniseries failed to transcend its genre, however, it added an exclamation point to the post-Eichmann, post–Six Day War attention to the Holocaust—more effectively, in many respects, than the equally rigged melodrama of Styron's novel. Taking a clear stand on the complex issues of Nazi intentionalism, Jewish resistance, and the singularity or uniqueness of the Jews' catastrophe, *Holocaust* illustrated that the question of comparability between Jews and Poles such as Sophie is a matter of interpreting the zone of likeness in which victims of genocide may be contained.[15]

In its critique of uniqueness, *Sophie's Choice* starts from the premise that the experience of Sophie, modeled on a Catholic Pole who had lost her father, husband, and two children to the gas chambers, and who lived briefly in 1949 in the same Brooklyn rooming house as Styron—a "lean and lonesome young Southerner wandering amid the Kingdom of the Jews," upholding the honor of his forefathers, William Faulkner and Thomas Wolfe, against "a pounding fast-footed horde of Bellows and Schwartzes and Levys and Mandelbaums"— is no less horrible than that of a Jew in Auschwitz. At the level of the individual, this is surely true, but Styron does not confine himself to this level. As Wanda, a member of the Polish resistance and Sophie's whilom lover, puts it, "in this war everyone suffers—Jews, Poles, Gypsies, Russians, Czechs, Yugoslavs, all the others. Everyone's a victim. The Jews are also victims of the victims, that's the main difference. But none of the suffering is precious and all die shitty deaths."[16] In this scene, Wanda rebukes a member of the Jewish resistance for naively expecting help from Poles and shows him photographs of boxcars full of dead Polish children abandoned after being kidnapped in the *Lebensborn* ("spring of life") program, part of the plans created by Heinrich Himmler, Adolf Hitler's minister of the interior and head of the SS, to breed a biological elite that would help to replenish an Aryan culture dangerously diluted by alien blood.[17] However it may implicitly acknowledge Polish anti-Semitism, Wanda's anachronistic formulation—Jews in 1943 were hardly in a position to conceive of, let alone portray, their suffering as "precious," regardless of what one member of the ghetto resistance might say—explicitly elides the experiences of victims.

Although she stops short of the platitudes about universal victimhood introduced into the American stage and film adaptations of *The Diary of Anne Frank* two decades earlier, Wanda's view is in keeping with Styron's argument, stated in the novel and elaborated in interviews, that "it is surprisingly difficult for many Jews to see beyond the consecrated nature of the Nazis' genocidal fury" and to recognize that "multitudes of non-Jews" were also "swallowed up in the apparatus of the camps, perishing just as surely as the Jews, though sometimes only less methodically." That Sophie herself turns out to be "a passionate, avid, tediously single-minded hater of Jews" makes this opinion ironically tortuous, of course, but it becomes a fine question, as we will see, whether Styron meant "consecration" to explain a quality in Jewish memory or a quality in Nazi conscience. Many years later, he would assert that "it never occurred to me that the Jewish experience under the Nazis was not unique, or that the victimization of the Jews was not of a far greater magnitude than the oppression of the others." In fact, he contended, the anti-Semitism of Sophie's father, the author of *Poland's Jewish Problem: Does National Socialism Have the Answer?* and an early prophet of the Final

Solution, provided evidence that "the book in large part has to be read as a parable of the devastation of anti-Semitism."[18] At the time he wrote the novel, however, Styron's reservations about the uniqueness of the Jews' experience were too obvious to ignore.

Styron forecast his perspective on the Holocaust in a preview essay entitled "Auschwitz," which appeared in 1974. Far shorter than "This Quiet Dust," his comparable prolegomenon to *The Confessions of Nat Turner*, Styron's essay on Auschwitz, prompted by his recent visit to the site, presents neatly the thesis that underlies his choice of a Christian heroine. Referring to a recent symposium on the Holocaust at St. John the Divine in New York, he writes:

> The Holocaust is so incomprehensible and so awesomely central to our present-day consciousness—Jewish and gentile—that one almost physically shrinks with reticence from attempting to point out again what was barely touched on in certain reports on the symposium: that at Auschwitz perished not only the Jews but at least one million other souls who were not Jews. Of many origins but mainly Slavs . . . they came from a despised people who almost certainly were fated to be butchered with the same genocidal ruthlessness as were the Jews had Hitler won the war, and they contained among them hundreds of thousands of Christians who went to their despairing deaths in the belief that *their* God, the Prince of Peace, was as dead as the God of Abraham and Moses. . . . For although the unparalleled tragedy of the Jews may have been [Nazism's] most terrible single handiwork, it was also anti-Christian. And it attempted to be more final than that, for its ultimate depravity lay in the fact that it was anti-human. Anti-life.

Like Sophie, Styron added, the woman on whom she was modeled was certain that "Christ had turned His face away from her, as He had from all mankind."[19]

Styron's rejection of the view that Jews were unique victims of Nazism or totalitarianism more generally—a rejection that D. G. Myers has placed under the heading of "liberal anti-Judaism"[20]—anticipated in some respects the *Historikerstreit*, the "historians' controversy" that erupted in Germany in the 1980s over the question of whether the Nazi crimes were unique, and specifically German, or instead a class of atrocity witnessed elsewhere—for example, under Joseph Stalin in the Soviet Union, where some 20 million people perished between 1926 and 1953 through purges, slave labor, and murder under the regime of collectivization. As Charles Maier has argued, however, singularity and comparability need not be contradictory,[21] an observation particularly apt in the case of Styron, who attempts to distinguish the experience of Jews—they are the victims of other victims, the slaves of other slaves—while at the same time he denies that they occupy a special position within the Nazi genocide.

Styron did not wish, nor should we wish, to forget the fact that Poles, not Jews, were the principal deportees to concentration camps before 1942, nor should we ignore the thousands of Poles who, at great risk, hid Jews or otherwise helped them to avoid persecution and death.[22] Of the 6 million people of Poland killed in the course of the war, half were not Jews, an onslaught that began with the decimation of the intellectual professions, the destruction of cultural institutions, the repression of the clergy, and a Nazification campaign in schools and other institutions meant to cripple the nation, so that its population could be replaced by a "master race" of ethnic Germans. Those with undesirable racial characteristics or unacceptable political loyalties were to be enslaved or killed. Children deemed able to be Germanized would be seized from their parents and sent to the Reich.[23]

At issue, however, is not the suffering of the Poles but the question of rightly interpreting the zone of likeness between Poland as a devastated nation and Poland as the main site of the attempted destruction of the European Jews—including more than 3 million of Poland's 1939 population of 3.5 million Jews. It was because Jews were an enemy different not in number but in kind that the Poland visited by Styron in 1974, no less than the Poland to which Sophie might have returned after the war, had become, in the later words of Thane Rosenbaum, "the blackest hole in the Jewish galaxy."[24]

Poles were executed for the crime of racial pollution, but according to more lenient standards, and pronouncements that they should be annihilated never matured into a policy, let alone a plan of implementation. Subject along with Czechs, Russians, and other Slavs to modes of classification and selection never applied to any Jews on racial grounds, Poles, said Himmler, might continue to provide slave labor so long as they did not "breed" within the Reich, whereas the Jews' demographic slate was to be made "quite clean."[25] In the euthanasia programs preparatory to the Holocaust, Jews were viewed as a group apart who did not have to meet criteria for killing such as mental deficiency or physical deformity. Defined as parasites on whose eradication rested the purity of the Aryan blood line and the fate of civilization itself, they were targeted for destruction as a biological group not confined to a geographical area or identified by specific political affiliations or economic connections. Instead, the group as such would be destroyed, wherever its members might be, with no option for conversion to a different creed and with confinement to ghettos or slave labor camps only a temporary respite. On this point, Styron might have referred to his own primary witness, Auschwitz commandant Rudolf Höss, who remembered Himmler's orders in the summer of 1941—it seems most likely to have been late July—as clear: "The Führer has ordered that the Jewish question be solved once and for all and that we, the SS, are to implement that order. . . . The Jews are the sworn enemies of the German people and must be eradicated. Every Jew that we can lay our hands on is to be destroyed now during the war, without exception. If we cannot now obliterate the biological basis of Jewry, the Jews will one day destroy the German people."[26]

Styron's interpretation of Auschwitz as "anti-life," wrote Cynthia Ozick in response to his 1974 essay, distracts attention from the brute fact that the Jewish presence in Poland was almost totally wiped out, while the language, culture, and institutions of Catholic Poland continued throughout the twentieth century very much intact, despite the depredations of Soviet tyranny.[27] Poland today is different enough from Poland then that readers might miss Ozick's point. As contemporary Poland has come to terms with its anti-Semitic past, memorials to the nation's lost Jewish population have become common, as have books and films on the subject. The collapse of communism marked a turning point in the nation's attitude toward Jews, one symbolized by President Lech Walesa's 1991 speech to the Israeli Knesset, a conciliatory effort that walked a fine line between praise for Israel and expression of the view that Poles and Jews faced the same murderers in the Nazis and the same opponents during communist rule. The fiftieth anniversary of the Warsaw Ghetto uprising in 1995 saw the most elaborate Holocaust commemoration in Polish history, while the publication a few years later of Jan Gross's *Neighbors*, which recounted the 1941 massacre of up to 1,600 Jews in the village of Jedwabne by local Poles, an atrocity previously attributed to German police units, stirred passionate debate and soul searching, but not blanket denial or government suppression.[28] Such events entailed facing a painful past—not only the genocide of the Jews and Polish cooperation in it but also the persecution of Jews and the erasure of the memory of Jewish civilization that continued in the postwar years leading up to the publication of *Sophie's Choice*.

Although the fate of Polish Jewry could not be reversed, its epilogue might have been different had the subsequent history of Poland negated Nazi anti-Semitism instead of carrying it forward in a different guise. Just as they had been scapegoated following World War I,[29] so in the next war's aftermath Jews were often blamed for its devastation, and survivors were subjected to ostracism and terror when they returned home to find out the fate of their families or to reclaim homes and businesses. In response to postwar violence such as the Kielce pogrom of 1946, between 100,000 and 200,000 Jews fled Poland, most to refugee camps in Germany where they awaited the opportunity to go to Palestine or the United States, thus reducing the Jewish population of Poland to about 50,000. A new wave of anti-Semitism accompanied the end of the Stalinist period in 1956, resulting in another large emigration to Israel. It flared up again more dramatically after the Six-Day War in 1967, when communist Poland, because of its allegiance to Arab states, ejected Jews from the Communist Party and professional positions, and fomented anti-Semitism under the cloak of anti-Zionism by encouraging the press and the public to revisit the "Jewish Problem." By 1980, according to one estimate, there were only some 6,000 Jews left in Poland, proving that it was indeed possible, to cite the title of a study of the Party's recourse to anti-Semitism in lands where Jews had been virtually wiped out, to have "anti-Semitism without Jews."[30]

Equally important was the rewriting of history. In major scholarly works, as well as in school textbooks and tourist guides, the history of the death camps subsumed Jews into the collective martyrology of Poland's wartime losses. The claim that there were 6 *million Poles* who were victims of the Nazi genocide thus contributed to what Iwona Irwin-Zarecka has termed Poland's "non-trauma of the Holocaust," part of the "neutralization of memory" that, in generalizing the targets of Nazi rapacity, ensured that claims of Jewish singularity were expunged from the historical record.[31]

The cleansing of public memory was nowhere more evident than at the Auschwitz visited by Styron before he composed his argument that the death camp was fundamentally anti-Christian, antilife. In 1947 the Polish parliament had declared that the main camp at Auschwitz would be "forever preserved as a memorial to the martyrdom of the Polish nation and other peoples." Although a reconstructed gas chamber and crematory were included in the memorial, Auschwitz II-Birkenau, the principal site of the extermination of the Jews, was excluded from the official tour. In 1967, the memorial erected at the selection ramp in Auschwitz II-Birkenau recorded a simple message in twenty languages, including Yiddish and Hebrew, on as many stone tablets: "Four million people suffered and died here [in Auschwitz] at the hands of the Nazi murderers between the years 1940 and 1945."[32] Insofar as the correct number was between 1.1 and 1.5 million, the vast majority Jews, the erroneous figure not only conflated all victims regardless of the scope of victimization but also exaggerated the number of Polish and Soviet martyrs, thereby diminishing Stalin's own crimes.[33] At the height of the anti-Jewish purges following the Six-Day War, the commemorative pavilion devoted to Jews was closed, ostensibly for renovation, and it was not opened again until 1978, four years after Styron's visit. Upon its rededication at that time, Jews and Poles were once again ranked together as equivalent kinds of victims, with biological elimination and political decimation placed on the same footing.

The presentation of Auschwitz as a Polish memorial was made more pronounced upon the elevation of Karol Wojtyla as Pope John Paul II in 1978. During his return visit to Poland a year later, the pope preached a message of spiritual freedom and, at Auschwitz, said a mass in which he clearly denounced anti-Semitism and recognized the Jews as a particular object of extermination. At the same time, he pronounced the beatification of Christians martyred in the Holocaust, described the Jews as a people that "draws its origins from Abraham, our father in faith," commemorated the "six million Poles [who] lost their lives during the Second World War: a fifth of a nation," and sanctified the site as "the Golgotha of the contemporary world."[34] As in his 1998 message "We Remember: A Reflection on the Shoah," Pope John Paul II did not deny the genocide of the Jews. But in turning Auschwitz into a site of Polish martyrdom and making the Catholic Church a victim alongside other victims—rather than an accomplice, or at least a bystander, in the Holocaust—he, like Styron, codified a Polish Catholic triumphalist tradition of incorporating the Holocaust into its own Christology.[35]

THE SLAVE ENTERPRISE

Styron makes much of the fact that Sophie arrives at Auschwitz just prior to a decree during the first week of April 1943—elsewhere Styron specified April 4, 1943—purportedly issued by Himmler, but "unquestionably originating with the Führer," that "the recently built gas chambers and crematoriums of Birkenau," employed to exterminate Jews, Poles, Russians, and other Slavs without differentiation according to the same rules of health and age, would henceforth be used with a "sudden unaccustomed exclusivity" only to kill Jews.[36] Although Styron admits that the number of non-Jews killed in the gas chambers or by other means of execution up to this point was probably only in the tens of thousands, even if many hundreds of thousands more died of illness, starvation, or being worked to death,[37] this seeming change in course is meant to highlight the fact that other races and nations had previously been at equal risk.

But was there such a change in course? Even though it coincides broadly with the liquidation of the Jewish ghettos and work camps, and precisely with the first use of one of four new crematoria constructed at Auschwitz II-Birkenau,[38] the April 4 order seems to have been invented by Styron and inserted into *Sophie's Choice* so as to buttress his contention that the death camps were chiefly a vast system of slavery and the Judeocide a function of wartime tactics or logistics rather than the result of a distinctive anti-Semitic ideology.[39] As we have already seen, however, Rudolf Höss placed Himmler's communication of the Führer's mandate to solve "the Jewish question" in the summer of 1941. The supposed April 4 order thus obscures the fact that the Final Solution had been inexorably unfolding for at least a year and probably closer to two years. Just as important, it confuses the meaning of slavery both within and beyond the Nazi regime.

In the midst of telling the story of Sophie's relationship with commandant Höss, Stingo pauses to explain that Auschwitz existed as both a depot for mass murder and "a vast enclave dedicated to the practice of slavery," albeit a new form of slavery in which murder was normal and humans were "continually replenished and expendable." Here he cites Richard Rubenstein's "masterful little book" *The Cunning of History* (1975), which extended the insights of Hannah Arendt and Stanley Elkins that the concentration camp was a "society of total domination."[40] Stingo quotes not only from Rubenstein but also from Styron's own essay on Rubenstein, published in 1978 under the title "Hell Reconsidered." In Elkins's much-debated thesis that the plantation, like the concentration camp, reduced slaves to childlike, dehumanized beings,

Styron had already found an explanation of slave psychology central to *The Confessions of Nat Turner*.[41] In Elkins's influence on Rubenstein, he found a retrospective bridge from chattel slavery to the destruction of the European Jews—or rather, to the Nazi destruction of millions of people, most of them Jews, since he also shared with Rubenstein the belief that the Holocaust was an act of totalitarian terror that swept up Jews and non-Jews alike.

Rubenstein's idiosyncratic but no doubt appealing contribution to Styron's argument lay in his theory that "the institution of chattel slavery as it was practiced by the great nations of the West" reached "its despotic apotheosis at Auschwitz," where the Nazis resolved slavery's contradiction between person and "thing" by eliminating it. In the kingdom of Auschwitz was created something worse than genocide, says Rubenstein in passages quoted by Styron: "The death-camp system became a society of total domination only when healthy inmates were kept alive and forced to become slaves rather than killed outright. . . . An extermination center can only manufacture corpses; a society of total domination creates a world of the living dead."[42] Although Styron and Rubenstein cited the Nazi practice of slavery in extremis for differing purposes, both failed to grasp—or chose to obscure the fact—that slave labor was ancillary to Hitler's plan to exterminate the Jews.

Styron bases his argument that the Holocaust was part of a vast slave enterprise on the labor provided for IG Farben's synthetic fuel and rubber plant erected near the village of Monowitz, seven kilometers from Auschwitz. Known also as "Buna," after the rubber product it was supposed to contribute to the war effort, Auschwitz III-Monowitz cost the lives of some 25,000 Jews, earned the Nazis some 20 million Reichsmark, and failed to produce a single pound of rubber.[43] Styron rightly depicts IG Farben's involvement in the Holocaust as the fruitful union of capitalism and totalitarianism—Rudolf Höss, says Styron, made himself a "vassal of IG Farben" in the "slave enterprise that he served"[44]—but the slave labor supplied to the firm by Auschwitz was, in the case of the Jews, an auxiliary to mass murder. Owing to a high death rate among Soviet prisoners and acute labor shortages in Germany, the Final Solution was periodically deferred in recognition of the temporary need for labor. Because the supply of Jews was easily replenished and work was never the first purpose, however, there was tension but never a breach between exploitation and extermination. The policy adopted for Jewish laborers was one of *Vernichtung durch Arbeit*, "destruction through work," and in this respect, Benjamin Ferencz has suggested, the term "slave" is appropriate only because English has no precise word to describe the status of workers marked for certain destruction, just as it has no good equivalent for *verbraucht* ("used up"), the term applied to such workers at the point their utility was gone and they had to be gassed and incinerated.[45] As Czech survivor Ctibor Wohl recalled, labor and death thus formed a perfect circle: "After extracting the maximum labour power from the prisoners, the firm [Farben] returned them to the SS for the gas chamber, for which the same concern supplied the poisonous gas, Zyklon B"—a reference to the fact that the Farben subsidiary Degesch controlled the manufacture and distribution of the gas pellets used by Höss's killing operation at Birkenau.[46]

By the time of Sophie's attempted seduction of Höss in October 1943, through which she hopes he will intervene to place her son in the *Lebensborn* program, it was clear, certainly in retrospect, that Jews were distinguished from other Nazi victims and that ghettos and slave labor camps provided only momentary sanctuary. "I must have more Jews," says Walter Dürrfeld, the director of Farben's rubber plant, to Höss in a fictional conversation created by Styron. Indeed, the dialogue between Höss and Dürrfeld, to whose telling relationship with Sophie we will return, depicts the vacillation in Nazi policy as a conflict between the Reich's commitment to "Special Action" and its commitment to sustain the war effort—between "the lust for murder and the need for labor"—in a metaphor already familiar in *Sophie's Choice*: "*Die Schizophrenie*." Insofar as it implies a more precise distinction between the zones of likeness inhabited by Jews and other laborers, however, this schizophrenia in purpose, coupled with Dürrfeld's demand for more Jews, brings Styron closer than he may have meant to an intentionalist interpretation of the Final Solution and therefore to the demented psychology of his key witness, Rudolf Höss.[47]

THE AUSCHWITZ SELF

Written in the months before he was hanged for war crimes in 1947, Höss's memoir, *Commandant of Auschwitz*, is one of the most disturbing expressions of the "schizophrenia" of Nazi ideology.[48] In a career marked not by overt signs of depravity but rather by routine military ambitions, Höss became a coldly efficient officer in the Nazi hierarchy.[49] Like Adolf Eichmann, Höss advanced the soldier's defense that he was only an unknowing "cog in the wheel of the great extermination machine created by the Third Reich," incapable of countermanding "sacred" orders issued in the name of the Führer and ultimately envious of those who faced a battlefield death rather than his inglorious execution.[50] It is not implausible to deduce Höss's moral effacement from his stoic focus upon technological problems, and Primo Levi found his story instructive for its description of a man who in different circumstances would have become a "drab functionary" but instead "evolved, step by step, into one of the greatest criminals in history."[51] One may likewise come away from the memoir, as Styron did, with contradictory sensations: Höss is at once an "organism so crushingly banal as to be a paradigm of the thesis eloquently stated by Hannah Arendt" and a "modern Gothic freak," his mind in thrall to "the rapture of totalitarianism."[52]

Through a mixture of subterfuge and blindness, Höss sought to mitigate his culpability even as he made no effort to disguise his heinous motives. "I see now that the extermination of the Jews was fundamentally wrong," he wrote in captivity, yet his apparent change of heart had nothing to do with remorse. "Precisely because of these mass exterminations," Höss said, "Germany has drawn upon herself the hatred of the entire world. It in no way served the cause of anti-Semitism, but on the contrary brought the Jews far closer to their ultimate objective," economic and political power, through resettlement in Palestine. From the outset, moreover, Höss conceived of the Jews' destruction in pragmatic terms. Although he was made apprehensive by the initial experiments with Zyklon B because he feared it would result in more violent, agonizing deaths, the victims were not his concern. Mindful of the morbid effects upon the *Einsatzgruppen* of the mass executions by firing squad on the eastern front (drinking, psychological breakdowns, suicide), Höss was pleased to see how quickly Zyklon B accomplished its task: "This gassing set my mind at rest, for the mass extermination of the Jews was to start soon and at that time neither Eichmann nor I was certain how these mass killings were to be carried out."[53]

Höss's peace of mind led Styron to a surprising judgment. Within the memoir, says Styron, one feels the "spectral presence" of a formerly innocent young man who "is stricken dumb at the unmentionable depravity in which the grown man is mired." Just as he identified a "certain idealism" in the attempt by Sophie's father to offer the Nazis his services as an expert anti-Semite, so Styron was determined to preserve in Höss a core not just of banality but of submerged goodness. Weaving Höss's idyllic account of life in Auschwitz into Sophie's narrative, Styron remained unaccountably persuaded that Höss was "sincere when he expresse[d] his misgivings, even his secret revulsion," at the acts he oversaw, just as he was convinced by the "equanimity" of Höss's claim that he "never personally hated the Jews" and only looked upon them as "enemies of our people." Styron was so eager to find Höss's text honest and reliable, in fact, that he turned to his fictional heroine for corroboration: "I do not recall Sophie's telling me about ever being the recipient of a present from Frau Höss," says Stingo, "but it confirms one's belief in the basic truthfulness of Höss's account to know that during Sophie's brief stay under the Commandant's roof she, like the other prisoners, just as he claimed, was never in any way or at any time badly treated." Yet even if some kind of "serviceable decency" could be retrieved from Höss's mendacious prose, perhaps by psychiatric means, it is immaterial to the moral man who must be judged.[54]

As the alternately clear-sighted and deluded judgments recorded in his memoir indicate, Höss showed a remarkable capacity to split himself into two selves, witness and actor, bystander and perpetrator. He is a striking instance of the "divided self" that Robert Jay Lifton adduced from the psychoanalytic concept of "splitting" in his study of racist biomedical theory.

Through a doubling of identity created by the duress of participating in genocide, Lifton suggests, conscience may be effectively transferred to an "Auschwitz self" who acts in loyalty to a skewed transcending vision seemingly beyond one's control. Just as Holocaust analysts such as Bruno Bettelheim have described a "split self" that emerged in the trauma of victims—a self to whom the horror was happening and a benumbed "vaguely interested, but essentially detached, observer" who registers the events—so it may be stipulated that the Nazis committed acts of extreme barbarism with relative equanimity by assigning responsibility to some "other" self acting in obedience to a mystified hierarchy.[55]

Averring that his acting and witnessing selves were irreconcilable, Höss claimed, in a confessional sequence largely quoted by Styron, that he had to suppress his own secret doubts while instilling in subordinates the same confidence that he had in Himmler and Hitler: "I had to exercise intense self-control in order to prevent my innermost doubts and feelings of oppression from becoming apparent. I had to appear cold and indifferent to events that must have wrung the heart of anyone possessed of human feelings. . . . I had to watch hour after hour, by day and by night, the removal and burning of the bodies, the extraction of the teeth, the cutting of the hair, the whole grisly, interminable business. . . . I had to look through the peep-hole of the gas-chambers and watch the process of death itself, because the doctors wanted me to see it."[56] Into Höss's self-presentation as a suffering witness Styron inserted Arendt's well-known assessment that Nazism protected the consciences of those committing genocide through a tactic of inversion whereby the perception of agony among the incarcerated was redirected toward the observing self: "So instead of saying: What horrible things I did to people!, the murderers would be able to say: What horrible things I had to watch in the pursuance of my duties, how heavily the task weighed upon my shoulders!" In this passage from *Eichmann in Jerusalem*, Arendt is speaking not of Höss but of Himmler, for her the Nazi most gifted in solving problems of conscience by coining slogans, employing euphemistic language rules ("migration," "final solution," "special treatment," and so forth), and presenting the genocide of the Jews as part of a grand, historic undertaking.[57]

The defining instance of this psychic strategy was Himmler's infamous speech to senior officers at Posen on October 4, 1943—a speech with an oblique but telling role in *Sophie's Choice*—in which he addressed the moral duty of the SS to exterminate the Jews. "I ask of you that what I say in this circle you really only hear and never speak of," Himmler requested, before discussing the necessity of killing Jewish women and children, as well as men, lest avengers from their germ culture be born to menace the children and grandchildren of Nazi Germany. He continued:

The difficult decision had to be taken, to cause this *Volk* to disappear from the face of the earth. To organize the execution of this mission was the most difficult task we had hitherto. It was accomplished without—as I believe I am able to say—our men or our officers suffering injury to spirit or soul. This danger was very close. The way between the two possibilities, either to become too crude, to become heartless and no longer to respect human life, or to become weak and crack up in a nervous breakdown—the path between this Scylla and Charybdis is horribly narrow. . . . The Jewish question in those countries occupied by us will be settled by the end of the year. Only a residue of individual Jews will remain in hiding. The question of the non-Jews married to Jews and the question of half-Jews will be sensibly and reasonably investigated, decided and then solved. . . . I believe it better that we—all of us—have borne [this task] for our *Volk*, have taken the responsibility on ourselves— the responsibility for a deed, not only for an idea—and that we take the secret with us to the grave.[58]

In his incredible proposition that the motives and means of the Holocaust might remain a secret, Himmler sought to lend genocide a sacrificial, mystical character, while at the same time making his officers bystanders to an event greater than themselves. By accepting the grave burden envisioned by Himmler and turning himself into a stoic witness, Höss likewise purported to steer a treacherous course between heartless strength and nervous breakdown, as though his part in the solution of the Jewish question might also be performed without injury to spirit or soul.

Styron depicts a subordinate but no less critical instance of Himmler's proposition in the doctor at the Auschwitz transport selection, Dr. Jemand von Niemand ("anybody from nobody"), who in allowing Sophie to save only one of her children from the gas chamber, thus becoming her daughter's executioner,[59] embodies the brittle psyche inferred by Lifton: he must have been "cracking apart like bamboo, disintegrating at the very moment that he was reaching out for spiritual salvation." Sophie's horrifying choice is thus prompted not by an evil act become bureaucratically banal but rather by an evil act cloaked in mental disintegration. Von Niemand's blasphemous response to Sophie's professed belief in Jesus—"I believe in Christ," the drunken von Niemand replies, "did He not say, 'Suffer the little children to come unto Me?' "—serves to demonstrate Styron's view that the Holocaust was first of all anti-Christian, anti-life.[60] What is most remarkable here, however, is the degree to which the Auschwitz selves of the commandant and the doctor anticipated Styron's 1990 memoir about his excruciating struggle with depression, *Darkness Visible*, self-consciously a narrative of survival in which an observing self splits off to witness helplessly the torment of the suffering self. Whether or not Styron's depression had begun to manifest itself during the composition of *Sophie's Choice*—his illness became full-blown and debilitating in 1985—the parallels between *Darkness Visible* and the novel's narrative self-projections are unmistakable.

Originating in 1988 as an op-ed piece for the *New York Times* entitled "Why Primo Levi Need Not Have Died," in which Styron argued that Levi's death, apparently by suicide, could have been prevented had he received proper care for his depression,[61] Styron's memoir details his rapid descent into a desperate state. In his blackest moments, he writes, the longing for annihilation, enacted in hideous fantasies of suicide that are to the depressed mind "what lascivious daydreams are to persons of robust sexuality," alternates with "near paralysis, psychic energy throttled back close to zero."[62] Styron here appears to have borrowed directly from the literature of Holocaust survival—the "zero" state of psychic exhaustion, as well as other physical symptoms he details, belongs very much to the realm of depleted selves that Levi, Bettelheim, Eugene Kogon, and other survivors made archetypes in the literature of the death camps—or perhaps from Stanley Elkins, who took the statements of such commentators as his own point of departure in elucidating the pathology of slave personality. In any case, the central component of Styron's "schizophrenia" is the differentiation of self into a brutalized object and "a wraithlike observer" who watches "with dispassionate curiosity as his companion struggles against the oncoming disaster."[63] Like Höss at the peephole of the gas chamber or von Niemand deciding who will live and who will die, Styron in the throes of depression becomes a voyeur to his own suffering. Understood as an epilogue to *Sophie's Choice*, *Darkness Visible* thus points to identification not only with Nazi victims but also with Nazi perpetrators, and therefore provides further reason to read the split figures of Stingo and Nathan Landau, contestants for the body of Holocaust survivor and anti-Semite Sophie Zawistowska, in an autobiographical light.

After "Planet Auschwitz," writes Emil Fackenheim, there can be no spiritual health, no psychic recovery, without a "mad midrash" to grapple, in counterpoint, with the madness of the Holocaust. Without such madness, a Jew cannot do "what a Voice From Sinai bids him do: choose life."[64] One can conceive of various ways in which Fackenheim's dictum might authorize wild satire or sacrilegious modes of artistic remembrance. Novels such as Tadeusz Borowski's *This Way to the Gas, Ladies and Gentlemen* and Leslie Epstein's *King of the Jews*, along with films such as Mel Brooks's *The Producers* and Lina Wertmüller's *Seven Beauties*, come to mind. Insatiable sexual desire might be another response to the trauma of the Holocaust—no less for a Polish Catholic like Sophie than for a Jew. Or, does *Sophie's Choice* belong to the genre of "porno-kitsch," necrophilia masquerading as art?[65] The answer to this question lies not in Sophie, the Holocaust survivor, but rather in the relationships Styron constructs for her with the insane Jew Nathan Landau and equally with the voyeuristic Stingo, the author's surrogate, who feeds vicariously off their psychotic passion as he brings the novel's several zones of likeness into final alignment.

Ecstatic Symbiosis

Having already lost her daughter through the cruel choice imposed by von Niemand, Sophie determines to use her assignment as Höss's secretary to save her son from the gas chamber. Although she is arrested with a resistance group (for smuggling meat) and judged to be guilty with them, Sophie has in fact done little to aid the resistance and is at Auschwitz, she insists, by mistake. When her declaration of innocence fails to win Höss's favor, she tries and fails to impress him with rancorous anti-Semitism (like his real-life counterpart, Höss dismisses her allegations that the Jew is a sexual defiler, "a diabolical debaucher with an enormous prick," as a mistaken stereotype counterproductive to the cause of anti-Semitism).[66] By itself, Sophie's attempt to save her son by seducing Höss is a maternal, not a collaborative act, but her secretarial role, as Styron plots it, thrusts her into a gray zone of complicity in which seduction and killing, the erotic and the nihilistic, become one.

Against the interior backdrop of Höss's tawdry decor—a pastel of Hitler as a Knight of the Holy Grail—and the exterior rumble of locomotives and boxcars arriving for the selection, Sophie takes Höss's dictation of a letter to Himmler in which the commandant complains about the miserable condition of Jews just arriving from Greece. She helps Höss with appropriately cordial phrasing in making the suggestion to Himmler that, since the "mechanism for Special Action" is taxed beyond its capacity, an alternative camp should have been considered. The transport having arrived and the "monstrous" having become commonplace, however, Sophie correctly interprets Höss's intention to assign the Greek Jews to the *Sonderkommando* unit at the crematoria, where they will "feed bodies to the furnaces until they too, exhausted beyond recall, are ready for the gas." Höss's dictated letter closes by mentioning his disappointment that he will miss Himmler's speech at Posen the following day, a telling detail that functions in two ways at once. Sophie's work for her father and for Höss, as Stingo later puts it, makes her a "filthy *collaboratrice*," simultaneously a victim and accomplice in the Nazis' decision "to cause this *Volk* to disappear from the face of the earth," to recall Himmler's words. By not revealing the contents of Himmler's speech to which her letter alludes, however, Styron condemns his heroine's struggle "with the demon of her own schizoid conscience" while purposefully obscuring the telling distinction between her own fate and that of those assigned to "special action," the distinction between Poles and Jews.[67]

If Sophie's attempt to rescue her son drags her into a twilight world of living death from which anguish and guilt can never save her, moreover, it does so by tangling her in a web of eroticism created as much by Styron's own collaboration, by his own "schizoid conscience," as by her own. The scene of Sophie's failed seduction of Höss and her role in preparing the letter to Himmler is intercut narratively with Stingo's meditations on his own lust and on Nat Turner's motives, as well as his account of Nathan's and Sophie's descent into sadomasochism. The place of Styron's hypersexualized black messiah within this constellation of symbolic forces only becomes evident at the end of the novel, but Turner's ghostly presence is verified earlier in Sophie's dream of sexual union with the "corporate prince" Walter Dürrfeld, portrayed by Styron as an acquaintance of Sophie's father, prior to her meeting him again in Höss's office. Set in a remote chapel overlooking an ocean—a setting whose details are vividly reminiscent of Nat Turner's reverie, which frames his narrative as prologue and epilogue in Styron's earlier novel—Sophie's dream unfolds in the symbolic language of erotic ecstasy in which her sensations are defined by submission to violent, death-seeking fascism. In a "frenzy of craving," she orally engulfs Dürrfeld's huge blue-black penis "with a choking sensation that wilt[s] her with pleasure." Accompanied by a Bach cantata, he then penetrates her from behind as she kneels at an altar beneath "the skeletal cruciform emblem of God's suffering, glowing like a naked bone."[68]

Seen from one angle, Styron's linkage between Nazism and eroticism is acute. Derived from the dominance of the Führer, at once fatherly and sadistic, and from a cult of obedience symbolized in mass public displays that drew upon a reserve of sexual energy, the Third Reich's conception of a purified racial universe has been said to resemble hardcore pornography in creating a "total universe" in which all is governed by the masculine erotic imperative.[69] In the more radical theory espoused by Andrea Dworkin, the death camp and pornography are, in fact, coequal expressions of sadistic power in which the Jew and the woman have the same status: "She is the Jew, the willing victim: the Jews walked willingly into the ovens. She is the woman, the volunteer for bondage." Dworkin's judgment that pornography is nothing less than "Dachau brought into the bedroom" has few adherents, but it has a compelling edge of truth as a gloss on the assumptions governing *Sophie's Choice*.[70] Whereas Sophie's sexual enslavement to Nathan could be interpreted as a psychotic reaction to her degradation in Auschwitz, her dream of Walter Dürrfeld precedes that degradation, concealing behind the glamour of fascist power the industrialized Judeocide taking place outside Höss's private quarters and making visceral, in Sophie, Styron's penchant for abridging sexual frenzy and Christian transcendence. Just as his depiction of Auschwitz subordinates anti-Semitism to totalitarianism and his depiction of IG Farben subordinates anti-Semitism to slave labor, so his depiction of Sophie's lust for Walter Dürrfeld subordinates anti-Semitism to religio-erotic ecstasy.

Far from penitential, Sophie's postwar life, like Styron's postwar plot, reprises these subordinations. In making Nathan Landau Sophie's "last executioner," who completes in Brooklyn her destruction begun in Auschwitz,[71] Styron in effect re-created what Primo Levi identified as the perverse "mimesis" of death camp existence, a state of psychosis wherein the roles of victim and accomplice become confused, even exchanged. But the magnetic power of that mimesis, Levi continues, should not blind us to the fact that the confusion of murderers with their victims (as in the pretended agonies of Himmler and Höss) or of victims with their murderers (as in the case of the *Sonderkommandos*) is "a moral disease or an aesthetic affectation or a sinister sign of complicity; above all, it is a precarious service rendered (intentionally or not) to the negators of truth."[72] Although Nathan speaks as a Jew, "an authority on anguish and suffering," his schizophrenic split between normality and madness also allies him with Rudolf Höss, a likeness meant to represent Styron's belief that "brutal sexuality and the pornography of violence" reflect the reality of Auschwitz.[73] By the time it is revealed that Nathan's job as a biomedical scientist is a sham and that he is a dangerous lunatic, Styron has almost fully inverted Jewish and gentile roles: the Polish anti-Semite has become the brutalized victim, the Jew the insane perpetrator whose mental illness and growing preoccupation with the Holocaust achieve cathexis in Sophie.

No doubt Styron recognized that the Judeophobic language of Nazism often sounded like the Negrophobic language of radical segregation. ("Systematically these black parasites of the nation defile our inexperienced young blond girls and thereby destroy something which can no longer be replaced in this world," wrote Hitler in a characteristic passage in *Mein Kampf*, while Christians "look on indifferently at this desecration and destruction of a noble and unique living creature, given to the earth by God's grace.")[74] Höss's rejection of it notwithstanding, anti-Semitic propaganda of the kind featured in the periodical *Der Stürmer*, a key feature of which was depictions of the Jew as sexual predator, constituted a prurient pornography that transferred to Jews repressed Aryan desires for the forbidden,[75] much as whites in the Jim Crow South may have transferred their own fearful desires to blacks. In this respect, Styron made Nathan's role structurally schizophrenic. In its orgiastic violation of the Nuremberg Laws, Nathan's relationship with Sophie, portrayed as a Pole whose complexion and features are nonetheless "typically Aryan," illustrates the Hitlerian thesis that the Aryan woman, the embodiment of nationhood, is threatened by the Jew's racial pollution. Yet in addressing Sophie as "Irma Griese Jew-burning cunt!" and commanding her to "suck the Jew-boy," in physically brutalizing her and attempting to urinate in her mouth,[76] Nathan behaves like a Nazi or, perhaps more aptly, like a *Kapo*, a death camp Jew whose collaboration with Nazism places him, according to Primo Levi, in the "hybrid class of the prisoner-functionary" where the roles of master and slave, oppressor and victim, have been exchanged.[77] Crack mimic and paranoid schizophrenic, a composite of Nat Turner and Rudolf Höss, Nathan acts as though a shard of Nazi criminality has entered his soul, giving him leave, as a Jew, to exact vengeance upon Sophie, the Nazi collaborator. In the end, however, the split between Nathan as Nazi and Nathan as Jew disappears. When he threatens to copy and then finally does copy Hermann Göring's suicide by cyanide in October 1946—Göring thus preempted the Nuremberg court's sentence that he be hanged, as did Himmler—Nathan dies as a Nazi *and* as a Jew, symbolically at one with the millions who died from the cyanide derivative Zyklon B, the pesticide that Höss determined would make the Final Solution technologically feasible.

Were Nathan Sophie's only American lover, their mimetic exchange of roles and their indulgence in a carnival of depravity and death would be an unexceptional, if vile, illustration of the wages of complicity in racism and genocide. But it is Styron's autobiographical narrator, "wraithlike observer" and sole survivor of the novel's moral wreckage, in whom mimetic exchange culminates. In narrating episodes of the "ecstatic symbiosis" between Sophie and Nathan he could not have witnessed, and then in narrating scenes in which he rivals the sexual hyperbolism of his mad alter ego, Stingo at last surmounts the "inward abiding Golgotha" of his virginity and folds into a single zone of likeness the roles of voyeur and actor, witness and perpetrator. The flamboyantly detailed scenes in which Sophie, "the world's most elegant cocksucker," massages Stingo's semen into her face while he fixes his eyes on her Auschwitz tattoo, or in which he ejaculates in her mouth, are literally the climax of the novel's lavish attention to his masturbation fantasies.[78] In short, they are the narrative equivalent of the "money shot" in pornographic film, where a stylized and artificial female orgasm coincides with an actual male orgasm rendered visible by its exteriority, its display of mastery.[79] What is most pornographic, however, is not the graphic detail of Stingo's escapades with Sophie but rather Styron's attempt to endow them, in the context of the Final Solution, with sacrificial, redemptive significance.

Here we may return to Styron's Nat Turner problem and compare the endings of the two novels. Punctuated by reiterations of the passage from Revelation announcing the return of Christ—"*Surely, I come quickly . . .*" (Rev. 3:11, 22:7, 20)—Nat's reverie also includes his imagining a last rapturous coupling with Margaret Whitehead: "with tender stroking motions I pour out my love within her; pulsing flood; she arches against me, cries out, and the twain—black and white—are one." The novel concludes, at the moment of Nat's execution, with the voice of God calling Nat—"'Come!' the voice booms, but commanding me now: 'Come, my son!' I turn in surrender"— accompanied by a lingering biblical coda, as though Margaret or even Christ were speaking in Nat's disembodied consciousness: "*Did He not say, I am the root and the offspring of David, and the bright and morning star*"[80] (Rev. 22:16). Although this crude conjunction of the erotic and the divine courts absurdity and justifies Vincent Harding's objection that Margaret Whitehead's "arched white body becomes Styron-Turner's pathway to their white, white God,"[81] the ecstasy of transcendence places Nat, in death, within a framework of millennial prophecy meant to reflect his life and preaching. No comparable defense is possible in the case of *Sophie's Choice*, however, and the falsification of Nat Turner's heroism with which Styron might be charged pales by comparison to his appropriation of the Nazi Judeocide to a scheme of Christian, as well as autobiographical, triumphalism.

The concurrence of the orgasmic and the apocalyptic is both replicated and made ridiculous in the case of Stingo, who proposes to make Sophie's life and death mean for the Holocaust what Nat Turner's life and death meant for American slavery. Stingo's resolve following Sophie's suicide to write about her someday, and thus to "*demonstrate how absolute evil is never extinguished from the world*," devolves into his capacious, theatrical tears for all the "beaten and butchered and betrayed and martyred children of the earth," followed by a vapid decree: "*Let your love flow out on all living things*." His own effort to find redemptive meaning and psychological healing in the awful spectacle of genocide's multitude unfolds in language comparable to that which he employs to capture the final act in the tragedy of Nathan and Sophie, who, in accompaniment of "their final anguish—or ecstasy, or whatever engulfing revelation may have united them just before the darkness," have been listening, like Walter Dürrfeld and Sophie earlier, to a Bach cantata, *Jesu, Joy of Man's Desiring*. When he awakes after a night of drunken soul searching, it is as though Stingo has undergone a comparable ordeal—indeed, as though he has come back from death. "Blessing my resurrection," he wakes "*at dawn to see / in glory, the bright, the morning star*," a borrowing from Revelation whose words and cathartic intent are a virtual replica of the ending of *The Confessions of Nat Turner*. This was not Judgment Day, he adds in this rendering, but only "morning: excellent and fair."[82]

Given Stingo's preoccupation with his erotic life, it is impossible to ignore the pun here on *Marjorie Morningstar*, just as the play on words in "blessing my resurrection" features his phallic preoccupations. On an even grander scale, Stingo-Styron, in a sublimated exhibition of authorial orgasm, now embraces "all living things," as though the cascade of his desire, released by Sophie's death, might be turned instead toward beatitude and his act of witness might redeem all the lives lost in the Nazi genocide, gentile and Jew alike. As in *The Confessions of Nat Turner*, so in *Sophie's Choice* the title character's destruction becomes the occasion for speaking in the language of ecstasy, as though the world-shattering acts for which each stands could be made to carry redemptive meaning. We need not look to Nat Turner for corroboration of Styron's triumphalism, however, for in Stingo's initial sexual encounter with Sophie his premature ejaculation is announced, we are told, by his "bleat of dismay like that of a ram being slaughtered." In subsuming both the binding of Isaac and the crucifixion of Christ into Stingo's libidinous solipsism, Styron completes, typologically, a final set of analogical substitutions.[83]

It is possible to discover sacrificial significance in the Holocaust, but arguments to that effect have focused not on Jews (or other victims)—not on the "holocaust," that is, a burnt offering, as in the case of the ram substituted for Isaac—but on the mentality of Nazism. Disguising murder within a racially mystified language of cleansing, it could be argued, the Third Reich mobilized collective fears of pollution and defilement such that genocide assumed the character of purification though sacrifice.[84] Or, consider the early assessment of David Rousset, one of Styron's sources, who ventured that the death camps were "high, sombre citadels of expiation" in which torture was more important than death since the Nazis wished, in exterminating them, to show that Jews were "creatures accursed, incarnations of Evil, not men." The "high priest of this punishment," the SS officer, thus found "a secret pleasure, an inner thrill of ecstasy, in wrecking their bodies."[85] In the case of *Sophie's Choice*, such a characterization could apply variously to the actual Nazi Rudolf Höss, to the insane Nazi-Jew, Nathan Landau, and by extension to their voyeuristic double, Stingo. But the fact remains that sacrifice and redemption are troubling terms to introduce into any dramatization of the Final Solution. Stingo's cathartic "resurrection" to the contrary, the one lesson to be drawn from the events he has narrated, to cite Cynthia Ozick's essay on Primo Levi, is that there is no redemption in Auschwitz: "if there is redemption in it, it cannot be Auschwitz; and if it is Auschwitz, it is nothing if not unholy."[86]

Imagine a Holocaust novel without Jews—or more precisely, in which the only Jew becomes a Nazi. As in post-Holocaust Poland, in which Auschwitz was "the Golgotha of the contemporary world," in the words of Pope John Paul II, Jews are everywhere present in *Sophie's Choice* and yet strangely vanquished, the centrality and singularity of their tragedy subservient to Styron's argument that their "totally proprietary notion of the Holocaust" distorts the fact that "the Nazis actually got everyone."[87] Of course, the Nazis did not get everyone, nor did they aim to get everyone. They only failed to get the world's Jews because they were stopped from doing so—stopped far too late but still stopped.

Like the Styron of *Darkness Visible*, who climbs up from the pit of depression as though he were Dante ascending from hell, Stingo has come back from the tragedy of Sophie and Nathan to bear witness. But to what? Just as the union of miscegenation and messianism provided Nat Turner's story a meaning Styron thought lacking in the historical record, so his placing Sophie's story within an eroticized framework of Christian redemption enforced a transcendent closure consistent with his view that it is "surprisingly difficult" for Jews to see beyond "the consecrated nature of the Nazis' genocidal fury." Reading the Holocaust through the lens provided by the Polish Catholic version of Auschwitz and consecrating his narrator's act of witness as his own, Styron made another bold incursion into alien territory. In doing so, however, he subordinated its essence, the destruction of the European Jews, to his own authorial passion play.

NOTES

1. William Styron, "A Wheel of Evil Come Full Circle: The Making of *Sophie's Choice*," *Sewanee Review* 105 (Summer 1997): 395–97.

2. William Styron, *Sophie's Choice* (1979; reprint, New York: Vintage, 1992), 491. On the black response to Styron's version of Nat Turner, see John Henrik Clarke, ed., *William Styron's Nat Turner: Ten Black Writers Respond* (Boston: Beacon Press, 1968); and Albert E. Stone, *The Return of Nat Turner: History, Literature, and Cultural Politics in Sixties America* (Athens: University of Georgia Press, 1992), 101–76.

3. See, for example, Lawrence J. Leblanc, *The United States and the Genocide Convention* (Durham, N.C.: Duke University Press, 1991); and Samantha Power, *"A Problem from Hell": America and the Age of Genocide* (New York: Basic Books, 2002), 31–60.

4. Styron, *Sophie's Choice*, 233–34, 491, 4. Styron took the phrase *l'univers concentrationnaire* ("the concentrationary universe") from the title of David Rousset's early work on the Holocaust, published in French in 1946 and in English a year later under the title *The Other Kingdom* (and thus contemporary with Sophie's life in Brooklyn), and he perhaps recalled as well that Norman Mailer appropriated it ten years later to describe the apocalyptic existential milieu of the hipster in "The White Negro" (1957). David Rousset, *L'Univers Concentrationnaire* (1946); *The Other Kingdom*, trans. Ramon Guthrie (New York: Reynal and Hitchcock, 1947); Norman Mailer, "The White Negro: Superficial Reflections on the Hipster," *Advertisements for Myself* (1959; reprint, New York: Signet, 1960), 303–4.

5. See Eric J. Sundquist, *To Wake the Nations: Race in the Making of American Literature* (Cambridge: Harvard University Press, 1992), 36–83.

6. W. J. Cash, *The Mind of the South* (1941; reprint, New York: Vintage, 1960), 117–19.

7. Styron found Rosenfeld's charge that he made Nathan a demonic Jew "absurd" and that he attributed Sophie's sexual allure to her death camp emaciation "stupid." He appeared to forget that Stingo recognizes in Sophie's "beautiful body" the "sickish plasticity" of someone who has suffered "severe emaciation and whose flesh is even now in the last stages of being restored" but who nevertheless exudes a "wonderfully negligent sexuality," thus setting the stage for an elision between voyeurism and witnessing that becomes more and more evident over the course of the novel. If Nathan and Stingo desire Sophie, he said, "it's really not because she has come back from hell but simply because she is a superb woman." Besides, he added on another occasion, the original Sophie looked like film star Ursula Andress. As Sharon Oster points out, however, traces of the Holocaust emerge through Sophie's skin in a kind of palimpsest, making her an object of erotic abuse and thus setting the stage for an elision between voyeurism and witnessing that becomes more and more disturbing over the course of the novel. Alvin H. Rosenfeld, "The Holocaust According to William Styron," *Midstream* 25 (December 1979): 43–49; Styron, interview with Michel Braudeau (1981),

in *Conversations with William Styron*, ed. James L. West III (Jackson: University Press of Mississippi, 1975), 251; Styron, *Sophie's Choice*, 55; Styron interview with Stephen Lewis (1983), in West, *Conversations with William Styron*, 259; Sharon Oster, "The 'Erotics of Auschwitz': Coming of Age in *The Painted Bird* and *Sophie's Choice*," in *Witnessing the Disaster: Essays on Representation and the Holocaust*, ed. Michael Bernard-Donals and Richard Glejzer (Madison: University of Wisconsin Press, 2003), 103.

8. The Jewish American princesses depicted (as Styron is careful to mention) by Herman Wouk in *Marjorie Morningstar* (1955) and Philip Roth in *Goodbye, Columbus* (1959) were decorous by comparison to his "Little Miss Cock Tease" Leslie Lapidus, who has been freed through psychoanalysis to express herself in a barrage of crude slang ("pussy," "blowjob," "jerking off") and the Lawrencian vulgarities of high culture ("to fuck is to go to the dark gods") but whose sexual life is limited to a torrent of words. Styron uses her to lampoon the Turner controversy, as well as his own authorial fantasies, when Stingo jokingly tells Nathan that Leslie "had been able to reach a climax only with large, muscular, coal-black Negroes with colossal penises," and Stingo's stymied amorous adventures, a portion of which are set down in the form of diary entries, are an amalgam of stylized tributes to the "'melon-heavy' Jewish breasts so dear to Thomas Wolfe," the surreal comic pornography of Terry Southern's *Candy* (1964), which Styron reviewed favorably, and the new benchmark of sexual liberation set by Roth's obsessive confessional in *Portnoy's Complaint* (1969), whose hero, like Stingo, is dedicated to the art of masturbation. No doubt Leslie Fiedler was correct to read the Leslie Lapidus episode, initially published as a short story in *Esquire*, as part of Styron's burlesque of the struggle over who would become the laureate of late-twentieth-century America, the southern WASP or the northern Jew. Styron, *Sophie's Choice*, 130–32, 187, 198; Leslie Fiedler, "Styron's Choice" (1979), in *Fiedler on the Roof: Essays on Literature and Jewish Identity* (Boston: David R. Godine, 1991), 105–7.

9. Styron, *Sophie's Choice*, 268–69.

10. Ibid., 269.

11. In what follows, especially in the case of Styron's account of his episode of severe depression in *Darkness Visible*, my intention is not to offer a clinical account of "splitting" (or "schizophrenia") but rather to consider how Styron deployed these concepts. Splitting and schizophrenia, as they are understood psychoanalytically, are different phenomena, although Melanie Klein points out that splitting, one of the earliest ego defense mechanisms against anxiety, is also "found in the later symptomatic picture of schizophrenia." More relevant here is Freud's observation that patients in a psychotic (or hallucinatory) state sometimes express the conviction that "in some corner of their minds . . . there was a normal person, who watched the hubbub of the illness go past, like a disinterested spectator." Insofar as splitting plays a role in the ego's defense against disruptive anxiety, differing from both denial and repression, it expresses conflicts marked by intense ambivalence in which contradictory attitudes or actions are ascribed to different selves, as though a normal person and a pathological person existed side by side. Melanie Klein, "Notes on Some Schizoid Mechanisms," *International Journal of Psychoanalysis* 27 (1940): 99–101; Sigmund Freud, "An Outline of Psychoanalysis," *International Journal of Psychoanalysis* 21 (January 1940): 78; Joseph D. Lichtenberg and Joseph William Slap, "Notes on the Concept of Splitting and the Defense Mechanism of the Splitting of Representations," *Journal of the Ameri-*

can *Psychoanalytic Association* 21 (1973): 773, 780–81. I am indebted to Janet Hadda for advice on this point.

12. The "gray zone" defines a convergence between perpetrators and victims where either through psychological identification of the prisoner with his captor—envying his power, wishing to share his attributes, ultimately admiring him—or through his active collaboration with the captor, intense moral ambiguity is created. Those prisoners who became *Kapos* (the chiefs of labor squads)—at first common criminals culled from the ranks of prisoners, but later Jews who saw a meager opportunity to save themselves—had great latitude to resemble the SS, even exercising sadistic power comparable to that of the Nazis in some instances. A more terrible instance of the gray zone appears in the *Sonderkommandos*, those prisoners, mainly Jews, detailed to dispose of the bodies of those gassed, cutting their hair and extracting their gold teeth before burning the bodies in crematoria. Isolated from other prisoners and deliberately consigned to destruction in their turn so that they would not survive to tell about the killing operation, the *Sonderkommandos* were afforded certain privileges and, indeed, in some ways entered onto the same footing with the SS, thus becoming the "bearers of a horrendous secret." Primo Levi, *The Drowned and the Saved*, trans. Raymond Rosenthal (1988; reprint, New York: Vintage, 1989), 36–69.

13. On the phenomenon of *Holocaust*, see, for example, Judith E. Doneson, *The Holocaust in American Film* (Philadelphia: Jewish Publication Society, 1987), 145, 188–89; Peter Novick, *The Holocaust in American Life* (Boston: Houghton Mifflin, 1999), 209–14; and Jeffrey Shandler, *While America Watches: Televising the Holocaust* (New York: Oxford University Press, 1999), 155–78.

14. Styron, "Hell Reconsidered," review of Richard L. Rubenstein, *The Cunning of History*, in *New York Review of Books* (1978), reprinted in *This Quiet Dust and Other Writings*, rev. ed. (New York: Vintage, 1993), 115.

15. *Holocaust* affirms the intentionalist thesis in part through the fictional character Erik Dorf. By virtue of his single-handed invention of the mutant language rules of Nazism and his presence as a witness and participant at virtually every stage in the escalation of the Final Solution—he advises Heydrich how un-uniformed SS can carry out *Kristallnacht* and gain popular sympathy; initiates the killing operations of the *Einsatzcommandos*; is present at the Wannsee Conference of 1942, where the decision was taken to enact the Final Solution; oversees the expansion of the concentration camp system into a death camp system; and discovers the virtues of Zyklon B as a means to quicken and systemize the murder of Jews—Dorf embodies in himself the Final Solution as an incremental but consciously "intentionalist" set of actions rather than the "functionalist" result of the exigencies of war, where the failure of various strategies, combined with the unpredictable complication of bureaucratic pressures, led to genocide on a scale not anticipated. As a number of commentators have argued, however, functionalism and intentionalism share many assumptions and may be understood as part of a continuum. See Berel Lang, *The Future of the Holocaust: Between History and Memory* (Ithaca, N.Y.: Cornell University Press, 1999), 71; Ian Kershaw, *Hitler, 1889–1936: Hubris* (New York: W. W. Norton, 1999), 529–91; and Christopher R. Browning, "Beyond 'Intentionalism' and 'Functionalism': The Decision for the Final Solution Reconsidered," in *The Path to Genocide* (New York: Cambridge University Press, 1992), 86–121. On the question of "uniqueness"—that is, the ideology and methodological

specificity governing the destruction of the Jews—see, for example, Stephen T. Katz, *Post-Holocaust Dialogues: Critical Studies in Modern Jewish Thought* (New York: New York University Press, 1983), 287–317; Gavriel D. Rosenfeld, "The Politics of Uniqueness: Reflections on the Recent Polemical Turn in Holocaust and Genocide Scholarship," *Holocaust and Genocide Studies* 13 (Spring 1999): 28–61; and Kenneth Seeskin, "What Philosophy Can and Cannot Say about Evil," in *A Holocaust Reader: Responses to the Nazi Extermination*, ed. Michael L. Morgan (New York: Oxford University Press, 2001), 321–33.

16. Styron, "Auschwitz" (1974), reprinted in *This Quiet Dust and Other Writings*, 338; Styron, interview with Braudeau, in West, *Conversations with William Styron*, 246; Styron, *Sophie's Choice*, 4, 125, 518.

17. By one estimate, the Nazis kidnapped some 200,000 Polish children deemed suitable for Germanization as soldiers or childbearers. Konnilyn Feig, "Non-Jewish Victims in the Concentration Camps," in *A Mosaic of Victims: Non-Jews Persecuted and Murdered by the Nazis*, ed. Michael Berenbaum (New York: New York University Press, 1999), 166.

18. Sophie's father is portrayed as a professor of jurisprudence at Cracow's Jagiellonian University, whose entire faculty, we are told, was deported to Sachsenhausen in November 1939. Styron's version of events notwithstanding, Rudolf Höss's memoir indicates that the professors were not executed but rather released after a few weeks owing to the intervention of German colleagues on their behalf. Styron, *Sophie's Choice*, 237–38, 261–64, 273; Styron, "A Wheel of Evil Come Full Circle," 398–99; Michael Burleigh, *The Third Reich: A New History* (New York: Hill and Wang, 2000), 441; Rudolf Höss, *Commandant of Auschwitz: The Autobiography of Rudolf Höss*, trans. Constantine Fitzgibbon (London: George Weidenfeld and Nicolson, 1959), 97; Rudolph Höss, *Death Dealer: The Memoirs of the SS Kommandant at Auschwitz*, ed. Steven Paskuly, trans. Andrew Pollinger (1992; reprint, New York: Da Capo, 1992), 110. See also Franz Link, "Auschwitz and the Literary Imagination: William Styron's *Sophie's Choice*," in *Jewish Life and Suffering as Mirrored in English and American Literature*, ed. Franz Link (Padenborn: Ferdinand Schöningh, 1987), 137n.

19. Styron, "Auschwitz," 337–38; Styron, *Sophie's Choice*, 92.

20. Faced with the demand of "modern secular liberalism" that their acceptance and assimilation is contingent upon giving up "the chauvinistic or even racist conception of themselves as a chosen people," writes Myers, emancipated Jews were made to surrender their status as unique victims. Styron's universalist interpretation of the Holocaust thus "divests the Jewish victims of their Jewishness and assigns their tragedy instead to the category of choiceless choice." Myers's compelling argument elides historical differences between Europe and America, as well as the era of emancipation and the era of genocide, and I find Sophie's Polish Catholicism, in particular its bearing on Styron's interpretation of Auschwitz, along with his reading the Holocaust through the lens of slavery, more to the point. D. G. Myers, "Jews without Memory: *Sophie's Choice* and the Ideology of Liberal Anti-Judaism," *American Literary History* 13 (Fall 2001): 520–22.

21. Charles S. Maier, The *Unmasterable Past: History, Holocaust, and German National Identity* (Cambridge: Harvard University Press, 1988), 66–99, 160–72 passim.

22. For convenience, I follow the practice of referring to non-Jewish Poles as "Poles," even though Polish Jews were Poles as well, whether or not they were so

regarded by others or by themselves. The commonplace nomenclature reflects, too, the propensity of Poles during the time in question, as well as later, to assert that there were no Jews in Poland, only people of "Jewish origin" or Poles of the "Mosaic faith."

23. By one count the total loss of Polish life itself during the war was 6,028,000–644,000 in war operations, 5,384,000 in executions, pacification killings, and deaths in labor or concentration camps—of which about half were Jews. Out of 280,000 Poles employed in what were deemed intellectual professions, 48,000 died during the course of the war, including 57 percent of judges and lawyers, and 29 percent of the clergy. Some 20,000–30,000 Poles were killed in 1939–40 in reprisals for resistance to the occupation and the so-called Extraordinary Pacification Campaign. Between 1939 and 1941, as many as 2 million Poles were deported to the annexed protectorate known as the General Government, to the Reich, or to Soviet labor camps. Norman Davies, *God's Playground: A History of Poland*, 2 vols. (New York: Columbia University Press, 1982), 2:447–50, 463; Burleigh, *The Third Reich*, 441–44; Richard C. Lukas, *The Forgotten Holocaust: The Poles under German Occupation, 1939–1944* (Lexington: University of Kentucky Press, 1986), 1–39, 127; Jan T. Gross, *Polish Society under German Occupation: The Generalgouvernement, 1939–1944* (Princeton: Princeton University Press, 1979), 72–78.

24. Thane Rosenbaum, *Second-Hand Smoke* (New York: St. Martin's Press, 1999), 180.

25. "Any slave families, of good Polish agricultural worker- and miner-origin we will radically destroy," said Himmler at the state funeral for Reinhard Heydrich on June 9, 1942. "If they want to breed, they should do it outside [the Reich]. Certainly we need new slaves, but not with us in Germany." In speaking of the Jews, Himmler employed a favorite euphemism while leaving no doubt about their very different fate: "The migration of the Jews will be dealt with for certain in a year: then none will wander again. Because now the slate must be made quite clean." Himmler quoted in Peter Padfield, *Himmler: Reichsführer-SS* (London: Macmillan, 1990), 383–86. Here and following I draw, in my comparison of Poles and Jews, on Erich Goldhagen, "Nazi Sexual Demonology," *Midstream* 27 (May 1981): 7–15; Lucy S. Dawidowicz, "Poles, Jews, and History" (1987), reprinted in Dawidowicz, *What Is the Use of Jewish History?* ed. Neal Kozodoy (New York: Schocken Books, 1992), 134–44; Götz Aly, *"Final Solution": Nazi Population Policy and the Murder of the European Jews*, trans. Belinda Cooper and Allison Brown (1995; reprint, New York: Oxford University Press, 1999), 245–49; Michael C. Steinlauf, "Poland," in *The World Reacts to the Holocaust*, ed. David S. Wyman (Baltimore: Johns Hopkins University Press, 1996), 81–155; and Richard C. Lukas, "The Polish Experience during the Holocaust," and Israel Gutman, "The Victimization of Poles," both in Berenbaum, *A Mosaic of Victims*, 88–95, 97–100. See also Joshua Zimmerman, ed., *Contested Memories: Poles and Jews during the Holocaust and Its Aftermath* (New Brunswick, N.J.: Rutgers University Press, 2003).

26. Although Höss's memory of the date has been questioned, it seems he was correct to remember the summer of 1941 rather than the summer of 1942. Höss, *Commandant of Auschwitz*, 183. Cf. Steven Paskuly's annotation in Höss, *Death Dealer*, 27 n. 2; Padfield, *Himmler*, 333–34; and Richard Breitman, *The Architect of Genocide: Himmler and the Final Solution* (New York: Alfred A. Knopf, 1991), 188–94.

27. Cynthia Ozick, "A Liberal's Auschwitz," in *The Pushcart Prize: Best of the Small Presses*, ed. Bill Henderson (New York: Pushcart Prize, 1976), 149–53. See also

Cynthia Ozick, "The Rights of History and the Rights of Imagination," *Commentary* 113 (March 1999): 25–27.

28. The Jews were accused of being Soviet collaborators, but even though the Nazis saw the value of promoting anti-Semitism, these murders, in contrast to the bureaucracy and technology of the Holocaust, seem to have been spawned by archaic hatred and mythologies such as the blood libel. The victims were dragged from their homes, tortured, and burned alive in a barn. See Jan T. Gross, *Neighbors: The Destruction of the Jewish Community in Jedwabne, Poland* (Princeton: Princeton University Press, 2001); and, for rejoinders to Gross, Antony Polonsky and Joanna B. Michlic, eds., *The Neighbors Respond: The Controversy over the Jedwabne Massacre in Poland* (Princeton: Princeton University Press, 2003).

29. International calls for the protection of Jews in Poland were answered by dozens of pogroms in the aftermath of World War I—some 8,000 Jews died in the winter of 1918–1919 alone—and Poland in the 1930s witnessed a surge of cultural and historical anti-Semitism comparable to that in Germany. Attacks on Jews were justified by a litany of populist accusations—the Jews murdered Christian children; they had collaborated with German occupiers and profited from the war; they were an advance guard for Communism, the newest threat to Poland—that were reiterated by Polish officials and by the Catholic Church throughout Nazification, when the Polish resistance was itself tainted by anti-Semitism. In Henryk Rolicki's *Zmierzch Izraela* (The Twilight of Israel), a 1933 work that achieved a significant popular audience, for example, Jews were held to be perfidious and treacherous, responsible for the fall of all great world powers over the course of history, even as they were also depicted, paradoxically, as weak and destined for subjugation (hence the book's title). Aleskander Hertz, *The Jew in Polish Culture*, trans. Richard Lourie (1961; reprint, Evanston, Ill.: Northwestern University Press, 1988), 188–90; David I. Kertzer, *The Popes against the Jews: The Vatican's Role in the Rise of Modern Anti-Semitism* (New York: Alfred A. Knopf, 2001), 244–78; Shmuel Krakowski, "The Polish Underground and the Extermination of the Jews," *POLIN: Studies in Polish Jewry* 9 (1996): 138–47.

30. On the declining Jewish presence in postwar Poland, see Lucy S. Dawidowicz, *The Holocaust and the Historians* (Cambridge: Harvard University Press, 1981), 88–124; Iwona Irwin-Zarecka, *Neutralizing Memory: The Jew in Contemporary Poland* (New Brunswick, N.J.: Transaction, 1989), 48–65; Aleksander Smolar, "Jews as a Polish Problem," *Daedalus* 116 (Spring 1987): 31–73; Krystyna Kersten and Jerzy Szapiro, "The Contexts of the So-Called Jewish Question after World War II," *POLIN: Studies in Polish Jewry* 4 (1989), 255–68; Robert S. Wistrich, *Antisemitism: The Longest Hatred* (New York: Schocken, 1991), 157–70; Bernard Wasserstein, *Vanishing Diaspora: The Jews in Europe since 1945* (Cambridge: Harvard University Press, 1996), 211–21; Michael C. Steinlauf, *Bondage to the Dead: Poland and the Memory of the Holocaust* (Syracuse, N.Y.: Syracuse University Press, 1997), 43–144; and Paul Lendvai, *Anti-Semitism without Jews: Communist Eastern Europe* (Garden City, N.Y.: Doubleday and Co., 1971), 89–239.

31. Gross, *Neighbors*, 143; Iwona Irwin-Zarecka, "Poland, after the Holocaust," in *Remembering for the Future: Working Papers and Addenda*, 3 vols., ed. Yehuda Bauer et al. (Oxford: Pergamon Press, 1989), 1:144.

32. On the evolving memorials at Auschwitz, see James E. Young, *The Texture of Memory: Holocaust Memorials and Meaning* (New Haven: Yale University Press, 1993),

128–54, quotes at 130 and 141; and Young, "Jewish Memory in Poland," in *Holocaust Remembrance: The Shapes of Memory*, ed. Geoffrey H. Hartman (Cambridge, Mass.: Blackwell, 1994), 211–31.

33. At the time he was composing *Sophie's Choice*, Styron believed that something on the order of 2.5–3 million Jews and 1 million non-Jews were killed in the gas chambers. Styron apparently took his numbers from then official Polish accounts, numbers derived in turn from estimates made by the Soviet army when it liberated the camp in 1945 (he elsewhere put the number of non-Jews at 750,000). Those numbers must be revised downward in that more recent and reliable estimates suggest that somewhere between 1.1 and 1.5 million people, some 90 percent of them Jews, died at Auschwitz, most in the gas chambers or by injection, others through starvation or disease, though the ways of dying were often in effect indistinguishable. Styron, interview with Michael West (1977), in West, *Conversations with William Styron*, 232; Styron, "Hell Reconsidered," 112; William L. Shirer, *The Rise and Fall of the Third Reich: A History of Nazi Germany* (1960; reprint, New York: Touchstone, 1990), 973. According to one count based on the camp registry, of the 215,409 Poles deported to Auschwitz, most of them political prisoners and members of the resistance, 3,665 were gassed and 79,345 died or were otherwise murdered, for a total of 83,010. Yehuda Bauer, "Auschwitz: The Dangers of Distortion," in *Memory Offended: The Auschwitz Convent Controversy*, ed. Carol Rittner and John K. Roth (New York: Praeger, 1991), 251–52; Franciszek Piper, "Auschwitz Concentration Camp," in *The Holocaust and History: The Known, the Unknown, the Disputed, and the Reexamined*, ed. Michael Berenbaum and Abraham J. Peck (Bloomington: Indiana University Press, 1998), 375–78; Franciszek Piper, "The Number of Victims," in *Anatomy of the Auschwitz Death Camp*, ed. Yisrael Gutman and Michael Berenbaum (Bloomington: Indiana University Press, 1994), 68–72.

34. The Pope recognized Father Maximilian Kolbe, who sacrificed himself so that another man might live in Auschwitz, but who was an outspoken anti-Semite before the war, and the Carmelite Sister Teresa Benedicta de Cruce (née Edith Stein), a converted Jew who was killed by the Nazis as a Jew, but whom the Church identified as a Christian martyr who died "for the glorification of the holy name of God." Pope Pius XII had already obfuscated the circumstances surrounding the deportation of Stein and other Catholic Jews in order to justify his reticence in the face of Hitler's onslaught and conceal his ingrained anti-Judaism, and Pope John Paul II in addition accepted fabricated evidence of the miracle attributed to her that was necessary for her later canonization in 1998. In the case of Father Kolbe, who was arrested on political charges, not because of his religion, and whose death was an act of conscience unrelated to his Catholicism as such, Pope John Paul II asserted his own apostolic authority as sufficient to decide the matter of Kolbe's martyrdom. The pope's appearance and the beatification of Sister Teresa spurred the highly controversial establishment of a Carmelite nunnery (marked by a twenty-three-foot wooden cross that dominated the landscape) at the site of Auschwitz in 1984. Although it was later moved to a more remote site after fierce protests, defenders of the nunnery and the cross asserted that Auschwitz was a proper site for ecumenical penance since Christians, too, had perished in the Nazi genocide. Controversy over the Christian memorials and the Carmelite convent has since diminished, but at the time that Styron visited Auschwitz both Polish nationalist appropriation of the Holocaust and the Christian triumphalism au-

thorized by the Catholic Church, perspectives constitutive for *Sophie's Choice*, were in full force. See Young, *The Texture of Memory*, 145; S. I. Minerbi, "Pope John Paul II and the Shoah," in Bauer et al., *Remembering for the Future*, 3:2974–76; John Cornwell, *Hitler's Pope: The Secret History of Pius XII* (New York: Viking Penguin, 1999), 286–97; Michael Phayer, *The Catholic Church and the Holocaust, 1930–1965* (Bloomington: Indiana University Press, 2000), 54–66; Debórah Dwork and Robert Jan van Pelt, "Reclaiming Auschwitz," in Hartman, *Holocaust Remembrance*, 239–46; and the essays in Rittner and Roth, *Memory Offended*.

35. I borrow this phrase from Daniel Jonah Goldhagen: "The Church's attempt at least in part to Christianize the Holocaust, to incorporate the Holocaust into its Christology, takes several forms: the invention of false Christian martyrs, false Christian heroes, and false Christian victims, and the appropriation of Jewish suffering falsely as its own." "What Would Jesus Have Done," *New Republic* 226 (January 21, 2002): 43. Although Pope John Paul II will be best remembered for his decisive opposition to Communism, he also forged an important reconciliation with Jews, however modest its extent. His foremost statement will surely turn out to have been "We Remember," prepared by the Vatican's Commission for Religious Relations with the Jews, a document that asserted that the Church objected to Jews only on religious, not racial, grounds. "We Remember" groups the Holocaust with other instances of modern genocide; apologizes for the actions of individuals but not the Church ("we deeply regret the errors and failures of those sons and daughters of the Church"); makes Pius XII out to be a protector of Jews during the Holocaust, while the record tells a different story; and distinguishes between "anti-Judaism," with which, unfortunately, the Church and Christians generally had been tainted in the past, and "anti-Semitism," a separate modern phenomenon purportedly unrelated to the Church's teachings or positions: "The Shoah was the work of a thoroughly modern neo-pagan regime. Its anti-Semitism had its roots outside of Christianity and, in pursuing its aims, it did not hesitate to oppose the Church and persecute her members also." "We Remember" clearly surpassed the declaration of the Second Vatican Council in 1965 to the effect that Jews were not to be blamed for the death of Jesus; but it did so by summing up the Church's decades-long evasion of its complicity in anti-Semitism and exonerating the Church of responsibility in the destruction of the Jews. Although it appeared two decades later, "We Remember" was consonant with Styron's view in *Sophie's Choice* that the Holocaust was less anti-Semitic than anti-Christian and antilife. "We Remember: A Reflection on the Shoah" (March 16, 1998), reprinted in "The Catholic Church and the Holocaust," *First Things* 83 (May 1998): 39–43; Garry Wills, *Papal Sin: Structures of Deceit* (New York: Doubleday, 2000), 15–65; David I. Kertzer, *The Popes against the Jews: The Vatican's Role in the Rise of Modern Anti-Semitism* (New York: Alfred A. Knopf, 2001), 3–9.

36. Styron, *Sophie's Choice*, pp. 254–55; Styron, "Hell Reconsidered," review of *The Cunning of History* in *New York Review of Books* (1978), reprinted in *This Quiet Dust and Other Writings*, 109, 111.

37. His interpretation here is in keeping with that of Höss, according to whom Poles calculated upon their own survival because they expected Germany to lose the war, and the primary question was therefore whether they would die by disease, by a work accident or abuse by a guard, or by execution as members of the resistance or

war hostages on order of the Reich Security office. Höss, *Commandant of Auschwitz*, 117–18.

38. Martin Gilbert, *The Holocaust: A History of the Jews of Europe during the Second World War* (New York: Holt, Rinehart, and Winston, 1986), 550–51.

39. It is not clear on what evidence Styron bases this apparently fictive order. It is certainly true that by the spring of 1943 Jews had become the principal object of genocidal intention, and something like 4 million had already been killed by that point. Facing defeat in Stalingrad and frustrated by reports of Jewish resistance in the Warsaw Ghetto, Hitler apparently came to understand that his only true victory might lie in the destruction of European Jewry. But this required only acceleration, not innovation. The date at which the Final Solution to the Jewish Question assumed the character of mass murder may be traced not just to the Wannsee Conference on January 20, 1942, when plans were formulated to exterminate the 11 million Jews of Europe as quickly as possible, but to the summer of 1941, when the phrase "Final Solution"—initially employed by Hitler in 1939 when he warned against the precipitation of another world war by "international Jewish finance" and advocated the annihilation of the Jews—assumed frequent usage, first as a concept that stopped short of systematic murder but soon thereafter as one signifying a campaign of extermination. Gerald Reitlinger, who may have been one of Styron's sources, wrote of the gassing facility overseen by Höss: "When it was ready for use, either in March, 1942, or a little earlier, it was not even intended specifically for Jews but for getting rid of the sick in the camp, and it was not till many months later that an order arrived restricting its use to Jews and Gipsies"; and further on, that "the advent of the racial murder programme brought an alleviation of the lot of the Aryan internees. . . . The gas chamber was restricted to the Jews." Reitlinger does not recur to this subject, however, and he offers no specific dates for such orders. No other major study of Auschwitz or its command verifies Styron's claim, and according to the exhaustive, day-by-day documentary chronicle of orders and actions pertaining to the establishment and implementation of the killing apparatus at Auschwitz compiled by Danuta Czech, no such order was received or at least recorded in early April 1943 or at any other time. Gerald Reitlinger, *The Final Solution: The Attempt to Exterminate the Jews of Europe, 1939–1945* (1953; reprint, New York: A. S. Barnes, 1961), 104, 107; Danuta Czech, *Auschwitz Chronicle, 1939–1945* (New York: Henry Holt, 1990); Walter Laqueur, *The Terrible Secret: Suppression of the Truth about Hitler's "Final Solution"* (1980; reprint, New York: Penguin, 1983), 17–18; Debórah Dwork and Robert Jan Van Pelt, *Auschwitz* (New York: Norton, 1996), 327–37; Ian Kershaw, *Hitler, 1936–1945: Nemesis* (New York: W. W. Norton, 2000), 521, 583.

40. Styron was no doubt equally influenced by one of Rubenstein's formulations in his landmark 1966 book *After Auschwitz*, which popularized the idea of the "Death of God": "To see any purpose in the death camps" requires one "to regard the most demonic, antihuman explosion in all history as a meaningful expression of God's purposes," an idea Rubenstein regarded as "too obscene for me to accept." Styron, *Sophie's Choice*, 255; Richard L. Rubenstein, *After Auschwitz: Radical Theology and Contemporary Judaism* (Indianapolis, Ind.: Bobbs-Merrill, 1966), 152–53.

41. As early as his 1963 review of Frank Tannenbaum's *Slave and Citizen*, Styron showed an allegiance to Elkins's thesis on slavery and the Holocaust in arguing that

the brutality of slavery resulted in the "total dehumanization of a race," the reduction of "an entire people to the status of children." Likewise, in explaining why American slavery was for the most part free from significant rebellions, Styron borrowed from Elkins, as well as from Bruno Bettelheim, in speaking of the nearly complete "degradation of slavery and of the concentration camps," each of them so "despotic and emasculating as to render organized revolt next to impossible." Nearly thirty years later, he continued to reiterate, unmodified, the Elkins thesis that slavery was "a closed system so powerful and totalitarian that organized insurrection was almost entirely precluded," although by this point the inclusion of the descriptor "totalitarian" was equally a defense of his own analogy between slavery and the death camps in *Sophie's Choice*. Styron, review of Frank Tannenbaum, *Slave and Citizen* (1963), in *This Quiet Dust*, 37; Styron, "This Quiet Dust," in *This Quiet Dust*, 14; Styron, interview with Ben Forkner and Gilbert Schricke (1974), in West, *Conversations with William Styron*, 199; William Stryon, "Nat Turner Revisited," afterword to *The Confessions of Nat Turner* (1966; reprint, New York: Vintage, 1993), 449.

42. For Rubenstein, although he does not share the Christian triumphalism on which Styron's novel rests, the idea of the Holocaust is even more capacious. The subtitle of his book when it first appeared was *Mass Death and the American Future*, and it was his conviction that the Jews "were the first to perish in the ultimate city of Western civilization, Necropolis, the new city of the dead that the Germans built and maintained at Auschwitz." Styron, *Sophie's Choice*, 255; Richard L. Rubenstein, *The Cunning of History: The Holocaust and the American Future* (New York: Harper and Row, 1975), 45–46, 79, 94; Styron, "Hell Reconsidered," 110–11. Rubenstein returned Styron's compliment by using his review as an introduction to a new edition of *The Cunning of History* and writing an admiring essay on *Sophie's Choice*, in which he quotes Styron quoting him. See Richard L. Rubenstein, "The South Encounters the Holocaust: William Styron's *Sophie's Choice*," *Michigan Quarterly Review* 20 (Fall 1981): 425–42.

43. Based on considerations of topography, transportation, and raw materials, IG Farben had determined to build its synthetic rubber and fuel plant on the site near Auschwitz before the camp became a killing center, but its choice contributed to the camp's expansion and had the advantage to the SS of laying a basis for the use of slave labor in other locales and providing managerial skills the SS lacked. See Danuta Czech, "The Auschwitz Sub-Camps," in Smolen, *From the History of KL-Auschwitz*, 35–54; Ota Kraus and Erich Kulka, *The Death Factory: Document on Auschwitz*, trans. Stephen Jolly (1946; reprint, London: Pergamon Press, 1966), 18–24; Peter Hayes, "State Policy and Corporate Involvement in the Holocaust," in Berenbaum and Peck, *The Holocaust and History*, 209; Peter Hayes, *Industry and Ideology: IG Farben in the Nazi Era*, rev. ed. (New York: Cambridge University Press, 2001), xii–xvi, 347–68; Christopher R. Browning, "Jewish Workers in Poland: Self-Maintenance, Exploitation, Destruction," in *Nazi Policy, Jewish Workers, German Killers* (New York: Cambridge University Press, 2000), 58–88; and Donald Bloxham, "Jewish Slave Labour and Its Relationship to the 'Final Solution,'" in *Remembering for the Future: The Holocaust in an Age of Genocide*, ed. John K. Roth and Elizabeth Maxwell, 3 vols. (New York: Palgrave, 2001), 1:163–86.

44. Styron, *Sophie's Choice*, 531.

45. Primo Levi, who by virtue of his professional training worked as a chemist at Buna, drew a distinction between the Jews' camp and those of the others prisoners: the Jews at Buna were "the slaves of the slaves, whom all could give orders to," and the *Judenlager* was also the *Vernichtungslager*, the "camp of destruction." (As recorded in his memoir *Night*, the young Elie Wiesel was also a worker at Monowitz-Buna.) Primo Levi, *Survival in Auschwitz: The Nazi Assault on Humanity*, trans. Stuart Woolf (1958; reprint, New York: Collier Books, 1961), 65–66; Benjamin B. Ferencz, *Less than Slaves: Jewish Forced Labor and the Quest for Compensation* (Cambridge: Harvard University Press, 1979), xvii, 13.

46. For this reason among others, IG Farben's claim that the firm, including director Walter Dürrfeld, knew nothing of the gas chambers and crematoria is not credible. The Nuremberg court found that Farben had participated in a "crime against humanity," but of the twenty-three directors indicted, only nine were found guilty of corporate plunder and five criminally liable for the abuse of slave labor; by 1951 all had served the mild prison terms to which they were sentenced. Dürrfeld received an eight-year sentence from the U.S. military tribunal but later became a director of a successful chemical concern. Farben settled a lawsuit brought by claimants in 1957, ultimately paying out some 27 million Reichsmark to survivors of the work camp. Ctibor Wohl quoted in Kraus and Kulka, *The Death Factory*, 23; Rubenstein, *The Cunning of History*, 63; Ferencz, *Less than Slaves*, 34–35, 66; Hayes, *Industry and Ideology*, 365–67; Peter Hayes, *From Cooperation to Complicity: Degussa in the Third Reich* (New York: Cambridge University Press, 2004), 272–300.

47. Styron, "Hell Reconsidered," 110; Styron, *Sophie's Choice*, 442–43.

48. Höss's memoir was published in a Polish translation in 1951 and in his original German in 1958. The English translation used by Styron was that of Constantine Fitzgibbon, *Commandant of Auschwitz*, cited above, which was also included in *KL Auschwitz Seen by the SS* (1972; reprint, New York: Howard Fertig, 1984). On Styron's use of Höss's memoir, as well as Olga Lengyel's *Five Chimneys*, see also Sue Vice, *Holocaust Fiction* (London: Routledge, 2000), 122–36.

49. In his youth Höss had been among the earliest converts to Hitler's vision, having joined the cause of Nationalist Socialism in 1922. Indeed, he was so committed that he participated in killing the leader of a rival political faction, for which he served six years in prison. After a short career in farming, he was recruited to the SS in 1934 by his old friend Heinrich Himmler and thereafter held a series of high-level positions, principally in managing concentration camps. As commandant at Auschwitz, Höss has even been credited with the accidental discovery, by men in his command, that Zyklon B, a chemical used in the camp laundry to kill lice, could be converted into an instrument of mass murder. Once the gas was tested on Soviet prisoners and determined to offer a significant improvement over the inefficient operation being used at Treblinka, Höss oversaw the construction of gas chambers able to accommodate up to 2,000 people at a time; worked out the logistics of the arrival of the transport and selection, so that prisoners, thinking they were being sent to disinfecting "showers," did not know what was happening to them; and thus presided over the murder of more than a million people, most by gassing and almost all of them Jews (Höss spoke erroneously of the number 3 million). Höss also took credit for a particularly cruel form of punishment in which the prisoner was suspended by his hands, which were crossed behind him and

tied with a rope attached to a beam. This alternative to incarceration was meant to prevent the prisoner's extended absence from work, which lends credence to the specu- lation that Höss may have devised the famous Auschwitz sign Arbeit Macht Frei, "work is liberating." Joseph E. Persico, *Nuremberg: Infamy on Trial* (New York: Viking Penguin, 1994), 316–20; Leni Yahil, *The Holocaust: The Fate of European Jewry, 1932– 1945* (1987), trans. Ina Friedman and Haya Galai (New York: Oxford University Press, 1990), 373; Otto Friedrich, *The Kingdom of Auschwitz* (New York: Harper, 1994), 2; Florent Brayard, "Humanitarian Concerns versus Zyklon B," trans. Helena Scott, in Roth and Maxwell, *Remembering for the Future: The Holocaust in an Age of Genocide*, 2:54–65.

50. Höss, *Commandant of Auschwitz*, 145, 178–79, 181.

51. Tzvetan Todorov, *Facing the Extreme: Moral Life in the Concentration Camps*, trans. Arthur Denner and Abigail Pollack (1991; reprint, New York: Henry Holt, 1996), 170–73; Primo Levi, "Foreward," in Höss, *Death Dealer*, 3.

52. Styron, *Sophie's Choice*, 159–61.

53. Höss, *Commandant of Auschwitz*, 178, 147–48.

54. Styron construes Höss's tone as "rueful, elegiac," and no doubt it is, but his fabricated sentimentalism concealed brutal truths about his life and that of his family. Höss's detailed descriptions of the workings of the gas chambers and crematoria, not least their difficulty in handling the numbers of people sent to death, fly in the face of his portrait of his villa as an idyllic plantation, and his indulgence in elements of pastoral—his description of the idyllic activities afforded by his private stables, ken- nels, and gardens, his declaration that the "prisoners never missed an opportunity for doing some little act of kindness to my wife or children," while his wife's "greatest pleasure would have been to give a present to every prisoner who was in any way connected to our household"—betrays a contentment shattered only by defeat, not by guilt. According to other accounts, his family was self-indulgent, extorting food and furnishings from the SS hierarchy, nor was it shielded from the purpose of the Final Solution. Charlotte Delbo, an Auschwitz prisoner, recalled seeing Höss's two sons play- ing "commandant and prisoner" in the environs of the rose garden, the elder pre- tending to brutalize the younger until he was close to lifeless, whereupon he ordered, "*Zum krematorium*" ("to the crematorium"). Not quite the paragon of fidelity to Aryan racial purity that he presents himself to be—as does Styron, who invents for him a youthful affair with an Aryan beauty, an actress with whom he once had an out-of- wedlock child—Höss in fact had an affair with an Italian prisoner at Auschwitz and, when she became pregnant, ordered her gassed. In 1943, moreover, Auschwitz became embroiled in a major scandal over corruption and the renegade killing of prisoners among the officer corps, an incident not mentioned in Höss's memoir or by Styron. As a result Höss was reassigned to a position as deputy to the inspector for all concen- tration camps, which was hardly a demotion but rather, as he rightly portrayed it with- out referring to the reason for the transfer, a promotion that allowed him to play a role in coordinating the functions of the whole camp system (Höss returned to Auschwitz as commandant later in 1944). Styron, *Sophie's Choice*, 161, 164–67; Höss, *Comman- dant of Auschwitz*, 132, 156; Charlotte Delbo, *None of Us Will Return* (1965), in *Ausch- witz and After*, trans. Rosette C. Lamont (New Haven, Conn.: Yale University Press, 1995), 100; Otto Friedrich, *The Kingdom of Auschwitz* (New York: Harper, 1994), 49–

51; and Aleksander Lasik, "Rudolf Höss: Manager of Crime," in Gutman and Berenbaum, *Anatomy of the Auschwitz Death Camp*, 294–95.

55. Robert Jay Lifton, *The Nazi Doctors: Medical Killing and the Psychology of Genocide* (New York: Basic Books, 1986), 419–25; Bruno Bettelheim, "Individual and Mass Behavior in Extreme Situations," in *Surviving and Other Essays* (New York: Random House, 1979), 65; Bettelheim, *The Informed Heart: Autonomy in a Mass Age* (Glencoe, Ill.: Free Press, 1960), 127. On Lifton's psychology of doubling, see also Laurence Mordekhai Thomas, *Vessels of Evil: American Slavery and the Holocaust* (Philadelphia: Temple University Press, 1993), 92–113.

56. Styron, *Sophie's Choice*, 165–66; Höss, *Commandant of Auschwitz*, 153–54.

57. Hannah Arendt, *Eichmann in Jerusalem: A Report on the Banality of Evil*, rev. ed. (1965; reprint, New York: Penguin, 1977), 85, 105–9. See also Nachman Blumenthal, "On Nazi Vocabulary," *Yad Vashem Studies* 1 (1957): 49–66; and Berel Lang, *Act and Idea in the Nazi Genocide* (Chicago: University of Chicago Press, 1990), 81–102. For Styron's further observation that Höss's "pain" belongs to the rhetorical register identified by Arendt, see Styron, interview with Braudeau, in West, *Conversations with William Styron*, 250.

58. Himmler's speech, Dominick LaCapra has argued, is a kind of prooftext of Nazi ideology for its invocation of a negative sublime, a distorted sacrificial process whereby it might be possible not just to preserve psychic coherence but, indeed, to attain moral beauty through turning transgression into a radical quest for purification. Himmler quoted in Padfield, *Himmler*, 469–70; Gilbert, *The Holocaust*, 615–16; Dominick LaCapra, *Writing History, Writing Trauma* (Baltimore: Johns Hopkins University Press, 2001), 94, 136–38.

59. To be "the executioner of your own children" is "perhaps the ultimate form of evil," Styron said of the incident, for which he apparently drew on both a story told by Hannah Arendt of a woman forced to choose which of her children would be gassed and Olga Lengyel's *Five Chimneys* (1947), in which she recounts inadvertently allowing her children to be led off with their grandmother to the gas chamber. Hannah Arendt, *The Origins of Totalitarianism*, 2d ed. (1968; reprint, New York: Harcourt Brace and Co., 1979), 452 (Arendt in turn seems to have taken the anecdote from Camus); Styron, interview with Braudeau, in West, *Conversations with William Styron*, 246–49; interview with Lewis, in West, *Conversations with William Styron*, 258; Styron, "A Wheel of Evil Come Full Circle," 396.

60. Styron, *Sophie's Choice*, 528, 531. Charlotte Wardi notes that Styron's attribution of von Niemand's moral depravity to a religiously inspired personality disorder represents a "stupefying interpretation of odious acts . . . a course falsification of history." The same question, though, is writ large in the conclusion of the novel. Charlotte Wardi, "A Device for the Falsification of History: The Staging of the Dialogue between Executioner and Victim," in *Comprehending the Holocaust: Historical and Literary Research*, ed. Asher Cohen et al., (Frankfurt am Main: Verlag Peter Lang, 1988), 331.

61. William Styron, "Why Primo Levi Need Not Have Died" (1988), in *This Quiet Dust*, 169–72. Although some commentators believe that his death from falling down a stairwell was an accident rather than suicide, recent biographers of Levi have concluded that deep depression, brought on primarily by the burden of caring for his paralytic mother, led to his suicide. See Carole Angier, *The Double Bond: Primo Levi* (New

York: Farrar, Straus & Giroux, 2002); and Ian Thompson, *Primo Levi* (London: Hutchinson, 2002).

62. Styron, *Darkness Visible: A Memoir of Madness* (New York: Random House, 1990), 47–48, 53.

63. Elkins, *Slavery*, 109; Bettleheim, "Schizophrenia as a Reaction to Extreme Situations" (1956), in *Surviving and Other Essays*, 112–24; Styron, *Darkness Visible*, 64.

64. Emil L. Fackenheim, *The Jewish Return into History* (New York: Schocken, 1978), 269.

65. James E. Young, *At Memory's Edge: After-Images of the Holocaust in Comtemporary Art and Architecture* (New Haven: Yale University Press, 2000), 55; Joan Smith, "Holocaust Girls," in *Misogynies: Reflections on Myths and Malice* (1989; reprint, New York: Fawcett Columbine, 1992), 127, 133.

66. Styron, *Sophie's Choice*, 302.

67. Ibid., 242–45, 497, 269.

68. Ibid., 423, 438–39.

69. I am drawing here on Lucy S. Dawidowicz, "Smut and Anti-Semitism," in *The Jewish Presence: Essays on Identity and History* (New York: Holt, Rinehart and Winston, 1977), 223–24; Susan Sontag, "Fascinating Fascism" (1975), in *Under the Sign of Saturn* (1980; reprint, New York: Vintage, 1981), 103–5; Susan Sontag, "The Pornographic Imagination," in *Styles of Radical Will* (New York: Anchor, 1969), 66, 71; and Susan Griffin, *Pornography and Silence: Culture's Revenge against Nature* (New York: Harper and Row, 1981), 183–84.

70. Andrea Dworkin, *Pornography: Men Possessing Women* (New York: G. P. Putnam's Sons, 1981), 68–69, 142–46.

71. Styron, interview with Braudeau, in West, *Conversations with William Styron*, 248.

72. It is notable, however, that Levi takes this occasion to reject the view of Liliana Cavani, director of *The Night Porter* (1973), that "we are all victims or murderers, and we accept these roles voluntarily," that "in every relationship, there is a victim-executioner dynamism more or less clearly expressed and generally lived on an unconscious level." The depiction in *The Night Porter* of a postwar sexual relationship between a former SS officer and one of his surviving prisoners, portrayed as sadomasochistic captivity in which the woman submits once again to the degradations of the camp, is false not because such a relationship of two damaged and damned people is inconceivable but because the sexual master-slave metaphor is in no way explanatory of the Holocaust. In making the Polish anti-Semite the victim and sexual slave, while displacing the Nazi master with a Jew, Styron combined aspects of Levi's deranged mimesis with Cavani's eroticization of fascism. In making the Holocaust safe for pornographic fantasy in the 1970s, whether in high culture forms such as *The Night Porter* or B movies such as *Ilsa: She-Wolf of the S.S.*, observes Laura Frost, liberalism demonstrated its inability to dissociate itself from fascism, an argument clearly applicable to *Sophie's Choice*. *The Night Porter*, it might be added, provides a more apt representation of this aspect of *Sophie's Choice* than does the film version of the novel, which, in replacing sadomasochism with manic romanticism, leaves the suicidal bondage of Sophie and Nathan largely inexplicable. Levi, *The Drowned and the Saved*, 48; Laura Frost, *Sex Drives: Fantasies of Fascism in Literary Modernism* (Ithaca: Cornell University Press, 2002), 151–60.

73. Styron, *Sophie's Choice*, 75; Styron, interview with Lewis, in West, *Conversations with William Styron*, 262–63.

74. Adolf Hitler, *Mein Kampf* (1925), trans. Ralph Mannheim (1943; reprint, Boston: Houghton Mifflin, 1971), 562. On the background of Hitler's views, see, for example, George L. Mosse, *Toward the Final Solution: A History of European Racism* (1978; reprint, Madison: University of Wisconsin Press, 1985), 113–27; and Klaus P. Fischer, *The History of an Obsession: German Judeophobia and the Holocaust* (New York: Continuum, 1998), 119–291.

75. Goldhagen, "Nazi Sexual Demonology," 12–15.

76. Nathan's knowledge of Irma Griese, "the blonde angel of death" of Auschwitz-Birkenau, known equally for her exceptional beauty and her inordinate cruelty, should be imagined to have been taken (as was Styron's) from Olga Lengyel's survivor memoir, *Five Chimneys*, published in 1947. Lengyel's book, which Styron had in mind when he began to write *Sophie's Choice* and which Nathan might plausibly have read, recounts both Griese's sexual slavery and sadism and her own brutal treatment at Griese's hands. A bisexual, Griese frequently had lesbian relationships with inmates and then sent the victims to their deaths. Styron, *Sophie's Choice*, 304, 367–71; Olga Lengyel, *Five Chimneys: A Woman Survivor's True Story of Auschwitz* (1947; reprint, Chicago: Academy Chicago Publishers, 1995), 103–8, 160–62, 197–203; Styron, interview with Lewis, in West, *Conversations with William Styron*, 257. Although the accounts are open to dispute, there has been conjecture that among Hitler's perversions was achieving sexual gratification from a woman urinating on him. Robert G. L. Waite, *The Psychopathic God: Adolf Hitler* (New York: Basic Books, 1977), 237–38.

77. Levi, *The Drowned and the Saved*, 42, 48.

78. Styron, *Sophie's Choice*, 369, 541–43, 391–92.

79. As Linda Williams has argued, the typical climactic scenario of film pornography insists that the "visual confession of a solitary male 'truth' coincides with the orgasmic bliss of the female," although its solipsistic withdrawal represents instead the inability to conceive a relation to the other in anything but the "phallic terms of self." Linda Williams, *Hard Core: Power, Pleasure, and the "Frenzy of the Visible,"* rev. ed. (Berkeley: University of California Press, 1999), 101, 113, 114.

80. William Styron, *The Confessions of Nat Turner* (1966; reprint, New York: Vintage, 1993), 421–28.

81. Vincent Harding, "You've Taken My Nat and Gone," in Clarke, *William Styron's Nat Turner*, 31.

82. Styron, *Sophie's Choice*, 554–55, 560–62.

83. Whether or not there is a corresponding undercurrent of anti-Semitism, Styron's Stingo, like his Nat Turner, contains echoes of Erik Erikson's *Young Man Luther*, a book that Styron cited for its study of the revolutionary impulse in a devout man whose sexual longings and involuntary seminal emissions, which increase when "a state of morbid watchfulness is heightened by spiritual terror," create a "divine sickness" in which libido and readiness for God's instruction are held in tense balance. Styron, *Sophie's Choice*, 391; Styron, "This Quiet Dust," 16n; Erik H. Erikson, *Young Man Luther: A Study in Psychoanalysis and History* (1958; reprint, New York: Norton, 1962), 158–61; Styron, *The Confessions of Nat Turner*, 178. Luther's infamous tract *The Jews*

and Their Lies (1543) characterized Jews as "vermin" who sought world domination, and he advocated burning their books, schools, and synagogues.

84. Lifton, *The Nazi Doctors*, 430–33, 451–58, 481–82.

85. Rousset, *The Other Kingdom*, 109–11.

86. Cynthia Ozick, "Primo Levi's Suicide Note," in *Metaphor and Memory* (1989; reprint, New York: Vintage, 1991), 45.

87. Styron, interview with Lewis, in West, *Conversations with William Styron*, 264.

CHAPTER 5

Planetary Circles: Philip Roth, Emerson, Kundera

Ross Posnock

EARLY ON CONVENTIONAL WISDOM cast Philip Roth in "the role of the rebellious Jewish son" and junior partner, born in Newark in 1933, of the firm Salinger, Bellow, Mailer, and Malamud.[1] While this grouping is more than the "journalistic cliché almost wholly devoid of content" as Roth described and dismissed it in 1981,[2] it has by now outlived its initial usefulness. For one thing, Roth's near half-century career of remarkable, indeed relentless, productivity—since 1959 twenty-two works of fiction and five of non-fiction—has left such early and parochial rubrics in the dustbin of literary history. And he has gone far from home (if only to return to Newark in *The Plot against America*, which seven-year-old Philip Roth narrates). For thirteen years Roth lived in London half the year; for five years in the seventies he was a regular visitor to Prague, where he "took a little crash course in political repression," became close with several writers, including Milan Kundera and Vaclav Havel, and was pivotal in publishing the English translations of some of the leading works of modern Eastern European literature (RMO, 140). Roth's own books have a large international audience (they have been translated into over thirty languages, and in fall 2004 two were best-sellers in France). All of these experiences, including his permanent return to the United States in 1989, which renewed his sense of the country and became a catalyst for his American trilogy (1997–2000), have significantly enlarged and deepened his art.

Roth's cosmopolitanism has created a body of work that is best understood in an international context—American, European, and Eastern European. This essay uses literary criticism to treat Roth in effect as a test case for seeing what happens when a familiar author's familiar moorings—national, ethnic, regional—are replaced by overlapping frames of reference that together form new configurations of intellectual history. What threads together my multiple contexts is the subject of immaturity. A fertile homegrown resistance to the renunciations required of adulthood began to appear in the American renaissance of the mid-nineteenth century as part of Romanticism's critique of Enlightenment scientism and rationalism, a critique that also informs modernist European and Eastern European novelists and thinkers. Emerson is the key figure (followed by Whitman and Melville) in revising the dominant models of rationality and maturity bequeathed by the Enlightenment. And Roth, I will argue, discerns that his antinomian predecessors' dismantling of rationalist, disciplinary models of knowledge, of success, and of selfhood is a countercultural endowment that he is free to use for his own purposes. Indeed, the title of his first novel, *Letting Go*, can be read as a neat summary of what the countermodel proposes as the goal of the dismantling—a relaxing of the constricted psyche.

It is not accidental that the Czech and Polish authors who are among those Roth most admires—Milan Kundera, Vaclav Havel, Witold Gombrowicz, and Bruno Schulz—are powerful theorists of immaturity. They fashion it, each in their own way, as a dissident stance against the coerced conformity of various modes of totalitarian oppression. Immaturity, then, is always already political for the Eastern Europeans I will discuss, as is true as well of the predecessor I most consistently invoke—Emerson. Initially this may be puzzling, for Emerson is conventionally regarded as the faintly embarrassing guardian of our most cherished American *isms*: optimism, exceptionalism, individualism, ahistoricism. But reading Emerson through Roth brings "Experience" and "Circles" center stage, brings forward the speaker of inadmissible, uncensored truth whom Nietzsche revered. Of Emerson, Nietzsche said: he contains "so many 'possibilities' that even virtue achieves esprit in his writings."[3] While the Emerson to be found here is a prophet of possibility, this is admittedly not the whole of Emerson—missing, for instance, are the metaphysician and transcendentalist. The Emerson who connects with Nietzsche and Roth thrives on the antagonistic energy released when one "abstain[s] from dogmatism and recognize[s] all the opposite negations, between which, as walls," one's "being is swung."[4] Two of the great enemies of ideology and of bourgeois pieties, Emerson and Nietzsche share with Roth a love of agonistic combat and of "speak[ing] the rude truth in all ways" (RWE, 262).

The "Nietzschean" Emerson I will be highlighting in my reading of Roth is an Emerson I have severed from his U.S. anchorage and set in "the world republic of letters" or "world literary space" that is "actual, albeit unseen," to borrow the phrases of Pascale Casanova.[5] This relocation or deracination is an act of appropriation, a word particularly congenial in this case, for in "Quotation and Originality" Emerson admiringly quotes the greatest cosmopolitan of the era and foremost proponent of world literature: "Goethe frankly said, 'what would remain to me if this art of appropriation were derogatory to genius. . . . My work is an aggregation of beings taken from the whole of Nature; it bears the name of Goethe.'"[6] We can understand acts of appropriation as allied to what Emerson calls the ceaseless "generation of circles" that forms the propulsive momentum and growth of nature, civilizations, and the individual, all testifying to the "truth" that "around every circle another can be drawn" (RWE, 403). To practice the "art of appropriation" is to treat Emerson not as a static touchstone for the ages, nor as only embedded in his historical moment, but as a fluid, metamorphic, living presence, one who can also serve as an emblem of my methodology: to regard regional or national points of origin (a Concord, a Newark, a United States) as simply the first circle around which a series of larger circles are drawn, spiraling out to encompass that republic of culture found on no map save the one drawn by literature.

"Depending on the force" of the individual, one's life is more or less "a self-evolving circle, which . . . rushes on all sides outwards to new and larger circles, and that without end" (RWE, 404). More than any American novelist in recent decades, Roth has answered Emerson's audacious imperative. Thus the responsible critic must be flexible enough to enter the circle and absorb its energy even as a new one is being formed. But until recently critics have tended to confine both writers to circles the latter drew early in their careers. Recall Roth the perennial bad boy, Roth the master of schtick-driven plots and satiric chronicler of Jewish American suburbia. Among Emerson's familiar circles consider: cultural nationalist cheerleading for "young America," dissenting minister leaving his Unitarian pulpit, inwardly migrating to preach the "infinitude of the private man." But, like Roth, Emerson had not stopped evolving and instead suited action to his word—that "there is no outside, no inclosing wall, no circumference to us" (405). The partisan of "young America" drew a new circle, eclipsing national boundary, and became, in his unquenchable curiosity about natural science, literature, and religion, a student of and participant in world culture; the man of the closed study became, in the 1850s, an influential figure on the antislavery platform.

Also pertinent here is Henry James, for Roth a crucial predecessor whom he appropriated as early as graduate school. Without using the word *appropriation* James makes vivid the spirit of its practice when he says in the 1870s, "to be an American is a great preparation for culture. . . . [W]e can deal freely with forms of civilization not our own, can pick and choose and . . . claim our property wherever we find it."[7] No wonder writers marginalized by class, ethnicity, or race were often drawn to the freewheeling picking and choosing of cultural property. Such freedom allows one to bypass the sacrificial ordeal of assimilation by rewriting it as appropriation. Thereby banished is the whole melodrama of assimilation, which requires the outsider to cast off old (ethnic) ways for new and submit to a culture assumed to possess a stable, homogenous identity; this sacrificial process affirms a hierarchy of insider/outsider, native/alien grounded in blood and origin.

In contrast, all that appropriation requires is a good library. In his fond recollections of the near magical power of transport he found in the city public library—where "property [was] held in common for the common good"—Roth joins Richard Wright and Ralph Ellison in recognizing that civic institution as nothing less than the essential power station for the individual's "generation of circles" that spiral out to form what Du Bois famously called "the kingdom of culture." Above the "veil," uncharted on any map, where neither the color line nor national boundary obtains, the kingdom is where "I sit with Shake-speare and he winces not," as Du Bois memorably put it in 1903.[8]

The practice of appropriation, the act of drawing a new circle, is insouciant regarding claims of ownership and identity and forms the basis of a cosmopoli-tan relation to culture. Its practice liberates culture goods from the proprietary grip of a single group; possessiveness—of the dismal and familiar "jazz is a black thing, Shakespeare a white" sort—is set aside for sampling, fixity for mobility. Cosmopolites refuse to know their place. The appropriation model combats a reductive tendency—promulgated by anthropology, embedded in separatist multiculturalism, and deeply influential upon literary study—of re-garding cultures as self-contained systems, discrete bounded groups—monads, in short. An antiproprietary view assails this notion of "culture" conceived as a fixed entity possessed of "the qualities of an internally homogenous and externally distinctive and bounded object." This view, in the words of the anthropologist Eric Wolf at the start of his famous book *Europe and the People without History*, propagates a "false model of reality," one that conceives "the world as a global pool hall in which the entities spin off each other like so many hard and round billiard balls."[9] Wolf's effort is to recover what the "global pool hall" obstructs—the fact that cultural groups are incessantly form-ing and reforming in mutually constitutive interchange with each other. This "energizing spirit" helps generate the evolving circles drawn by my authors and inspires my own drawing of spiraling circles between America and Eastern Europe, the nineteenth and twentieth centuries, affiliations that together form a new "world literary space."

Because it imputes literary agency to authors as readers and writers, the art of appropriation, the claiming of cultural property, and the drawing of circles can also help rethink the relation of author and historical context. Recall that the most prestigious understanding of context of the last quarter century, New Historicism, under the formative influence of Foucault's antihumanism and his notion of the death of the author, assimilates author to context, the former the creature of the latter. Under the weight of context, the possibility of autho-rial agency is severely limited, indeed becomes an oxymoron; and equally con-fined is the critic's agency, his or her freedom to draw circles of relation that are not anchored to historical circumstance. A vivid sense of this constricted view of how author and context relate is evident in the most famous critical judgment against Roth, not one by a New Historicist but by an earlier critic who shares their rigid construction of that relation. In "Philip Roth Reconsid-ered" (1972), Irving Howe declared that the novelist wrote out of a "thin personal culture" which evidently occurs when an author "comes at the end of a tradition which can no longer nourish his imagination or [when] he has, through an act of fiat, chosen to tear himself away from that tradition." This is a "severe predicament," declares Howe, and forces the writer (Roth is his example) into "self-consciousness, improvisation, and false starts; but if he is genuinely serious, he will try, like a farmer determined to get what he can from poor soil, to make a usable theme of his dilemmas."[10] The stoic farmer he salutes as a model of heroic perseverance not only exposes Howe's organicism but his determinism—one is stuck with the soil one has. Absent is any notion of imaginative autonomy that might liberate one from "poor soil" or "thin culture." The present essay aims to restore a measure of aesthetic autonomy and imaginative energy to writers and critics by redescribing context as significantly more fluid and plastic than is usually assumed. And in making the drawing of circles one of the metaphors for this fluidity I have appropriated Emerson, another writer for whom Howe had small regard. In his small book on that author, Howe arrests him in the first circle of caricature, reading Emerson as a hapless romantic individualist soon dwarfed by modernity.[11]

Earlier I suggested that Roth's "immaturity" draws on his American predecessors, especially Emerson. Emerson, in turn, derives his notion of immaturity from an engagement with Kant and, more immediately, with Coleridge. The widening circle of these entanglements comprises Emerson's complex relation to the Enlightenment's twin pillars, maturity and reason. This matter is worth sketching because from Emerson's renovation of both terms emerged a new way to think about immaturity. In 1784 Kant published his famous "motto" for the Enlightenment—"have the courage to use your *own* understanding!" Only by thinking for himself does man emerge from his "self-incurred immaturity" (the gender exclusiveness of this will soon concern us).[12] And "it is so easy to be immature," remarks Kant; all one need do is rely on the panoply of authorities that surround one—starting with the books one reads. But maturity requires, says Kant, that one always "look within oneself . . . for the supreme touchstone of truth."[13] This reverence for the spiritual sanctity of the individual's inwardness and his access to intuitive truth untethered to empirical evidence is one reason Kantian idealism was welcomed in 1830s New England intellectual culture, inspiring the Transcendentalism of Emerson and his circle. Kantianism was also a philosophical ground of Romanticism, that other liberating European thought intoxicating American intellectuals at the time. Both movements accorded the mind's shaping powers of perception an unprecedented dignity, a respect for inwardness that developed out of an earlier foundational tenet of Enlightenment, Descartes's cogito—"I think therefore I am"—and its bracketing of custom and tradition. Descartes "is a founder of modern individualism, because his theory throws the individual thinker back on his own responsibility"[14]

In the 1830s Samuel Taylor Coleridge was a key mediator of Romantic and Kantian thought to New England, and he borrowed his crucial distinction—between Reason and Understanding—from Kant. "I think it a philosophy itself," an excited Emerson said of this distinction, for it furnished an alternative to what was stultifying in Descartes—his deadening reduction of reason to mathematical certainty and calculation, a reduction that entailed the stark divorce of reason from emotions. In light of Coleridge's Kantian terms, this impoverishing dimension of the Enlightenment legacy could be averted. Now Cartesian reason was resituated as closer to Understanding, which Emerson in an 1834 letter characterized as a "wrinkled calculator" who "toils all the time, compares, contrives, adds, argues," and relies on the "expedient" and "customary." In contrast, Reason (capitalized to distinguish it from earlier uses), according to an enthusiastic Emerson in the same letter, "is the highest faculty of the soul—what we mean often by the soul itself; it never *reasons*, never proves, it simply perceives; it is vision. . . . The thoughts of youth & 'first thoughts' are the revelations of Reason." And poetry is one of the things that resides in the province of Reason.[15]

Most striking for my purposes is Emerson's paradoxical formulation that Reason "never *reasons*" for it embodies the impatience of youth, what in "Self-Reliance" he extols as the "nonchalance" of a boy—"independent, irresponsible"—who "cumbers himself never about consequences, about interests" (RWE, 261). "Whim" is the brusque boy's angle of vision, his zigzagging moodiness in tune with nature's incessant, incorrigible movements. Emerson's audacious reversal of Enlightenment reason and maturity also feeds on the anarchy and spontaneity latent and untapped in Kant's demand to shed reliance on authority and to think for oneself. Emersonian anti-Enlightenment Reason forms the basis of the vision of exhilarating, defiant immaturity that Emerson calls self-reliance. His undoing and remaking of reason and maturity can be regarded as a model for what Emerson means by abstaining from dogmatism so to recognize "all the opposite negations." For the self, as if an extension of nature, is riven by volatility and ambivalence; and Emerson invites us to stay attuned to this by inhabiting contradiction and perversity. Both will, in his word, give "edge" to one's feelings: "your goodness must have some edge to it—else it is none. The doctrine of hatred must be preached as the counteraction of the doctrine of love when that pules and whines" (RWE, 262).

Reason "never *reasons*" and maturity is never mature: in this essay, maturity suffers a reversal analogous to Cartesian rationalism when exposed to Emersonian Reason. The premise of Kant's notion of Enlightenment, maturity is emptied of its project of mastery and remade in effect as immaturity, disrespectful of dogma, authority, bounded form, all that insulates one from a more open, less censored engagement with and in the moment. Rather than goal centered, immaturity is ludic, seeking not to dominate but to mime or to enter the turbulent flow of what Emerson calls "counteraction" and Roth will call "counterlife," rhythms that prosper in the refractory domain of the aesthetic, if we allow that term to include ways of being in the world.

Roth's fertile immaturity has sustained a career nearing a half-century, encompassing by 2006 a corpus of twenty-seven books. Even more remarkable is that the preponderance of major works, by my estimate, leans toward the later decades. Before looking at one of his major late works, *The Human Stain*

(2000), and a bit at another, *Sabbath's Theater* (1995), I will sketch the ground rules of Roth's turbulent fictive world. In it characters are never immune from being "blindsided by the terrifyingly provisional nature of everything,"[16] from the raw force of history ceaselessly proliferating. Underwriting Roth's world is the impersonal fact that "what we are in the hands of *is not protection*"; "*We have no idea how it's going to turn out*," says the stumblebum Mickey Sabbath to a wealthy friend: "even you are exposed. . . . Fucking naked, even in that suit." Our nakedness has a corollary for Sabbath—that we "are destined to lead stupid" lives "*because there is no other kind.* There is nothing personal in it."[17] Shielding us from the humiliating fact of stupidity—the frailty of our powers—is the blessed obliviousness of American Adamism or exceptionalism. This ahistoricism comprises part of what Roth condemns as "pastoral" at the end of *The Counterlife*, sounding a major chord in his subsequent books. Pastoral's inertia deadens life, as Zuckerman explains at the end of *I Married a Communist*, "because everything that lives is in movement. Because purity is petrifaction. Because purity is a lie."[18] And a particularly compelling form of this lie is romantic American individualism.

The Human Stain depicts a man trapped in its antinomies. Coleman Silk seizes individualism as his birthright but his defiant willfulness blinds him to limits, to the simple fact that "history claims everybody, whether they know it or not and whether they like it or not."[19] Roth made this remark in an essay about *The Plot against America* (2004), but it derives from a passage in *The Human Stain* that sums up the unraveling of Coleman Silk's "life as a created self." He is a mulatto who, in the early 1950s, decides to pass for what many people routinely take him to be—a white man and Jew. Neither to the Jewish woman whom he marries, nor to their four children, does he ever reveal his secret. But eventually, through uncanny accident, he falls from grace and finds his life in shambles. Yet in the year before his sudden death, he is "freed into the natural thing" and "let[s] the brute out" in his affair with Faunia, a cleaning woman and self-described illiterate (HS, 32). The intrusive history that upends Coleman is the nineties era of political correctness, a national "purity binge" that culminates in the outbreak of pious sanctimony surrounding the Clinton/Lewinsky sex scandal, which indirectly triggers Silk's downfall and eventual remaking.

Prior to its unraveling, Silk's is the counterlife to Sabbath's flowing mess of a life. A low-rent noble savage, Sabbath is a relic of the 1960s, when he won brief notoriety for his avant-garde puppetry. He is a "squat man . . . obviously very sexed-up and lawless, who didn't give a damn what anybody thought" (ST, 123). One way to articulate the distinct shape of their lives is that Sabbath understands his as a problem, not as a project: "the problem that was his life was never to be solved. His wasn't the kind of life where there are aims that are clear and means that are clear and where it is possible to say, 'This is essential and that is not essential'" (ST, 108). Juxtaposed, Sabbath and Silk (before his fall) appear as two extremes—the naked and the defended. What can ameliorate the severity of this stark contrast and find access to the realm Emerson commends as the "mid-world"? One answer, we shall see below, is Roth's admiration for and Coleman's late embrace of being "game."

Until he meets Faunia and "lets the whole creature out" unfurled, Coleman regards his life as an artifact, sculpted by decisions and acts produced by his executive will. That this understanding is at once brave and deeply inadequate is part of the perplexing irreconcilability that Silk will grapple with in a novel that is framed by the terms of Greek tragedy. *The Human Stain* starts, in an epigraph, with Oedipus's question to Creon in *Oedipus the King*, "What is the rite of purification?" The answer is provided in the novel's final chapter, entitled "The Purifying Ritual." The epigraph and the chapter title are sharply ironic, for Roth, as we know, is skeptical, to put it mildly, of purification. Belief in purifying ritual comports with the effort to treat one's life as a project; each of these enterprises breeds violence and attracts those allergic to "everything that flows," those who can "no longer bear the spectacle of life's outrageous chaos and mysterious fertility." [20]

These last words are Vaclav Havel's, part of his critique of the utopian sensibility with its "desperate impatience" that "drives . . . compulsively to construct and impose various projects." The purpose of the utopian is "to make sure that, at long last, things will be clear and comprehensible, that the world will stride onward toward a goal, finally putting an end to all the infuriating contingency of history" (LT, 173). In other words, the utopian visionary pursues a fantasy of transparency first hatched by the dream of Cartesian rationality; the latter Havel calls the "grand self-delusion of the modern spirit" (LT, 159). Fueled by the certitude of Cartesian rationality, utopians—Havel mentions Robespierre, Lenin, and Pol Pot—cast the "cold" light of "objective" reason upon any mystery or ambiguity, insisting on the "'mental short-cut'" and the "clarity of the pamphlet" in their impatience to impose their projects. In the process, man is transformed from a naked, questioning being "into an existing answer" (LT, 174).

Havel's tempering of Enlightenment rationality, which has striking affinities with Emerson's germinal reversal of Cartesianism described earlier, informs his portrait of the dissident's "distinctive central European skepticism." Careful to avoid starkly opposing the dissident against the utopian, Havel notes that "a trace of the heroic dreamer, something mad and unrealistic, is hidden in the very genesis of the dissident perspective. In the very nature of things, the dissident is something of a Don Quixote" (LT, 192). As the resemblance to Quixote would suggest, the dissident is not immune to utopian imagination; indeed within him is "the germ of utopianism" (LT, 192, 175). "Visions of a better world and dreams about it are surely a fundamental aspect of authentic humanity," and without this "transcendence of the given" human life loses meaning (LT, 175). But this "germ" contains a "devilish temptation" that if left unchecked can end up "degenerating" and enslaving one to an abstraction—a "project for a better world." Often, megalomania ensues, followed by zealous indoctrination of the masses.[21]

The ambition of the "fanatic of the abstract project, that practicing Utopian," in Havel's words, produces what his countryman Kundera calls "idyll" and their friend Roth calls "pastoral." All three authors are preoccupied in their various ways with anatomizing the utopian impulse that, in Kundera's words, wants "to leave nothing but an unstained age of an unstained idyll" (*Laughter and Forgetting*, 33).[22] Havel's critique is in texts published in English in 1985 ("An Anatomy of Reticence") and 1988 (*Letters to Olga*), and Kundera's relevant texts are from 1980 (*The Book of Laughter and Forgetting*) and 1984 (*The Unbearable Lightness of Being*). Given Roth's deep familiarity with these writers and the political context of their thinking, it seems reasonable to suggest that their antiutopian skepticism helped inspire his own rejection of American pastoralism that concluded *The Counterlife* in 1986 and has oriented his major novels ever since.

Outside Czechoslovakia, other Eastern European intellectuals were making similar points. The Polish dissident Adam Michnik in *Letters from Prison* (translated in 1985) spoke of the dangerous "Manichean simplicity"—"the curse of captive peoples"—that divides the world between "maggots and angels," a mentality that is lodged deep in the Polish romantic tradition. [23] The heroic rebel, ready to die a martyr, "denies the value of compromise," favoring instead "self-idealization. . . . Seeing maggots in the cowed population, he 'angelized' himself and his friends, fighters for a sovereign and just Poland" (LP, 196, 194). These angels, often justifying their actions "with the jargon of . . . a socialist-universalist utopia," are "already sowing the seeds of future hatred. . . . And the angel who is not criticized, the angel who is convinced of his angelic character, may metamorphose into the devil. . . . Read *The Possessed*" (LP, 197).[24]

Although contempt for purist politics clearly links Roth to the Eastern European dissident sensibility, a subtler continuity among Roth, Havel, and Kundera is founded on their esteem of nakedness and recognition that we lead a "stupid" life, for "*We have no idea how it's going to turn out*" (ST, 344). I want to suggest that Kundera's notion of the "planet of inexperience," the original title of *The Unbearable Lightness of Being*, and expounded in that novel and in his "Sixty-three Words" (in *The Art of the Novel*), is a distinctive version of what Roth in *Sabbath's Theater* calls "stupid life" and Havel describes as "existential nakedness."[25] And Kundera's planet bears an uncanny resemblance to the vertiginous world Emerson discloses in "Experience." "Inexperience," says Kundera, is a "quality of the human condition. We are born one time only, we can never start a new life equipped with the experience we've gained from a previous one . . . even when we enter old age, we don't know what it is we're heading for: the old are innocent children of their old age. In that sense, man's world is the planet of inexperience."[26] Kundera makes this a motif of his novel, first rehearsing it soon after the opening, where Tomas is perplexed about what he should do with Tereza:

> He remained annoyed with himself until he realized that not knowing what he wanted was actually quite natural. We can never know what to want, because, living only one life, we can neither compare it with our previous lives nor perfect it in our lives to come. . . . We live everything as it comes, without warning, like an actor going on cold. And what can life be worth if the first rehearsal of life is life itself? That is why life is always like a sketch. No, 'sketch' is not quite the word, because a sketch is an outline of something, the groundwork for a picture, whereas the sketch that is our life is a sketch for nothing, an outline with no picture.[27]

Our irremediable inexperience makes human beings "unbearably light." Sabina realizes this when she grasps that "the thing that gives our every move its meaning is always totally unknown to us. Sabina was unaware of the goal that lay behind her longing to betray. The unbearable lightness of being—was that the goal?" (ULB, 122). Man's "fateful inexperience" is also what makes history "light as individual human life, unbearably light" (ULB, 223). With this Kundera implicitly dismisses the ponderous certitude of Hegelian-Marxist historicism and its "'geometric conception of the future' . . . that would like to have assurances in advance through science about the future, without running any risk."[28] What are the prospects for maturity if we are like actors going on cold, if the "first rehearsal of life is life itself"?

Given that maturity is funded by the steady amassing and assessing of experience, it seems forever out of our reach. Tomas imagines that "somewhere out in space there was a planet where all people would be born again" and imbued with the lessons of their previous life experience. "And perhaps there were yet more and more planets, where mankind would be born one degree (one life) more mature." But since we are stuck on the first planet, the planet of inexperience, "we can only fabricate vague fantasies of what will happen to man on those other planets. Will he be wiser? Is maturity within man's power?" (ULB, 224). Sabbath shares Kundera's and Tomas's doubts about attaining maturity, shares especially their sense of being stalled (in Sabbath's words) in "this always-beginning, never-ending present" (204). Whereas Kundera and his character are calmly resigned, Sabbath finds "repugnant" the "inexhaustibility of the present."

"You can only be young once, but you can be immature forever"; Sabbath likes to invoke this saying; and both novels, Kundera's and Roth's, can agree on that bit of folk wisdom, for each is compelled in its own way by the unbearable lightness of the perpetual present. Sabbath, like Kundera and Havel, would detect a flight from the fact of our endemic immaturity, our "inexperience," in those electing to pursue "the relatively undemanding duty of devoted service to a given project" which provides one with a specious sense of mastery

(Havel, *Olga*, 363). For instance, Tomas knows an editor who acts "as though history were a finished picture rather than a sketch" (223). Belief in the "finished picture" assumes coherence and control and predictability—all elements required for executing projects. But they unravel in the weightless air of the "planet of inexperience."

Strangely enough, yet not so strange, this is the air and this is the planet where Emerson's "Experience" uneasily, woozily, finds itself, unable to "shake off the lethargy now at noonday" (RWE, 471). We realize with a shock that the gliding, sliding, swimming, and skating that suffuses Emerson's opening pages describes our unbearable lightness of being on the "planet of inexperience." "Where do we find ourselves?" are the first words of "Experience," and this disorienting query initiates the essay's oblique and casual passage, depicting a world and a self weirdly lethargic, unmoored, adrift in a place where "all things swim and glitter" and "we thrive by casualties." The "results of life are uncalculated and uncalculable" for "all objects slip through our fingers." Although we crave "reality, sharp peaks and edges of truth" as boundary lines to guide us and as seedbeds of wisdom that might nurture us, they seem always beyond our grasp (RWE, 471–73). As we stumble along slippery surfaces, "all our blows glance, all our hits are accidents. Our relations to each other are oblique and casual." Emerson teases out the deathly randomness instilled in the casual: "we thrive by casualties. Our chief experiences have been casual" (RWE, 473).

If in "Circles" the self's fluidity is a cause for exuberance ("the way of life is wonderful: it is by abandonment"), in "Experience" abandonment is shadowed by the unmovable fact that "the whole frame of things preaches indifferency" (RWE, 478). Life seems immune to our designs and all we can count on is the unaccountable. Suddenly at risk is the Enlightenment assumption of man's dominion over experience. "Experience" exposes as self-flattering fantasy our normally taken-for-granted belief that from the rigors of experience we create the ballast of hard-won, communicable wisdom. Early on Emerson writes: "We do not know today whether we are busy or idle. . . . All our days are so unprofitable while they pass, that 'tis wonderful where or when we ever got anything of this which we call wisdom, poetry, virtue. We never got it on any dated calendar day" (RWE, 471).

For much of the essay, grief (at the death of his infant son) is the "subject-lens" through which Emerson views experience as a ceaseless, sliding procession. That grief would accentuate this careening movement is at first paradoxical, for grief would seem to be one of those "sharp peaks and edges of truth" that will provide the anchorage we crave. After all, grief is deemed to be experience saturated with meaning, a crucible that forges strength, wisdom, maturity. In sum, grief is assumed to be a supreme teacher; it introduces us into reality. Or so Emerson believed. But grief's prestige turns out to be conventional and the spur of histrionics ("people grieve and bemoan themselves") more than anything else. The sharp peaks of truth turn "out to be scene-painting and counterfeit." In the essay's most famous words, Emerson confides: "the only thing grief has taught me, is to know how shallow it is. . . . I grieve that grief can teach me nothing, nor carry me one step into real nature" (RWE, 473). Instead of providing anchorage, grief reveals the quicksand of nonmeaning normally hidden by the merciful quotidian routines of the midworld. Grief's scripted glibness—it "plays about the surface"—exposes the usually concealed fact that experience is neither friend nor teacher, nor a repository of painful but redemptive lessons in living. We project these meanings *into* experience, as if desperate to populate the vacancy of its stark, casual indifferency.

When Sabbath grieves for his long dead brother Morty at the Jersey shore, he discovers nothing save how "immoderate" is grief ; "staring into the sea and up at the sky and seeing nothing and everything and nothing," he reaches no sharp peaks and edges of epiphanic illumination (ST, 407). The chronic self-befuddlement ("If any of us knew what we were doing, or where we are going, then when we think we best know!") that Emerson would have us accept as our lot, is Kundera's attitude as well ("not knowing what he wanted was actually quite natural"). Kundera's conviction of our vulnerability, our endemic "inexperience" and "lightness" as we "live everything as it comes, without warning," tallies with Emerson's exposure of selfhood as little more than a "flux of moods," of ghostly gliding on life's surfaces. These glimpses into the "quicksand" (Emerson) that lurks in supposedly solid foundations and anchorages, are "unbearable." So is the power of chance in our lives. "We all reject out of hand the idea that the love of our life may be something light or weightless," says Kundera's narrator; "we presume our love is what must be" (ULB, 35). Though Tomas refuses the comforting notion of fated necessity that would drape over the unflattering power of "absolute fortuity," his refusal gives him little solace.

Reading Emerson and Kundera together suggests that "Experience" might be retitled "Inexperience" and that the words turn out to be synonymous for both writers. Reading *Sabbath's Theater* with Kundera and Emerson prepares for *The Human Stain*; Coleman Silk will come to learn that he dwells, with Mickey Sabbath, Nathan Zuckerman (who narrates the novel), and their creator, on the planet of inexperience. The slippery world of Roth's late fiction is shaped in part by the radical skepticism of two vastly different times and places, one from an antinomian living in a mid-nineteenth-century laboratory of democracy, the other from a dissident in exile from totalitarian occupation in Eastern Europe. The currents of both flow into and help propel a capacious late-twentieth-century cosmopolitan's art of appropriation.

"We could have great times as Homo Ludens and wife, inventing the imperfect future. . . . All it takes is impersonation," quips Nathan Zuckerman to Maria at the end of *The Counterlife*. [29] Nathan's playful remark about Man the player sums up his plea to become emancipated from myths of the natural, the "pastoral," with its "idyllic scenario[s] of redemption." The novel that is about to conclude—replete with vertiginous acts of literary artifice and self-conscious self-fashioning—has exuberantly enacted and affirmed Nathan's late hymn to Homo Ludens. *The Human Stain* (2000) renews and enlarges the emphasis on man's propensity for play, for mimicry and invention, but in a key more somber and searching and capacious. Here the *costs* of conceiving identity and artifice as synonymous are weighed, as the limits and illusions of freedom inscribed in extravagant self-making are revealed. And experimental ventures in self-*unmaking*—composing less brutal and entrapping models of self-fashioning—suddenly emerge near the end of the protagonist's life. Being "game" in the face of death becomes the fate of Homo Ludens in *The Human Stain*. Being game is what immaturity matures into when it retains its undefended immersion in the present moment and attunement to the precarious.

The novel also asks its readers to be game, invites them to tap their own capacity for interpretive play. Roth in effect encourages this by foregrounding the power of language in a number of scenes that dramatize intense acts of reading, as if to inspire our own. When Coleman receives the "everyone knows" anonymous letter exposing his affair with Faunia, he and Nathan "appraised the choice of words and their linear deployment as if they'd been composed not by Delphine Roux but by Emily Dickinson" (HS, 39–40). The preacher's intoning of "the word 'valiant'" in reading an excerpt from *Julius Caesar* at the funeral of Clarence Silk, strips away his son Coleman's "manly effort at sober, stoical self-control," a rare lapse from his unflappable "impregnability" (HS, 107). Soon after "valiant," the words of a poem sent by Steena Palsson, Coleman's first love, so intrigue him that "at the desk in his room, he battled into the morning with the paradoxical implications" of her writing (HS, 114). Later he subjects her farewell letter to "numerous rereadings" and hears in it a "subaudible apology" (HS, 126).

The prominence of language and of acts of analytical scrutiny in *The Human Stain* alert us to the impact words have, including, as in "spooks," their incorrigible consequences that take on a life of their own, beyond our control. And alert us as well to the solicitations that artifacts great and small make upon us, demands that are analogous to what brings this novel into being—Nathan feeling "seized" by Coleman's "story" (HS, 337). I will eventually dilate upon this crucial moment at graveside where the novel is born. But here I want to show how Roth's dense weave of literary allusion is not to be regarded as ornamental or the occasion for scavenger hunts but works rather as a vehicle of solicitation, inviting us to pursue clues, hazard guesses, make connections, activities analogous to how Nathan reconstructs Coleman's life. In repeating scenes where characters are seized by language and literature, seized that is by the claims of otherness, the novel dramatizes the primal moment of aesthetic action as intersubjective, even if the other has to be reclaimed from death and imagined back into being (just as a mute text has to be made to speak). In a novel where the intersubjective is not a given but achieved—Nathan must be wooed out of his isolation, Coleman must be weaned from the insulation of his secret—Roth invites his reader to engage with otherness by pursuing textual moments that expand or open out in ways that defy control, a submission to the possible but unprovable that encourages being game.

Consider the workings of one allusion that initially seems straightforward but upon further scrutiny exfoliates into a model of volatile experience that ensnares both reader and character in *The Human Stain*. Late in the novel we learn that Delphine Roux, the twenty-nine-year-old French feminist colleague of Coleman's, is seized emotionally by Milan Kundera after hearing him lecture in Paris; "basking" in his insights, she and a friend feel "infected" by the "Kundera disease." His "playfulness did not appear to be frivolous, not at all. *The Book of Laughter and Forgetting* they loved. There was something trustworthy about him. His Eastern Europeaness. The restless nature of the intellectual. That everything appeared to be difficult for him" (HS, 261). Delphine admires not only his work but his "poetically prizefighterish looks," and turns him into a moral ideal, on occasion calling him to mind to "ask his forgiveness" (HS, 266). Roth is having a bit of fun at Delphine's idolatry but is also is saluting his friend Kundera. And other things are going on as well. Her crush on the "prizefighterish" Kundera echoes another—Delphine's fascination with a former prizefighter, a "snub-nosed, goat-footed Pan," Dean Coleman Silk. He is the man who hired her and with whom she bitterly clashes, eventually exposing his affair with Faunia. But these are surface connections; less visible ones emerge when we examine "Lost Letters," the opening story of Delphine's favorite, *The Book of Laughter and Forgetting*.

"Lost Letters" concerns Mirek, a dissident Czech scientist, who has never believed in the Communist "idyll of justice for all," a "realm of harmony" that requires the liquidation of any discordant element, including the cropping of pictures and imprisonment of dissenters.[30] As an opponent of the state, Mirek had years earlier lost his job when he refused to "renounce his convictions"; he finds work in construction, avoids prison but is often followed by the police. We first meet him as he is meticulously preserving documents, diaries, lists of his activities from the earliest days of the Russian occupation. Dismissing the alarm of friends who fear he is making himself vulnerable to arrest, his reasoning is impeccably heroic: "the struggle of man against power is the struggle of memory against forgetting" (LL, 4). The police do indeed seize his cache of papers and Mirek, "who had been drawn irresistibly to the idea of prison," is sentenced to six years, and though his son and ten friends are also sentenced, Mirek seems fulfilled: the Communists "wanted to efface hundreds of thousands of lives from memory and leave nothing but an unstained age of unstained idyll. But Mirek is going to land his whole body on that idyll, like a stain" (LL, 33).

But the story is more complicated than a portrait of a martyr to memory. And its resonance with Roth's novel exceeds the clearly shared interest in staining pastoral idylls. Mirek has for many years been "in love with his destiny" and even finds his ruined career "noble and beautiful. . . . His connection to his life was that of a sculptor to his statue or a novelist to his novel. It is an inviolable right of a novelist to rework his novel. If the opening does not please him, he can rewrite or delete it" (LL, 14–15). The potential moral ambiguity of this attitude becomes clear when Mirek seeks to confiscate his old letters to a former lover, a homely, still devout party member. "That a piece of his life remained in Zdena's hands was unbearable" (LL, 25). So are his fleeting memories of his love for her. At one point the narrator intrudes: "I call on that memory to linger awhile" and discovers that it turns out Mirek wants to "efface her from the photograph of his life" because he is ashamed that he once loved the ugly Zdena. So he has erased her, rewriting history "just like the Communist Party, like all political parties, like all peoples, like mankind" (LL, 30).

In Mirek, Kundera has created a thoroughly ambiguous protagonist—at once the "stain" on the Communist "idyll" yet a purist who is bent, like his despised enemies, on airbrushing out whatever doesn't fit. The narrator is intent, however, on staining Mirek, intent on drawing out the irony, for us at least, of Mirek's flight from the (personal) past in the name of keeping the (political) past alive. In *The Art of the Novel* Kundera notes that Mirek's belief that "the struggle of man against power is the struggle of memory against forgetting" is "often cited as the book's message. This is because the first thing a reader recognizes in a novel is the 'already known.' The 'already known' in that novel is Orwell's famous theme: the forgetting that a totalitarian regime imposes. But to me the originality of Mirek's story lay somewhere else entirely"—the contradiction of his character's struggle. "Before it becomes a political issue," says Kundera, "the will to forget is an anthropological one: man has always harbored the desire to rewrite his own biography, to change the past." [31] "Lost Letters" charts the tension between these different meanings of the will to forget.

The protagonist of *The Human Stain* is, like Mirek, a master of self-revision; what Kundera says of Mirek could be said of Coleman: "his connection to his life was that of a sculptor to his statue or a novelist to his novel." This intersection, like the notions of "idyll" and "stain," clearly anticipates *The Human Stain*. And there are other resemblances. Kundera's active narrator who intervenes on behalf of memory and stains Mirek's purist project of forgetting prefigures Nathan's recovery of Coleman's life of immaculate insulation and exposure of his secret. But perhaps most notable is the disruption of expectation Kundera has built into "Lost Letters," a certain shiftiness achieved by baiting his story with the "already known"—Orwell's theme of the power of memory—that evidently has diverted readers from discerning Mirek's compromised plan. What seems like a tale of heroic resistance turns out to concern a self-divided protagonist. Mirek remains stubbornly oblivious to his contradictions; indeed, now under arrest he "could not imagine a better ending for the novel of his life" (LL, 33). The story's last lines, noting the prison sentences handed down to his son and circle of friends, underscore the perfect solipsism of his aesthetic relation to his life.

In sum: to pursue Kundera's playful, not frivolous presence in *The Human Stain* discloses that Roth shares his commitment to staining idylls, but also to volatility, to double moves that keep readers off balance. Such unsettlement is particularly apt for *The Human Stain* because it is fascinated not only by Mirek-like self-fashioning but also the boomeranging contradictions that emerge when one vows, as Delphine, a self-described Cartesian, vows, to be "the author of my life. . . . I will construct myself outside the orthodoxy of my family's given, I will fight *against* the given, impassioned subjectivity carried to the limit, individualism at its best—and she winds up instead in a drama beyond her control" (HS, 273). The abrupt reversal from subject to object is mirrored in the pronoun shift from the active "I" to the subjected "she." The sudden loss of control, a slipperiness also observed in "Lost Letters" via Kundera's feinting with Orwell, becomes in *The Human Stain* the leitmotif of the novel.

This lability starts on the level of the sentence, threading itself through a wealth of narrative and descriptive detail, turning the title phrase inside out, accumulating thematic significance. At the fluid center is the smooth counterpunching boxer "Silky" Silk, adept at both "slipping the punch" and "rolling" with it, a suppleness that extends to his smooth and seamless transition from black to white. He is master of the art of passing and its "sliding relationship with everything" that is the liberating opposite of the "tyranny of the we" that burdened his father's generation of race loyalists (HS, 108). Yet all his crafty, graceful movement in the service of control is eventually tripped up by the equally artful counterpoint of accident and reversal—ironic life at its slippery work. So Coleman will come to bruising awareness of the traps hidden in the fine art of passing and suffer as well other twists of fortune, suffer them as blind spots, for he has encountered premonitions of them before. Peripeteia haunts the classical Greek drama he reads: "freedom is dangerous," "nothing is on your own terms for long," and "how easily life can be one thing rather than another" (HS, 145, 125).

Shiftiness and reversal, both startling and subtle, are the very stuff of *The Human Stain*. For instance, many read it as a meditation upon race in America, but race is, arguably, closer to the status of Orwell in "Lost Letters"—"the first thing a reader recognizes," an "already known." More pivotal than race in explaining Coleman is "the *gift* to be secretive" that he possesses; indeed, his self-understanding equates having a self with having a secret. "It's like being fluent in another language," he says of the latter.[32] This gift for secrets is a gift for fluency and is the source of the "sliding relationship with every-thing" that Roth makes the thematic and stylistic spine of the novel (HS, 135–36).

Nathan's graveyard pledge to tell Coleman's story will become a recurring reference point, for that scene entwines the novel's birth with the power of being game. This latter theme will open out to reveal Roth's exuberantly inventive engagement with his nineteenth-century predecessors, Hawthorne and especially Melville. Roth makes the seeds of that engagement quite visible in the text. A colleague eulogizes Coleman as an "American individualist" who, in the tradition of "Hawthorne, Melville, and Thoreau," resisted the "coercions of a censorious community" (HS, 310).[33]

Not only is *The Human Stain* a novel where the main character fabricates an identity, but Roth foregrounds the artful fabrication that is the novel itself, as late in the book he presents Zuckerman narrating the moment when he decides to write *The Human Stain*: "not quite knowing what was happening, standing in the falling darkness beside the uneven earth mound roughly heaped over Coleman's coffin, I was completely seized by his story, by its end and by its beginning, and, then and there, I began this book" (HS, 337). Roth has arranged here a stark, primal collision between life and art. But, as always in his work, life and art also intermix and mingle. The graveside "competition with death" inspires Nathan to reveal "how all this began"—both how Cole-man and Faunia's affair began and how the making of *The Human Stain* began. These two beginnings turn out to have much in common and tell a good deal about the conditions and motives enabling the making of life and art. But they also clarify a difference that the novel has earlier dramatized—a differ-ence between two understandings of how art and life and freedom are entan-gled. One is Coleman's art of being white, which ends up imprisoning him in his secret, and the other is his late affair with Faunia, where he is "freed into the natural thing," "free to be abandoned" (HS, 32–33). The contrast, how-ever, does not reduce to artifice versus nature; the "natural thing," for Roth, is itself a mode of artifice, with its own elusive rhythms and rigors. It is a difficult thing to acquire.

"I waited and I waited for him to speak." Standing alone at the graveside, Nathan at last hears an inaugural vibration—Coleman asking Faunia what was the worst job she'd ever had. The answer Zuckerman imagines for her is a graphic recollection of being paid a hundred dollars an hour to clean up a cabin where a man had blown his brains out with a shotgun. Faunia had been enlisted by a friend for this grisly work, a friend who knew she had a "strong stomach" and could "handle things." But even Faunia needs a mask and almost gags: "Blood on the walls everywhere. Ba-boom, he's all over the walls, all over everything. . . . I had to put on a mask, because even *I* couldn't take this anymore" (HS, 339). She is in the cabin cleaning for five hours.

And it is Faunia's act of scrubbing and affirming the human stain—that mental picture Coleman imagines as she tells the story that he has elicited (what was your worst job?) according to Nathan's imagination, according to Roth's imagination—this four-part invention of a woman determinedly scrubbing becomes a visceral bolt of an epiphany for Coleman, an epiphany of love and trust.

> Because he loved her at that moment, imagining her scrubbing the blood. It was the closest he ever felt to her. Could it be? It was the closest Coleman ever felt to anyone! He loved her. Because that is when you love somebody—when you see them being game in the face of the worst. Not courageous. Not heroic. Just game. He had no reservations about her. None. . . . He trusts her—that's what it is. He trusts her: she scrubbed the blood off the floor. She's not religious, she's not sanctimonious, she is not deformed by the fairy tale of purity. . . . She's not interested in judging—she's seen too much for all that shit." (HS, 340–41)

And then Coleman tells Faunia his secret.

Although Roth's novels are usually regarded as bleakly cynical and despairing, *The Human Stain* is, improbably, but intensely, a portrayal of the efficacy of art and love when nourished by a certain stance toward the world. Ishmael invokes that stance, or one close to it, in *Moby Dick* when he invokes the spirit of "godly gamesomeness" in saluting the "Huzza Porpoise": "they are the lads that always live before the wind."[34] Their animal, uncontainable exuberance gives a clue to why human versions of being "game" are so potent an elixir for love and art, as if Roth is suggesting that what defies death is not simply artistic creation but creation imbued with the spirit of being game.

Roth's esteem of being game serves, most immediately, as a rebuke to the national "purity binge" aroused by the Clinton/Lewinsky affair in the novel's opening pages. Nathan Zuckerman derides the "ecstasy of sanctimony" abroad in the land in summer 1998, a censorious moral climate that will foster the campus scandal that erupts around Coleman.[35] In *Sabbath's Theater* and *The Human Stain* Roth's contempt for sanctimony becomes a catalyst for fashioning a new moral vocabulary—"stupid" and "naked" and "game," for instance. What grounds these words is the fact of the human stain—the realization that "there's no other way to be here"—and sponsoring this recognition is not the Jewish or Christian God but pagan Greek polytheism. Indeed, Nathan invokes them immediately after Faunia first remarks the human stain; creatures such as Zeus are fully "reconciled to the horrible, elemental imperfection"—"a god of life if there ever was one. God in the image of man" (HS, 242–43). Under this pagan aegis (as Coleman the classics professor might have told Faunia), we accept that our lives are "unprotected" or "naked" (Mickey Sabbath's words), shorn of the traditional scaffolding of "grace or salvation or redemption." This is the life of "quicksand" on the "planet of inexperience," to borrow Roth's and Emerson's word and Kundera's phrase. What makes the bravado of being game so reverberant for Roth, we shall see below, is its long genealogy, both within his oeuvre and in American literature.

Distrusting projects, preferring to let the moment take its impress, the knack for being game withers under the reign of absolutes and the routine of convention; instead it flowers in extremity, in moments when survival is at stake and all bets are off. In other words, being game makes a virtue of the fact that we live amid the unbearable lightness of the perpetual present. In other words, to be game is to be alert to the massive cultural bias toward sentimentality, the customary, and self-congratulation with its various modes of inertia, reflex, and habit deeply imbibed and socially encouraged, modes that constitute for many the comfortably complacent basis of personal and moral identity. A deflationary or skeptical stance expressed on the body and in language ("all the social ways of thinking, shut 'em down," says Faunia, naked, dancing), gameness has an element of ascetic rigor but does not wholly abjure the pleasure principle. Rather, it finds pleasure in experience dislocated from routine.

Faunia utters the phrase the "human stain" about Prince, a crow she loves. Orphaned and twice abandoned, Prince is now caged in a local Audubon Society, where Faunia visits him and fantasizes about becoming a crow. Faunia's intimacy and identification with Prince, like her pretense of illiteracy, cuts two ways—it appears at first simply to permit Faunia to revel in the primitive and dramatize her alienation. But simultaneously her identification with the crow, like her illiteracy, does nearly the opposite—it works to immunize her from the lure of the natural or authentic. Prince turns out to be an artist. Faunia finds Prince compelling not as a figure of nature but as a misfit, a wild bird unsuited for the wild since he has been hand-raised by humans and made into a pet. He caws but "not in a true crow caw but in that caw that he had stumbled on himself and that drove the other crows nuts" (HS, 243). Prince has devised his caw by imitating the school kids that visit and imitate him. Explains his keeper: "That's his impression of the kids. The kids do that. He's invented his own language. From kids" (HS, 243). Like Nathan, Faunia, and Coleman, Prince participates in the unstoppable circulation of mimetic and inferential impressions; his mimicry of mimicry infers and fashions a voice. "I love that strange voice he invented," remarks Faunia "in a strange voice of her own." Here, in her mimetic receptivity to Prince, Faunia unwittingly underlines the novel's animating technique—the impersonations Nathan assembles into a collocation of invented voices.

"I am a theater and nothing more than a theater," a younger Nathan Zuckerman had declared at the end of The Counterlife. The Human Stain ratifies this emptying out of the self as a "natural being" rooted in a solid core of fixed identity. But here Nathan renovates the theater of the self, not to repudiate his commitment to the primacy of impersonation but to enlarge its scope, to include the fact that the elemental impulse to imitate—the mimetic faculty—is shared by man and beast. The bond of mimesis means, in effect, that Art lurks in the heart of Nature; and this mingling topples the primordial opposition between them, the opposition that grounds the always lethal "fantasy of purity."

Prince's mimicry leaves him a misfit among his own species. Whenever he leaves his cage to fly around, crows attack him. The keeper tells Faunia that Prince "doesn't have the right voice. He doesn't know the crow language," and Faunia remarks: "That's what comes of being hand-raised. . . . [T]hat's what comes of hanging around all his life with people like us. The human stain . . ." Nathan then dilates about Faunia's enigmatic comment: "*That's how it is*—in her own dry way, that is all Faunia was telling the girl feeding the snake: we leave a stain, we leave a trail, we leave our imprint." One of the oddities of this pivotal scene is that an animal elicits Faunia's (and Nathan's) epiphany of the human stain, a statement that purports to define the human condition, to declare what "we" humans do. If read out of context, the "human stain" would seem a phrase that unequivocally defines the "we" by setting off the human species' distinction and distinctiveness. But in the novel the phrase does precisely the opposite—the "human stain" links us to the animal; stains, trails, imprints are common to both species.

This equivocation makes sense when we consider that if the "stain" was understood to function as an absolute, as an essentialist term of immutable difference, the stain would embody the very "fantasy of purity" that it is intended to rupture. The phrase, in other words, to enact its slippery ubiquity, rather than marking a limit, must embody transit or transfiguration. The mimetic impulse (as Prince reveals) is precisely that nexus of reciprocal imitation or exchange, is a practice that crosses boundaries and species, destabilizes reference. In sum: inhabiting the "human stain" is the stain of mimesis, its disruptive energies unraveling Roth's titular phrase from within. In pushing the concept of a strictly "*human* stain" to the edge of coherence, opening it to the nonhuman, Roth enacts the experience of volatility, a commitment to unsettlement that he shares with Kundera and Emerson.[36]

If Prince is a strutting black category mistake—described as a "crow that doesn't know how to be a crow"—Coleman Silk is a human version, a black man who won't be a black man. After arriving at Howard abruptly to discover "he was a Negro and nothing else," Coleman rejects the "tyranny of the we and its we-talk" (HS, 108). Analogously, Faunia is a middle-class woman who refuses to be one, who insists on a white-trash life. Her rejection of her original class membership is not an act of political solidarity with the lumpen but an act of aggressive disaffiliation from any collective "we" with its expectations about "what you're supposed to be . . . supposed to do." Instead, she grasps freedom as being game; when she takes up with Coleman, they are both in it "for the ride": "not for learning, not for planning, but for adventure" (HS, 33).

After her two children had died (in a fire likely set by her ex-husband), Faunia visited Prince almost daily, a time when she was "looking for ways to leave the human race" (HS, 239) and attempted suicide twice. Her intimacy with Prince functions as a kind of liminal space of suspension between the human and animal and her "marriage" to the crow declares her radical alienation from human hope, what she terms contemptuously "the fantasy of forever." Her affair with Coleman, with its rigorous adherence to the moment and its prohibition on believing it is "something more than" the immediate, approximates her kinship with Prince. In sum, Faunia's is a terminal gameness, the other side of "the tragedy of her strangeness" (HS, 208). She seals her intimacy with Prince by humming, "imitating the bird" after it had hummed to her and "exploded with its special noise": "Caw. Caw. Caw. Caw. Right into her face" (HS, 244).

"Caw! caw! caw! caw! caw! caw! Ain't I a crow?" So little Pip in *Moby-Dick* babbles in mimicry, with his "unearthly idiot face"; soon he will mime a limb, as he begs Ahab if he can act as his Captain's second leg ("use poor me for your one lost leg . . . so I remain a part of ye"). "The little negro Pippin," by nickname Pip, is the cabin boy who survives abandonment at sea, suffers a "strange sweet lunacy," and is the one person on the *Pequod* for whom Ahab has affection (MD, 450, 475). Not long after, Pip pops up when Queequeg, ill and assuming death imminent, stoically prepares his coffin. "Queequeg dies game! I say; game, game, game! But base little Pip, he died a coward" (MD, 523). Game, game, game, caw, caw, caw: in his own frantic way, Pip shares some of the language of *The Human Stain*. Intentionally or not, Pip, the loneliest figure in American literature, is discernible on the far horizon of Roth's novel.

"Left behind on the sea, like a hurried traveller's trunk" in the endless ocean, Pip experiences an "intolerable," "awful lonesomeness." The extremity of his dilemma leaves Ishmael at a loss for words: "The intense concentration of self in the middle of such a heartless immensity, my God! who can tell it?" (MD, 453). Ishmael falters here, a preliminary indication of the linguistic disturbance that will mark Pip's own agitated speech in the wake of his traumatized survival. What Pip has suffered is an ontological dislocation so severe that it fractures his psyche—"the sea had jeeringly kept his finite body up, but drowned the infinite of his soul"—and he registers the severance of soul from body by addressing himself in the third person. And addressing himself as if dead ("Seek out one Pip, who's now been missing long," he implores Queequeg). Pip's indeterminate status—"not drowned entirely" in Melville's eerie phrase—leaves him permanently estranged in the aftermath of having been "carried down alive to wondrous depths" where the "unwarped primal world" glided before his "passive eyes" and then bobbing up to live (MD, 453). He has achieved what Faunia sought—an existence at once within and outside the human race, a stance of uncanny elusiveness that resists any single description; "crazy-witty," Ahab calls him, and his shipmates call him mad, though in his insanity he possesses "heaven's sense," and Ahab reveres his "holiness" (MD, 454, 567). Pip is a madman who doesn't know how to be a madman.

Why does Pip, however improbably, circulate at the margins of *The Human Stain*? A short answer is that Roth has invited him. After all, at the funeral, the principal eulogist puts Coleman in company with Melville, along with Hawthorne and Thoreau, as exemplary "American individualists" (HS, 311). But unlike the eulogist, Roth, like his predecessors, does not simply revere "American individualism" but subjects it to skeptical scrutiny. Like them, Roth anatomizes the orthodoxy of individualism's cardinal tenet—the self-mastery of self-possession—and reveals its compulsive hostility to relation. As we have seen, Roth and Nathan expose the limits and costs of Coleman's self-making, but also depict its *unmaking*, embodied in his late-blooming abandonment of propriety that sheds his defensiveness.

Something like Coleman's two modes of selfhood are found in *Moby-Dick*, distributed between the monomaniacal Ahab and the melancholy, insouciant, "gamesome" sole survivor, Ishmael. Pip—who is both Ahab's only friend and the herald, as Ishmael notes, of Ishmael's own "like abandonment" at sea—functions as a kind of pivot between these disparate modes of being (MD, 454). So Pip's inferential presence in *The Human Stain* is a way for Roth to engage Melville, much as Nathan, early on in the novel, wishes he could have known his onetime Berkshires neighbor Hawthorne.

Pip's solitude amid the "heartless immensity" of ocean enacts, as Sharon Cameron has noted in the most searching discussion of this character, "the antithesis of a Narcissus fall in which the self is lost in fusion with the universe. In Pip's fall, self and world are rent, opposites turned toward each other."[37] Although Pip knows firsthand the stark terror of the world's indifference, his response, Cameron argues, "is not to become heartless himself" but rather to "mourn his fate" and in his pervasive grief to "complete" Ahab's pervasive rage. These characters are "halves of the same consciousness." "It is precisely this grief . . . that Ahab will find intolerable." Grief is never expressed by Ahab, except once, fleetingly. And though Ahab feels that Pip touches his "inmost center" and is "tied" to him "by cords woven" of his "heart-strings," Ahab will banish Pip below deck and reject his extraordinary offer to act as a second leg. Ahab's rejection of Pip, says Cameron, repudiates not only their particular relationship but "the fact of relationship itself." Instead, "grief is purged from the body, is that feeling rage will not have in its midst, because it threatens the uniformity of conception it would both invade and divide" (CS, 29). Nothing must dilute Ahab's tenacious commitment.

Ahab's banishment of grief takes to an extreme Coleman's coldness, his willfulness, his fantasy of self-birth. The latter contrives the ultimate test of becoming "the man he has chosen to be" by turning his back on his mother forever: "There was no explanation that could begin to address the outrage of what he was doing to her. . . . He was murdering her . . . murdering her on behalf of his exhilarating notion of freedom!" (HS, 138). Ahab is preeminently a man with a consuming project. The incubus of unfettered autonomy in the form of a "supreme purpose" turns him into a zombie who sleeps "with clenched hands; and wakes with his own bloody nails in his palms" (MD, 219). As is often observed, Ishmael seems of markedly different disposition than Ahab. An easygoing democrat, suspicious of hierarchy, indifferent to capital accumulation, content to float and drift in reverie, Ishmael has no animating project or "supreme purpose" in life. Yet he is also susceptible to Ahab's obsession because Ishmael "loves to sail forbidden seas" both mentally—his reveries at times express a morbidity verging on the suicidal—and literally. Whenever he feels too morbid he ships off as a sailor.

Melville implicitly identifies with Ishmael's abjuring of instrumentality, of profit, when, in a famous letter to Hawthorne, he says that "irresponsibility" is "my profoundest sense of being."[38] Melville means in part to demystify that allegedly natural birthright of American maturity—the mastery bequeathed by Cartesian individualism. Its sterile arrogance relies on repressing the subterranean urges of irresponsibility. "Who ain't a slave," Ishmael remarks early on (MD, 6), as he redefines mastery to be at best a provisional role granted by the "stage managers, the Fates," who cajole us into the "delusion" that our "unbiased free will and discriminating judgment" guide our choices (MD, 7). Ishmael's matter-of-fact attitude about our precarious and frail powers of self-mastery expresses not despair but fellowship; for him, slavery's ubiquity engenders communion: "so the universal thump [administered by the old sea-captains] is passed round and all hands should rub each other's shoulder-blades, and be content" (MD, 6).

Amid the wreckage of the *Pequod* he alone lives; "for almost one whole day and night," Ishmael drifts at sea buoyed up by Queequeg's coffin, "floating on the margin," relaxing the purposive will. For all his "romantic, melancholy" moodiness and dreaminess, Ishmael is also imbued with the spirit of "godly gamesomeness." This spirit, which Ishmael also dubs a "genial, desperado philosophy," is second nature to sailors, he says, for they are constantly exposed to danger and incipient disaster. Tempered by "extreme tribulation," sailors banish the grim and earnest demeanor of the conventionally responsible and instead welcome the ludic, the "free and easy" stance in which one takes the "whole universe for a vast practical joke" at one's own expense. A psychic calm ensues wherein "nothing dispirits, and nothing seems worth while disputing" in this stance of stoic aplomb (MD, 247). Being game is at one with this "odd sort of wayward mood" that Ishmael cultivates amid "the perils of whaling." In his capacity for letting go and floating, for "gamesomeness" and love of the "landless"—all that is hazardous, unfinished, and flowing—Ishmael is the consummate survivor. Which, as *The Human Stain* suggests, is a way of saying he has the makings of a great novelist. As Nathan Zuckerman discovers, writing puts one "in professional competition with death" (indeed Ishmael is saved by a text—Queequeg's coffin that buoys him up has inscribed on it drawings and figures, making it a "riddle to unfold") and functions to disinter and recover those consigned to oblivion.

Roth's acts of appropriation produce the seamlessly allusive capaciousness of *The Human Stain*—embracing nineteenth-century native predecessors and Eastern European contemporaries, classical tragedy and contemporary French theory[39]—and make this novel arguably the summit of his cosmopolitan narrative art. We have seen that under pressure of the novel's own self-interrogating energy the human stain itself is revealed not as essence but attachment, the gift of mimesis that links human to animal. This titular dynamism is the emblem of the text's boundary crossing movement, its fertility of affiliations, a connective power that from the start of this essay we have allied with Emerson's perpetual drawing of new circles. All this commitment to acts of unsettling makes *The Human Stain* an apt test case for revaluating our scholarly devotion to nationalist categories and historical context. The prestige of the former is already beginning to wane, but materialist and New Historicist approaches seem hardier, given that they anchor (or, more radically, dissolve) the individual author in a web of contextual affiliations. Undeniably salutary as a corrective, this turn from author to context is grounded in skepticism of aesthetic autonomy. But this distrust has calcified into orthodoxy. In some historicism a suspicion of the literary has become a hobbling reflex, reducing writers to their historical circumstances. What the anchorage of context tends to smother is what I have attempted to release here: the spatial realm beyond or above the strict linearity of the historical—the spiraling circles of "world literary space" as it has recently been called, the "kingdom of culture," to use Du Bois's still stirring image of freedom.

Notes

1. Ruth Wisse, *The Modern Jewish Canon* (New York, 2000), 317.

2. Philip Roth, *Reading Myself and Others* (New York, 2001), 104; hereafter RMO.

3. Quoted in Lawrence Buell, *Emerson* (Cambridge, Mass., 2003), 239.

4. Ralph Waldo Emerson, *Essays and Lectures* (New York, 1983), 426; hereafter RWE.

5. Pascale Casanova, *The World Republic of Letters*, trans. M. DeBevoise (1999; Cambridge, Mass., 2004), 3. This book is a major effort to "break with the national habits of thought that create the illusion of uniqueness and insularity" (5).

6. "Quotation and Originality," *Emerson's Prose and Poetry*, ed. J. Porte and S. Morris (New York, 2001), 329.

7. Henry James *Letters*, vol. 1, *1843–1875*, ed. Leon Edel (Cambridge, Mass., 1974), 77.

8. W.E.B. Du Bois, *Writings* (New York, 1986), 365. Ellison calls himself, Wright, and James Baldwin as much products of the library as of painful experiences (*Collected Essays* [New York, 1995], 163.) And no reader of *Black Boy* will forget the importance of the library for Wright. Roth's salute to the Newark Public Library is in *Reading Myself and Others*, 216–19. The quotation is on 217. He honors the centrality of the library for Jewish American and African American intellectuals in his first long work of fiction, *Goodbye, Columbus*, where a Jewish librarian befriends a black boy who loves going to the library to look at art books of Gauguin.

9. Eric Wolf, *Europe and the People without History* (Berkeley and Los Angeles, 1982), 6.

10. Irving Howe, "Philip Roth Reconsidered" (1972), in *Modern Critical Views: Philip Roth*, ed. Irving Howe, Harold Bloom (New York, 1986), 71–88. Quotation is on 80.

11. *The American Newness: Culture and Politics in the Age of Emerson* (Cambridge, Mass., 1986).

12. Immanuel Kant, "An Answer to the Question: What Is Enlightenment?" reprinted in James Schmidt, ed., *What Is Enlightenment? Eighteenth-Century Answers and Twentieth-Century Questions* (Berkeley and Los Angeles, 1996), 58.

13. Quoted in Schmidt, "Introduction," in *What Is Enlightenment?* 17.

14. Charles Taylor, *Sources of the Self* (Cambridge, Mass., 1989), 182.

15. Emerson, *Selected Letters*, ed. Joel Myerson (New York, 1997), 133. It should be added that in the same letter, Emerson concedes that by the end of life Understanding will have proved to be the more reliable bearer of truth. My bare sketch leaves out the often observed fact that Emerson's use of Reason misunderstands Kant's notion, a perhaps inevitable result of Emerson's reliance on Coleridge's own misunderstanding. But as Barbara Packer notes, "few of Coleridge's American readers knew *The Critique of Pure Reason* (1781), and most were happy to use Coleridge's terms as if they were Kant's." See Packer for a splendid intellectual history of the period: "The Transcendentalists." in *The Cambridge History of American Literature*, ed. Sacvan Bercovitch, vol. 2, *Prose Writing 1820–1865* (New York, 1995), 329–604. Quotation is on 355. See also Lawrence Buell, *Emerson*, on Emerson, Coleridge and Kant (61), and David Van Leer, *Emerson's Epistemology* (New York, 1986), 4–5, for a summary of how commentators have described Emerson's misuses of Kant.

16. Philip Roth, *The Human Stain* (Boston, 2000), 336; hereafter HS.

17. Philip Roth, *Sabbath's Theater* (Boston, 1995), 344, 204; hereafter ST.

18. Philip Roth, *I Married a Communist* (Boston, 1998), 318.

19. Philip Roth, "The Story Behind *The Plot against America*." *New York Times Book Review*, Sept. 12, 2004, 12.

20. Vaclav Havel, *Living in Truth*, ed. John Vladislav (London, 1989), 173; hereafter LT.

21. As if the antidote to such overreaching, the dissident sensibility, in Havel's portrayal, is full of irony, self-irony, and black humor and desires "to desecrate the altar." The dissident has a "fear of pathos and sentimentality, of overstatement and of what Kundera calls the lyric relation to the world" (LT, 180, 183). A capacity to make light of and rise above oneself, qualities that ridicule taking oneself too seriously, are anathema to the earnest, bloated Stalinist aesthetics of the utopian fanatic.

22. Roth expresses his admiration for Havel in *Shoptalk* in the course of an interview with Ivan Klima (Boston, 2001), 70. The same volume includes Roth's conversations

with Kundera, whose exile to France and international fame made him a controversial figure for Czech intellectuals who stayed at home, working and suffering. Havel discusses his differences with Kundera in a book of interviews, *Disturbing the Peace* (New York, 1991), 171–80.

23. Adam Michnik, *Letters From Prison*, trans. Maya Latynski (Berkeley and Los Angeles, 1987), 194–95; hereafter LP.

24. Roth's own diatribes against "Manichean simplicity" in *Sabbath's Theater* and *The Human Stain* inevitably lack the urgency and immediacy of his Eastern European contemporaries (American identity politics and resurgent Puritanism, after all, are hardly in the same league as totalitarian occupation). *I Married a Communist* is the most direct assault on the intellectual abasement, the moral and political gullibility, required to be an American member of the Party from the late thirties to midfifties. And in *Sabbath's Theater* he writes that ideologies traffic in Manichean polarities; "the holder of the ideology is pure and good and clean and the other is wicked. . . . The ideology *institutionalizes* the pathology" (ST, 274).

25. Vaclav Havel, *Letters to Olga*, trans. Paul Wilson (New York, 1988), 364.

26. Milan Kundera, *The Art of the Novel*, trans. Linda Asher (New York, 1988), 132–33.

27. Milan Kundera, *The Unbearable Lightness of Being*, trans. Michael Henry Heim (New York, 1999), 8; hereafter ULB.

28. "Geometric conception" is George Bataille's phrase and the rest of the sentence is Denis Hollier's gloss; *Against Architecture: The Writings of Georges Bataille* (Cambridge, Mass., 1992), 55. Bataille is an archenemy of projects.

29. Philip Roth, *The Counterlife* (New York, 1986), 321.

30. Milan Kundera, "Lost Letters," in *The Book of Laughter and Forgetting*, trans. Aaron Asher (New York, 1999), 11; hereafter LL.

31. Milan Kundera, *The Art of the Novel*, trans. Linda Asher (New York, 1988), 130.

32. My emphasis coincides with Amy Hungerford's argument that in Coleman Silk Roth is "creating a character whose true identity has nothing to do with race—understood either biologically or as a social construction." Instead, it is "the inherent secrecy of individual consciousness that defines who Coleman 'really' was" (*The Holocaust of Texts* [Chicago, 2003], 143–45). In stressing secrets against the many readers who have eyes only for race, I, like Hungerford, am taking my cue from Roth's own emphasis: "Could it be because who he [Coleman] really was was entirely his secret?" Nathan asks rhetorically about Coleman's early experience of passing while a boxer (HS, 100).

33. Zuckerman, lonely in the Berkshires, wishes he could "find sustenance in *people like Hawthorne*, in the wisdom of the brilliant deceased" (44). Zuckerman does find sustenance in *The Scarlet Letter*, both in general ways—linking Puritan censoriousness with its contemporary resurgence during the Clinton/Lewinsky scandals—and in more particular ones—troping the "The Minister in a Maze" chapter that narrates Dimmesdale's inner reversal, the "revolution" that incites him to do "wicked" things.

34. Herman Melville, *Moby-Dick* (New York, 1992), 156; hereafter MD.

35. The late-nineties censoriousness repeats on the national level a version of what Roth personally confronted in the early and late sixties—outrage over "Defender of the Faith," and of course *Portnoy's Complaint*. The latter book was Roth's most brazen assault on the stereotype of the Jew as embodiment of the superego, suspicious of appe-

tite and excess, eagerly embracing renunciation and virtue. (The compulsion of respectability is a residue from historical circumstance—the effort starting in late-eighteenth-century Germany to keep the Jew on social probation, allowing him civil rights so long as he makes good on the opportunity to become German.)

36. In undoing his own effort to define the human stain, Roth performs an act akin to Emersonian troping, as he turns against a privileged piece of language. "Why, then, do we prate of self-reliance?" asks Emerson in the middle of "Self-Reliance." Emerson's "derisive rejoinder," as Richard Poirier describes it, is "a rejection of his dependence on the phrase that serves as his title" (*Poetry and Pragmatism* [Cambridge, Mass., 1992], 28). In *Poetry and Pragmatism*, Poirier was the first to make us aware of the pivotal importance of troping in Emerson's writing, which aims to enact, rather than merely describe, his struggle with language's inevitable betrayal (or purifying) of reality.

37. Sharon Cameron, *The Corporeal Self: Allegories of the Body in Melville and Hawthorne* (Baltimore, 1981), 26; hereafter CS.

38. Herman Melville, *Moby-Dick*, Norton ed. (New York, 2001), 545. We know that Roth read Melville's letter because in 1973 he reports he was inspired by the declaration "I have written a wicked book" that appears a few lines before Melville's admission of "irresponsibility."

39. Delphine Roux wrote her Yale dissertation on Bataille, and his Nietzschean animus against humanism finds its way into the novel.

PART THREE

Local and Global

CHAPTER 6

World Bank Drama

Joseph Roach

> Green grow the lilacs, all sparkling with dew,
> I'm lonely my darling, since parting with you,
> And by our next meeting I hope to prove true
> To change the green lilacs to the red, white, and blue.

This lyric comes from the 1931 Theatre Guild production of *Green Grow the Lilacs*, Lynn Riggs's "folk play" of conventional romance and dark ritual set in Indian Territory before it became a state at the closing of the American frontier a century ago. The title song was one of a dozen ballads gathered locally and transcribed by the playwright, who was a gifted singer himself, for production on Broadway and on national tour. Of his ambitions for the play, Riggs modestly wrote: "It must be fairly obvious from reading or seeing the play that it might have been subtitled *An Old Song*. The intent has been solely to recapture in a kind of nostalgic glow (but in dramatic dialogue more than in song) the great range of mood which characterized the old folk songs and ballads I used to hear in my Oklahoma childhood—their quaintness, their sadness, their robustness, their simplicity, their hearty or bawdy humors, their sentimentalities, their melodrama, their touching sweetness."[1] Riggs succeeded far beyond expectation, but not ultimately in the venue he intended. *Green Grow the Lilacs* is better known today (though still perhaps not as well known as it should be) as the play adapted by Richard Rodgers and Oscar Hammerstein II as the revolutionary American musical comedy *Oklahoma!*, which opened in 1943. The plot, the characters, and much of the dialogue reappear from the play unchanged in the musical, and even the new tunes and lyrics follow Riggs's intentions by evoking a distinctive mood, one that presaged, in its nostalgia and unnervingly self-satisfied mystifications, the highly effective theme from Ronald Reagan's 1984 reelection campaign: "It's Morning in America."

Riggs's opening stage direction for *Green Grow the Lilacs* sets the time and place in which the action will unfold: "It is a radiant summer morning several years ago, the kind of morning which, enveloping the shapes of the earth—men, cattle in a meadow, blades of young corn, streams—makes them seem to exist now for the first time, their images giving off a visible golden emanation that is partly true and partly a trick of the imagination focusing to keep alive a loveliness that may pass away" (3). Giving material form to the verbal cognates *voice, invocation, evocation,* and *vocation,* the playwright calls for the first entrance to be made by a singing cowboy: "And, like the voice of the morning, a rich male voice outside somewhere begins to sing" (3). So deeply has Rodgers and Hammerstein's bucolic "Oh, What a Beautiful Mornin'" in-sinuated itself into popular memory that in retrospect Riggs's own introduc-tory song, meant to establish Curly McLain's character, sounds like a bump-tious parody:

> Ta whoop ti aye ay, git along, you little doggies!
> Way out in Wyoming shall be your bright home—
> A-whooping and a-yelling and a-driving those doggies,
> And a-riding those bronchos that are none of my own. (4)

The original folk tune does directly assert, in ways its successor does not, the fact that *cowboy* was a one-word job description for the geographically dispossessed.

This is "an old song" indeed, at least by the standards of American popular culture, one of many derived from the so-called common domain, that folk-loric limbo of unclaimed intellectual property where Lynn Riggs found it, but by no means where Rodgers and Hammerstein left it. Even in its transforma-tion beyond recognition into a show tune, however, the preexisting, authorless ballad, by the very fact of its priority and anonymity, adds authenticity and hence value to the commercial work. Like the exploitation of natural re-sources and environments, such borrowing from the residual stock of common cultural ownership—generally summed up in words like *tradition* or *heritage*—has been a significant force in shaping modern performing arts. What Adorno and Horkheimer call the culture industry stands on the shoulders of giants.[2] It has financed its operations on the strength of artistic capital secured, very often interest free, from world-historic traditions, including music and dance forms, folk dramas, and ancient rituals. These in turn have been influenced, some would say ruined, in the process of being absorbed, by their counter-appropriation of commercial techniques. Borrowing heavily from one another, cultural heritage and the culture industry have created a global network of mutual but largely inequitable indebtedness. That is what I am calling, from the perspective of my specialty in theatrical history, "World Bank Drama."

The size of First World debt to the world bank of culture remains unwieldy, no matter how often it has been forgiven or simply disavowed. In 1926, when the nearly simultaneous development of the phonograph and radio had made possible the broadcast of American popular music worldwide, German com-poser Kurt Weill, collaborator with Bertolt Brecht on *The Threepenny Opera,* wrote: "The rhythm of our time is jazz. In it the slow but sure Americanisation of all our physical life finds its most notable manifestation. The shimmy outweighs everything else."[3] But as everyone knows (or ought to know), commercialized jazz itself was produced only by deep borrowing from vast cultural reserves belonging to others. On a microcosmic scale, but with similar procedures, the Theatre Guild billed *Green Grow the Lilacs* as a "regional folk drama" and brought in real working cowboys from a visiting rodeo to lend authenticity to the New York cast as "Others of the Countryside." From this generous loan, drawn from local folkways and passing through many hands, ultimately came the definitive Broadway musical: *Oklahoma!* realized huge returns, not only in the obvious way, for its investors, but also for the genre of musical theater as a global attraction. In connection with this transfer of American cultural capital, originating in the exchange between Lynn Riggs and Rodgers and Hammerstein, I will be considering two Australian performance texts, *Bran Nue Dae* by Jimmy Chi and Kuckles, known widely as "the first Aboriginal musical," which premiered in 1990, and *Ningali*, a solo performance piece by Josie Ningali Lawford, one of the original cast members of *Bran Nue Dae*. The concatenation of these texts and performances offers an occasion to reveal the open but unremarked transactions of world-bank drama, which continue to grow between retail centers and the deep reserves of local cultures, especially indigenous and hence "authentic" ones, under the aegis of modern global institutions.

While the subject is indebtedness, I must acknowledge mine to the phrase coined by Amitava Kumar in *World Bank Literature*.[4] This anthology probes the place of culture in the global marketplace, centered metaphorically and to some extent materially on the policies and practices of the World Bank and its affiliates. The authors who appear in Kumar's collection—literary theorists, cultural critics, and economists—imagine their subject in a number of registers: as either adversarial critique or superstructural product of the unholy trinity of globalization—the World Bank, the International Monetary Fund, and the World Trade Organization; alternatively, they imagine World Bank Literature as the experiential link between the people living in the global system shaped by these institutions, including "nomadic," displaced postcolonial subjects of many points of origin and "freeway flyers," the adjunct writing teachers of the contemporary North American academy. Some of Kumar's contributors imagine World Bank Lit as the discourse of the World Bank itself, a growing mass of published reports and white papers that would seem to them to qualify as creative writing; while others, more appetizingly, imagine it as a syllabus of literary works from contemporary writers, especially those from the Subcontinent and Latin America, who take up the local social costs of global economic decisions—Arundhati Roy's *The God of Small Things*, Amit Chaudhuri's *A New World*, Bharati Mukherjee's *Darkness* or *Jasmine*; detective fiction on the U.S.-Mexican border; the "Zapatistas' Storybook." The diverse essays are joined together by a common skepticism about the World Bank's stated mission, which is, according to its Web site at worldbank.org, "to fight poverty and improve living standards for people in the developing world."

In order to go from world-bank literature to world-bank drama, the most obvious move would be simply to expand the syllabus to embrace this most neglected genre. In service of that expansion, one could propose some likely offerings from the growing and increasingly interesting repertoire of postcolonial theatre. Let Manjula Padmanabhan's *Harvest*, winner of the inaugural Onassis Prize for Drama in 1997, serve as one instance among many. A dystopic fantasy set in the year 2010, *Harvest* dramatizes the predatory operations of the World Bank by means of a mordant allegory. Third World families, in return for a guarantee of decent housing, food, and health care (for as long as they live), contract with corporate middlemen to pool their organs for donation to First World recipients, those who can afford to extend their lives indefinitely by means of a well-stocked world bank of spare parts, calling in their investments when the need arises; hence: "harvest." Setting the scene, an early stage direction reads: "For the sake of coherence, this play is set in Bombay, the DONORS are Indian and the RECEIVERS, North American. Ideally, however, the DONORS and RECEIVERS should take on the racial identities, names, costumes, and accents most suited to the location of the production."[5] Of the innovative immigration patterns imposed by these transactions between donor and recipient peoples—those who are (bad luck) merely "developing" and those who are very well developed indeed—one donor says nostalgically to another, "No one goes abroad these days"; to which complaint his sardonic interlocutor replies: "Not whole people, anyway!"[6] This adds a new twist to the well-known phenomenon of "the brain drain," but the communication between the intimate strangers from poles apart is not only one-way. In each Donor's home, technicians install a "Contact Module." Through this two-way camera-eye the Recipients can monitor the health and hygiene of their investments via satellite; and, if they choose, beam down cyber-enhanced effigies of themselves, speaking with American accents in what the stage directions call "a youthful, glamorous First World manner," to inspire the patient bearers of their future kidneys and corneas to greater efforts toward health and general well-being. Even if only as urban legend, such a cannibalistic nightmare chillingly recalls a platitude on the World Bank Web site, meant to reassure: "The Bank believes that people who live in poverty should not be treated as a liability, but as a resource" (worldbank.org).

What kind of bank is this? What kind of world?

As unsettling as the answer to these questions posed by *Harvest* must be, world-bank drama suggests something else, perhaps equally sinister, perhaps less so. The world bank of drama is a loosely organized network of transnational performances that overlap and invest one another or, more precisely, invest *in* one another. These performances intertwine with the global economy, assigning values asymmetrically but reciprocally between and among their constituents. They may be observed most clearly in transactions of cultural capital between the First World and so-called First Peoples, the long-term indigenous inhabitants of particular regions or environments. With tenure that precedes the nation-state, the colony, the empire, autochthons have priority in claiming a particular place on the face of the earth, in contrast to the tenuousness that is the condition of "postmodern feudalism."[7] Let postmodern feudalism be defined as the reappearance in the contemporary world of power that is fragmented into a patchwork of duchies and fiefdoms as in feudal Europe, multinational corporate entities, organized as vertical hierarchies, kept secure against regulation by the weakness of central authority as in medieval times, but no longer attached to any one place on the land as a locus of wealth and prestige. Jack Welch, former chief executive officer of General Electric, said this about the most efficacious setup for modern manufacture: "Ideally, you'd have every plant you own on a barge";[8] that is, always easily towable to the source of the cheapest labor and least intrusive environmental law. Such mobility is no doubt good for the bottom line at multinational corporations, but it leaves something of a shortfall in the area of authenticating narratives and local color, likely to be a strong suit of First Peoples anywhere.

There is, I hypothesize, a peculiar algebra involved in the financial performances of the World Bank, on the one hand, with its mind-numbing abstraction of value into blips on computer screens, transferred at the speed of light, and on the other, the world's perceived accumulation of cultural capital, categorized under the portmanteau term *heritage*, which is also increasingly treated as an intangible but "bankable" abstraction, global in scope but most readily authenticated only in local, preferably indigenous detail. Barbara Kirshenblatt-Gimblett defines the paradox of global abstraction and local cultural specificity in "World Heritage and Cultural Economics." She writes: "World heritage is a vehicle for envisioning and constituting a global polity within the conceptual space of a global cultural commons. The asymmetry between the *diversity* of those who produce cultural assets in the first place and the *humanity* to which those assets come to belong as world heritage gives to this commons its paradoxical character."[9] The vehicle of which Kirshenblatt-Gimblett speaks can be seen most clearly in the recent initiative at UNESCO, supported in part by the World Bank, called "Intangible Heritage." This is the logical development of two previous UNESCO policy initiatives in World Heritage, and the three of them together might be imagined as the World Bank of culture. The premise of all three is that certain local sources of value belong to the common heritage of all humankind; its corollary is that these sources should be commonly identified, protected, and shared. But such a universal resource must be located and validated in the practices and traditions of a "folk," most desirably an indigenous one. Their culture is potentially everyone's heritage—whether they like it or not.

Toward the end of securing the assets of a world bank of culture, the earliest UNESCO initiative was "Tangible Heritage," encompassing monuments and sites of world-historic significance, from Angkor Wat in Cambodia to Robbin Island in South Africa, where Nelson Mandela was imprisoned. The second was "Natural Heritage," seeking to protect natural sites, habitats, or ecological systems of special beauty or importance, from the Central Amazon Conservation Complex to the Grand Canyon. The third, and the one most pertinent to performance, is "Intangible Heritage." The UNESCO Web site at unesco.org/culture/heritage/intangible begins with an apology and a play for sympathy: "It is not easy to map out the boundaries of what is called the cultural heritage of humanity." It goes on to define the scope of Intangible Heritage "as embracing all forms of traditional and popular or folk culture, [that is] collective works originating in a given community and based on tradition. These creations are transmitted orally or by gesture, and are modified over a period of time through a process of collective recreation. They include oral traditions, customs, languages, music, dance, rituals, festivities, traditional medicine and pharmacopoeia, the culinary arts and all kinds of special skills connected with the material aspects of culture, such as tools and the habitat." UNESCO here defines Intangible Heritage very broadly as performance: a conscious repetition and occasional revision of previous collective behaviors, as in formal or improvised public events such as carnival, and precise enactments of scripted scenarios, as in theatrical representation or obligatory ritual. Performance implies a certain level of shared expectation about the way in which the participants will behave, even if that expectation is for free-wheeling spontaneity, predisposing them to special efforts in the ways in which they will make use of the time and place of the event. This prior disposition rests on fundamental assumptions about the assignment of roles and the conduct appropriate to their execution. Such a broad conception opens up an all but limitless range of activities that might qualify as heritage, so UNESCO must propose some additional principles of selection to validate deposits in the world drama bank.

Currently, the three major categories in which traditions are to be identified and prioritized for "urgent" preservation efforts are: (1) "Masterpieces of Oral and Intangible Heritage of Humanity," which contemplates particular masterworks (something of a contradiction, it might seem, of the ecologically minded conceptual premise of "collective works originating in a community"); (2) "Living National Treasures," a global appropriation of the enlightened policy of the Japanese government since the 1950s of identifying and honoring supremely accomplished individual artists and master teachers, especially of the traditional forms of theater; and (3) "Endangered Languages." Having set these parameters, the narrative of Intangible Heritage continues by asking, "What for, and for whom?" and answering: "For many populations (especially minority groups and indigenous populations), the intangible heritage is the vital source of an identity that is deeply rooted in history. The philosophy, values, moral code and ways of thinking transmitted by oral traditions, languages and the various forms taken by its culture constitute the foundation of a community's life. The essentially ephemeral nature of this intangible heritage makes it highly vulnerable. It is urgent to take action!" Here the emphasis falls on the value concentrated in the local and the indigenous—"diversity" in Kirshenblatt-Gimblett's sense—but the context of the global imperative of universal heritage suggests that the ultimate interests at stake are those of "humanity." "What for, and for whom?" is a question that dogs the world bank of culture as it does the World Bank itself, and it is here that the algebra of abstract borrowing between the two systems of intangible resources—those of world capital and those of world heritage—must be viewed not only on the global scale, with loans transacted willy-nilly between the First World and First Peoples, but also in the particularities of actual performance at specific sites where authenticity and value are created.

Bran Nue Dae by Jimmy Chi and Kuckles premiered in the Octagon Theatre in Perth, Australia, in 1990. It is celebrated in recent Australian theatrical history as "the first Aboriginal musical."[10] Chi hails from the isolated town of Broome, where he performed during the 1980s with his rock band Kuckles, mixing rhythm and blues, calypso, reggae, country and western, and indigenous musical sounds. Subtitled "a musical journey," *Bran Nue Dae* depicts the comic pilgrimage of the Aboriginal and hybrid characters from the urban hub of Perth back to Broome, evoking a variety of sites and landscapes along the way. In this sense, it takes the form of the peripatetic Aboriginal song-cycle, in popular association a "walkabout," a sacred journey through the outback along a track where the topography is charged with deep meaning, expressive of the relationship of the people to the land. The people are not owners in the Western sense of property holders, but spiritual sharers, those who are too often misidentified as "nomads" because, laying claim to no one place as belonging to them, they belong to the whole place. The tone of the show is lighthearted and celebratory, but it also contains pointed lyrics protesting two hundred years of genocidal displacement. The Aboriginal and mixed-race chorus sings: "There's nothing I would rather be / than to be an Aborigine / and watch you take my precious land away! Ohhhhhh no."[11]

As evidence of the show's ritual efficacy for at least one of its performers, we have the autobiographical testimony of Josie Ningali Lawford, an original cast member of *Bran Nue Dae*. In her solo performance piece *Ningali*, written in collaboration with Angela Chapin and Robyn Archer, Lawford narrates her life's journey, the climactic scene of which concerns her casting in *Bran Nue Dae*. Raised on Wankatjunka station (or reservation) near Fitzroy Crossing in the Australian outback, "Ningali" builds her identity around the land of her childhood: "The station was good, I had the best time, I suppose the land I knew was only little because I was only little. But it felt endless, there were no fences, we could go wherever we wanted. I knew all that big country of my people, our dreaming was all over the land."[12] Her indigenous worldview is at once transformed and affirmed by the great event of her early teens, her winning of a scholarship to study in the United States. She had applied to go to "Hollywood" but inexplicably (at least it is not explained in *Ningali*) she ends up being sent to Anchorage, Alaska. There she discovers, in a reversal of the oft-cited example of the copiousness of the Eskimo lexicon relating to snow, that Wambajarri speakers have no words at all for ice. But her true epiphany comes about through another kind of discovery. Placed in the Native American club at East Anchorage High School, she comes to know her Inuit peers and to learn about their culture in relationship to her own: "I hadn't realized things on the station, I hadn't realized how Mum and Dad were just slave labor, hadn't realized that our stuff was beautiful, and important like Inuit things."[13] This borrowed affirmation of her First Person identity dramatically prepares for the climactic scene of *Ningali*, her performance in the original cast of *Bran Nue Day*. She sings a medley, going out on the stirringly optimistic title number, which envisions a utopian future for the First Peoples of Australia and the world: "On the way to a Bran Nue Day / Everybody everybody say / On the way to a Bran Nue Day / Everybody everybody say."[14]

From Lawford's perspective, then, the indigenousness of *Bran Nue Dae* outweighs its other possible derivations and heightens its claims to "diversity" as one of the preconditions of intangible heritage to be deposited in the world bank of culture. But with its alternation of spoken dialogue and sung and danced musical numbers, with its book featuring three intertwined romance plots (Willie partners Rosie/Tadpole partners Theresa/Slippery partners Marijuana Annie), with its structure of character-building and plot-driving production numbers for soloists, ensembles, and chorus, with its superabundance of feel-good razzle-dazzle to salve the threats raised by its own dramatic conflicts, and with its huge box office and long run (it was the hottest ticket among white audiences in Perth, Sydney, and Melbourne from 1990 to 1993), *Bran Nue Dae* looked and sounded an awful lot like American musical comedy. This indebtedness concerns Chi's postcolonial critics, one of whom rationalizes: "The construction of an Aboriginal musical would seem deliberately to appropriate the most Westernised and commercialised of theatre forms—the Broadway production—for oppositional ends: to make a political protest while broadly appealing to the popular imagination."[15] The question of who is appropriating what from whom is at the heart of the debt restructuring performed by world-bank drama.

The Broadway production from which *Bran Nue Day* most clearly borrows is *Oklahoma!* by Rodgers and Hammerstein. The debt is evident not only the triple pairing of the love plot at the final curtain (Curly partners Laurey, Will Parker partners Aido Annie, and Ali Hakim, the "Persian Peddler," partners the ugliest girl at the box-lunch social), but in specific verbal echoes as well, such as Laurey's "Many a New Day" and the expansive claim of identity and entitlement, forecast throughout the musical but saved for the rousing chorus of the title number: "We know we belong to the land, / And the land we belong to is grand."[16] After opening at the Shubert Theatre in New Haven for tryouts as *Away We Go*, the show found its title (with exclamation point) and its final structure in Boston before opening on Broadway on March 31, 1943. The story of the genesis of the title song is suggestive in the present context. Riding home dejected in a taxi after an unsuccessful sing-through for potential backers who didn't show any interest, one of the Theatre Guild producers, Theresa Helburn, suggested offhandedly to Hammerstein, "I wish you and Dick would write a song about the earth." Puzzled, Hammerstein asked, "What do you mean, Terry?" She elaborated only slightly but decisively, "Oh, I don't know, just a song about the earth—the land."[17] The title song first appeared in New Haven as a tap dance specialty number. In Boston it became a solo for Curly. Neither worked. Then one of the chorus girls, whose name was Faye Elizabeth Smith, entered into the annals of theatrical history when she suggested rearranging "Oklahoma" in harmony for the full ensemble of principals and chorus.[18] This spot-on play-doctor's insight resulted in the concussive showstopping number around which the plot and thematic material coalesce, hallowing the land and the people of one state as synecdoche for all the United States. It became a hymn of reassurance during wartime: "You're doin' fine, Oklahoma! / Oklahoma, O.K."[19] Famed as the breakthrough production of a new kind of musical theater in which a strong book unifies tunes, lyrics, and dance components into a compelling dramatic narrative, *Oklahoma!* might be cited as a "masterpiece of intangible heritage," if that designation is understood to encompass a unique interlocking system of performance skills—not solely singing, dancing, and acting (or writing, directing, and designing)—but all of those together, not subordinated to music as in opera, but coordinated as an integrated ensemble of autonomous elements. No one can possibly write down all the things you need to know to do this well, even in the job description for a humble chorus girl. In the words of the UNESCO Web site: "These creations are transmitted orally or by gesture, and are modified over a period of time by collective recreation." This is no doubt part of what Jimmy Chi and Kuckles found in American musical theater that seemed worth borrowing, but in the case of *Green Grow the Lilacs* and *Oklahoma!* there is another dimension to the hidden balance sheet between cultural heritage and the culture industry.

UNESCO policies show a predilection for the intangible heritage of "indigenous populations." That question would seem to be perversely set aside by Hammerstein's book for *Oklahoma!* Set in the decade after Frederick Jackson Turner's enunciation of the "frontier hypothesis" and just before statehood for the eponymous territory, the show makes no mention of the prior history of Oklahoma. That would have had necessarily included its role as the terminus for the genocidal Trail of Tears of the Five Civilized Tribes—Cherokee, Chickasaw, Choctaw, Creek, and Seminole—and its preservation as Indian Territory until the Dawes Commission of 1893 compelled the survivors to substitute individual for tribal land ownership. The reader or audience would never know that from the book of the musical. But Hammerstein was personally more generous in acknowledging the author who wrote the original stage play from which the book is borrowed—scene for scene, character for character, and even line for line. The title page for the first edition of *Oklahoma!* reads: "A musical Play by Richard Rodgers and Oscar Hammerstein, 2nd based on Lynn Riggs' *Green Grow the Lilacs*." Hammerstein later confessed, "Mr. Riggs' play is the well-spring of almost all that is good in *Oklahoma!*"[20] The silence of the libretto on the history of the territory it depicts is all the more imposing in view of Riggs's personal history. Rollie Lynn Riggs (1899–1954), a Cherokee descendant of the Trail of Tears on his mother's side, was entitled his portion of tribal land under the Dawes Allotment act of 1887, as amended in 1893.[21] This was his tangible heritage—not just the land he belonged to, but the land that belonged to him. Unlike *Oklahoma! Green Grow the Lilacs* acknowledges (though it does not foreground) the tortured issue of "land" for Native Americans and the ambivalence toward approaching statehood in the context of mixed racial identities and tensions. Asked to accept as sovereign the authority of the U.S. marshall over the lives of "Territory Folk," one character exclaims, "No! My papy and mammy was *both* borned in Indian Territory! Why I'm jist plumb full of Indian blood myself." To which another adds proudly, "Me, too! An I c'n prove it." Aunt Eller, the sympathetic matriarch of the play, puts the sentiment forthrightly: "What's the United States? It's jist a furrin country to me" (161).

In the algebra of borrowing from world heritage, tangible and intangible, Hammerstein cancels out the Indians and abstracts the "Territory folks'" identification with the land, which is a powerful part of *Green Grow the Lilacs*, into a pastoral idyll of Oklahoma as synecdoche for the United States as a whole. In doing that, he substitutes for interracial antagonism and the specter of miscegenation the ersatz competition of "The Farmer and the Cowman" for the prize: "The farmer and the cowman should be friends, / Oh, the farmer and the cowman should be friends. / One man likes to push a plow, / The other likes to chase a cow, / But that's no reason why they cain't be friends. Territory folks should stick together, / Territory folks should all be pals, / Cowboys, dance with the farmers' daughters! / Farmers, dance with the ranchers' gals!"[22] In such a homogenized dramatization of ethnic conflict, "humanity" can readily find its own abstracted image, while "diversity" recedes as the authenticating footnote. Riggs, by contrast, lets the genius of the place speak for itself quietly but eloquently through bits of local color, such as Laurey's incidental archaeological report on a mound that marked the attack of Osage on Cherokee: "In Verdigree bottom the other day, a man found thirty-tree arrow heads—thirty-three—whur they'd been a Indian battle" (33).

If Riggs was unhappy with the fate of his play, he never said so: the residuals gave him an income for the rest of his career, which was already assimilated into the American literary and theatrical avant-garde. *Green Grow the Lilacs* was written, not in sight of Oklahoma's "bright golden haze on the meadow," so tenderly evoked by the opening lines of the play and the musical, but in Paris on a grant from the Guggenheim Foundation, where Riggs occupied a table in the same café where Ernest Hemingway wrote *The Sun Also Rises*. He did work on and off for many years on *Cherokee Night*, a play he hoped would cover "the entire field of Indian-White relationships in one dramatic incident, not a protest—but a triumphant comprehension."[23] Although Aaron Copland considered turning it into an opera, *Cherokee Night* never made it to Broadway. The more successful *Green Grow the Lilacs* aligned itself with a well-articulated movement in the American drama of the 1930s. Featuring customs, dialects, legends, and myths from around the country, folk plays celebrated ethnicities, regions, and localities. Their performance entailed the ethnomusicological recovery of songs, such as the ones Riggs collected from the "folk" of his native Oklahoma, to drive home the emotion at each dramatic turn. This includes the title song, "Green Grow the Lilacs," in which Curly laments his apparent loss of Laurey to the half-breed Jeeter Fry (Jud in the musical). Curly vows to demonstrate the depth of his love by joining the U.S. Army, "to change the green lilacs to the red, white, and blue." Brooks Atkinson, writing in the commemorative edition of *Green Grow the Lilacs* in 1954, illustrated by Thomas Hart Benton, reflected on the absorption of the folk play by "plays of universal significance" (namely those by Tennessee Williams and Arthur Miller) after World War Two.[24] In the case of *Oklahoma!* however, the absorption was more in the nature of a bank loan, the success of which retrospectively bestows an aura of authenticity on the original, the true "folk play." The authentic in this sense is that which has not yet been borrowed. The authentic in this sense is the apparent touchstone of heritage, its gold standard, as land once was, and that is why brokers like Jimmy Chi, an exile in his own land, are likely to be called upon to carry out the transactions of world-bank drama by mediating between the performances cherished by their people and the performances underwritten by paying subscribers.

World-bank drama is a metaphor, but it is not only that. The expansion of travel and tourism into the largest single source of jobs in the global economy has fueled a boom called "the heritage industry." The World Bank sees its promise and invests in its future. Sites such as the West African slave forts or the Galapagos Islands nature reserve have become very hot tickets for world tourists. Aboriginal painting is now a hugely successful attraction in Sydney galleries and at Sotheby's, which has recently added a department specializing in native Australian work. Unlike tangible monuments and ecosystems, however, which are fragile, the works of intangible heritage are (paradoxically) sustainable, renewable. The temple site or the tropical waterfall may be irreversibly degraded by overuse, but the corn feast comes back every year as picturesque as ever. The American musical is itself a successful destination, created to sustain long runs by appealing to tourists above and beyond the local New York City theatergoers. After 9/11 the musical theater was vital to the reconstruction of the Manhattan economy. As world-bank drama, why wouldn't it be?

Performance is the perfect commodity under conditions of postmodern feudalism: it disappears entirely at each iteration, leaving behind only a desire for more, which is the motive for its perpetual return. It dramatizes its intangibility and hence its authenticating value as heritage. As Dean MacCannell puts it in *The Tourist*: "Increasingly, pure experience, which leaves no material trace, is manufactured and sold like a commodity."[25] In *Bran Nue Dae*, Slippery and Marijuana Annie are German tourists arriving in Australia, where they seek spiritual renewal through contact with First Peoples and purer cannabis sativa. The Aborigines humorously decide to oblige them by improvising a "traditional lizard hunt" complete with loincloths and spears, every ritual element of which, except for passing around the joint, is a first-time experience for performers and spectators alike. First Peoples stage themselves ironically for visitors from the First World in search of "heritage." Looking for a loan, the visitors seek a source of regeneration for their own failing cultural economies.

Under postmodern feudalism, intangible heritage replaces the land as the principal touchstone of value, but only so that it can be turned into "gold." First peoples are so rich in heritage, who needs land? The State of Connecticut has an answer for the Mashantucket-Pequot tribe of Native Americans: as much land as is needed to accommodate the footprint of the world's largest casino, with just enough left over for a heritage museum. To get a loan from the World Bank, the borrowers need put up not their organs as collateral, but their authenticity. At the same time, however, they can hope for a substantial return in the form of gaming revenues and heritage tours. Some have done very well indeed. The refrain of the chorus in "Oklahoma"—"We belong to the land, and the land we belong to is grand"—echoes ironically as one flies across the United States over the Middle West and the Great Plains and beholds, as far as the eye can see, the land atomized by the work of rotary-irrigated agribusiness, the appanage of postmodern feudalism. North America, the largest, most rapidly constructed artifact in history, cleared of what Riggs evokes in his Edenic description of "the kind of morning which, enveloping the shapes of the earth—men, cattle in a meadow, blades of corn, streams— makes them seem to exist now for the first time," is succeeding in its quest "to change the green lilacs to the red, white, and blue."

NOTES

1. Lynn Riggs, *Green Grow the Lilacs, A Play* (New York: Samuel French, 1931), 3. Subsequent references to this edition parenthetical.

2. Max Horkheimer and Theodor Adorno, "The Culture Industry: Enlightenment as Mass Deception," in *Dialectic of Enlightenment*, trans. John Cumming (New York: Continuum, 1997), 120–67.

3. Kurt Weill, "Dancemusic: Jazz" (1926), quoted in Douglas Jarman, *Kurt Weill* (Bloomington: Indiana University Press, 1982), 108–9.

4. Amitava Kumar, *World Bank Literature* (Minneapolis: University of Minnesota Press, 2002).

5. Manjula Padmanabhan, *Harvest*, in *Postcolonial Plays*, ed. Helen Gilbert (London: Routledge, 2001), 217.

6. Ibid., 223.

7. The phrase is Richard Schechner's, coined in a personal conversation, November 4, 2003.

8. Jack Welch, quoted in Andrew Ross, "The Uneven Development of Tactics," in Kumar, *World Bank Literature*, 99.

9. Barbara Kirshenblatt-Gimblett, "World Heritage and Cultural Economics," forthcoming in *Museum Frictions: Public Cultures/Global Transformations* (in press).

10. Jimmy Chi and Kuckles, *Bran Nue Dae*, in Gilbert, *Postcolonial Plays*, 320–21.

11. Ibid., 344.

12. Josie Ningali Lawford, Angela Chapin, and Robyn Archer, *Ningali* (unpublished performance script), 4. See Helena Grehan, *Mapping Cultural Identity in Contemporary Australian Performance* (Bruxelles: Peter Lang, 2001), passim. I am grateful to Professor Grehan for kindly providing me with the script for *Ningali*.

13. Ibid., 15.

14. Ibid., 22.

15. Helen Gilbert, introduction to *Bran Nue Dae*, in *Postcolonial Plays*, 320.

16. Richard Rodgers and Oscar Hammerstein II, *Oklahoma! A Musical Play based on Lynn Riggs' "Green Grow the Lilacs"* (New York: Random House, 1943), 132. See Andrea Most, " 'We Know We Belong to the Land': The Theatricality of Assimilation in Rodgers and Hammerstein's *Oklahoma!*" *PMLA* 112 (1998): 77–89.

17. Quoted in Hugh Fordin, *Getting to Know Him: A Biography of Oscar Hammerstein II* (New York: Random House, 1977), 197.

18. Max Wilk, *OK! The Story of Oklahoma!* (New York: Applause, 2002), 200–203.

19. Rodgers and Hammerstein, *Oklahoma!* 132.

20. Quoted in Brooks Atkinson, introduction to the commemorative edition of *Green Grow the Lilacs* (Norman: University of Oklahoma Press, 1954), viii.

21. Phyllis Cole Braunlich, *Haunted by Home: The Life and Letters of Lynn Riggs* (Norman: University of Oklahoma Press, 1988), 23–24.

22. Rodgers and Hammerstein, *Oklahoma!*, 85.

23. Quoted in Braunlich, *Haunted by Home*, 95.

24. Atkinson, introduction, x.

25. Dean MacCannell, *The Tourist: A New Theory of the Leisure Class* (reprint, New York: Shocken Books, 1989), 21.

CHAPTER 7

Global Minoritarian Culture

Homi K. Bhabha

> The problem of a minority group in a world torn by old and
> new national and racial division was of enormous difficulty: it
> was idle for us simply to repeat the old slogans of democracy in
> an oligarchic world; no matter how strongly we, with all forward-
> looking thinkers, might envisage a birth of democracy . . . amid
> turmoil and contradiction, beclouded by a thousand irrelevances
> and bedeviled by every art of selfishness, but nevertheless clearly
> in progress. My problem was—How can American Negroes join
> this movement and intelligently reenforce it, for their own good
> and the good of all men.
> —W.E.B. Du Bois, A *Pageant in Seven Decades:*
> *1868–1938* (1938)

W.E.B. Du Bois's Bollywood-style bildungsroman, *Dark Princess* (1928), presents a strange juxtaposition of the race-man Matthew Towns, figure of forbearance, and his revolutionary leader and lover, Kautilya, the Dark Princess
of the Tibetan Kingdom of Bwodpur, "Princess of the wide, wide world." The
race-man struggles with beauty and death in the treacherous folds of the Veil
of the color-line where "the Doer never sees the Deed and the Victim knows
not the Victor"; the high-caste Hindu princess imperiously commands a pa-
trician posse of cosmopolitan modernists with Bolshevist leanings, banded
together in an antiimperialist Council of Darker Peoples. In this odd coupling, the celebrated "two-ness" of "double-consciousness"—an American
and a Negro—seems to lose its predominantly national mooring; and
strangely beside, *abseits*, there opens up a form of global thirdness, embodied
in the histrionic, even hysterical, diva, Kautilya, who emerges on the American scene with all the Sturm und Drang of the Du Boisian persona now
culturally cross-dressed in silks, turbans, and sarees. This allegorical configuration of characters, countries, and commitments prefigures a method of representing the particularity of racial antagonism and ambivalence that Du
Bois was to frame as the rule of "juxtaposition" in the later elegiac encounters
of *Darkwater* (1920): racial conflicts, striated selves, barriers between bodies
and spaces—these signatures of segregation and separation also enforce an
ethical proximity and a political contiguity in between social and cultural

differences. The rule of juxtaposition represents what is intolerable in the "local" lifeworld of racial injustice and inequality; and yet, by juxtaposing it with "extraterritorial" symbolic and social orders—Nature's sublimity, transnational transitions, and aesthetic transcriptions—the authority and transparency of the domestic norms of discrimination and despair are displaced, their mimetic measure over-shadowed.[1]

> Here, then, is beauty and ugliness, a wide vision of world-sacrifice, a fierce gleam of world-hate. Which is life and what is death and how shall we face so tantalizing a contradiction? Any explanation must necessarily be subtle and involved. No pert and easy word of encouragement, no merely dark despair, can lay hold of the roots of these things. . . . There is not in the world a more disgraceful denial of human brotherhood than the "Jim-Crow" car of the southern United States; but, too, just as true, there is nothing more beautiful in the universe than sunset and moonlight on Montego Bay in far Jamaica. And both things are true and both belong to this our world, and neither can be denied.[2]

These juxtaposed scenes of a double truth—at times incommensurable, at others, almost unbearable—cannot be transcended or rendered whole. Their contradictory mode of coexistence—be it aesthetic or ethical—requires us to acknowledge the importance of the "counterfactual" in the realm of political discourse and the desire for freedom. "And both things are true and both belong to this our world, and neither can be denied" is a statement neither of passivity nor of quietism. To make an imaginative appeal to freedom through counterfactual choice—the freedom from humiliation, suffering, racism—cannot be dismissed as mere rhetoric. Such a counterfactual rhetoric "of freedom as an effective power to achieve what one would choose," as Amartya Sen writes in *Inequality Reexamined*, is an essential value of the language and idea of freedom. "The role of counterfactual choice becomes relevant—indeed central . . . in . . . being able to live as one would value, desire and choose, is a contribution to one's freedom [and agency] and not just to one's well-being or achievement, though it is also that."[3]

Du Bois's concept of the "American" gift of "second-sight," from which the aesthetic "rule of juxtaposition" emerges, reaches beyond its immediate ontological or existential concerns and moves toward an ethical-political project. Stanley Cavell's fine essay on *King Lear* yields a useful insight into the trope of double-consciousness as ethical agency. Doubling as the rule of juxtaposition "taunts the characters with their lack of wholeness, their separation from themselves, by loss or denial or opposition. . . . But in either way, either by putting freedom or by putting integrity into question, doubling sets a task, of discovery, of acknowledgement."[4]

What, then, is the task of discovery narrated in *Dark Princess*? Princess Kautilya describes the common mission of the anticolonial confederation in terms familiar to any reader of Du Bois. Their goal, she says, is [the recognition of] democracy as a method of discovering real aristocracy. We looked frankly forward to raising not all the dead, sluggish, brutalized masses of men, but discovering among them genius, gift, and ability in far larger number than among the privileged and the ruling classes. Search, weed out, encourage; educate, train, and open all doors! Democracy is not an end; it is a method of aristocracy. (225)

An aesthetic education for democracy lies at the very heart of Du Bois's theory of the Talented Tenth and derives its aspirational activism from the art and ethic of forbearance. "Entbehren sollst du, sollst entbehren" (Forbear you must, you must forbear), Du Bois echoes Goethe's *Faust* (part 1) in "Of the Wings of Atalanta," where he defines his aims of education against what he describes as the "scattered," "haphazard" educational practices of Booker T. Washington and others.[5] Democracy as a method of seeking the aristocracy of talent is a phrase that resonates suggestively with the Deweyan influence on Du Bois as well as with the Hind Swaraj and Arya Samaj movements for Indian independence, both mentioned in *Dark Princess*. Du Bois's Indian friend Lala Lajpat Rai, one of the founders of the Arya Samaj movement, believed that colonized Indians had to be prepared for political independence by being educated in the best traditions of classical Hindu thought and culture.

Following this line of transnational inquiry might also yield an intriguing historical lead to a shadowy figure who, I believe, might have provided Du Bois with a model for the passionate Kautilya. Far be it from me to dispel the dream of faery shared by critics from Herbert Aptheker to Arnold Rampersad who have endorsed Mary White Ovington's account of her sighting of the dark lady:

I think I saw the dark Indian Princess in 1911 as she came down the steps of the ballroom at the last meeting of the First Universal Races Congress in London. By the Princess's side was one of the most distinguished men at the Conference, Burghardt Du Bois. They were talking earnestly of the race problem. Did this Indian Princess remain in the American Negro's memory to become the Titania of his midsummer night's dream?[6]

My recent researches, however, have turned up another, more plausible, source for the lingering memory of the Indian princess in the mind and art of the Black Savant. In 1907 Du Bois took a summer sojourn in England and Europe, cycling through the Lake District and being entertained by the liberal, even radical, members of the European upper classes. In these weeks of respite from the lacerating color-line of America, Du Bois abandoned himself to a Europe "of past beauty and present culture, fit as [he] fondly dreamed to realize a democracy in which [he] and [his] people could find a welcome place."[7] Had he, perchance, heard tell that very summer of a diasporic Indian revolutionary, daughter of a well-to-do Parsi family from Bombay, Madame Bhikaji Cama, who had lived in exile in Europe since 1902, finally settling in a small pension in Paris? Madame Cama was a fervent and fearless radical in the cause of

Indian independence, but one who saw the horizon of freedom stopping at no national border or regional boundary. She was, beyond her Indian interests, the inspiring leader of a group of Asian revolutionary anticolonialists who had gathered in Europe. In August 1907, while Du Bois was in Europe, Madame Cama attended the International Socialist Congress in Stuttgart, where she famously unfurled the Indian national flag with its middle band bearing "emblems to represent the Hindus, Mohammedans, Budhists [sic] and Parsis"[8]— emblems that echo the passage in which Du Bois's Princess Kautilya gathers the many peoples of India, Africa, and the Americas around the symbol of the rice dish:

> "I and my Buddhist priest, a Mohammedan Mullah, and a Hindu leader of Swaraj, were India. . . . We came in every guise, at my command when around the world I sent the symbol of the rice dish; we came as laborers, as cotton pickers, as peddlers, as fortune tellers, as travelers and tourists. . . . The Day has dawned, Matthew—the Great Plan is on its way." (297–98)

Madame Cama spoke out against the "slavery of the fifth of the whole of the human race. . . . The perfect social state demands that no people should be subject to any despotic or tyrannical forms of Government." The Leipziger Zeitung commented on the rousing impact of Madame Cama (Mrs. Kramas) on the gathered delegates: dressed in shimmering silken garments, she "displayed a silken tricolour, the banner of the oppressed, then the cheers of the International would not end." Later that very summer, on September 21, 1907, a group of antiimperialist revolutionaries, Indians and Egyptians prominent amongst them, held a soiree at the Hotel Palais on the Champs Elysées. Madame Cama, the dark princess no less, was the centerpiece of this gathering.[9] Was this figure of romance and revolution the inspiration for Dark Princess? Had Du Bois read of Madame Cama as he was traveling in Europe in the summer of 1907, turning frequently to German newspapers as was his wont when in Europe? Or was Madame Cama mentioned to him by her comrade and compatriot, Du Bois's faithful friend, Lala Lajpat Rai, to whom he sent the manuscript of Dark Princess for comment and advice?

Having fled to Berlin to take refuge from segregation in America, Du Bois's protagonist Matthew Towns falls in with a group of Third World aristocrats who have formed themselves into an antiimperialist Council of Darker Peoples. At a soiree in a Berlin hotel suite, presided over by the Princess of Bwodpur, Towns is enraptured by the modernist, cosmopolitan knowledge of these pan-Asian and North African leaders. His mind turned by their conversational fluency and savoir faire—Kandinsky with the canapés and Schönberg with socialism—Towns is persuaded that he is, at last, in the emancipatory embrace of the finest flower of the antiracist representatives of the Culture Societies (as Du Bois called the "old world" in the early 1900s). To the gathered revolutionaries, however, Towns is quite literally a bête noire; his blood, his low caste, and his African American origin are all anathema to their foundational belief in the "natural aristocracy" of blood and talent. The Japanese member speaks for the group when he states, "For us here and for the larger company we represent, there is a deeper question—that of the ability, qualifications, and real possibilities of the black race in Africa and elsewhere." The genealogy of such a discourse of natural aristocracy ("Superior races—the right to rule—born to command—inferior breeds—the lower classes—the rabble," to quote the book) is itself a rich mélange of the imperial racial imaginary (25, 21, 24). Elements of Edward Augustus Freeman's mid-Victorian version of the Teutonic myth of "the community of blood" are mixed with a late-nineteenth-century "anthropocentric" theme of the backward and advanced races, all of it staged on the Roman imperial model turned into baroque kitsch that rationalized the imperial despotism of the late Victorian Raj.[10]

The princess protests at the emergent color-line that seems to shadow the thinking of her revolutionary anticolonial cohort. She has heard tell in Moscow that "the Negroes of America . . . are a nation today, a modern nation worthy to stand beside any nation here." The Egyptians and Japanese desperately want to change the topic. They turn the conversation to Schönberg's recent transcription of Bach's choral prelude "Komm, Gott, Schöpfer." Matthew, who has so far "felt this lack of culture audible," is gripped suddenly by the passionate memory of the "sodden masses" of men "in Black Africa," the "old log church" in Virgina, the strong arm of his father conducting the church choir. Then, from the depths of oppression and obscurity, rises the resounding anthem "The Great Song of Emancipation": Go down, Moses! (22, 25).

What sounds, at times, like an "open bouffé" in Berlin—Wyndham Lewis calls the novel a film-farrago[11]—is, indeed, a primal scene of Dark Princess. Such scenes prepare us for the great theme of the novel, which is the betrayal of common purpose amongst minorities who share a common historic condition of racial oppression. How do we account for the "shadow of the color-line within the color-line" (22), the stain of prejudice amongst those who have themselves been the victims of prejudice? Is this the negation of human and ethical solidarity, or the necessary negotiation of cultural differences in constructing our inter-national claims to human "rights"?

By way of the "shadow of the color-line within the color-line," Du Bois introduces a feminized form of Asiatic "archaism" into the verbal and visual staging of the narrative, a style of cultural difference that is sensuously embodied in the Dark Princess. She signifies, through her Orientalist affect, a political passion and charisma that are kept distinct from her progressive, quasi-materialist, or Marxist political opinions. It is, indeed, this engendering split between the deep inheritance of aristocracy, royal blood, Indian caste hierarchy, and her profoundly "high modernist" tastes for Picasso, Proust, Meyerhold, Kandinsky, Schönberg—even Marx!—that turns her into an incandescent icon of world-service and inter-national emancipation. Archaic and avant-garde, all at once. What could so easily be read as an ideological or "class" contradiction, a capitulation to oligarchy, is transformed by the "rule of juxtaposition" into a wily and wise political message. Indeed, Matthew suggests that although it is hard for a stranger such as the cosmopolitan Indian princess to see beneath the "unlovely surface of this racial tangle [of American segregation] somehow he had counted on this woman—on her subtlety and vision; on her knowledge of the color line" (59). What could her specific knowledge of the color-line be? How could she, as an antiimperialist Asian woman, part of the Indian freedom movement, be counted upon to illuminate the struggle around and against the segregationist color-line?

"It is dominating Europe that has flung the color-line and we cannot avoid it," a (Chinese) character in *Dark Princess* declares. The cosmopolitan princess is now entering the terrain of the Du Boisian minority: "When a minority group is thus segregated and forced out of the nation they can in reason do but one thing—take advantage of the disadvantage."[12] To understand how the Asian anticolonialists dealt with the discriminatory divisions of imperial westernization and modernization gives us an intimation of the reasons why Matthew may find the Asiatics so compelling. Partha Chatterjee, the political philosopher, explains this process as a form of "subaltern" action:

> Anticolonial nationalism creates its own domain of sovereignty within colonial society. . . . It does this by dividing the world of social institutions and practices into two domains—the material and the spiritual. The material is the domain of the "outside," of the economy and of statecraft, of science and technology, a domain where the West had proved its superiority and the East had succumbed. In this domain, then, Western superiority had to be acknowledged and its accomplishments carefully studied and replicated. The spiritual, on the other hand, is an "inner" domain bearing the "essential" marks of cultural identity. The greater one's success in imitating Western skills in the material domain, therefore, the greater the need to preserve the distinctness of one's spiritual culture. This formula is, I think, a fundamental feature of anticolonial nationalisms in Asia and Africa.[13]

The colonialist color-line in Asia and Africa demanded that native populations should "prove their humanity," by adapting to the norms of "westernization"—law, police, land reform, utilitarian urban planning, a sharper distinction between polis and peasantry, the public/private distinction, the redemptive gospel of muscular Christianity. The civilizing mission initiated a cultural project similar to what Du Bois describes as the anomaly of "amalgamation" in a segregationist context—the assumption that you want to be white or westernized or "modern," which is then only partially or selectively permitted, so that your own difference is "normalized" and your desire naturalized into majoritarian claims. The anticolonial realignment of the spiritual and the material, the inner and the outer, mimics the colonialist's color-line of archaism and modernity, up to a point.

At each end of the binary divisions of discriminatory power—modernity/ archaism, democracy/despotism, law/custom, culture/folk mythology, secular/ sacred—I suggest, the anticolonialist strategy introduces an inappropriatable or untranslatable element of juxtaposition that unsettles the temporal framing and the political spacing of polarities. For example, the colonialist assumption that Indian political systems are premodern—ascriptive and kin-based, for instance—will now be "doubled" by the fact that the nationalist minority acknowledges and attempts to replicate the "material" institutions of the modern state, while maintaining, in that very same public domain or civil society, a political morality that derives from Hindu or Muslim customary law. Deploying the minority strategy of taking advantage of disadvantage, this anticolonial double-consciousness seeks to establish an alternative contramodernity that is tolerant of the "enduring hyphenation" of the Vedas (or the Koran) and modern science. As an Indian historian of science has picturesquely described it, "Navigating between the bank of the Vedas and the bank of modern science and technology, but holding neither one or the other fixed, India appears simultaneously as something altogether new and unmistakably old, at once undoubtedly modern and irreducibly Indian."[14]

In keeping with the Du Boisian "structure of juxtaposition," the double mimesis involved in the anticolonial strategy—the shadowing and subverting of the colonialist color-line, replicating the material realm while recognizing oneself in the cultural realm—allows the race-man, like Towns, to envisage a coevality of cultural "difference," to strive for a right to an equality-in-difference. Having interleaved the antisegregationist and anticolonialist perspectives on the minority, American and Asian, we can now proceed toward the novel's "great synthesis" of an inter-national, minoritarian civil society built around a reformed nation. Du Bois projects a mode of nationhood that interestingly decenters the "state" by locating it in a region, the Midwest, and localizing it in a city, Chicago, and from there he traces an inter-national routing of the political periphery—the Black Belt. "New York is a province of England. Virginia, Charleston, and New Orleans are memories"; "California is just beyond the world. . . . Chicago is the American world and the modern world, and the worst of it. We Americans are caught here in our own machinery" (284). Six years earlier than *Dark Princess*, Du Bois had ventured this very vision of a synthetic, minoritarian nation in a condemnation of British imperialism and the cultural hegemony of the East Coast. In "Americanization" (1922) he made an appeal to the Midwest of the nation to envision a democracy that goes beyond the "Englishmen and New Englander; a democracy that marches forth in a great alliance between the darker people of the world, between disadvantaged groups like the Irish and the Jews, the working classes everywhere." This "quasi-colonial" alliance displaces the national perspective onto a local regional focus—the Midwest, the "finer flower of democracy."[15] The alliance constitutes a community of minorities, racialized populations, workers, women, and the unwaged—a transcultural alliance, now often the subjects of what we have come to call, at the end of the century, a culture of rights. Two decades after the publication of *Dark Princess* and "Americanization," the concept of the "quasi-colonial" emerged in 1945 to remind us that the moral strains of racism and oppression had not passed, that the poetics of forbearance requires us to live and work within the contradiction of double aims. Du Bois's concept of the quasicolonial, with its metaphoricity and its moral fervor, has lost none of its demographic and democratic relevance, a half-century later:

> Thus we must conceive of colonies in the nineteenth and twentieth centuries as not something far away from the centers of civilization; not as comprehending problems which are not our problem [but also] the local problems of London, Paris and New York. . . . We must remember also that in the organized and dominated states there are groups of people who occupy the quasi-colonial status: laborers who are settled in the slums of large cities; groups like Negroes in the United States who are segregated physically and discriminated against spiritually in law and custom. . . . All these people occupy what is really a colonial status and make the kernel and substance of the problem of minorities.[16]

It is the mission of the quasicolonial to take on the challenge of the "contradiction of double aims," to use Du Bois's canonical phrase,[17] and struggle to produce a world-open message through the aesthetic and political rule of juxtaposition. For Du Bois, minoritarian agency is envisaged as a process of enunciation—the enslaved or the colonized represent their community in the very act of political poesis. The burden of the minoritarian "message" is not merely the demand for the respect and recognition of cultural or political differences. This very aesthetic act of communication or narration is also an ethical practice "that is complete not in opening to the spectacle of, or the recognition of, the other, but in becoming a responsibility for him/her."[18] The responsibility of the minoritarian agent lies in creating a world-open forum of communication in which "the crankiest, humblest and poorest . . . people are the . . . key to the consent of the governed."[19]

Du Bois's central insight lies in emphasizing the "contiguous" and contingent nature of the making of minorities, where solidarity depends on surpassing autonomy or sovereignty in favor of an intercultural articulation of differences. This is a dynamic and dialectical concept of the minority as a process of affiliation, an ongoing translation of aims and interests through which minorities emerge to communicate their messages adjacently across communities. This enunciative concept of minoritization is much in advance of the anthropological concept of the minority that is in place in Article 27 of the International Covenant on Civil and Political Rights. For Article 27, minorities, in the main, are groups that have existed in a state before becoming beneficiaries of protection. It is their "cohesion" as a minority that has to be protected, for "minorities have been conceived of [in the article] as social entities wholly sustainable in their separateness." Immigrants and women, for example, have had problems being recognized by Article 27 because, it is argued, they do not closely approximate to a "jural order with institutions shared by the whole category," and they do not demand the right to sustain their culture as a "fundamental group quality sought to be maintained as an end in itself."[20] Such a strong preference for cultural "holism" prevents Article 27 from envisaging, or providing protection for, new and affiliative forms of minoritarian agents and institutions who do not necessarily choose to signify their lifeworlds in the political forms of nationness and nationalisms.

Du Bois stands, with the ethical minorities of his aspirational imagination, at the limits of national society, adjacent to both the white and the black worlds, sending his double-aimed message in an "inter-national" or quasicolonial direction (to use Du Bois's concepts of "enduring hyphenation").[21] He paradoxically declares that of all modern peoples it is the dispossessed—the colonized and the enslaved—who are convinced, in some profound way, of the ethical impossibility of perpetuating discrimination, segregation, or global injustice in the modern world. "It is not possible in a modern world to separate people by vertical partitions," W.E.B. Du Bois declared in 1929. "And who was it that made such group and racial separation impossible under modern methods? Who brought 15 million black folks over-seas? . . . The world has come together in an organization which you can no more unscramble than you can unscramble eggs."[22]

As any advanced cook knows, and we have no reason to believe that Du Bois was anything less, scrambling eggs is one of the great challenges to the enduring problem of integration: once the heat is on there is a running battle between the whites (of eggs) and those Others, unjustly "yoked" together in the process of ethnic or racial emulsification. How do we arrive at the right consistency and constituency for freedom?

There is a less obvious reading of the parable of the scrambled eggs, which hinges more directly on Du Bois's critique of the modern nation and its "organization" of majorities and minorities. In his statement from 1929, we see the anticipatory traces of a wider critique of the nation-state from the minoritarian perspective that Du Bois was to launch much later, at a 1944 Department of State meeting of Americans United for World Organization, where he represented the NAACP, against the resolutions of the Dumbarton Oaks Conference. He argued that the conference's "emphasis on nations and states and the indifference to races, groups or organizations indicate that the welfare and protection of colonial peoples are beyond the jurisdiction of the conference's proposed governments." Du Bois's "challenge to the idea that human beings had rights and agency only as citizens of a nation-state" was taken up at the UN in 1946–47, as Penny von Eschen notes, by an alliance of black Americans, Indian and black South Africans, and the government of India. It was with such doubts about the "statist" representation of the rights of minorities in mind that, in a speech in New York on human rights, Du Bois called for a transnational gathering of the "quasi-colonial" not as a racial or ethnic community but as a "community of condition," to borrow a beautiful phrase from Albert Memmi.[23]

Du Bois's enduring doubts about the protection and representation of minorities by the nation-state were to echo menacingly more than half a century later, in conference rooms in Durban decked out with smoke and mirrors. At the World Congress of Races in September 2001, the cabals and collusions of national sovereignty cynically trumped the cause of sexual and racial minorities. The unseemly rush, on the part of many major states, to run from their historical pasts, like Lady Macbeth fleeing the bedchamber, was only matched by those great stalwarts of international democracy who stormed out of the conference at the very mention of the deep divisions and discriminations that survive in their countries. As the *New York Times* reported it: "India successfully lobbied fellow nations to prevent mention of caste discrimination. Before walking out of the conference over criticism of Israel, the United States objected to any discussion of reparations for the descendants of African slaves. Others refused to consider gays as victims of discrimination" (September 10, 2001).[24]

To ensure that "no human group is so small as to deserve to be ignored as a part, and as a respected and integral part, of the mass of men" is also to say that in the narrative of global history there is no mode of historical "time and development"—that is, culture—so small or insignificant that it can be dismissed from democratic representation on the grounds of its lack of power, or its refusal to share the "same desire to be alike."[25] Du Bois's combination of praxis and poesis—of advocacy and aspiration—places his work at the center of some of the most urgent global, democratic dilemmas of our time. He gives us courage and hope because he takes the measure of existence from its most melancholic metaphors—the color-line, the shadow of the Veil, the divided self, enduring hyphenation. We know these things as we know the frail and fragile survival of life itself. It is from the fine adjustments of everyday alienations and agonies, everyday epiphanies and visions, that Du Bois makes us part of the community of those "gifted" with second sight in this "American world."[26]

NOTES

I am immensely grateful to Lawrence Buell for casting his brilliant eye over this piece. Wai Chee Dimock has been remarkably supportive and appreciative, for which I am most grateful. I would like to thank Mark Jerng for impeccable research assistance.

1. See W.E.B. Du Bois, *Dark Princess: A Romance* (Jackson: University Press of Mississippi, 1995), 307, hereafter cited parenthetically; *The Autobiography of W.E.B. Du Bois: A Soliloquy on Viewing My Life from the Last Decade of Its First Century* (New York: International Publishers Co., 1968), 412; and Du Bois, "Of Our Spiritual Strivings," chap. 1 in *The Souls of Black Folk*, ed. David W. Blight and Robert Gooding-Williams (1903; reprint, Boston: Bedford Books, 1997), 38. On "juxtaposition," see, for example, Du Bois, *Darkwater: Voices from within the Veil* (New York: Harcourt, Brace and Howe, 1920), 225–26.

2. Du Bois, *Darkwater*, 225, 230.

3. Amartya Kumar Sen, *Inequality Reexamined* (Cambridge: Harvard University Press, 1992), 69, 68.

4. Du Bois, "Of Our Spiritual Strivings," 38; Stanley Cavell, *Must We Mean What We Say? A Book of Essays* (New York: Charles Scribner's Sons, 1969), 308.

5. W.E.B. Du Bois, "Of the Wings of Atalanta," chap. 5 in *Souls of Black Folk*, 86–87.

6. Mary White Ovington, review of *Dark Princess*, by W.E.B. Du Bois, *Chicago Bee*, August 4, 1928; quoted in Arnold Rampersad, "Du Bois's Passage to India: *Dark Princess*," in *W.E.B. Du Bois on Race and Culture: Philosophy, Politics, and Poetics*, ed. Bernard W. Bell, Emily Grosholz, and James B. Stewart (New York: Routledge, 1996), 165.

7. W.E.B. Du Bois, *Dusk of Dawn: An Essay toward an Autobiography of a Race Concept* (1940; reprint, New York: Schocken Books, 1968), 223.

8. Panchanan Saha (Madam Cama) (Bhikaji Rustom K. R.), *Mother of Indian Revolution* (Calcutta: Manisha, 1975), 18.

9. Ibid., 17, 19–20.

10. See Edward Augustus Freeman, "Race and Language" (1879), in *Essays, English and American* (New York: P. F. Collier, 1910), 240.

11. Wyndham Lewis, *Paleface: The Philosophy of the Melting Pot* (London: Chatto and Windus, 1929), 41.

12. Du Bois, *Autobiography*, 266.

13. Partha Chatterjee, *The Nation and Its Fragments: Colonial and Postcolonial Histories* (Princeton: Princeton University Press, 1993), 6.

14. Gyan Prakash, *Another Reason: Science and the Imagination of Modern India* (Princeton: Princeton University Press, 1999), 14. "Enduring hyphenation" is David Levering Lewis's resonant summation of the "permanent tension" embedded in the racial dialectic of *The Souls of Black Folk* (see *W.E.B. Du Bois: Biography of a Race, 1868–1919* [New York: Holt, 1993], 281).

15. W.E.B. Du Bois, "Americanization," in *The Oxford W.E.B. Du Bois Reader*, ed. Eric J. Sundquist (New York: Oxford University Press, 1996), 384.

16. W.E.B. Du Bois, "Human Rights for All Minorities," in *W.E.B. Du Bois Speaks: Speeches and Addresses, 1920–1963*, ed. Philip S. Foner (New York: Pathfinder Press, 1972), 183–84.

17. Du Bois, "Of Our Spiritual Strivings," 39.

18. *The Levinas Reader*, ed. Seán Hand (1989; reprint, Oxford: Blackwell, 1994), 108.

19. Du Bois, *Darkwater*, 153.

20. Philip Vuciri Ramaga, "The Group Concept in Minority Protection," in *Human Rights Quarterly* 15 (1993): 581.

21. "International" always appears hyphenated in Du Bois in order to emphasize his notion of a minoritarian global alliance rather than one based on national or nationalist populations. I have therefore adhered to his usage throughout the essay.

22. "Rebuttal Statement by Dr. Du Bois," in W.E.B. Du Bois, Theodore L. Stoddard, and Lothrop Stoddard, "Shall the Negro Be Encouraged to Seek Cultural Equality?" in *Report of Debate Conducted by the Chicago Forum*: "Shall the Negro Be Encouraged to Seek Cultural Equality?" (Chicago: Chicago Forum Council, 1929), 21.

23. "Dumbarton Oaks Proposals Exclude Colonies—Du Bois," *Baltimore Afro-American*, October 28, 1944, 3; and "Dr. Du Bois 'Depressed' Colonial Questions Ignored at Dumbarton Oaks Peace Session," *Pittsburgh Courier*, October 28, 1944, 4; quoted in Penny M. von Eschen, *Race against Empire: Black Americans and Anticolonialism, 1937–1957* (Ithaca: Cornell University Press, 1997), 74–75. Also see Albert Memmi, *Dominated Man: Notes towards a Portrait* (New York: Orion, 1968), 38.

24. Rachel L. Swarns, "After the Race Conference: Relief, and Doubt over Whether It Will Matter," *New York Times*, September 10, 2001, late ed. (East Coast), A10.

25. Du Bois, *Darkwater*, 154.

26. Du Bois, "Of Our Spiritual Strivings," 38.

CHAPTER 8

Atlantic to Pacific: James, Todorov, Blackmur, and Intercontinental Form

David Palumbo-Liu

> The reach is into the dark places where the Muses are, and all the rest is the work we do to bring into the performance of our own language the underlying classic form in which they speak.
> —R. P. Blackmur, "The Loose and Baggy Monsters of Henry James." (1951)[1]

> The native architecture of the particular time, which could rejoice so in the multiplication of doors—the opposite extreme to the modern, the actual almost complete proscription of them; but it had fairly contributed to provoke this obsession of the presence encountered telescopically, as he might say, focused and studied in diminishing perspective and as by a rest for the elbow.
> —Henry James, "The Jolly Corner," 358–59[1]

In discussing the topic of the "planetary" in American literature, we need to attend to the question of how, exactly, even imagining that figure itself involves a moment of transfer and an attempt at legibility. The questions then become—how does the "planet" become (newly) imaginable over and against the particularities of national identity and understanding? How is the planet itself figured and mediated particularly? In attempting to answer these questions, we find ourselves embarking on a project to find some mode of translating across that distance, to find a point in common, to discover, in short, an intermediate and mediating Form. The two quotes above illustrate precisely both the notion that there is some abiding "classic form" of which all other forms, even modern ones, seem simply a variation, *and* that the precise nature of form is mediated variously from different angles of vision, which have their own ways of reconstituting the "classic." In short, Form is the meeting place of a number of aesthetic and psychic investments, both the common ground and vehicle for planetary thinking.

Crucially, this is not a problem (at this stage) of representation—it precedes such inquiries. I will be arguing a critical connection between form, planetary thinking, and community or social space. Since a transnational community cannot, by definition, be a "representation" derived from the lexicon and assumptions of the nation-state, it can only emerge through the mediated space of nonrepresentation.[2] Here I argue that on the one hand, Form is a space in which neither "American" nor "global" appear totally foreign to each other, but imagine a space of mutual legibility, a space that is mutually habitable. On the other hand, neither "American" nor "global" simply disappear into a seamless and indistinct sameness. In such a reading we discover instead a tension, a recognition of incommensurateness or irresolvable difference that does not obliterate the project, but rather casts it into another domain—again, not of representation (which would ask the question: "is the form adequate to the concept?") but of the desire to find a form that allegorizes the near/far dynamics of in-forming planetary thinking. I will focus on one possible angle onto these questions, exploring closely the function and valorizations of Form as it appears in James and his critics, not as an end to itself, but as a window onto precisely the topic of modernity and a new sense of the planet, a sense that cannot (yet) be represented directly.

In mapping the circulation, revaluation, and replenishment of Form as an object and construction of imaginative will, this essay follows an admittedly circuitous route. Chronologically, it can be mapped as emanating from that memory of a ghostly, formless escapade in the Galerie d'Apollon to the composition and narrative content of James's 1908 short story, "The Jolly Corner," to another appreciation of James as found in the reinvention of poetics and formalism in the work of an expatriate Bulgarian in France, Tzvetan Todorov, and finally to the rich and complex critical appreciation of James found in the works of the American critic R. P. Blackmur and articulated forcefully in a series of seminars Blackmur delivered in postwar Japan. We trace, therefore, a transatlantic circuit from America to Europe, and then back to the United States, and across the Pacific to East Asia.[3] Each of these moves is necessary (though perhaps not completely adequate) for an imagining of the planetary, testing out the capaciousness of such a notion in the moment of transoceanic transfer. And, if I may be allowed to insert myself explicitly into this hazardous trajectory, it would find next a Chinese American graduate student at Berkeley in the 1980s, studying with Todorov and writing a seminar paper on Blackmur's talks on literary criticism that were delivered in postwar Japan. The title of that course was, of course, "French Literary Theory."

My interest in following this circuit is to disclose how the author whom Blackmur called the "grandfather" of formal literary criticism thematized the problematics of Form and Formlessness, of European-ness and American-ness, of Self and Other, and, most especially, how he set forth a critical engagement with the status of the individual in a time of radical historical change that had a view onto planetary significance. Not only did James articulate these key problematics, his writings also prompted the imaginative rehabilitation

198 • David Palumbo-Liu

(and reinhabiting) of each of those terms by Blackmur and Todorov. I will be arguing that because the instantiation of Form in each of these particular evocations occurs at precise and critical historical moments (the turn of the century; the post-1968 cultural and political scene in Paris; the period of the Second World War and its aftermath; the allied occupation of Japan), the particular value and currency of Form as well as its aforementioned thematics take on specific meanings that tell us much about not only how American literature and criticism is linked globally, but also how these moments of literary criticism and theory can productively be read as involving a specific sense of history and historical crisis, moments in which the notion of Form itself calls on the capacity to discover or imagine the mediation of individual subjects across the troubled terrains of modern life and onto planetary scale.

And this project to discover or imagine afresh a Form that may accommodate this new social life is evident as well in the actual built and lived environment. I will thus investigate how the architectural trope in "The Jolly Corner" is not arbitrary or merely symbolic, but motivated by a sense of changing material and social history that is registered as well in contemporary debates about Form and architecture in both Todorov's and Blackmur's ages—that is, debates about how social memory is to be enshrined in the cityscapes and archaeological spaces of the nation, and where the new and old cultural habits of contemporary peoples are to interact and be manifested. How does Form come to stand as mediation at the turn of the century, when the "American scene" seems to overflow the capaciousness of imaginative Forms left over from its days of standing in Europe's shadow, or in the postwar period, which witnesses both the emerging superpower of the United States and the occupied, eclipsed empire of Japan (Blackmur), or in the aftermath of the great revolts of Paris in 1968 (Todorov)? Each of these issues is in fact foreshadowed in James's late tale, "The Jolly Corner." It is here that we can discern its immense powers of evocation, powers that strike so immediately upon both the New Critical sensibilities of Blackmur and the formalist and poetic sensibilities of Todorov.

"The Jolly Corner" and the Euro-American Grotesque

In a journal entry from August 9, 1900, James writes of beginning *The Sense of the Past* as an " 'international' tale, something expressive of the peculiarly acute Modern, the current polyglot, the American-experience-abroad line. I saw something; it glimmered in me; but I didn't in my then uncertainty, follow it up. *Is* there anything to follow up? *Vedremo bene.*"[4] Before continuing the drafting of *The Sense of the Past*, James then decides that he wants "something *simpler* than *The S. of the P.* . . . The *fantasticated* is, for this job, my probable formula . . . something in the general glimmer of the notion of what the quasi-grotesque Europeo-American situation, in the way of the gruesome, may, *pushed to the full and right expression of its grotesqueness.*"[5]

What was, exactly, this "Europeo-American situation"? One answer to this open question can be found in a moment James witnesses, as if regarding that house of fiction, the disorientation of a group of Americans in England, whose rapid shuttlings back and forth disclose both their appetite for "Europe" and their inability to register their surroundings: "I see the *picture* somehow—saw it, that night, in the train back from Brighton—the picture of 3 or 4 'scared' and slightly modern American figures moving against the background of three or four European *milieux*, different European conditions, out of which their obsession, their visitation, is projected. I seemed to see them *going*—hurried by their fate—from one of these places to the other, in search of, in flight from, something or other, and encountering also everywhere the something or other which the successive *milieux* threw up for them."[6]

These "slightly modern American figures" are pursued as much as they are pursuers, "in search of, and in flight from, something or other." What this is, we do not know, but it is rather in the movement of projection, of cathexis, that we are occupied. It is, in the terms of this essay, a search for a Form, and a haunting by Form, in which these "slightly modern Americans" find themselves having the very milieux casting unassimilable forms up to their senses. The very liminality of their status ("slightly") points to the crux of the problem—they are decidedly not modern, but not not modern either. They may have intimations of the world beyond themselves, but are as yet utterly unhabituated to whatever place or time that may be that will eventually be their new chronotope. The thematic of pursuing, and of being pursued, is of course a key theme in "The Jolly Corner," as we noted above. But that fictional tale is complemented not only by the episode in Brighton witnessed by James, but narrated in a famous autobiographical anecdote as well. At the Galerie d'Apollon James experiences "the most appalling yet most admirable night-mare of my life." He espies there "a just dimly-descried figure that retreated in terror before my rush and dash (a glare of inspired reaction from irresistible but shameful dread)." "The Jolly Corner" takes up this ghostly encounter and retreat and thematizes the issue of doubleness and haunting. However, the element I wish to foreground in this essay is again that of Form, of the englob-ing of the sameness/difference dialectic, as it is construed as a common ground in an uncommon age.

It is crucial to note then that the encounter with the ghostly figure takes place in a specific chronotope: Form itself acts upon James, the form of not only these relics of European art and culture, but also that space which houses these shapes and objects. And the totality of the form and its inhabitants overflows the capacity of the viewer to absorb it in much the same way as, on the other side of the Atlantic, the forms of modern life exceed the capacity of James's character to locate himself amongst them:

The bliss in fact I think I scarce disengaged itself at all, but only the sense of a freedom of contact and appreciation really too big for one, and leaving such a mark on the very place, the pictures, the frames themselves, the figures within them, the particular parts and features of each, the look of the rich light, the smell of the massively enclosed air, that I have never since renewed the old exposure without renewing again the old emotion and take up the small scared consciousness. (198)

This disturbance in James's ability to fully absorb what he finds confronting him in the Louvre involves also the temporal dimension, one in which he seeks not only to reconcile discrepant histories and temporalities, but also to possess them. And these themes of form and possession are exactly those found in "The Jolly Corner."

"The Jolly Corner" is one of James's most famous and one of his last literary creations. Its protagonist, Spencer Brydon, returns to the United States after a long absence abroad. His property in America consists of two buildings in New York City. [7] One is being reconstructed, parceled out into apartments that he will let out, thereby increasing exponentially the income he has been deriving from it, income that has formed a key part of the material support of his life in Europe. The other building, his family's traditional abode and the scene of his birth and childhood, is "the jolly corner," empty now, but still resonant of his past memories. Brydon has kept it vacant intentionally; it is visited only by an old housekeeper who dusts and maintains the structure. He intends to keep it empty, and intact.

As he confides to an old friend, Alice Staverton, Brydon wishes to discover there what he might have been had he not emigrated to Europe. He stealthily begins to "creep" about the Jolly Corner's spaces during the night, hoping to encounter there the answer to his question. The precise Form of that "thing" or person (the nature of the embodiment is never explicitly assumed) would presumably reveal to Brydon the exact dimensions of his immanent American identity. However, in the course of this stalking, the Form turns against the subject, and the hunter becomes the hunted. Upon finally confronting (and being confronted by) this other life, Brydon faints, and is revived by Staverton, who declaims at once both her sympathy for the poor Form of the Other, and her love for Brydon.

The tale has been read variously as a classic doppelgänger tale, a tale of haunting, of self and otherness, of Europe and America, of tradition and modernity, of queerness, of the act of writing itself. But again, here I use the tale as the starting point for a discussion of how Form in this instance becomes transcoded, made both the repository of and open space for a desire to posit at once and perhaps paradoxically both selfhood and otherness. And I use these terms here not only in an ontological sense, but also in a humanistic and historically social sense. James measures this by mapping the distance between what Brydon registers upon returning to America and what he would have expected to produce such an enormous effect on his senses, marking the disparity between what Brydon encounters as an assault on his vision and what Brydon imagines might have led to these effects—history has accelerated at such a pace as to outstrip any former rhythm of change: "It would have taken a century . . . it would have taken a longer absence and a more averted mind than those even of which he had been guilty, to pile up the differences, the newnesses, the queernesses, above all the bignesses, for the better or the worse, that at present assaulted his vision wherever he looked" (341). Scalar models have exponentially blossomed into strange new forms of the new, the queer, the big, which are no match for his newly outmoded senses of time and history: "He actually saw that he had allowed for nothing; he missed what he would have been sure of finding, he found what he would never have imagined. Proportions and values were upside-down" (342).

And it is not merely a matter of proportion and scale—James now draws together a string of adjectives to attempt to describe the new world—it is characterized by an entirely new materiality and inhabited by "the modern, the monstrous, the famous things" (342). In sum, the forms of modern life have exceeded Brydon's ability to map them, to measure and calibrate them according to his preexisting sense of Form, mass, and proportion. The delineation of difference along the scale, rhythm, and values of the past and the modern worlds, of, to be more precise, Europe and America, are transcoded onto the self-imaging of the protagonist. Brydon hypothetically locates himself in a different past, with a different, American identity: "If he had but stayed at home he would have anticipated the inventor of the sky-scraper. If he had but stayed at home he would have discovered his genius in time really to start some new variety of awful architectural hare and run it till it burrowed in a gold-mine" (344).

And yet again, we find that the imagining of self cannot take place formlessly; rather, identity is converted into the coinage of Form—it is Form that circulates in the visual, the sensual, the experiential fields of social, intersubjective life on the streets, in the boulevards. The difficulty is finding the Form that is commensurate to this imaging, for it is in the spatial distributions and figurations of Form that the Other is imagined, incarnated, and animated: "'Not to have followed my perverse young course—and almost in the teeth of my father's curse, as I may say; not to have kept it up, so, 'over there,' from that day to this, without a doubt or a pang; not, above all, to have liked it, to have loved it, so much, loved it, no doubt, with such an abysmal conceit of my own preference: some variation from *that*, I say, must have produced some different effect for my life and for my 'form.'" (349). The whole idea of measurement, gradation, calibration breaks apart the easy dichotomies with which we have been discussing this narrative of form and imagination, past and present, Europe and America. For what emerges in this tale is a complication of the function of Form in literary texts, and this complication has everything to do with extraformal, that is to say, historical and contingent matters that destabilize all prior forms of measurement and comprehension, and question the capacities of any imagining of commensurability or transfer, in short, of imagining planetary being.

The historical dimension enters into consideration precisely in that the fissures and gaps that trouble the conversion of Form are the products themselves of a tectonic shift in temporality and historicity that brings with it new ways of evaluating social and historical space and temporality. This is a formal problematic situated in an eminently worldly space and time, one that is characterized by displacement, migration, the reinhabiting of the modern world by new forms and ideologies. Under these circumstances, Form becomes freighted with the obligation to encase an as yet unsettled and indeterminate admixture of projected desire and repressed fear—the postmodern problematic of "mapping" finds in this modern piece the problematic of envisioning a Form commensurate with the will to know the obverse facets of the modern and the "traditional" (for lack of a better word). This is graphically depicted in "The Jolly Corner" as we have seen in Brydon's difficulty in mapping the "newnesses and queernesses" of the modern world, as found in, among other places, the new architectural forms that house the modern man and woman, new forms that operate on both aesthetic and financial imperatives.[8]

Tellingly, it is precisely as a "house" that James describes fiction itself, and it is in this moment of transference back upon the act of literary imagination itself that the potential of Form as common ground is fully articulated. In the following passage from the 1908 preface to *The Portrait of a Lady* (1881), James famously writes:

[T]he house of fiction has in short not one window, but a million—a number of possible windows not to be reckoned, rather; every one of which has been pierced, or is still pierceable, in its vast front, by the need of the individual vision and by *the pressure of the individual will* [my emphasis]. These apertures, of dissimilar shape and size, hang so, all together, over the human scene that we might have expected of them a greater sameness of report than we find. They are but windows at the best, mere holes in a dead wall, disconnected, perched aloft; they are not hinged doors opening straight upon life. But they have this mark of their own that at each of them stand a figure with a pair of eyes, or at least with a field-glass, which forms, again and again, for observation, a unique instrument, insuring to the person making use of it an impression distinct from every other. . . . He and his neighbors are watching the same show, but one seeing more where the other sees less, one seeing black where the other sees white. . . . The spreading field, the human scene, is the "choice of subject"; the pierced aperture, either broad or balconied or slit-like and low-browed, is the "literary form"; but they are, singly or together, as nothing without the posted presence of the watcher—without, in other words, the consciousness of the artist.[9]

This convergence of self and other, of individual artist who watches a scene that has been perceived in multiple and incommensurate manners, marks a relation between multiply occupied spaces and at least two distinct forms—that of the "house" and that inhabited by the artist who is inventing that form from without. In this tale, James, the "watcher," sets Brydon, his other, and Staverton at their respective windows, each with a different view onto the scene, but whose views are housed, englobed, as it were, by James's narrative. The weirdness of the tale is colored precisely by the incommensurability, the mixedness of not only the views, but also of the "individual wills" that shape and seek to find in Form the adequate embodiment of a desire to be present to both self and other. And thus it is in Form that the planetary can be imagined. And, finally, this new imaginary extends out to and helps concretely construct a new social world.

The (Re)built Forms of Modernity

What was, exactly, the historical moment that so forcefully compels both James and Brydon to reassess the idea of Form? And how was this moment inscribed not only in literary form, but also in the actual built environment, in the actual structures that were to embody a new historical age and a new mode of living together in it? James left the United States in 1875 to live in England. He returned to America thirty years later in 1905 and recorded his impressions in *The American Scene*. While Leon Edel asserts that "The Jolly Corner" is a "story about what it means to be an American in an increasingly international world," this "scene" was also and unavoidably quantitatively different from that which James left behind in 1875. For instance, between 1860 and 1914 New York's population had increased from 850,000 to more than 4 million people, many of them immigrants. We can thus see the tale as linking the "global" to "America" both in terms of the modern identity of "American" and "international" and in terms of a marked shift in the material forms of America and the world—cultural, architecture, urban planning, financial districts, domestic spaces, et cetera.

Indeed, *The Real Estate Record* of New York declared that by end of nineteenth century, "[n]o one who will study the development of the architecture of New York City in the last quarter century will fail to observe how completely it reflects the chief social facts of the time."[10] Hawes notes that these facts include the tremendous increase in wealth, the explosion of commercial energy, the development of technology, and a pronounced show of public spirit, thinking specifically of the neoclassic mansion, the skyscraper, the hotel, and the apartment house as illustrations.[11] It is precisely these new architectural forms that displaced the material Forms that had oriented James before he left the United States. Upon his return to America, James found "his birthplace on

Figure 8.1. St. Regis Hotel. From Robert A. M. Stern, *New York 1880: Architecture and Urbanism in the Gilded Age* (New York: Monacelli Press, 1999). Permission from Museum of the City of New York.

Washington Square harbored a shirt factory, his childhood home on 14th Street was gone, and the church across the way had been replaced by a faceless row of stores. Elsewhere his favorite buildings seemed lost at sea, deprived of their old dignity and visibility by a crude new dimension to the city.[12] James deplored the destruction of old houses: "He declared the destruction of these recent nineteenth-century residences comparable to sending young men to the guillotine."[13] James described the new apartment houses on the Upper West Side in 1904 as "a colossal hair-comb turned upward and so deprived of half its teeth that the others, at their uneven intervals, count doubly as sharp spikes . . . crudely-extemporized . . . interrogative feelers of a society trying to build itself into some coherent sense of itself."[14] In this attempt to find some "coherent" form to contain and express modern American society, architects turned to Paris. The modern apartment house appeared in 1870, when entrepreneur Dr. David H. Haight rebuilt two houses at Fifteenth Street and Fifth Avenue into a more refined rendition of a multiple dwelling. These new forms showed the particular influence of Parisian design: "The Stevens House, eight stories tall and occupied the whole block between Fifth Avenue and Broadway on 27th street, larger, bolder, more patently Parisian. . . . [It] recalled Haussmann's buildings in Paris."[15] Ironically, the invention of modern American architecture looked to Europe's reinvention of its own city spaces—and as in the case of Haussmann's Paris, it is important to note that the expression of modernity in material form was not simply a matter of aesthetics; it was also an index to a new set of social arrangements. One of the most striking examples of the effect of new forms was the invention of the modern apartment out of the carving up and redesigning of single family dwellings, which prompted new forms of living together. Along with the emergence of the apartment house came the invention of the cooperative apartment. According to Hawes, it was "idealistic in purpose, economical in plan, extravagant in nature." These co-ops first appeared in 1880s as the Hubert Home Clubs.

James wrote precisely of the link between the reconstruction of urban and social spaces, and the concomitant effect of this merger upon social interaction and indeed the rescripting of national culture: "The moral in question, the high interest of the tale, is that you are in the presence of a revelation of the possibilities of the hotel—for which the American spirit has for so unprecedented a use and a value; leading it on to express so a social, indeed positively an aesthetic ideal, and making it so, at this supreme pitch, a synonym for civilization, for the capture of conceived manners themselves, that one is verily tempted to ask of the hotel-spirit may not just *be* the American spirit most seeking and most finding itself."[16]

This "spirit" that so informs social life was undetachable from the new financial world of the turn of the century—we should recall that Spencer Brydon's life in Europe is financed precisely by his rental income in New York. In turn, the financial world is inseparable from the new advances in technology that not only spurred on the production of new commodities, but created inventions that themselves fueled the imagining of new structures. Nothing better emblematizes this circuit of influence than the first building dubbed a "skyscraper." The term comes from Winston Weisman, and is first applied to the Equitable Life Assurance Society Building (1868–70): "the first business building in which the possibilities of the elevator were realized."[17] Equitable had been organized in 1859 with a small capital investment of $100,000; by 1870 its assets were worth more than $11 million. Thus when Brydon thinks with horror that he might have anticipated the inventor of the skyscraper, he is referencing not only a grotesque architectural form, but also a radically alienated economic, social, and aesthetic life.

In regarding James's tale and its address to issues of Form, we should not therefore too quickly metaphorize the materiality of "The Jolly Corner." The radical changes Brydon registers correlate the transformation of the city and the country itself under the pressures of social, cultural, and economic changes that all are manifested in the lived environment, which witnesses nothing less than the reconceptualization of social life and Form. The problem becomes how to find any way that Form can still serve as both the aesthetic expression of a newly modern life and a mediating space in which subjects can interact and communicate.

BACK TO EUROPE: THE ACCOMMODATION OF OTHERNESS IN POETICS

The appeal to Form as a constant (albeit variously imaginable) element amid radical historical change is felt as well in the new poetics founded by Tzvetan Todorov in the late 1960s in Paris and influenced strongly by American formalist criticism. The notion of Form as a mediating space, rather than (only) a complete and independent aesthetic object, appears also in even Todorov's rigorously formalist poetics. This rigor contains its own degree of radicalness; in the late 1960s to the late 1970s, Tzvetan Todorov will approach form as the proper object of a poetic theorization of literature that will precisely displace literary criticism and instead instantiate a prescriptive poetics. In his "Introduction: French Poetics Today," Todorov begins by locating this project temporally: "*Today* is evidently a synecdoche for 'recent': the texts which follow . . .. were written between 1968 and 1978. This period was not chosen at random: before 1968 there were only sporadic publications in the area of poetics; today, however, it is reasonable to say, the time has arrived for a preliminary assessment."[18] Poetics is then defined thusly: "the object of poetics is the general laws which govern the function of literature, its forms and varieties. . . . [I]t has its own way of carving out its object of study. . . . [It] is primarily concerned with the verbal structures which are to be found in works of literature. . . . [T]he object of poetics is furnished by literary discourse, as opposed to other types of discourse. . . . It is to be contrasted in aim and nature to interpretation and criticism." Poetics, is, to put it bluntly, "[a] way of looking at facts."[19] We can mark here the attempt to rationalize and make objective "life."

One of the key organs of this endeavor became the periodical founded by Todorov, Barthes, and others, *Poetique*, whose manifesto follows exactly the prescription found above, and includes as well the goal of publishing critical and theoretical articles from abroad. In both the "domestic" and "foreign" essays, one discovers a particular fascination with Henry James. Essays on James by Ian Watt, Seymour Chatman, Leo Bersani, and others were translated into French; and contributions on James from Hélène Cixous and others were published. Blackmur's assertion that James was the "grandfather" of formalist criticism is borne out anachronistically in this latter incarnation of formalist criticism, one that saw in James's literary texts as well as his criticism a particularly amenable set of "facts" and a way of looking at them. The reinvention of formalist criticism in the 1960s in France was of course itself influenced enormously by the translation into French of key texts from a group of critics that came to be known as the Russian Formalists, a project carried out by Todorov himself, as an intermediary between Eastern and Western Europe.[20]

Yet as much as the initial impulse of poetic criticism was toward the technical attributes of verbal art, even in the essays Todorov published between 1964 and 1969, and translated by Jonathan Culler as *The Poetics of Prose*, we find a slippage between purely formal criticism and literary and social interpretation, that hermeneutic act banished from "poetics" in Todorov's introductory essay, and this slippage echoes precisely the movement between Form and social life in James.[21] Essays on James in this collection include "The Secret of Narrative" and "The Ghosts of Henry James," and it is in the latter that we find a specific address to "The Jolly Corner":

> This text ["The Jolly Corner"] thereby signifies the reversal of the figure we see recurring throughout the Jamesian *oeuvre*. The essential absence and the insignificant presence no longer dominate his universe: the relation with another, even the humblest presence, is affirmed against the selfish (solitary) quest for absence. The self does not exist outside its relation with others, with another; essence is an illusion. Thus James pivots, at the end of his *oeuvre*, to the other side of the great thematic dichotomy we evoked earlier: the problematics of man alone confronting the world gives way to another, that of the relation of human being to human being. *To be* is supplanted by *to have*, *I* by *you*.[22]

The "problematic" that emerges as the product of a "poetic" analytic revolves back, with great logic, to precisely the issue that James outlines—how is otherness not only given form, but how can Form itself be both the allegorical *articulation* of the mediation of self and other and at the same time be that mediating *space* that accommodates both? In that sense, the "house of fiction" is both the symbol of fiction and of common ground, and again, of possibilities of reading beyond the local and the individual.

If we accept that notion, then the ending passages of Todorov's essay can be envisioned as not as bleak as they sound: "As soon as I speak, I enter the universe of abstraction, of generality, of concepts, and no longer of things. How to name the individual, when the names themselves, as we all know, do not belong to the individual himself? If the absence of difference equals nonexistence, pure difference is unnameable: it is nonexistent for language."[23] The impossibility of "pure difference" resides precisely in the world of shared abstractions, that is, in the world of language, that mediate and mediating form of otherness and sameness which offers individuals a conduit through which they might meet, however contingently. That universal condition, as discovered by Todorov in James's story, cannot stand alone as the sole possible incarnation of Form in a time of historical crisis.[24]

Indeed, shortly after Todorov's program for poetics was established, Henri Lefebvre published his magisterial *The Production of Space* (1974), in which an entirely new understanding of form and space was articulated, specifically with regard to issues of social and political habitations and negotiations. Although in significantly different ways, both the poetician and the Marxist geographer reapproach the forms of social life. If the formalist's quest for Form has led Todorov back into the world of hermeneutics and semantics and living social beings, it has done so because the very structures of the Jamesian narratives that most fascinate Todorov are those that both mimic and articulate the thematic of social being, of being with others at a time of radical historical change. The movement back into language has yielded not a pure form of abstraction, but a social contract that is struck precisely in the intermediate spaces carved out by the literary Form, and it is to this space that the final phrases of Todorov's quotation point. Again, albeit in a different manner, Lefebvre's program moves abstract language aside to get at forms of social being via a radically revised way of understanding space.

Consider Lefebvre's critique of semiology: "Semiology raises difficult questions precisely because it is an incomplete body of knowledge which is expanding without any sense of its own limitations; its very dynamism creates a need for such limits to be set, as difficult as that might be. When codes worked up from literary texts are applied to spaces—to urban spaces, say—we remain, as may easily be shown, on the purely descriptive level. Any attempt to use such codes as a means of deciphering social space must surely reduce that space itself to the status of a *message*, and the inhabiting of it to the status of a *reading*. This is to evade both history and practice."[25] Lefebvre, in quite a different way, and for different purposes, names another sort of dialectic that nonetheless joins the later Todorov in its attention to the dialectic between subjects and their environment: "The shift I am proposing in analytic orientation relative to the work of specialists in this area ought by now to be clear: instead of emphasizing the rigorously formal aspect of codes, I shall instead be putting the stress on their dialectical character. Codes will be seen as part of a practical relationship, as part of an interaction between 'subjects' and their space and surroundings" (18). It would not be illegitimate to argue that the radical shift that Lefebvre advocates, away from the dry formalist view toward "codes" and toward intersubjective social interactions, is at least sentimentally present in Todorov's own thematization of form. Todorov too finds, even within his formalist poetics, an accommodation of a social interpretation. Semantics, heretofore banished, or at least held in abeyance by poetics, finds its return precisely in the form of social interaction.

And the tensions and stress of social interaction were registered as well in the city planning of Paris. The early 1960s also witnessed a rapid change in Paris's city planning, prompted in no small part by the fact that it was now defined as a self-governing municipal unit. The city launched a review of the building regulations of 1902, and in 1959 "various additions and amendments to were included in a comprehensive *Plan d'urbanisme directeur*, which was applied progressively over the following years until the plan was formally approved in 1967. . . . New system use of zoning, building regulations, and plot ratios."[26] In 1955 national legislation established the basis for large-scale urban renewal: "Planners and officials spoke optimistically of the 'reconquest' of Paris. . . . [B]etween 1955 and 1960, Parisian renovation included seventeen projects with a total area of 89.7 hectares."[27] By "reconquest" the planners meant "renovation," but more precisely the term referenced the reassessment of "tradition" and the need to reconsider what was vital and what was moribund. In 1959 the prefect of the Seine, Jean Benedetti, "painted a picture of a dynamic, commercial capital of the future, retaining all the forms of its historic and aesthetic prestige but continuing to decentralize population and employment into both the suburbs and the provinces."[28] According to Everson, the *Plan d'urbanisme directeur* "provided the charter for the biggest transformation of the Paris townscape since the Second Empire."[29] Two zones were invented—inner zone, central and historic, and outer rings of the city, more modernist. However, "the results [of French modernism] will be apparent to anyone looking through the compilation of highlights of French modernism by Maurice Besset, published in 1967. This tedious parade of untreated concrete, bleak symmetry and constant repetition represents the emergence of a world of modern architecture which lacks many of the qualities of the old while retaining some of its defects, such as obsessive symmetry, and conformity."[30] And it was in the "historical" core that power was concentrated. This was the moment that saw a tremendous development of highrises, which the planners insisted had to be built back from the street in order not to block the sunlight. It was also the start of the planning for the construction of the huge tower projects, one near the Port Maillot, and the Tour Montparnasse, which was started in 1969, finished in 1973. The developers, consulting architects, and consulting engineers were all American, though the projects were designed by French architects.

It was into this hyperrationalized and institutionalized world that the Paris revolt of 1968 emerged, fueled, according to one observer, by the following conditions and contradictions:

> The first industrial revolution in France occurred in a country which, fifteen years ago, was still largely rural. The second industrial revolution—atomic energy, automation, space communications, computers—is now bypassing the very areas that have been most advanced. The breaking down of frontiers in the Common Market has forced the industries of France and Europe to adapt or perish. . . .
>
> Add to this a psychological mutation. None of the eighteenth- or nineteenth-century ideologies are able to cope with the new problems of society. Pure capitalism is no longer satisfactory, and it is changing rapidly in the United States. Socialism, as it has been practiced in Eastern Europe, has also failed and is going through a radical transformation in Russia itself.[31]

Immanuel Wallerstein takes this critique further. Speaking of the nature of the 1968 world revolutions, he writes, "they legitimated and strengthened the sense of disillusionment not only with the old antisystemic movements but also with the state structures these movements had been fortifying. The long-term certainties of evolutionary hope had become transformed into fears that the world-system might be unchanging."[32] The tension between a sense of possible radical change and pessimistic attitudes toward conservative continuities were met by the partitioning and centralization evinced in the new plan for Paris, which redistributed power and authority while graphically marking the line between the core and periphery:

> Those who live in the provinces resent this humiliating and paralyzing centralization even more than Parisians do. . . . Whether the subject be education, housing, urban planning, the water supply, or recreational equipment, the municipalities have had virtually no freedom. . . . Caught in this crossfire between a mounting pace of change and a petrified society, the nation has tried to follow two contradictory objectives at the same time: the expansion of the economy and the conservation of the old political mechanism.[33]

These dramatic changes, occurring at once in the social, political, economic, and cultural spheres and often in contradiction, spill out as well into the lived environments and physical Forms of social space, just as they did during the period that saw the composition of "The Jolly Corner." Todorov appreciates in James precisely his attention to form, but, equally important, both these formal appreciations of James's craft are themselves set within historical eras that witness similar demands being placed on Form to mediate between divergent worlds, to imagine the planet as an inhabited and animated social space. The appeal of Form was felt not only transatlantically during a time of political and social upheaval, but also transpacifically. Again, it is James who stands out as that figure who is seen to best articulate a notion of Form that can serve planetary purposes of cohesion, continuity, and sociality amidst difference.

This time he is delivered into the other spaces of the globe not by an East European expatriate, but by an American academic invited to lecture the Japanese on literary criticism.

FROM THE ATLANTIC TO THE PACIFIC

Interestingly for this essay on American literature, the notion of the planetary, and Form, one of the first attempts to build an American-designed building in postwar Japan was the design and construction of the Reader's Digest Building, which was to house that eminent attempt to condense and disseminate literature throughout America and the rest of the world. At the start of the Allied occupation of Japan, architect Antonin Raymond petitioned General MacArthur to be able to reenter Japan in order to participate in the work of reconstructing the country. One of his first projects, requested by Mrs. DeWitt Wallace, was the Reader's Digest Building: "The latest technical innovations and materials available in the United States were now copied in Japan under his supervision. . . . [U]nlike the Imperial Hotel down the street, the building's oblique profile was 'international' rather than continental."[34] In it we can find the critical tension between intimations of planetariness ("international style") and the counterweights of national and racial history, between aesthetics and politics.

With regard to this style, one of the most influential postwar architects in Japan was Kenzo Tange, a widely read cosmopolitan intellectual who was well versed in Valéry, Gide, Proust, and Dostoyevsky. Tange studied Le Corbusier's work closely, but particularly as it was itself influenced by Michelangelo, writing a "Eulogy for Michelangelo as an Introduction to the Study of Le Corbusier." His response to the position documents of the Congrès Internationaux d'Architecture Moderne were particularly influential.

The significance of the postwar meetings of the CIAM cannot be overemphasized, as they set an agenda that had to be reckoned with, either positively or negatively, by the international architectural community. After the war, the issue of renovation and renewal took center stage. In 1949 the congress issued this challenge: "Death overcomes buildings and cities as well as human beings. Who will make the choice between what should remain and what must disappear?" The response was as follows:

> The spirit which prevails in the oldest part of the city is built up over the years; ordinary buildings acquire an everlasting significance insomuch as they come to symbolize collective consciousness; they provide the skeleton of a tradition, which, without attempting to limit future progress, nevertheless conditions and forms individuals in much the same way as do climate, country, race or custom. Since cities, and especially historic town centers, are nations unto themselves, there is a sense of moral value that holds a meaning and to which they are indivisibly linked.[35]

(This quote could very well describe the issues at stake at the turn of the century in James's New York.)

Nevertheless, in Japan this "collective consciousness," a term that emanates out of Le Corbusier, was deeply shaken by the war, the massive fire bombings and the devastation of the atomic bombs. Regarding Tange's design of the Atomic Memorial Museum, Stewart notes that "the compulsive attraction which Hiroshima suddenly came to exercise, and which it holds for us today, is that all such considerations were obliterated at a single stroke. As a result, a new 'soul' or collective focus was created as a function of national and, eventually, of world attention. This imposed meaning, having nothing to do with the monumental features of the town itself, creates its own unique situational ethos as a kind of antithesis."[36] That is to say, the global effects of history impede any notion that a city could be a nation unto itself.

Still, at the 1960 Tokyo World Design Conference, Tange employed such words as "cell"and "metabolism" in an attempt to evoke the city, once again, as a kind of self-enclosed organism. A member of his group, Noriaki Kurokawa, published a manifesto, *Metabolism 1960: Proposals for a New Urbanism*, which deployed keywords such as "mobility," "cluster," "growth/change," "urbanism and habitat," and biological rhythm, which Stewart notes implied "a degree of order and control, on a new invisible scale or level."[37]

The idea of Metabolism attached itself to the program of CIAM, but also inescapably ran up against its problematic attempt to ascertain what was to be preserved from what was to be created, and the premises upon which such a determination was to be made:

> The conceit of transforming ruins into a city of the future in Isozaki's imagination lies midway between such behavioral extremes, and the "Future City" illustration itself is concerned, above all, with establishing transience as a monumental datum. This vision of a contemporary city arising amid classical ruins of a markedly primitive type and bespeaking an already known capacity for future growth—but also decline—is supremely an image of its time. . . . Interestingly, in diverging from the biorhythmical imagery of the main Metabolist personalities, "Future City" raises the ante for the Metabolist stakes. By admitting a free-floating metaphor of classicity, it also permits us to glimpse a crack in the Metabolist's spotless utopia.[38]

The tension between the notion of residual traditional forms and independent forms of modernity must be understood as taking place within a particular national political history. The formalist and self-enclosed aesthetic may be related to a general revision of the historical and political realm in which Japanese architects were working. For example, Hajime Yatsuka argues that Tange's Tokyo Bay Project "was a negative picture of his 'Greater Asian Co-prosperity Sphere Monument,' just as the political background had reversed from a totalitarian regime to a democratic one. By adopting an axial composition, Tange argued that limitations on the scope of expansion in the existing

Figure 8.2. Modern Tokyo building. Photo by Ari Seligman.

radial-concentric structure of Tokyo would be greatly alleviated."[39] This re-alignment of aesthetics with the postwar historical and political contingencies is noted as well by Wendelken:

> Japanese architects . . . reforged links with the international design community and its values. . . . In the broadest sense, the reappearance of modernist design must be understood beyond its link to architects or architectural movements overseas. The rehabilitation of modernist architecture of the late 1940s and early 1950s, with its

214 • David Palumbo-Liu

emphasis on the rational use of industrial materials, functional planning, and rejection of historical or regional references, was part of a larger cultural climate. Historian Victor Koschman has proposed that a "community of contrition" be created in Japan during the first decade after the war, characterized by universalist concerns: "humanity, the abstract individual, the working class."[40] There was thus "an overt agenda to transcend national boundaries."[41]

Yet this move toward an ahistorical internationalist aesthetic could not maintain itself for long—by the 1950s and 1960s, one witnesses the emergence of *machinami hozon undô*, grassroots preservation societies seeking to preserve, revive, and even invent "tradition." In 1955, the Society for International Cultural Relations published *Architectural Beauty in Japan*: "the division of the book into pre-modern and modern sections seeks both to mask, and to minimize, the pervasive, catastrophic environmental and cultural rupture of the Second World War, by constructing a visual narrative of continuity at the very moment when continuities were little felt or seen" (199).

The repudiation of both the aspirations of the Metabolist rational response to contingency and the internationalist aesthetic of transcendent form, which each in their own way attempted the containment of chaos, came in 1960, when more than 5 million demonstrators took to the streets to protest renewal of the U.S.-Japan Security Pact in Tokyo: "The psychological breach became more firmly established as Japan's power in the economic sphere evolved and the conservatism of her political establishment was openly accepted as a way of life; disenchantment and frustration among intellectuals reached a high point in the futile revolt of the universities later in the decade. . . . [A]s the social goals of the protest movement aborted, the expected pursuit by younger men of the 'architect's modern' practiced by Maekawa, Tange, and others was subtly undermined. In brief, events of the sixties imposed a tacit recognition that a specifically Japanese 'new tradition' was as empty as Antonin Raymond had warned."[42] That is to say, the very reinvention of Japan after the war was predicated upon its reformation by the United States as an economic nation integrated into the postwar capitalist world economic system now dominated by the United States.

Under these circumstances, "Le Corbusier's concept of 'La Ville Radieuse' (the Radiant City) as a 'rational and poetic monument set up in the midst of contingencies,' though it may contradict Japanese sensibilities, would never prove thoroughly alien in a milieu of an industrialized, or industrializing, cultural setting."[43] The borders between "tradition" and the modern, the city as self-enclosed nation with its own memory and the city as part of a global historical moment, and the nation as cultural nation and as nodal point in a network of transnational capitalist life, could not be maintained. The postwar reconstruction of Tokyo as precisely an economically and financially organized "global city" insinuated it automatically into the circuits of postwar capitalism, and broke apart the seemingly easy boundaries between past and future forms. Ichikawa Hiroo notes precisely the intimate connection between the project to reconstruct Tokyo and the project to construct it as a global financial center. According to the Tokyo War Damage Rehabilitation Plan, "Tokyo was to become an industrial city in the future, the priority at that time should be on development as a political, economic and cultural centre."[44] In fact, with the Korean War, Tokyo benefited from the huge influx of U.S. military dollars: "Once the Korean War began in June 1950, Tokyo experienced a burst of new energy and an economic 'special procurements boom' that sparked Tokyo's resurrection. . . . The number of offices, only 281,000 in 1947, totaled 359,000 only seven years later. The land created through the filling in of streams and moats with the ashes of the war-damaged city provided the foundations for the rise of the business sector" (54–55). Yet with this economic surge came too "a lack of balance in the use of land and in the disorderly construction of the city's landscape. This foretold the city's general lack of coherence and logical order in its urban forms" (55).

Not only was it a matter of "urban forms," but, in much the same way as we witnessed in James's New York City and Todorov's Paris, it was a matter too of new social forms: "The public sector responded with the construction of the apartment buildings know as *danchi* complexes to meet the urgent demand for housing. . . . [T]he huge apartment complexes rose one after the other to house what became the '*danchi* clan.' Soon friction appeared between the newer and older inhabitants of the area because of differences in values and style of living. In other ways too, these enormous apartment complexes caused problems for the municipal government, which had to provide the infrastructure to support such large numbers" (55).

In his preface to *Tokyo for the People: Concepts for Urban Renewal*, the then-mayor of Tokyo, Ryokichi Minobe, writes, "in giving priority to Tokyo's development as the economic and industrial hub of the nation after World War II, the welfare of its citizens was forced to take a back seat."[45] This municipal report notes, "The US recommendations, known as the 'Dodge Line' after the US financial authority Mr. Joseph Dodge, gave priority to putting the Japanese economy back on an independent footing, and establishing a sound capital base. . . . City planning to date has been formulated without the people" (11).

If above we noted the moment in which a transcendental notion of the individual was appealed to as an essential element for postwar internationalist architecture, by this time any innocent notion of the individual has been modified according to the inescapable pressures of new modern urban life. In this regard, an essay by Masao Maruyama is instructive.[46] According to Maruyama, one of the fundamental questions of the 1960 Hakone Conference on the "Modernization of Japan" was "whether we should incorporate such concepts as 'democracy,' 'liberalism,' and 'socialism' into the conceptual framework with which to deal with the problems involved in modernization"

216 • David Palumbo-Liu

(489). Importantly, even as these academic questions were posed, Maruyama notes too that "Professor J. Hall, in his capacity as chairman of the conference, doubted 'whether in the tense political environment of the summer demonstrations, these subjects could be objectively discussed' " (489). The reference to demonstrations points to precisely the protests described above in my treatment of modern Japanese architecture.

Maruyama's essay focuses on "the disparity between what is expected of modern institutions—legal, political, and economic—and the interpersonal relations which in fact are at work within the framework of such institutions," noting that "it is beyond dispute that the degree of inconsistency in Japan, or in other non-Western countries where all modern institutions and ideas were imported from outside as 'ready-made articles,' is far greater than in the Western countries" (491). Thus, while individuals are formed in relation to the institutional frames in which they operate socially, in modernizing Japan we have this ponderous "degree of inconsistency": "The dominant personality type in any society experiencing modernization seems to have a definite interrelationship with the kind of political and social system the society develops; and that different patterns in the disintegration of 'traditional' attitudes, as well as their variances from one social strata to another or from one generation to another, may be one of the crucial factors in determining the political dynamics of modernization" (492). In a standard sociological gesture, Maruyama agrees with one of his coconferees: "Thus, [Schwartz] concludes that 'modernization' can be given a universal definition only with regard to the appropriate means by which man controls his physical and social environments" (493).[47] Nevertheless, recalling Tange's "metabolistic" manifesto for architecture, we find such appeals to controlling the environment rather dubious.

Maruyama thus focuses on that newly complex interstitial space between individual and collective bodies, which are then plotted along a temporal and spatial line: "Four possible patterns of such an individuation process which can be distinguished according to the attitude of the person experiencing various phases of modernization, and which determine his sense of relationship with his community. These four are: individualization, democratization, privatization, and atomization. . . . Individualization is centrifugal and yet associative; democratization is associative and centripetal; privatization is centrifugal and dissociative; finally, atomization is dissociative and yet centripetal" (494). This is the Japan that Blackmur will enter into, one that sees its rebirth take place within a debate over the containability of the city, as an organic form, as a self-enclosed system, as a monument to nuclear devastation, as a relic of tradition, or, predominately, as the New Japan of modernity, economic ascension, and late capitalist development as a global city.[48] All these questions inform the constitution of social space, the interstitial elements between these newly invented and inconsistent "individuals."

And in the Japanese project to understand the *formal* modulation of new social life, R. P. Blackmur will find a common interest. Indeed, "form" here will be the critical analytic and imaginative category with which he will approach modern literature and society.

BLACKMUR ON FORM

Blackmur's appreciation of James is multifaceted and wide ranging, but it is not unjust to assert that the essential element that Blackmur isolated within both James's literary and critical texts was that of Form. For instance, in his introduction to his edition of James's critical prefaces, Blackmur notes "James' exceeding conviction that the art of fiction is an organic form."[49] Indeed, it was precisely the job of art to give form to life:

> Life itself—the subject of art—was formless and likely to be a waste, with its situations leading to endless bewilderment; while art, the imaginative representation of life, selected, formed, made lucid and intelligent, gave value and meaning to, the contrasts and oppositions and processions of the society that confronted the artist. The emphases were on intelligence—James was avowedly the novelist of the free spirit, the liberated intelligence—on feeling, and on form. . . . Everything must be sacrificed to the exigence of that form, it must never be loose or overflowing but always tight and contained. There was the "coercive charm" of Form, so conceived, which would achieve, dramatise or enact, the moral intent of the theme by making it finely intelligible, better than anything else.[50]

The struggle for Form becomes explicitly articulated as a struggle to find a medial form between author and reader that might, finally, produce a particular effect: "The greater complexity, the superior truth, was all more or less present to me; the only question was, too dreadfully, how to make it present to the reader? How to boil down so many facts in the alembic, so that the distilled result, the produced appearance, should have intensity, lucidity, brevity, beauty, all the merits required for my effect?"[51] The goal is thus not only to reshape Life into a Form that would be commensurate with Life, but also to complete that act of predication required the connection with the reader, and the success of that connection was evinced by the production of a specific effect. That effect counted on the potency of the "coercion" of Form, a coercion found in another form in James's tale of haunting, in which Brydon is both "charmed" and "coerced" by the Form of otherness, indeed, rendered unconscious by it finally, and that tale itself was the product of an effect posited upon the young James at the Galerie d'Apollon by Form itself. We begin to see then the double currency of Form, as it acts both as subject and as it is posited as object. But we should not lose sight of the fact that there is a third manifestation of Form—that is of the emptied and always potential space of positing, of depositing an imaginative will.

The pun on the idea of currency, the cash value of Form, is meant to draw out, or better yet, to not leave silent, the economic facet of "The Jolly Corner," and of Form. Recall that Brydon mentions again and again the cash value of the newly re-formed house, the other house. A corollary question emerges— what would Brydon have "been worth" if he had indeed stayed in America? The transactional value of Form as it receives and conveys the imagined forms of modern life, as it exchanges value, is indeed not too subtly found in the passage above, which ends by saying that the successful work of art would make the theme "finely intelligible, *better* than anything else [my emphasis]." The problem I wish to trace is exactly the problem of how value is both assigned and conveyed when the rates of exchange are unsettled, volatile, when history has produced multiple and differentiated ways of measuring Form and value. The Jolly Corner contains one, the "other" house another, for instance. The pressure on Form is thus increased—it must reconcile difference (then and now, the two Brydons, America and Europe), not to make them the same (that would be impossible), but to find some way of having them speak to each other, to have some convertibility to the same currency, some common way of marking value and communicating meaning.

In his 1951 essay, "The Loose and Baggy Monsters of Henry James: Notes on the Underlying Classic Form in the Novel," Blackmur not only reasserts the value of Form in art in much the same terms as James (and in the terms in which he interprets James), but also foregrounds its specific value in his contemporary postwar age. To begin with, he sees technical form as "our means of getting at, of finding, and then making something of, what we feel the form of life itself is: the tensions, the stresses, the deep relations and the terrible disrelations that inhabit them as they are made to come together in a particular struggle between manners and behavior, between the ideal insight and the actual momentum in which the form of life is found."[52] Crucially, both "manners and behaviors" and "actual momentum" are located by Blackmur within a specific sense of history and contingency. In the following passage we glimpse Blackmur's sensitivity to the crisis in his age, one characterized by the absence (or silence) of resonant forms and active subjects mutually engaged in social and cultural exchange:

What we see is the disappearance of the old establishment of culture—culture safe from the ravages of economy—and we do not know whether another culture is emerging from the massive dark, or if it is, whether we like it. . . . What has above all survived in our new mass society is the sense of the pure individual—by himself, or herself, heir to all the ages. Because of the loss of the cultural establishment we have put a tremendous burden on the pure individual consciousness. . . . Sometimes this burden of consciousness seems to obscure, if not to replace, the individuals we create,

Figure 8.3. Richard P. Blackmur at Zenkoji Temple, August 1956.

whether in ourselves or in our arts. At any rate, this burden of consciousness is what has happened to our culture. There is no longer any establishment, no longer any formula, and we like to say only vestigial forms, to call on outside ourselves. (144)

Thus Blackmur approaches the question of reanimating literary critical formal sensibilities that have been with us since antiquity as a way to reconnect to the social world as a pedagogical and ethical problem, produced by and in an age when a particular brand of modern individualism appears at a point of historical rupture. The burden placed on individual consciousness is precisely the burden of invention in the absence of tradition. Unanchored by the radical change in historical context, modern "individuals" are set loose to find their own path. The imperative to be oneself finds no modeling system, no form that suffices, and instead individuals cannot but fall back upon themselves. The best that can be hoped for is that some might imagine what in forms they might be mutually apprehended.

Crucially, Blackmur then draws a relation between his age and its crisis and that of James: "His [James's] own experience of 'America' and of 'Europe,'

Figure 8.4. Blackmur at Nagano Seminar.

where America had apparently moved faster than Europe toward the mass society, toward the disinheritance but not the disappearance of the individual, had moved him ahead of his contemporaries" (145). That is to say, James's place ahead of his contemporaries is enabled by James's co-occupation of America and Europe, in his bearing witness in stereoscopic form to their mutual yet incommensurate existence.

This sense of history and cultural change, and the concomitant pressure now exerted upon art, is found again, and with added conviction and urgency, in a series of lectures Blackmur delivered in Japan in 1956 at the Nagano Summer Seminar in American Literature. In these lectures, Blackmur gives specific attention to James's notion of Form, asserting that for James "Life itself—the subject of art—was formless and likely to be a waste, with its situations leading to endless bewilderment; while art, the imaginative representation of life, selected, formed, made lucid and intelligent, gave value and meaning to, the contrasts and oppositions and processions of the society that confronted the artist."[53]

But "life itself" and all artistic attempts to represent it are to be read historically. Continuing his historical critique of the role of Form, Blackmur explains to his Japanese audience "why we developed formal and technical criticism":

Is it not because literature, and especially poetry, in the last forty years has operated in a medium both formal and technical, increasingly unavailable, either by skill or literacy, to the little audience that was desirous of reading it and for whom it was intended? Further, was not its separable content also increasingly unavailable, more obscure, more private so that the only possible approach to it was by formal and technical criticism; and this may be historically the most important aspect of the matter. Has not the professionalization of literary studies itself set up in the study of old authors the foundation for the formal and technical methods? (7–8)

In this passage, Blackmur indicts both the increasingly individualistic manners in which literature is being produced in his age and the fact that such a private mode of composition has resulted in an increasingly diminished audience capable of appreciating such literature. It is to the task of forging a possible space of understanding that formal criticism will be called. As this is the case, the notion of Form itself takes on a special status, as it is that space of mediation that one must first inhabit with the Other, a point of transfer and mutual movement into Art. And yet Blackmur follows this assertion with a bolder one, one that seeks to legitimize this seemingly "modern" problem by claiming that the "foundation" for the formal and technical methods was set up at once with the professionalization of literary studies. That is, the instantiation of "professional" literary studies had within its founding pedagogy a sensitivity toward and use for Form that has stayed with it, and now serves it well in grappling with another sort of obscurity—not that of past ages, but of an alienated present, a historical time in which "traditional" modes of being together have evaporated and "individuals" are set forth on their own to negotiate intersubjective discourse. And it is precisely in the multivalent, transhistorical (that is, "classic") aspects of Form that we can imagine a transcendental notion of Literature.

In this case, Form and our apprehension of it links not only individual to individual in the modern age, but also all living humans to others, past and present in a truly planetary existence. Formalist critics (throughout the ages) have in common "a tendency to make the analyzable features of the forms and techniques of poetry both the only means of access to poetry and somehow the equivalent of its content" (16). The genius of this turn of phrase resides exactly in the equating ("somehow") of Form and Content, and, by a corollary logic, one individual "life" with another. It is precisely the analog James sets forth in the "house of fiction"—multiple views out of the house to the scene set before it, multiple individuals at each window, and the author, watching them watch the scene, who gives shape and Form to discrepant life views. The faith that Blackmur places in Form seems absolute, and yet it is precisely the indecidable human agent that must, ultimately, find the capacity to read Form adequately. And when it comes to this thing called "human agency" we find Blackmur's cultural and historical limitations, limitations that precisely disallow him from making the connection between the ways Form houses crises of James's turn-of-the-century and postwar America *and* postwar Japan, where it seems the discrepancies of life views seem too great to be accommodated in the same space.

Blackmur's former student, Edward Said, writes eloquently of Blackmur in very similar ways, and it is useful to note how Said's critical assessment of Blackmur also brings out not only the primacy of form, but form as involved in social and economic history. I want to use one of Said's central works on Blackmur to help chart a trajectory that is not explicit in Blackmur's writings, but essential to the present essay, and that is the ways in which Blackmur's postwar writings, as we have seen above, point to an apparently transcendental notion of art and form, but also inscribe a potential obstacle that lies exactly at the boundaries between the West and non-West. And I would suggest that it is Said's position as a "postcolonial" and Todorov's as an exile to Europe from Bulgaria that give them each a particular mode of appreciating James and these issues of Form. Both subscribe to a "planetary" conceptualization of Form and yet each staunchly anchors it in a social and material world. If Todorov readmits the social world of language users back into formalist poetics, Said insists on the political nature and the historicity of englobing forms.

In his essay, "The Horizon of R. P. Blackmur," Said awards Blackmur a "position of intransigent honor."[54] For him, Blackmur "seemed to locate himself at the source of the poet's creativity, as it deployed forms, idioms, figures to negotiate the disorder of modernity" (247). He quotes extensively from Blackmur's collection, *The Lion and the Honeycomb*: "the work of art itself almost gets outside art to make a shape—a form of the forms—of our total recognition of the force that moves us."[55] In both Said's and Blackmur's phrasing there is again the attention to the connection of form and space—for Said, Blackmur's first gesture is one of situating himself and his ideal critic "at the source" of creativity, but not just "creativity" as a thing, but as a form-generating process. And it is that process-originating space that seems "almost" to exceed itself, as it creates "a form of the forms." As Said puts it, Blackmur "describe[s] literary experience as a zone rather than as an inert place" (255). It is crucial to note that this "space" is not unworldly, but precisely of the world—of social and historical materiality.

Criticism, similarly, "chart[s] a novel space between history, society, and the author" (259). Said credits James for instilling this notion into Blackmur's critical sensibilities: "His model for such a critical attitude was Henry James" (259). Said notes that James was "an American writer confronting a world of cultural forms fundamentally alien to the new and overburdened sensibility. . . . Consequently, Blackmur's consideration of James stressed the relationship between consciousness and form as a social, and not just an aesthetic, issue" (261). As I noted above, it is the problematic of reading both the forms of the old and of the new, from respectively different sensibilities, that haunts both James and Blackmur. James's wonderful description of the Americans in Europe dashing from one end of the Louvre to the other, rapaciously inhaling the scent of the traditional cultural forms, but unable to absorb them; and Blackmur's poignant invention of a line of formal and "technical" criticism reaching back to Aristotle to bolster the claims of 1960s formal criticism, in addition to numerous other instances in the works of both writers, gives us a strong sense of the social burden and historical significance placed upon the critical act. Said describes precisely that evocative movement back into classical antiquity that we saw in Blackmur: "The net effect of Blackmur's later work therefore is, I think, that of a negative dialectic, a process by which the stabilities and continuities of twentieth-century capitalism are de-defined, worn back down by a difficult, dissolving prose to the instability which the forms of art, intellect, and society had resorted to when in the first instance they tried to give permanence and shape to their apprehension" (263).[56]

Nevertheless, even as Blackmur lectures to the Japanese about the need to find the "form outside the form," that classical form that undergirds all literary production (or at least seems to), we find him reticent to make any universal claim ("Now I want to suggest something that seems to me to be a possible thing to do in the West—the language would not be your language; I don't know your language and I couldn't suddenly jump into your language to find terms" [New Criticism in the United States, 37]). And while the generous reader might see this gesture as an act of discretion, Said asserts instead that in his postwar criticism Blackmur displayed an "astonishing ignorance and condescension about the non-Western world" (261). Indeed, at exactly the same time as Blackmur is assuming a conceptual gulf between East and West, at another conference being held in Hakone in 1960, we discover a number of Western and Japanese scholars debating exactly the real possibilities that the very concept of modernity was not only transposed to Japan, but lived out in various forms. Blackmur simply assumes this gulf, this incommensurate space, between his brilliant and poignant evocation of Form as a redemptive sociocultural phenomenon, a transhistorical bridge for both individuals and societies, and whatever issues might be on the minds of his Japanese audience. And yet, as we have seen, it is precisely these issues that inform the core of postwar Japanese debates about modernization. The impossibility of fully sequestering "Form" from social ontology is evident even in the most rigorously formal criticism of the late twentieth century, in the poetics of Tzvetan Todorov, and even more elaborated in Said's critique, as appreciative as he is of Blackmur. Thus, while we must regard Form as an indispensable concept in and through which to mediate our imagining of planetariness, we cannot sequester it from the material world.

Using "The Jolly Corner" as a starting point, and situating my reading of the text within a discussion of Form in both literature and the built environment, I have hoped to show that the "house of fiction" is manifested as well in the actual shifting forms of the built environment, which itself links up to an overarching change in material history that affects at once both the production of art and the mediating function the forms of art play between social subjects. At these particulary significant times and places—turn-of-the-century America; postwar Japan; and post '68 Paris, we find the repercussions of historical change impact as well the conception of Form as housing the possibilities of intersubjective being together. This thesis thus strives to make a broader claim about formal criticism, as it has appeared in James, Todorov, and Blackmur: that Form is always, in addition to its formal literary properties, an integral aspect of a meditation on the possibilities of being together, and the conditions in which such being can be not only imagined, but built. If American literature can be seen to be "planetary," then, it is only with an accounting as well of the forms in which such "englobalization" take place sociohistorically.

NOTES

1. R. P. Blackmur, *Studies in Henry James*, ed. with an introduction by Veronica A. Makowsky (New York: New Directions, 1983), 146; Henry James, "The Jolly Corner," in Henry James, *The Portable Henry James*, ed. John Auchard (New York: Penguin Classics, 2003). All further references are to this edition.

2. I thank Wai Chee Dimock for suggesting this formulation, and for many other useful suggestions.

3. And in this catalog of exiles, expatriates, and marginals, let us not forget that Blackmur, for an act of insubordination, was banished from elementary school and never received a formal education beyond that.

4. *The Complete Notebooks of Henry James*, ed. with introductions and notes by Leon Edel and Lyall H. Powers (New York and Oxford: Oxford University Press, 1987), 189.

5. Ibid., 190.

6. Ibid., 190–91.

7. The Jolly Corner is located at Fifth Avenue near Washington Square.

8. For a fascinating study, see William Righter, *American Memory in Henry James*, ed. Rosemary Righter (Hampshire, England: Ashgate, 2004).

9. In Henry James, *The Art of the Novel: Critical Prefaces*, introduction by R. P. Blackmur (New York and London: C. Scribner's Sons, 1934).

10. Cited in Elizabeth Hawes, *New York, New York: How the Apartment House Transformed the Life of the City (1869–1930)* (New York: Knopf, 1993), 129–30.

11. Ibid.

12. Ibid., 152.

13. Ibid., 190.

14. Henry James, *The American Scene* (New York: Harper and Bros, 1907; reprint, Bloomington: Indiana University Press, 1968), 139–41.

15. Hawes, *New York, New York*, 35.

16. James, *The American* Scene, 102.

17. Sarah Bradford Landau and Carl W. Condit, *The Rise of the New York Skyscraper, 1865–1913* (New Haven: Yale University Press, 1996), 62.

18. From *French Literary Theory Today*, ed. Tzvetan Todorov, trans. R. Carter (Cambridge: Cambridge University Press, 1982), 1.

19. Ibid., 2–3.

20. Tzvetan Todorov, *Théorie de la littérature: Texts des formalists russes* (Paris: Seuil, 1965).

21. Tzvetan Todorov, *The Poetics of Prose*, trans. Richard Howard, foreword by Jonathan Culler (Ithaca, N.Y.: Cornell University Press, 1977).

22. Ibid., 188.

23. Ibid., 189.

24. Indeed, since his work on poetics, Todorov has produced an astonishing number of works addressing the idea of otherness and being together. Among many other titles (and I list only these which are in English translation), see: *The Conquest of America: The Question of the Other* (Normen: University of Oklahoma Press, 1982); *On Human Diversity: Nationalism, Racism, and Exoticism in French Thought* (Cambridge: Harvard University Press, 1993); *Life in Common: An Essay in General Anthropology* (2001); *Imperfect Garden: The Legacy of Humanism* (Princeton: Princeton University Press, 2002). For a concise and acute consideration of this topic, see Todorov, "Living Alone Together," *New Literary History* 27, no. 1 (1996): 1–14, in which he concentrates on the topic of "the social dimension, the fact of living with others."

25. Henri Lefebvre, *The Production of Space* (Paris: Anthropos, 1974; reprint, Oxford: Blackwell, 1992), 7.

26. Norma Evenson, *Paris: A Century of Change, 1878–1978* (New Haven: Yale University Press, 1979), 165.

27. Ibid., 287–88.

28. Ibid., 166.

29. Ibid., 167.

30. Ibid., 171.

31. J.-J. Servan-Schreiber, *The Spirit of May*, trans. Ronald Steel (New York: McGraw-Hill, 1969), 21–22.

32. Immanuel Wallerstein, *World-Systems Analysis* (Durham, N.C.: Duke University Press, 2004), 84.

33. Ibid., 24–25.

34. David B. Stewart, *The Making of Modern Japanese Architecture, 1868 to the Present* (Tokyo and New York: Kodansha International, 1987), 165.

35. Ibid., 173.

36. Ibid., 174.

37. Ibid., 184.

38. Ibid., 184.

39. Hajime Yatsuka, "The 1960 Tokyo Bay Project of Kenzo Tange," in *Cities in Transition*, ed. Deborah Hauptmann (Rotterdam: 010 Publishers, 2001), 187–88.

40. J Victor Koschman, "Intellectuals and Politics," in *Postwar Japan as History*, ed. Andrew Gordon (Berkeley: University of California Press, 1933), 395–423.

41. Cherie Wendelken, "Aesthetics and Reconstruction: Japanese Architectural Culture in the 1950s," in *Rebuilding Urban Japan after 1945*, ed. Carol Hein, Jeffry M. Diefendorf, and Ishida Yorifusa, 192. References appear in the text.

42. Stewart, *The Making of Modern Japanese Architecture*, 189.

43. Ibid.

44. Ichikawa Hiroo, "Reconstructing Tokyo: The Attempt to Transform a Metropolis," in *Rebuilding Urban Japan after 1945*, ed. Carol Hein, Jeffry M. Diefendorf, and Ishida Yorifusa (London: Palgrave Macmillan, 2003), 53. References appear in the text.

45. *Tokyo for the People: Concepts for Urban Renewal*, ed. by the Liaison and Protocol, Bureau of General Affairs (Tokyo: Tokyo Metropolitan Government, 1972), i.

46. Masao Maruyama, "Patterns of Individuation and the Case of Japan: A Conceptual Scheme," in *Changing Japanese Attitudes toward Modernization*, ed. Marius B. Jansen (Princeton: Princeton University Press, 1965), 489–532.

47. B. I. Schwartz, "Modernization and Its Ambiguities," unpublished conference paper, Conference on Modern Japan, August 29—September 2, 1960, Hakone, Japan.

48. For this term, see Saskia Sassen, *The Global City: New York, London, Tokyo* (Princeton: Princeton University Press, 2001).

49. From R. P. Blackmur, *The Art of the Novel: Critical Prefaces*, with an introduction by Richard P. Blackmur (New York: Charles Scribner's Sons, 1934), xxiii.

50. Ibid., xxxviii. Consider as well Blackmur's assertion that "James was impervious to every force to which he could not give a form and what makes him a writer of great stature was the gradual deepening of the themes which beset him to find them form." *The Outsider at the Heart of Things: Essays by R. P. Blackmur*, ed. with an introduction by James T. Jones (Urbana: University of Illinois Press, 1989), 192.

51. Ibid., 13.

52. R. P. Blackmur, *Studies in Henry James*, ed. with an introduction by Veronica A. Makowsky (New York: New Directions, 1983), 129.

53. R. P. Blackmur, *New Criticism in the United States* (Tokyo: Kenkyusha, 1959), 3–4.

54. Edward W. Said, *Reflections on Exile and Other Essays* (Cambridge: Harvard University Press, 2002), 246–67, 247.

55. R. P. Blackmur, *The Lion and the Honeycomb: Essays in Solitude and Critique* (New York: Harcourt, Brace and Co., 1955).

56. Said, 263.

CHAPTER 9

Ecoglobalist Affects: The Emergence of U.S. Environmental Imagination on a Planetary Scale

Lawrence Buell

To THINK "ENVIRONMENTALLY" or "ecologically" requires thinking "against" or "beyond" nationness even more self-evidently than thinking "culturally" does. Seldom do jurisdictional borders correspond to ecological borders. For the island nation of Iceland, yes. For the U.S.-Canada and the U.S.-Mexico borders, clearly not. Arguably "the oldest form of globalization" is environmental rather than economic or political.[1] Species have been migrating ever since life on earth began. Individual states have never effectively legislated against disease, toxic fallout, plant and animal invasions—less so in recent times than ever before. Smallpox took three millennia to spread worldwide, AIDS three decades. Particularly during the last half century, supposedly integral "landscapes" have become "timescapes" subject to inexorable reshaping by exotic permeations we are just starting to learn how to measure.[2] The Rachel Carson of social theory, Ulrich Beck, may be right in asserting that a global "risk society"—a shared climate of anxiety about the threats of environmental deterioration—has come into being that comprehends the rich as well as the poor.[3] During the past quarter century, the prospect of global warming, whatever the culture of denial within the present U.S. administration, has reinforced a tendency to think of environmental belonging and citizenship in planetary terms, and for international accords unprecedented in seeking to guard against predicted catastrophes that are still a long time off.[4]

From this standpoint the case for a planetary perspective over against a nation-centered approach to environmentality seems open and shut. The whole earth image taken from the moon a third of a century ago has long since become a logo, a cultural cliché.[5] But ecoglobalism, that is a whole-earth way of thinking and feeling about environmentality, is at this time of writing more a model that has begun to take root than an achieved result: a model for inquiry, furthermore, that is quite unevenly distributed across the disciplines. The average contemporary geologist or ecologist or environmental economist is better equipped to operate on a global scale than is the average sociologist or historian, and the average ethicist more so than the average literary critic. This essay, then, will be a partial account of an emergent critical project that for understandable substantive and pragmatic reasons is almost certainly destined to remain a work in progress, well in arrears of the bolder acts of ecoliterary imagination for decades to come.

THE AMBIGUOUS PLACE OF NATIONNESS IN THE CONTEXT OF ECOLOGICAL MODERNIZATION

What might account for the slow and uneven advance of ecoglobalism as a settled conviction and critical modus operandi relative to its ostensible cogency, relative to nationness, as an image or notion? One hypothesis would be aversiveness toward "globalization" or "globalism" conceived as the aspiration of a particular nation (the United States, for instance) or block of nations (the G-8 or the permanent members of the U.N. Security Council, for instance) to control world affairs. A more satisfactorily comprehensive explanation, however, suggested by these same examples, would be that there's simply no possibility that the nation form, however much nation-centrism be deplored or deconstructed, will go away any time soon, even in an arena like environmentality that is inherently border crossing in nature and planetary in ultimate scope. Transnational accords on environmental policy are cobbled together by national representatives. Decisions made unilaterally from national self-interest increasingly have the potential for altering environments on a planetary scale, especially if the country in question has the world's biggest economy.

Meanwhile, in the arts, literary production and academic study have been from Enlightenment even into Postmodernism profoundly shaped by a "Herderian imperative" to conceive of literary cultures as expressions of national cultures, an imperative that has been in certain respects reinforced even as it has been increasingly regulated by a global system of print culture channeled through a handful of cultural centers.[6] Discourses that aspire self-consciously to transnational or global reach can easily wind up recontained by nation-centered mentalities.

Ecocriticism—as the burgeoning movement of environmentally oriented literary studies of the last fifteen years has come to be called—is ironically a typical case in point. Most ecocritics tend in practice to adopt a single-country-focused approach, notwithstanding that most, like me, believe in principle that thinking about environmentality in terms that are either more microscopic (e.g., local, regional) or macroscopic (e.g., bioregional-transnational, continental, oceanic, or planetary) than the nation-level. Ecocriticism started as an insurgency that located itself explicitly within U.S. literary studies; and despite having spread long since throughout the Anglophone world and beyond, its practitioners still tend to direct what from a planetary standpoint seems disproportionate attention to putatively national modes and myths of landscape imagination, such as the value traditionally set on "nature" and "wilderness" as definers of U.S. cultural-geographic distinctiveness.[7] Even when conducted skeptically, concentration on such topics can wind up reinforcing a nation-centripetal disposition toward environmentality.

Not that this *need* be a problem in and of itself. After all, most if not all modernized nations, for example, have myths of nationness that identify it with "heartland" and traditions of pastoral nostalgia for a more land-based existence than their intelligentsia now enjoy. The problem arises when these phenomena are studied in isolation rather than in conversation with each other.[8]

Obviously national environments do have repertoires of unique environmental features. Just to name a few physiographic basics, this nation has numerous unique plant and animal species and unique geologic "wonders": Yellowstone, Niagara Falls, the South Dakota badlands, Death Valley, and so forth. No nation-state has greater extremes of climate. A hundred or so miles inland from its coasts, the U.S. population thins out to a degree that might astonish one whose entry point or primary base of operations is New York or Los Angeles. (But also remember Australia, Canada, Siberia.) Homeland myths, furthermore, are hardly interchangeable. German valorization of *Heimat* does not *equate* to U.S.-style "nature's nation"-ism, which hardly equates to (say) Chicano Atzlan or Jewish Zion or Hopi Túwanasavi. It is rather the complex, tangled, coevolving interaction between what seem to be the environmental "givens" and emergent cultural imaginaries—a process typically not autonomous and hermetically sealed like a controlled laboratory experiment but syncretic and porous to extrinsic influences—that produces a *national* environmental imaginary, which in turn acquires to a lesser or greater extent the powers to produce what pass as distinctive myths of landscape that then inscribe themselves on the physical environment, partly to underscore and partly to produce what passes as distinctively national environmental forms. In U.S. history, the most important strand of this imaginary, as long observed by celebrators and detractors alike, has been the vision of a vast land of abundant resources whose natural advantages promised an inexhaustible opportunity for settlers and a guarantee of future national greatness.[9]

The first grand-scale example of the hybrid fusion of ideology and physical landscape was the legacy of the late-eighteenth-century Jeffersonian land survey that mapped the vast transappalachian hinterland in rectilinear grids, which in turn became the units of purchase and settlement for much of the lower forty-eight states. This gridwork reflected a vision of "democratic social space," a potential distribution of landscape at least notionally egalitarian (however compromised in practice by land speculation), in terms of which land parcels were defined as interchangeable and fungible commodities in utter disregard of topographic contours, differential rainfall and soil fertility, and the like. The patchwork quilt of Mondrian squares stretching across the midcontinent is the engineered result.[10] During the past century, an even more proliferate, transregional form of U.S. "democratic" landscape reengineering is postage-stamp pastoral suburbanization, of which the "development" of multiple single-family tract houses is the typical icon.[11]

The fact that national land(scape) myths and ideologies can produce large-scale refashioning of a nation's physical landscape does not justify studying these effects only at the level of the nation, however. Indeed, quite the contrary. On the one hand, there are family resemblances among national landscape ideologies. The Australian settler ideology of *terra nullius*, the notion of a vast vacant land available for the taking, has close affinities with American promised-land ideology. On the other hand, landscape engineering may bespeak transnational repercussions and/or interdependencies. Neither of the two paradigmatic landscape forms just described, the Jefferson-instigated hinterland gridwork and the suburban subdivision, has been sustained by national resources alone. The former depends for its prosperity upon a lavishly expensive system of price supports that have destabilizing effects on world markets. The latter requires ever larger conurbations of increasingly remote exurban parcels dependent upon further proliferation of automotive-based transportation networks that make the United States increasingly energy-dependent on foreign suppliers. Neither the domestic agricultural subsidy system as such nor the consumer culture that canonizes the suburban "dream house" and the "love affair with the American lawn" are more unique to the United States than are the basic types of pastoral nationalism they reflect and perpetuate: the myth of a national agricultural heartland and the myth of a green "middle landscape" between urban and outback. The exceptionalism is more of degree than of kind. Writing in the days of the early republic of the transformation of the American northeast from "wilderness" into orderly self-sufficient agricultural villages, Calvinist minister Timothy Dwight insisted, with only slight excess of zeal, that such an achievement was a phenomenon "of which the eastern continent and the records of past ages furnish neither an example, nor a resemblance." But what understandably amazed Dwight most was the scale and speed of the experiment. It would be interesting to know how he would have reacted to megascale American suburbanization.[12] From a turn-of-the-twenty-first-century standpoint, this seems especially responsible for the fact that the United States leaves by far the largest "ecological footprint" of any nation on earth,[13] and for its being bound for the foreseeable future within a web of global entanglements around the procurement of such extracted resources as oil, rare minerals, and timber.

In quotidian middle-class existence, this side of American ecoglobalism tends to be hidden in plain sight. How many people, including even intellectuals, regularly ponder where ordinary household objects come from? Hence the value of a book like John Ryan and Alan Thein During's *Stuff*, a primer on common products on which middle American families depend: coffee, newspapers, T-shirts, bikes, and so forth. The authors track the transcontinental flows of raw materials, the story of their assemblage across space and time, the hidden as well as the nominal costs involved.[14] Yet by other standards of measurement national ecoglobal imagination is self-consciously alert. U.S. citizens are also the world's largest bankrollers of environmental nongovernmental organizations (NGOs), even if not the most generous contributor on a per capita basis.

Prima facie, this is a mendacious paradox: to purport to care for what amounts to the distant impact of the chronic indulgence of which one remains negligently unaware—whether the "one" is a person or a populace. It is hardly consoling that the paradox more or less holds for other economically potent nation-states—the United Kingdom, Germany, and Japan, for example. Yet the self-contradiction also makes sense. Nothing is commoner than disparities between notional assent to a principle and full internalization. The gap between environmental attitudes and behavior specifically is largely explicable by the alienation of modern daily living from the processes of extraction and production, as well as by a lack of felt urgency among even the moderately well-off, not to mention the truly affluent. U.S. public opinion polls indicate that the state and fate of "the environment" matters much more to respondents in principle than as a top-priority crisis in the here and now. Environment is expected to become a pressing concern a few decades hence, but not imminently. Everyone wants a safe and attractive environment, but enough citizens—poll respondents, anyhow—are buffered from immediate bad effects to make environmental welfare seem more like an amenity to be expected than a emergency that calls for drastic changes in behavior.[15]

To the extent that this paradoxical mentality of half-awakeness and self-division with regard to the responsibilities of ecological citizenship at national and individual levels can be credited with an implicit ethos of any sort, it can be typed as a semiconscious version of the mentality that European social theorists have started to call "ecological modernization." Like its more familiar semisynonym "sustainable development,"[16] ecological modernization favors a mode of economic evolution that will somehow be regulated by respect for environmental risks and constraints, and holds that something like a worldwide network of environmental policy-making institutions has begun to gain a "momentum and internal 'logic' which can no longer be reduced to a narrow economic rationality."[17]

To a considerable extent, this vision of the birth of a semiautonomous global environmental public sphere may be wishful thinking. (N.b.: the writer in question cites NAFTA and the World Bank as venues traditionally associated with free market values in which an "increasing advance of environmental considerations" is visible.) At best we are talking about two steps forward, one step back. Be that as it may, to the extent that there is a "paradigmatic" or normative disposition that marks ecoglobalist sentiment within the United States today, and in other modernized nations as well, ecological modernization is probably it.

The sections that follow will attempt to show how this state of affairs makes literary-historical sense. The emergence of U.S. ecoglobal imagination is symbiotic with the history of economic modernization. I hope to unfold some of the key stages in this history in such a way as to avoid the facile extremes of capitalism-bashing (which blocks one from understanding how a "responsible" ecoglobalism might arise as a messily partial yet partially honorable reaction against the conquest mentality itself) and of maintaining that any actor in this drama no matter how admirable can be exonerated from the culture of economic entrepreneurialism that has largely driven American settlement from its inception. Beyond this, I hope also to help clarify both why U.S. environmental imagination might crystallize in nationalistic ways and yet at the same time remain markedy transnational or global in character.

LITERARY U.S. ECOGLOBALISM AS LITERARY AFFECT: SOME CONTEMPORARY EXAMPLES

By "ecoglobalist affect" I mean, in broadest terms, an emotion-laden preoccupation with a finite, near-at-hand physical environment defined, at least in part, by an imagined inextricable linkage of some sort between that specific site and a context of planetary reach. Either the feel of the near-at-hand or the sense of its connection to the remote may be experienced as either consoling or painful or both. Diaspora can feel wrenching and liberatory by turns. Ecoglobalist affect entails a widening of the customary aperture of vision as unsettling as it is epiphanic in a positive sense, and a perception of raised stakes as to the significance of whatever is transpiring locally in the here and now that tends to bring with it either a fatalistic sense of the inexorable or a daunting sense of responsibility as the price of prophetic vision.

Three late-twentieth-century literary excerpts will ramify.[18]

> I sit in the shade of the trees of the land I was born in.
> As they are native I am native, and I hold to this place as carefully as
>   they hold to it,
> I do not see the national flag flying from the staff of the sycamore,
> or any decree of the government written on the leaves of the walnut,
> nor has the elm bowed before monuments or sworn the oath of allegiance.
> They have not declared to whom they stand in welcome.
> In the thought of you I imagine myself free of the weapons and the official
>   hates that I have borne on my back like a hump,
> and in the thought of myself I imagine you free of weapons and official hates,
> so that if we should meet we would not go by each other looking at the ground
>   like slaves sullen under their burdens,
> but would stand clear in the gaze of each other.
> —Wendell Berry, from "To a Siberian Woodsman" (1968)

There was no end to it; it knew no boundaries; and he had arrived at the point of convergence where the fate of all living things, and even the earth, had been laid. From the jungles of his dreaming he recognized why the Japanese voices had merged with Laguna voices, with Josiah's voice and Rocky's voice; the lines of cultures and worlds were drawn in flat dark lines on fine light sand, converging in the middle of witchery's final ceremonial sand painting. From that time on, human beings were one clan again, united by the fate the destroyers planned for all of them, for all living things; united by a circle of death that devoured people in cities twelve thousand miles away, victims who had never known these mesas, who had never seen the delicate colors of the rocks which boiled up their slaughter.

— Leslie Marmon Silko, from *Ceremony*

The Matacão, scientists asserted, had been formed for the most part within the last century, paralleling the development of the more common forms of plastic, polyurethane and styrofoam. Enormous landfills of nonbiodegradable material buried under virtually every populated part of the Earth had undergone tremendous pressure, pushed ever farther into the lower layers of the Earth's mantle. The liquid deposits of the molten mass had been squeezed through underground veins to virgin areas of the Earth. The Amazon Forest, being one of the last virgin areas on Earth, got plenty.

— Karen Tei Yamashita, from *Through the Arc of the Rain Forest*

Kentucky regionalist Wendell Berry's Vietnam-era Cold War poem hopes that similarity of ecocultural context might unite rustic husbandmen across the world and thereby neutralize official enmity. By distinguishing culturally representative figures who will never meet, and by itemizing a local landscape on the American side that includes only native tree species, the poem creates an effect of "solidarity" without presuming to claim "identity" (ecophilosopher Val Plumwood's prescription for the most responsible sort of environmental caring).[19] Ecoglobalism for Berry means parallel worlds of analogous but distinct niches, in which like ecocultural backgrounds produce like results. He imagines a traditional land-based stay-at-home existence for both himself and his Soviet counterpart in a world made safe from Cold War madness by a sodality of sturdy, sensible peasants for whom *patria* still bears its original Latin meaning: not bonding to "nation" but to one's home place.

Such is too the denouement awaiting Laguna Pueblo novelist Leslie Silko's protagonist. But by contrast to Berry, Silko and Japanese American fabulist Karen Tei Yamashita evoke what cultural geographer Doreen Massey calls a global sense of place: the vision of a particular site understood to be a nodal point of interconnected force fields of planetary scope.[20]

In *Ceremony*, the site in question is the unholy birthplace of the atomic age: an abandoned uranium mine on Laguna land, whence came raw materials for the atomic bombs developed and tested close by. In addition to evoking the sense and memory of the "nuclear sublime,"[21] the place provokes two planet-fusing epiphanies for the war-damaged Indian veteran Tayo, the seeds of both having been planted earlier by his medicine man mentor Betonie. One is the perception of the bomb as the work of the white "destroyers" anciently let loose on the world, according to a widely told Native American story. The other is Tayo's realization of the logic of his own "irrational" fantasies of the likeness between Japanese faces and familiar Indian faces. The link, he now fully sees, goes all the way back to the ancient continuum of (nonwhite) aboriginal via the prehistoric land bridge from Asia to the Americas, and forward to their mutual victimage by the forces of destruction.

In *Through the Arc*, a fast-paced boom-and-bust magical-realist narrative, the site is a vast area of former Amazonian jungle laid bare by soil erosion. The so-called Matacão turns out to be a hard plasticoid substance made up of the compacted residue of the world's trash dumps. In the short run, it proves amenable to a mind-boggling array of commercial uses, from artificial feathers to ferris wheels, from which the U.S.-based multinational corporation exploiting it profits enormously. But it also proves vulnerable to an invasive bacterium that reduces the burgeoning commercial empire's regional base and global affluence to nothing in a matter of days. After which, the rainforest takes over again.

Much might be also said about how Silko's and Yamashita's narratives are minoritized as Berry's poem is not, based as it is around a figure offered as a typical ordinary American. And about the fact that *Through the Arc*, a Brazil-set novel with a Japanese expatriate protagonist, is only marginally an *"American"* or "ethnic American" literary text. (Asian Americanists have found Yamashita's work tricky to categorize.)[22] But the point I want to stress here is the common thread of conceiving the United States as connected to or impinging upon far-distant lands via its environmentality, whether this be its groves, its uranium, or its garbage. Each text offers an identifiably late-twentieth-century image of remote points on earth linked by remembered or hypothetical global cataclysm: the solemn image of the *omphalos* of the atomic age, the zany image of Amazonia as *literally* a first-world dumping ground, the homey image of the hinterland rustic haunted by the struggle between superpowers that he hopes his Soviet counterpart hates as much as he does. Yet the possibility of planetary consciousness these images render is prefigured in U.S. writing more than a century before. Let's now turn to that backstory.

Early American Anticipations: Transnational Landscapes of Possession and Displacement

The oldest and most familiar form of ecoglobalist affect in the writings of the settler cultures that populated what later became the United States was of course the dream of transhemispheric migration and possession by advocates of colonization. Such as Puritan chief John Winthrop commending New England as "the Lord's Garden" "given to the sons of men," lying in wait for "improvement." Or colonial poetaster William Becket imagining the apotheosis of Philadelphia. ("There stately Oaks, shall lofty Piles adorn; / and yet preplex'd with various Weeds and Thorn / Here Industry & Peace shall fix their Seat, / & Plenty make her Pleasant, Happy, Great.") Or early national poet Philip Freneau imagining the prototypical emigrant fleeing "Europe's proud, despotic shores" for "fair plains" and "rural seats" vacated by "the unsocial Indian," where in time he will help "happier systems bring to view, / Than all the eastern sages knew."[23] In painting, this utopic-expansionist urge reached its apogee during the mid-nineteenth century, in Romantic artifacts of the "magisterial gaze" like Emanuel Leutze's *Westward the Course of Empire Takes Its Way* (1862), a mural commissioned for the national capitol that depicts a pioneer band scaling the Continental Divide, and John Gast's painting *American Progress* (1872), in which a large scantily clad pseudoclassical goddess floats over the Great Plains stringing telegraph wire, as Indians retreat from the scene before a covered wagon and a group of prospectors, and below the goddess appear a farm scene and a stagecoach, with several railroad trains close behind, and beyond that, in the far distance, a glimpse of the urbanized East Coast and a hint of the old world from which the pioneers have come.[24]

It is tempting to read such settler-culture fantasies as expansionist hubris pure and simple.[25] For often they were, and doubtless almost always to some extent, although the elements of disinterested moral-religious idealism, aggrandizement, rapacity, racism, and sheer fortuity were blended differently from case to case. In U.S. settler culture history, land has always been defined predominantly as commodity.[26] Even more basic to the visionary rhetoric of continental settlement than possession per se, however, is what the scholar of British-American emigrant discourse Stephen Fender calls "the figure of anticipation": the anticipation of a "future culture" destined to spring up from "a present natural setting."[27] The rhetoric of possession, whether it bespoke motives mainly high-minded or avaricious, embedded a rudimentary ecoglobalist calculus: a visionary fusion of cisatlantic landscape (seen as raw material and future habitat) against the background of a distant transcontinental landscape of origin to yield a wishful vision of an ideal landscape of the future of world-historical import. Hence de Tocqueville's dry insistence that Americans "are insensible to the wonders of inanimate nature" because "their eyes are fixed" on the "magnificent image of themselves" marching "across these wilds, draining swamps, turning the course of rivers, peopling solitudes, and subduing nature."[28]

The figure of anticipation, Fender cautions, is often complicated by a range of characteristic anxieties, one of them the "anxiety about broken connections."[29] For many first-generation colonists, the affect was not landscape as possession but as displacement. As William Bradford, Winthrop's Plymouth counterpart, famously bemoans the Pilgrims' "safe arrival" at Cape Cod:

"What could they see but a hideous and desolate wilderness," without a Mount Pisgah from which to view a promised land as Moses did. Although "the affections and love of their brethren at Leyden was cordial and entire," the thought of this was more dreary than consoling, stuck at the edge of the world as they were.[30] This passage has been claimed as the inception of what late-twentieth-century Americanist criticism, following Harold Bloom, who followed Wallace Stevens, has called the "American sublime": the trope of a vast, "empty"-seeming landscape that the spectatorial consciousness must transfuse and sublate.[31] But strictly speaking the landscape Bradford describes isn't empty. It's charged with ritual significance. It's a tapestry of retrospective symbol-making sharply different from the documentary report of the Pilgrim band's first foragings in *Mourt's Relation* ("Here is sand, gravel, and excellent clay, no better in the world . . . and the best water we ever drank, and the brooks now begin to be full of fish").[32] Bradford deliteralizes the vista in order to reinvent it diasporically and biblically—and classically too. (Of the company's relief at reaching harbor, he effuses: "no marvel if they were thus joyful, seeing wise Seneca was so affected with sailing a few miles on the coast of his own Italy.") The point is not that the new world is a nowhere. But the actual "where" is here *felt* only in terms of where one had come from: tribally, intellectually, spiritually.

Few early colonial texts embed the paradox of virtual nonexistence *versus* symbolic plenitude of new world landscape more complexly than Mary Rowlandson's *Narrative* of her captivity during King Philip's War (1676):[33]

> And here I cannot but remember how many times sitting in their wigwams, and musing on things past, I should suddenly leap up and run out, as if I had been at home, forgetting where I was, and what my condition was; but when I was without, and saw nothing but wilderness, and woods, and a company of barbarous heathens, my mind quickly returned to me, which made me think of that, spoken concerning Sampson, who said, "I will go out and shake myself as at other times, but he wist not that the Lord was departed from him."

By this account, not once but repeatedly was the author brought to grief by the "hallucination of the displaced terrain"—the superimposition of a habituated landscape upon the place one actually is.[34] Rowlandson, so she claims, momentarily beholds the forests of Massachusetts as if they *were* her actual "home," the neo-English village landscape into which the Puritan settlers had been transforming the New England region. Even after awakening to where she "really" is, the persona still sees the forest in symbolic terms, taking refuge from the trauma of her predicament by identifying with another tribally sanctioned, biblical, landscape. She is a modern Sampson waking up to the discovery of impotence now that his locks have been shorn. Ironically, as the *Narrative* has just explained, Rowlandson has just now also begun to wake up to how to read the woods with a literality that her stylized rendering of her predicament belies. By the end of her ordeal, she has picked up at least a few wilderness survival skills and begun to understand Native American coping strategies there. But she can't bring herself, at least in public, to assign any significance to the forest except as an antiplace.

To experience landscape through the lens of cultural displacement, one might think, would disenable a person from engaging its materiality on its own terms. But Rowlandson's *Narrative* shows that pragmatic savvy can override ideology, even though the author's investment in representing her experience as an exemplum of communal affliction keeps her from expressing, maybe even from realizing, this point. Mary Austin's turn-of-the-twentieth-century sketches of the forbidding aridlands along the California-Nevada border, *Land of Little Rain*, similarly describes an English "pocket hunter" or small-time prospector who never bonds to the region where he hunts for gold as a native would, or even as the Illinois-born author comes to do; his ambition is simply "to strike it rich and set himself up among the eminently bourgeois of London." Yet he manages to thrive in this alien, unforgiving locale through his seeming "faculty of small hunted things of taking the color of his surroundings."[35]

In some versions of immigrant experience, importation of old-country ways can produce acute maladaptation to new-world conditions and exemplary environmental citizenship at the same time. Such has been the case with Amish culture, much praised by Wendell Berry (who would object to "maladaptation" as a diagnosis of Amish tribal separation in self-consciously distinct and culturally coherent communities). Willa Cather's *O Pioneers!* a novel of Scandanavian immigration to the Nebraska plains in the late nineteenth century, scripts this paradox explicitly through the figure of old Ivar and his relation to the protagonist, Alexandra Bergson. Prone to emotional seizures and religious fanaticism, Ivar is the book's most culturally regressive figure. He never even learns to speak English. But he is also the most intimately linked to the natural world. Alexandra turns to him as a kind of environmental guru for guidance about livestock, crops, soil. In the long run, her farming prospers while his fails because she has the entrepreneurial shrewdness to negotiate modern agribusiness; but her respect for old-country peasant culture is correlated with her ability to make the shrewd decisions as to what to buy and build and what to plant when that gives her the jump on her brothers and neighbors.

At first sight, Alexandra might seem a quintessential figure of anticipation, hankering to enact the Freneauvian dream of eager emigrants bringing the primordial hinterland to a new state of fruition and prosperity. For a book written by an author reared only a generation later in the same region who must have known that the Native dispensation didn't just vanish into thin air, the novel seems only too willing to indulge the expansionist stereotype of landscape primordialism.[36] The climax of the first section is Alexandra's mystical encounter with the "Genius of the Divide," an unmediated experience of connectedness with "the land" that gives rise to her vision of how to farm it successfully. But the environmental psychology of this "aha experience" is actually the obverse of that of the magisterial gaze. Alexandra, or so the text asserts, does not conquer; she opens herself up to the feeling of the land and submits. Her capacity to do so is congruent with and follows from the receptivity to land-wisdom that draws her to Ivar. That is what enables her, unlike the stereotypical Whitmanian pioneers to which the title alludes ("We the virgin soil upheaving," etc.), to reverse the customary order of the transaction between settlers and new-world environment encapsulated by the opening line of the poem Robert Frost delivered at the Kennedy inaugural: "The land was ours before we were the land's."[37] To be sure, Alexandra's submission to the land enables control of the land. But to insist on submission first is a significant revisionist move. And so is the novel's insistence that diasporic land-memory can actually solidify place-connectedness in a strange new world as well as the old. When Alexandra starts to feel out of place again near the end, it is because the system of agrarian modernization that has profited her materially now threatens to destroy the traditional values for which she likes to think she stands—although the assertive role she plays as clan leader is anything but traditional.[38]

INDUSTRIAL REVOLUTION AND/AS THE EMERGENCE OF MODERN U.S. ECOGLOBALISM

In the discourse of displacement as well as possession, the emergence of a sense of environmentality of transnational reach is inseparable from a sense of the incipient commodification of environment, exuberant in the former and troubled in the latter, in itself also potentially transnational. U.S. ecoglobalist consciousness emerges in symbiotic tension with, first, the rise of imperial commerce and then of entrepreneurial capitalism, both perceived in succession as world orders in which the nation is destined to play a central if not *the* central role. By the mid-nineteenth century, a generation before the advent of institutionalized environmentalism, this mentality is already well in place.

In canonical U.S. literature, Henry Thoreau's *Walden* is an especially notable case precisely because it is so doggedly local in its focus.[39] Concord, Massachusetts, the oldest inland town in British America, had been settled for more than two centuries before Thoreau began to write; and he remained fiercely loyal to his home place. But Thoreau cannot think locally without bringing in the rest of the world. He can't walk over the expanse of snow-covered ice on nearby Flint's Pond without being reminded of Baffin's Bay (271). In order to relish the view from his cabin across Walden Pond, he must imagine the vista stretching "away toward the prairies of the West and the steppes of Tar-

tary, affording ample room for all the roving families of men" (87). Here and repeatedly, Thoreau doesn't merely succumb to but positively riots in the hallucination of the displaced terrain. Why? That he was compensating for cabin fever, that his stay-at-home habits concealed a hankering for armchair travel and travel books—Thoreau's favorite genre of contemporary literature—are true but insufficient.[40] Thoreau is also betraying consciousness of the fact that Concord's environment was indissolubly connected with the rest of the world and defining himself not as a local character but as a local cosmopolitan.

In *Walden* this comes out especially in a wintertime passage that starts out as a complaint at the invasion of his hermitage by a gang of ice harvesters dispatched by a Boston merchant to collect a shipment for export to India. Once the persona manages to strike the right aesthetic distance, beholding the workmen from the distance of his cabin as if they were "a picture as we see on the first page of the almanac," he warms to his subject and tranquilly imagines "the pure Walden water . . . mingled with the sacred water of the Ganges." This symbolizes *and* literalizes the potential payoff of his own discursive stream, which has been inspired by the Bhagavad Gita and other Indian sacred texts. ("I lay down the book and go to my well for water, and lo! there I meet the servant of the Brahmin . . . come to draw water for his master, and our buckets as it were grate together in the same well.") Thoreauvian ecoglobalism transparently depends upon even while resisting the momentum of economic history: that Yankee-spearheaded maritime capitalism was making the world smaller. Massachusetts ice baron Frederic Tudor had been conducting trade with Asia for more than forty years.[41] An inveterate punster, Thoreau may even intend a wry double entendre here. This may be the first usage of "Brahmin" to connote New England blue blood or grandee.[42] Elsewhere, stirred by the sound of the railroad train whistling past the west end of Walden Pond, Thoreau is momentarily suffused with excitement at the romance of commerce. ("I feel more like a citizen of the world at the sight of the palm-leaf which will cover so many flaxen New England heads the next summer, the Manilla hemp and cocoa-nut husks" [119].) Ultimately, he valued the groves of Walden far more than the business of cutting them down for railroad ties and engine fuel. And his one-man revolt against the work ethic protests the standardization of labor ushered in by industrial revolution. Yet the new technology helped instill in him a global sense of place.

To Herman Melville, the first canonical U.S. author to have sojourned in the developing world and to have perceived the effects of gunboat diplomacy there from the standpoint of its indigenous victims,[43] the rise of U.S. industrial might on a global scale was an issue of far deeper interest. Whereas *Walden*'s scene of Thoreau meeting the Brahmin's servant looks forward to Wendell Berry's apostrophe to the antipodal Siberian woodsman, *Moby-Dick* more closely anticipates the whole-earth ecoglobalisms of Silko and Yamashita. It was indeed the first canonical novel about an extractive industry of global scope, dominated by Yankee entrepreneurs for a brief but spectacular interval during the antebellum years. Even if Cesare Caserino's arresting conjecture is ruled out, that Melville's archaization of whaling as epic tragedy uncannily anticipates the industry's imminent collapse that nobody in 1851 could have been expected to foresee, the scene of factory-ship confinement and disciplined regimen makes *Moby-Dick* in important ways a paradigmatic exposé of early industrial overreach. Ahab's overruling of Starbuck's sound business sense can be read as symptomatic of that excess at least as plausibly as it can be read as a rejection of standard bourgeois values.[44]

Ishmael/Melville's passion for cetological detail cannot be accounted for simply in these terms, however. Until recently this aspect of the book was short-shrifted by students and specialists alike. Fortunately, during the last two decades the situation has changed. In particular, new Americanist-inflected scholarship on literary texts as ideological representations have scrutinized *Moby-Dick*'s cetological dimension more closely. William Spanos, for example, reads Ishmael's rompish classification of whales in "Cetology" as a "carnivalesque parody" of the Linnean mode of "the high imperial Linnean ground and the schematizing imperatives of natural science," whose pretensions to objective knowledge production were concurrently underwriting expansionist and technodominationist subjugation of the American wilderness. Samuel Otter, in a different application of somewhat similar premises, reads the cetology chapters as undermining the racist pseudoscience of anthropometry.[45] Yet neither quite accounts for the element of encyclopedic *zest* this novel evinces for whaling. Doubtless this passion is as overdetermined as the deconstructive satire. But one dimension of it, surely, is fascination with the global reach of both cetacean ecology and whaling praxis. Something like this is at the bottom of the effusion "To produce a mighty book, you must choose a mighty theme," a whale and not a flea.[46] The gusto arises as much from the gigantic spatial scale of the endeavor as from the giganticism of the cetaceans.

The chapter "The Chart" is especially instructive here. Ishmael ponders Ahab pondering the charts of whale migration routes. These charts are a form of knowledge production that Ishmael takes much more seriously than his classification system and his later measurements of the whale's skeleton, although he also stresses that Ahab will not and should not go by them alone, despite studying them to the point that his furrowed brow itself looks like a chart. There is also a predictable unpredictability to whale behavior that the seasoned mariner needs to anticipate. Though appalled by Ahab's monomania, Ishmael is fascinated by both the phenomenon of whale migration, the claim that the global movements of sperm whales might "be found to correspond in invariability to those of the herring-shoals or the flights of swallows," and the evidence of whalemen's sagacity in negotiating the combination of predictability and fortuity, its mixture of systematic empirical knowledge and intuition.[47] Despite whatever might be said either in praise or denigration about its farcical spoofing and overheated symbolistic byplay, the novel responds excitedly and also elegantly to the challenge of representing the global proportions of whaling ecology and the business of whaling. As I have shown elsewhere, although the case for *Moby-Dick* as a protoecological text is not so strong as is the case for *Walden*, Melville's novel is striking for interrogating speciesism (the assumption of a solid human/nonhuman borderline in an ethical pyramid of the orders of creation where humans occupy a place of special privilege at the top) no less vigorously than dominationism in the social sphere.[48] And with respect to eco*globalism*, *Moby-Dick* on cetology far surpasses *Walden* on limnology.

Neither Thoreau's local cosmopolitanism nor Melville's global epic devote more than a limited amount of attention to theorizing global environmentality as such. But to the extent they do, both anticipate the work of their fellow northeasterner, George Perkins Marsh, whose magnum opus *Man and Nature* (1864) became the first significant conservationist manifesto in the English language. An intellectually hyperactive polymath who knew twenty languages and had tried out almost as many professions by the time he settled into a consular career that allowed him ample time to research and write, Marsh was the first American clearly to grasp the planetary scope of the environmental side effects of modernization. Like Melville, Marsh wondered if whales were destined for extinction.[49] Like Thoreau and Dwight (both of whom he read attentively), Marsh was deeply impressed by the consequences of rapid New England deforestation, which as a one-time agricultural and industrial entrepreneur he himself had helped perpetrate. But unlike them, Marsh sensed the history of new world landscape—or rather landscapes, plural, since he viewed U.S. environmental history comparatively, with a broader interest in Euro-settlement worldwide—in relation to the much longer history of species transfer/migration/extinction, of deforestation, desertification, and land reclamation in the Mediterranean world from prehistoric antiquity to the present. Marsh felt forced to conclude that even "in his earliest known stages of existence, [man] was probably a destructive power upon the earth," and that modern European settler colonies, the United States chief among them, were showing unmistakable "signs of that melancholy dilapidation which is now driving so many of the [European] peasantry from their native hearths." Although American natural resources were still abundant, without major changes in environmental policy and practice, a "desolation, like that which has overwhelmed many once beautiful and fertile regions of Europe," Marsh prophesied, "awaits an important part of the territory of the United States, and of other comparatively new countries over which European civilization is now extending its sway."[50]

Environmental historians customarily set Marsh and Thoreau at odds as anticipators of the split between "preservationist" and "conservationist" camps at the turn of the twentieth century.[51] This is justifiable insofar as Marsh consistently argued that the remedy for environmental mismanagement was better management. It is hard to imagine Thoreau enthusing about "harbor and coast improvements," sea walls and the like, as "among the great works of man"; or praising the Suez Canal, had he lived to see its day, as "the greatest and most truly cosmopolite physical improvement ever undertaken." Marsh took for granted the legitimacy of anthropogenic environmental modification, not just locally but on a planetary scale; the question for him was how to make man "a co-worker with nature in the reconstruction of the damaged fabric which the negligence or the wantonness of former [generations] has rendered untenantable." On the other hand, Marsh's denunciations of man in practice as "everywhere a disturbing agent," a perennial disruptor of nature's harmonies,[52] often sound neo-Romantic and resonate with his late-life recollection that as a youth "the bubbling brook, the trees, the flowers, the wild animals were to me persons, not things."[53] It is telling that Marsh's single most far-reaching instance of possible ecoglobal management in *Man and Nature*, "the most colossal project" of human engineering ever proposed, inspires fear rather than hope. This is the proposal for a Panama canal in the form of "an open cut between the two seas." The audacity of the prospect intrigues him, but Marsh fears dire unintended consequences of global scope. In a striking anticipation of contemporary anxieties about the effects of global warming on polar glaciers, he imagines a rerouting of both the Pacific currents and the Gulf Stream, such as might precipitate "an immediate depression of the mean temperature of Western Europe to the level of that of Eastern America," possibly even ushering in "a new 'ice period'" as a result of "the withdrawal of so important a source of warmth from the northern seas."[54]

What most crucially links *Walden*, *Moby-Dick*, and *Man and Nature* as harbingers of contemporary ecoglobalist imagination is a combination of susceptibility to and skepticism about the ongoing conquest of natural environment on a planetary scale. Although the contribution of Yankee entrepreneurship specifically to this process is obviously of great interest to each, in the long run issues of cultural nationalism and national politics become subsidiary to a vision of Western culture in a state of ongoing, transnational modernization and with it the vexed question of what "man"'s relation to "nature" properly is or should be. "From that time on, human beings were one clan again," writes the narrator of *Ceremony* a century later, as we have seen. What Silko specifically had in mind, the nuclear age, those nineteenth-century writers could not have known. But they had seen enough of modernization to be able to intuit it. In Thoreau, Melville, and Marsh, something like the full range of contemporary ecoglobalist affects has begun to emerge.

Notes

1. Joseph Nye, *The Paradox of American Power* (New York: Oxford University Press, 2002), 82.

2. Barbara Adam, *Timescapes of Modernity: The Environment and Invisible Hazards* (London: Routledge, 1998), which concentrates especially on the slow-working pervasive effects of nuclear toxification (with the Chernobyl disaster especially in mind) and Bovine Spongiform Encephalopathy (mad cow disease).

3. Ulrich Beck, *Risk Society: Towards a New Modernity*, trans. Mark Ritter (1986; reprint, London: Sage, 1992), esp. 19–84; Beck and Johannes Willms, "Global Risk Society," in *Conversations with Ulrich Beck*, trans. Michael Pollak (Cambridge: Polity, 2004), 109–52.

4. Karen Litfin, *Ozone Discourses: Science and Politics in Global Environmental Cooperations* (Ithaca: Cornell University Press, 1994), 78–116, notes the unprecedentedness of the so-called precautionary principle as a motive for the ozone accords. See Peter Singer, "One Atmosphere," in *One World: The Ethics of Globalization* (New Haven: Yale University Press, 2002), 14–50, for discussion of global warming discourse as a harbinger and promoter of an ethic of global citizenship.

5. For an analysis of the uses and significance of this image, see Sheila Jasanoff, "Heaven and Earth: The Politics of Environmental Images," in *Earthly Politics: Local and Global in Environmental Governance*, ed. Jasanoff and David Rothenberg (Cambridge: MIT Press, 2000), 231–52.

6. Pascale Casanova, *The World Republic of Letters*, trans. M. B. DeBevoise (1999; reprint, Cambridge: Harvard University Press, 2004), 75–81 and passim.

7. See for example *Literature of Nature: An International Sourcebook*, ed. Patrick D. Murphy with Terry Gifford and Katsunori Yamazato (Chicago: Fitzroy Dearborn, 1998), a unique and useful but also balkanized collection of essays on traditions of environmental writing around the world. Chapters 1 and 3 of my *The Future of Environmental Criticism* (Oxford: Blackwell, 2005) comment, respectively, on the history of the ecocritical movement and its preferences both in principle and de facto as to subnational, national, and global scales of analysis.

8. A striking example is the nation-specificity of the two most significant precontemporary works on American and British pastoral, respectively, as culturally symptomatic modes: Leo Marx, *The Machine in the Garden: Technology and the Pastoral Ideal in America* (New York: Oxford University Press, 1964); and Raymond Williams, *The Country and the City* (New York: Oxford University Press, 1973). Marx did publish a complimentary review of Williams's book, but neither seems to have been in any way influenced by the other. For a further discussion, see Buell, *The Future of Environmental Criticism*, 13–16 (on Marx and Williams) and (for pastoral as a transhemispheric formation) Buell, *The Environmental Imagination* (Cambridge: Harvard University Press, 1995), 53–77; and Terry Gifford, *Pastoral* (London: Routledge, 1999).

9. The classic study is Henry Nash Smith, *Virgin Land: The American West as Symbol and Myth* (Cambridge: Harvard University Press, 1950). Revisionist scholars, including to some extent Smith himself in a retrospective essay, have tended to dismantle the myth as self-justifying ideology. See in particular Myra Jehlen, *American Incarnation:*

The Individual, the Nation, and the Continent (Cambridge: Harvard University Press, 1985).

10. On ideology, see Philip Fisher, "Democratic Social Space: Whitman, Melville, and the Promise of American Transparency," *Representations* 24 (Fall 1988): 60–101. For the gridwork as lived experience, see Curt Meine, "Inherit the Grid," in *Placing Nature: Culture and Landscape Ecology*, ed. Joan Iverson Nassauer (Washington, D.C.: Island Press, 1997), 45–62.

11. On suburbanization as postage-stamp pastoral, see Kenneth T. Jackson, *Crabgrass Frontier: The Suburbanization of the United States* (New York: Oxford University Press, 1985); Peter Rowe, *Making a Middle Landscape* (Cambridge: MIT Press, 1991); and Virginia Scott Jenkins, *The Lawn: A History of an American Obsession* (Washington, D.C.: Smithsonian Institution Press, 1994). See Adam Ward Rome, *The Bulldozer in the Countryside: Suburban Sprawl and the Rise of American Environmentalism* (Cambridge: Cambridge University Press, 2001), for a history of suburbanization as an incentive to (certain forms of) environmentalist activism and regulation.

12. Timothy Dwight, *Travels; in New-England and New-York*, ed. Barbara Miller Solomon (1821; reprint, Cambridge: Harvard University Press, 1969), 1:6.

13. "Ecological footprint" is a term coined by environmental reformers and sympathetic environmental scholars to refer to "the land area necessary to sustain current levels of resource consumption and waste discharge by that population" (Mathis Wackernagel and William E. Rees, *Our Ecological Footprint: Reducing Human Impact on the Earth* [Gabriola Island, B.C.: New Society Publishers, 1996], 5).

14. John C. Ryan and Alan Thein During, *Stuff: The Secret Lives of Everyday Things* (Seattle: Northwest Environment Watch, 1997).

15. On environmental polling, see Deborah Lynn Gubar, *The Grassroots of a Green Revolution: Polling America on the Environment* (Cambridge: MIT Press, 2003). On American attitudes toward environment(alism) as amenity, see Samuel Hays, *Beauty, Health, and Permanence: Environmental Politics in the United States, 1955–1985* (Cambridge: Cambridge University Press, 1985).

16. I rely especially here on Maarten A. Hajer, *The Politics of Environmental Discourse: Ecological Modernization and the Policy Process* (Oxford: Clarendon Press, 1995); and Arthur P. J. Mol, *Globalization and Environmental Reform: The Ecological Modernization of the Global Economy* (Cambridge: MIT Press, 2001). Mol views sustainable development and ecological modernization as equivalent (111); Hajer, more elegantly and plausibly, sees sustainable development as one strand in a braided rope of heterogeneous and sometimes conflicting "story-lines" comprising the discourse of ecological modernization. For a bottom-line, but relatively detailed, summary of its premises relative to "traditional pragmatism," see Hajer, *The Politics of Environmental Discourse*, 164–65.

17. Mol, *Globalization and Environmental Reform*, 101.

18. Wendell Berry, "To a Siberian Woodsman," *Collected Poems, 1957–1982* (San Francisco: North Point, 1985), 97–98; Leslie Marmon Silko, *Ceremony* (New York: Penguin, 1977), 246; Karen Tei Yamashita, *Through the Arc of the Rain Forest* (Minneapolis: Coffee House Press, 1990), 202.

19. Val Plumwood, *Environmental Culture: The Ecological Crisis of Reason* (London: Routledge, 2002), 196–217—a critique of deep ecology's emphasis on "identification"

with nature that seems to anticipate the respectful distance Berry's persona tries to strike here ("Such an ethic cannot address the other as a communicative or potentially communicative subject").

20. Doreen Massey, "A Global Sense of Place," in *Space, Place, and Gender* (Minneapolis: University of Minnesota Press, 1994), 146–56.

21. "Nuclear sublime" is Rob Wilson's term for "the terror of a technological determination within the Cold War period." Wilson, *American Sublime: The Genealogy of a Poetic Genre* (Madison: University of Wisconsin Press, 1991), 231, 228–63.

22. Rachel C. Lee, *The Americas of Asian American Literature: Gendered Fictions of Nation and Transnation* (Princeton: Princeton University Press, 1999), 106–38, frames the problem thoughtfully, seeing Yamashita's two Brazilian books as a kind of limit case in what might count as Asian American writing, although I'm not convinced by Lee's solution of decoding *Rain Forest*'s hero, Kasumasa, as a proxy for the traditional Chinese American railroad worker. Yamashita herself has demurred from the classification of this novel as either "an Asian-American book" pure and simple *or* as an environmental(ist) text pure and simple (Jean Vengue Gier and Carla Alicia Tejada, "An Interview with Karen Tei Yamashita" [1998], http://social.chass.ncsu.edu/jouvert/ v2i2/yamishi.htm).

23. John Winthrop, *Reasons to Be Considered for . . . the Intended Plantation in New England* (1629), in Alan Heimert and Andrew Delbanco, eds., *The Puritans in America: A Narrative Anthology* (Cambridge: Harvard University Press, 1985), 72; William Becket, "Fragment from an Ancient Poet . . . ," quoted in David Shields, *Oracles of Empire: Poetry, Politics, and Commerce in British America, 1690–1750* (Chicago: University of Chicago Press, 1990), 45; Philip Freneau, "On the Emigration to America and Peopling the Western Country," *Poems of Freneau*, ed. Harry Hayden Clark (1929; reprint, New York: Harper, 1960), 92–93. Regarding Winthrop, note that Heimert and Delbanco plausibly surmise that he was arguing to some extent against his own doubts as well as others'.

24. Both images are reprinted in (at least) two works of revisionist art history: *The West as America: Reinterpreting Images of the Frontier, 1820–1920*, ed. William H. Truettner (Washington, D.C.: Smithsonian Institution Press, 1991), 118, 135; and Albert Boime, *The Magisterial Gaze: Manifest Destiny and American Landscape Painting c. 1830–1865* (Washington, D.C.: Smithsonian Institution Press, 1991), 44, 132.

25. The analyses of Truettner and Boime both point that way. In literary studies, probably the most significant of the many revisionist interventions during the past several decades that have established the plot of "from genocidal conquest to new imperium" as the new and regnant grand narrative of U.S. settlement culture history have been Myra Jehlen, *American Incarnation*; and *Cultures of United States Imperialism*, ed. Amy Kaplan and Donald E. Pease (Durham, N.C.: Duke University Press, 1993). (See especially the opening essays by each coeditor.) These books were defining expressions of new historicist and new Americanist revisionisms, respectively.

26. Richard N. L. Andrews, "Land in America: A Brief History," in *Land in America: Commodity or Natural Resource*, ed. Andrews (Lexington, Mass.: Lexington Books, 1979), 27–40.

27. Stephen Fender, "American Landscape and the Figure of Anticipation," in *Views of American Landscapes*, ed. Mick Gidley and Robert Lawson-Peebles (Cam-

bridge: Cambridge University Press, 1989), 57. Fender takes the term from a British traveler's account of 1817—expressing disappointment that the Pittsburgh he beheld did not, in fact, measure up to "the Birmingham of America."

28. Alexis de Tocqueville, *Democracy in America*, trans. Henry Reeve, rev. Francis Bowen, ed. Phillips Bradley (New York: Vintage, 1945), 2:78.

29. Ibid., 59–60. The exemplary text here is the denouement of Crèvecoeur's *Letters from an American Farmer*, which produces, Fender argues, "the first characteristic dislocation at the end of American fiction, in which a disenchanted hero lights out for the Territory, at the same time as his author 'lights in' back to the metropolis."

30. William Bradford, *Of Plymouth Plantation, 1620–1647*, ed. Francis Murphy (New York: Modern Library, 1981), 69–71. Bradford was also probably mourning the loss of Plymouth, which had been absorbed into the Massachusetts Bay colony.

31. David Laurence, "William Bradford's American Sublime," *PMLA* 102 (January 1987): 55–65.

32. "G. Mourt," *Mourt's Relation* (1622), in Heimert and Delbanco, *The Puritans in America*, 46.

33. Mary Rowlandson, *A Narrative of the Captivity and Restoration of Mrs. Mary Rowlandson*, in *Norton Anthology of American Literature: Literature to 1820*, ed. Wayne Franklin, 6th ed. (New York: Norton), 324.

34. This term, coined by art critic Harold Rosenberg, is adapted by Robert Lawson-Peebles, *Landscape and Written Expression in Revolutionary America* (Cambridge: Cambridge University Press, 1988), 22–62 and passim. Lawson-Peebles cogently applies to colonial and early national British-American art and literature Rosenberg's example of the ill-fated British General Braddock during the French and Indian War, who tried with disastrous result to march his army of redcoats through the woods of western Pennsylvania as if it were a conventional European battleground. "The more that American writers struggled to assert a unique American culture," as Lawson-Peebles tellingly puts it, "the more they were trapped in the hallucination of displaced terrain" (45).

35. Mary Austin, "The Pocket-Hunter," in *Land of Little Rain* (1903), *Stories from the Country of Lost Borders*, ed. Marjorie Pryse (New Brunswick, N.J.: Rutgers University Press, 1987), 49, 43.

36. Technically the novel starts in 1883, just six years after "Custer's last stand," but of tangible marks of Plains Indians in the vicinity the novel admits only to "feeble scratches on stone left by prehistoric races, so indeterminate that they may, after all, be only the markings of glaciers, and not a record of human strivings" (Willa Cather, *O Pioneers!* [1913; reprint, New York: Vintage, 1992], 3, 11). This is a notorious problem with Cather's Nebraska novels. All are similarly insouciant of the aboriginal dispensation.

37. Cather, *O Pioneers!* 33; Walt Whitman, "Pioneers! O Pioneers" (1865), in *Leaves of Grass: Comprehensive Reader's Edition*, ed. Harold W. Blodgett and Sculley Bradley (New York: New York University Press, 1965), 230; Robert Frost, "The Gift Outright" (1941), in *The Poetry of Robert Frost*, ed. Edward Connery Lathem (New York: Holt, 1975), 348. Frost intended to declaim his new poem "For John F. Kennedy: His Inauguration" (ibid., 422–24), but the weather kept him from reading his notes.

38. As Tom Lutz bemusedly sums up the novel's cross-currents, "*O Pioneers!* is antimodern in its rejection of mass culture, promodern in its respect for agricultural science

and psychology, antimodern in its respect for old Ivar, promodern in its rejection of social convention" (*Cosmopolitan Vistas: American Regionalism and Literary Value* [Ithaca: Cornell University Press, 2004], 114).

39. Henry David Thoreau, *Walden*, ed. J. Lyndon Shanley (Princeton: Princeton University Press, 1971).

40. John Christie, *Thoreau as World Traveler* (New York: Columbia University Press, 1965); and Robert Sattelmeyer, *Thoreau's Reading: A Study in Intellectual History with Bibliographical Catalogue* (Princeton: Princeton University Press, 1988), document Thoreau's interest in travel writing.

41. Thoreau, *Walden*, 298. On Thoreau and the ice merchant, see Lewis Simpson, "The Tudor Brothers: Boston Ice and Boston Letters," in *The Man of Letters in New England and the South: Essays on the History of the Literary Vocation in America* (Baton Rouge: Louisiana State University Press, 1973), 32–61.

42. The first figurative use of "Brahmin" in this sense is usually credited (*v. OED*) to Oliver Wendell Holmes Sr.'s preface to *Elsie Venner* (1859), though Byron's *Don Juan* (1823) uses "Brahmin" in a similar sense as a nickname for English gentry.

43. I refer of course to Melville's several weeks in Taipivai, Nukuheva, in the Marquesas Islands, at the very moment of the island's French imperial appropriation (1842) and a quarter century after the Taipi community had been laid waste by Captain David Porter of the U.S. Navy, often called "the first imperialist" for having briefly conquered Nukuheva, renaming it "Madison Island" and claiming the Marquesas as U.S. territory—a claim the U.S. administration refused to acknowledge. T. Walter Herbert, Jr., *Marquesan Encounters: Melville and the Meaning of Civilization* (Cambridge: Harvard University Press, 1980), provides an admirably scrupulous comparative portrayal of Porter's and Melville's sorties, as both antithetical and complementary instances of Yankee encounters with Polynesian indigenes in the contact zone.

44. Cesare Casarino, *Modernity at Sea: Melville, Marx, Conrad in Crisis* (Minneapolis: University of Minnesota Press, 2002), 75–83. The modern tradition of envisaging Ahab as a warped captain of industry entered American literary studies most influentially with F. O. Matthiessen's *American Renaissance* (London: Oxford University Press, 1941), 459; and Matthiessen's student Leo Marx, *The Machine in the Garden*, 278–319. But see also C.L.R. James, *Mariners, Renegades and Castaways: The Story of Herman Melville and the World We Live In* (1953; reprint, London: Allison & Busby, 1985).

45. William Spanos, *The Errant Art of "Moby-Dick": The Canon, the Cold War, and the Struggle for American Studies* (Durham, N.C.: Duke University Press, 1995), 191–92; Samuel Otter, *Melville's Anatomies* (Berkeley: University of California Press, 1999), 132–49.

46. Herman Melville, *Moby-Dick*, ed. Hershel Parker and Harrison Hayford (1851; reprint, New York: Norton, 2002), 349.

47. Ibid., 167.

48. Lawrence Buell, *Writing for an Endangered World: Literature, Culture, and Environment in the United States and Beyond* (Cambridge: Harvard University Press, 2001), 205–23.

49. Ironically, the most authoritative history of nineteenth-century American whaling sides with the novelist's surmise that hot pursuit has made whales warier, not with Marsh's inference that whale elusiveness signified species depletion. See Lance E.

Davis, Robert E. Gallman, and Karin Gleiter, *In Pursuit of Leviathan: Technology, Institutions, Productivity, and Profits in American Whaling, 1816–1906* (Chicago: University of Chicago Press, 1997), 131–49.

50. George Perkins Marsh, *Man and Nature: Or, Physical Geography as Modified by Human Action*, ed. David Lowenthal (Cambridge: Harvard University Press, 1964), 70, 46, 201.

51. See for example Nash, *Wilderness and the American Mind*, 3rd ed. (New Haven: Yale Unversity Press, 1982), 104–5.

52. Marsh, *Man and Nature*, 282–83, 439, 65, 36.

53. To Charles Eliot Norton, May 24, 1871, quoted in Lowenthal's "Introduction" to Marsh, *Man and Nature*, xi.

54. Marsh, *Man and Nature*, 441–42.

CHAPTER 10

At the Borders of American Crime Fiction

Rachel Adams

A CASE INVOLVING WOMEN, MONEY, AND MURDER. A darkened room where two men confront one another. A disillusioned investigator. The friend who betrayed him by "going Mexican." The intimacies of male bonding sundered. Forty years after the publication of Raymond Chandler's *The Long Goodbye* (1951), Michael Connelly revives these plot elements for his best-selling crime novel, *The Black Ice* (1993).[1] Both novels are set in Los Angeles, where their detective-protagonists struggle to preserve the reputations of men who appear to have committed suicide under suspicious circumstances. Both crimes have ties to Mexico that require the detective to cross the border during the course of his investigation. In the end, the alleged victims are found alive, having faked their own deaths to get away with murder. Each man's slide into degeneracy is indicated by his increasing identification with Mexico, and the transformation of his physical features from white to "Mexican." His passage across the border signals the surrender of his values, relationships, and core aspects of his identity.

This is where the similarities between Connelly and Chandler come to an end. Published in the same year as the signing of NAFTA, *The Black Ice* reflects the extent to which relations between the United States and Mexico have changed in the decades since the publication of *The Long Goodbye*. Although Connelly's protagonist Harry Bosch is as tough-minded and individualistic as Chandler's Philip Marlowe, he operates in a world where the professional private eye is obsolete. A lone detective is no match for the transnational crime rings that plague contemporary Los Angeles. The files, computer databases, and institutional resources needed to track their movements are available only to those working within a law enforcement agency. Bosch is a member of the Los Angeles Police Department, where his breaches of protocol cause constant friction with his superiors. Whereas Marlowe's case concerns interpersonal, domestic matters—a bad marriage leads to conflicts over love, money, and, ultimately, murder—Bosch's concerns rivalry among powerful international drug cartels. And whereas Marlowe perceives the border as a sparsely populated, liminal wasteland, Bosch's borderlands are teeming with vehicular traffic, commerce, and industrial activity. In order to continue his investigation on the other side, he must contend with a foreign system of law enforcement that requires him to collaborate with his Mexican counterparts. The forty years from the publication of *The Long Goodbye* to *The Black Ice* mark not only material changes in U.S.-Mexico relations, but also the evolution of detective fiction itself, which has increasingly recognized links between crimes against individuals and the transnational criminal networks that operate on the underside of the global economy. The evolution of this popular genre should encourage us to read beyond the borders of the nation to trace out the circuits of intercultural contact and cross-pollination that are becoming increasingly important to understandings of American literary history.

As the detective novel turns to the globalization of crime, it acknowledges borders as an ever more important narrative locale. When Chandler's Marlowe remarked that "Tijuana is not Mexico. No border town is anything but a border town," he indicated the marginality of the region.[2] As a resident of Los Angeles, he perceives border towns as isolated, provincial, and unique unto themselves. This view would become increasingly untenable once contemporary globalization began to affect the U.S.-Mexico border in the 1960s and 1970s. The decades following World War II saw a period of rapid development spurred by the buildup of U.S. military bases, a booming tourist industry, and the arrival of the *maquiladoras* in the 1960s. The implementation of NAFTA in 1994 turned the region into a primary artery in the global economy, of vital concern to national and international relations.[3] During the same period, the U.S. government was coming to recognize cross-border crime as a national security concern.[4] The erosion of economic borders that gave rise to legally sanctioned forms of globalization also encouraged the internationalization of a brand of criminals political scientist Peter Andreas has labeled "clandestine transnational actors, . . . nonstate actors who operate across national borders in violation of state laws and who attempt to evade law enforcement efforts."[5] This new type of criminal poses a problem for law enforcement, whose jurisdictional authority typically ends at national borders.[6] As Bartosz H. Stanislawski and Margaret G. Hermann have argued, international policing efforts have lagged far behind the evolution of powerful clandestine networks, which seek out "black spots" in the vicinity of national borders where "weak state structures and high levels of corruption [provide] a lawless and relatively sovereignty-free environment."[7] So wealthy and powerful are these networks that their influence is often dispersed far beyond the borderlands where their operations are based.

These new circumstances have made the U.S.-Mexico border a popular setting for contemporary crime fiction, which takes its cue, in part, from the changing face of North American crime. However, the detective novel has never been a simple reflection of its historical context. At its most basic level, the genre registers disruptions in the social order, seeking imagined resolution to problems of morality, injustice, and the law that may seem insurmountable outside the domain of fiction. Because their themes and conventions have proved to be extremely portable, detective novels can now be found in virtually any part of the world.[8] North America, where hard-boiled crime writers first transformed the genre in the 1920s, is now home to a rich array of revisionist detective fictions. One of the most remarkable features of these newer works is a geographic diversity that stretches from Quebec to Chiapas. But a survey of contemporary detective fiction also reveals the extent to which crime continues to be associated with particular locations and communities. While murder is almost unthinkable in the sleepy Canadian town of Algonquin Bay depicted by Giles Blunt's *Forty Words for Sorrow*, "going Mexican" continues to be as potent a signifier of corruption in literature today as it was in 1951.[9] Thus, although there is a growing body of crime writing focused on the U.S.-Canadian border, the U.S.-Mexico borderlands are a far more common setting for American detective fiction because of the region's long-standing association with lawlessness and violence, and its current struggles with the most negative consequences of globalization.[10]

Contemporary crime writing set along the U.S.-Mexico border exemplifies the globalization of the detective novel since it is at once regionally specific—in that it substitutes Ciudad Juárez, El Paso, Tijuana, or Calexico for the mean streets of Los Angeles and New York—and conscious of the international, and potentially planetary, implications of the crimes it represents.[11] As such, it provides an opportunity to link local problems to global concerns. In what follows, I consider the work of three authors—Rolando Hinojosa, Paco Ignacio Taibo II, and Alicia Gaspar de Alba—whose revisionist crime writing presses at the boundaries of the genre's traditional forms and purposes. Whereas the detective's most fundamental task has always been to bring new perspective to the scene of the crime, these authors grant the investigator a special form of knowledge that Walter Mignolo has called "border gnosis." Derived "from the exterior borders of the modern/colonial world system," border gnosis provides the detective with alternative understandings of the relations among crime, lawfulness, and community.[12] For Hinojosa, this means introducing new characters and settings to the police procedural, a subgenre of detective fiction ideally suited to his concern with community and cross-border collaboration. His imagined solution to the problem of global crime is the solidification of regional, transnational ties. The more radical and nihilistic Taibo revives the figure of the independent hard-boiled investigator in a context where law enforcement and all other forms of institutional authority are as immoral as the worst criminals he encounters. Addressing an international readership, Taibo's detective fiction produces counterhistories intended to create possibilities for identification across the boundaries of language and nation as a corrective to government corruption and the breakdown of community. Gaspar de Alba turns to the detective novel to bring a single, real-life crime—the deaths of hundreds of women in the El Paso/Ciudad Juárez area—to the attention of English-language readers, who have largely remained ignorant of the problems plaguing the region. Focusing on a female investigator who uncovers the particularly brutal consequences of globalization for poor women, Gaspar de Alba draws attention to the gendering of transnational crime, as well as the crime writing tradition. Her work seeks to expose violence and injustice, but it also recognizes the detective novel's potential to galvanize political action. Rarely do detectives in any of these works find satisfaction in identifying individual culprits, whose crimes are linked to networks too vast to be apprehended or brought to justice. Yet despite this apparent failure of the genre, each author suggests that globalization has opened up new possibilities for the production and circulation of literature, making it a more potent tool for addressing social problems, seeking justice, and forging solidarities across the lines of nation and community.

CULTURE AND "THE MYTH OF THE CONTINENTS"

While this essay is focused on detective fiction from a particular region, it is also inspired by the broader question of what it would mean to reframe the study of American literature in transnational, rather than national, terms. My own approach to this question is to consider the continent as a unit of cultural analysis. Continents provide an ideal, and largely untapped, opportunity to examine the interrelationship of geography, culture, and politics that has been central to much recent work in American literary studies. Because they are neither sovereign political territories nor determined by any particular topographical logic, continents may be the most unstable and fallacious of all geographic configurations. In their book *The Myth of the Continents*, Martin W. Lewis and Kären E. Wigen argue that this spatial fiction has had particularly deleterious effects on geographical understanding. Yet what makes myths troubling to geographers is precisely why they are valuable to cultural critics, because they are rich repositories of collective beliefs and values. Acknowledging the fictitiousness of continents helps to expose the constructedness of the more familiar spatial metaphors—regions, nations, hemispheres, worlds—that are used to understand and categorize literature. Yet continents are a fiction with very real consequences, as is evidenced by recent debates over membership in the European Union. They are the building blocks of our most basic understanding of the globe. From elementary school to the highest levels of foreign policy and international governance, continents determine economic and political alignments, as well as the flow of people and goods around the world. Given their vital role in geopolitical relations, it is worth asking about the *cultural* impact of "the myth of the continents,"[13] which seems destined to persist despite the protests of professional geographers.

Intracontinental borders, which are the focus of this essay, have played a crucial part in the formation of North American cultural history. Traditionally, these borders have provided a rationale for the division of North American literature into three discrete categories, which suggest, artificially, that Canadian, U.S., and Mexican cultures can be best understood as self-enclosed units, each defined by questions of national identity and history.[14] Some specialists in Canadian and Mexican studies have sought to maintain those categories against what they perceive as an imperialistic attempt by American studies to engulf contiguous fields. However, others see the mutual benefits of situating American literatures within histories of transnational, diasporic, and cross-border contact. Many scholars, including those collected in this volume, have proposed that new understandings of geography offer promising ways to reconfigure Americanist literary study. My attention to the continent, a spatial unit that is widely used by geographers, sociologists, economists, and historians, but rarely by literary or cultural critics, is intended as a contribution to these efforts. One potential benefit of this approach is that it can examine localities, such as the U.S.-Mexico border regions, within the context of broader national, and international, relations, as this essay will attempt to do by analyzing literary responses to NAFTA and the impact of globalization.

My understanding of North America treats it as a subset of the more well-developed field of hemispheric studies. Recent scholarship that takes the hemisphere as a unit of analysis has produced new maps of multilingual, trans-American cultural filiation. Yet "the Americas" can often seem an inchoate and unwieldy category. North America is a region of the American hemisphere that emphasizes cultural relations between the U.S. and its closest neighbors. To study the continent is to foreground the question of neighborliness, to acknowledge the impact of geography and shared borders on the cultures of the United States, Mexico, and Canada, which necessarily have a different relationship to one another than to other nations. With the onset of Cold War and the declining emphasis on hemispheric alignments, these neighborly relations became all the more important. The implementation of NAFTA and heightened security concerns since September 11, 2001, solidified the notion of North America as a geopolitical unit, which some feared might become a "fortress continent"[15] cordoned off from a world community. A continental perspective seeks to better understand how the fiction of "North America" might reverberate at the level of cultural production. For the purposes of this essay, I will focus on how a particular genre has registered the impact of NAFTA—a potent symptom of the perils and possibilities of "North America" within the global economy—on a specific region. Although I discuss the problems of neighborliness, border management, and cultural and linguistic diversity within particular communities, I hope it will also serve as a model for the comparative study of popular genres at other North American borders, or on other continents.

The Borderlanders and the Police

Until the late twentieth century, the law stopped at the United States' southern border. At least that is the conclusion one might draw from reading hard-boiled fiction, a genre invented on North American soil. In the work of classic practitioners of the genre, Mexico is essentially outside the law, a space where the police are incompetent and corrupt, and where criminals, perverts, and losers go to indulge their appetites for vice. Mexican lawlessness is at once dangerous and seductive to streetwise detectives who walk a fine line at the edge of morality and lawfulness. Criminals who flee south to escape identification often end up losing themselves altogether, engulfed by the tantalizing prospect of "going Mexican." As we have seen, the association of Mexico with moral degeneracy can be found in a novel as recent as Connelly's *The Black Ice*. It can be traced to such early works of hard-boiled fiction as Dashiell Hammett's 1927 story "The Golden Horseshoe," in which a petty criminal escapes into Mexico, where he assumes the identity of a dead man in order to extort money from his wife back in the United States.[16] The more extreme case occurs in Chandler's *The Long Goodbye*, where the fickle and deceptive Terry Lennox undergoes plastic surgery, his darkened skin and changed features literally transforming him into a Mexican. He enhances the surgical alterations to his body with cosmetic changes such as an effeminate perfume and dainty eyebrows, as well as the adoption of overly expressive body language.[17] The extent of Lennox's fall is figured as a geographic descent from North to South when he explains to Marlowe, "I was born in Montreal. I'll be a Mexican national pretty soon now."[18] His statement implies that becoming a "Mexican national" will conclude his slide into utter degradation, permanently severing the bond of friendship he shared with Marlowe. James M. Cain's *Serenade* (1937) emphasizes the primitive aspects of Mexico, where Americans go to indulge their most naked, bestial instincts. His protagonist, the American John Howard Sharp, describes the penchant for violence he discovers in the Mexican populace: "About half the population of the country go around with pearl-handled automatics on their hips, and the bad part about these guns is that they shoot, and after they shoot nothing is ever done about it."[19] Cain's Mexico is a place of primitive savagery, where an innate brutality combines with a total absence of law enforcement.

Orson Welles would try to challenge these stereotypes in his 1957 film noir *Touch of Evil*, which pits the tough, honest Mexican detective Miguel Vargas against the corrupt American Hank Quinlan. *Touch of Evil* reverses the conventions of hard-boiled fiction by making a Mexican its hero and advocating collaboration between law enforcement agencies on both sides of the border. But Welles's vision of neighborly community is undermined by his decision to cast Charleton Heston as Vargas, suggesting that an actual Mexican would be unsuited to play the part. The spectacle of a white actor in brownface turns the character's Mexican nationality into a matter of race, while Heston's garbled Spanish further distinguishes him from the actual Spanish speakers in the film. And despite the fact that Vargas is part of a police force, he is the only Mexican law enforcement figure to appear during the entire movie, which otherwise relegates Mexicans to predictable roles as cartoonish villains, drug addicts, and vandals. Many of these clichés endure in Steven Soderbergh's more recent depiction of cross-border crime in *Traffic* (2000). The film is intended to indict the U.S. War on Drugs for its failure to combat the drug habits of U.S. consumers and the powerful Mexican drug cartels that supply them. Yet despite its manifest effort to lay the blame on both sides of the border, *Traffic* relies uncritically on an array of familiar stereotypes. Whereas the United States is pictured in cool blues, the Mexican scenes are shot through a lurid yellow filter that suggests an atmosphere of corruption and decay. This visual device is echoed at the level of plot, which is weighted heavily toward the well-rounded stories of families in the United States while focusing its Mexican sequences almost exclusively on the corruption that extends from ordinary cops to wealthy drug cartels, the military, and the highest levels of government.

Beginning in the 1980s, Chicano/a authors began to challenge such narrative clichés about the border by writing detective fiction that featured more well-developed Mexican and Mexican American characters in the context of complex, historically informed representations of border culture. The Chicano detective novel is one instance of the general diversification of crime writing in the United States. In place of the working-class white protagonists created by Hammett, Chandler, and Cain are investigators who come from many different cultures. In keeping with the detective's changing complexion, the mean streets of Los Angeles, Chicago, and New York city have relocated to a variety of geographic locales.[20] The new face of the genre is reflected in Karen Tei Yamashita's 1997 *Tropic of Orange*, where Gabriel, a Mexican American character who is a fan of Southern California's hard-boiled tradition, fantasizes about writing his own novel featuring "an L.A. Chicano private dick."[21] It is not surprising that Gabriel imagines the detective in his own image since identitarian concerns have become an important aspect of U.S. crime writing, which now includes detectives of every conceivable gender, racial, and ethnic background.

Rolando Hinojosa is one of the earliest and most acclaimed Chicano authors to work in the detective genre. His crime novels are part of an ongoing fictional project that creates a thick portrait of Mexican American community through the use of multiple perspectives and literary genres. Hinojosa's Klail City cycle, which has been compared in complexity and scope to William Faulkner's Yoknapatawpha or Gabriel García Marquez's Macondo, consists of a series of interrelated novels about the fictional communities of Barrones,

Tamaulipas, and Belken County, Texas, the southernmost point of land entry into Mexico. A scholar and teacher, as well as a novelist, Hinojosa has dedicated his career to the study and representation of regional Chicano culture. The portrait of a hybrid border culture provided by the Klail City novels is rooted in his own experiences as a native of Mercedes, Texas, who was born and raised by an Anglo mother and Latino father. But Hinojosa's concern with a specific region does not make him provincial. As he described it, "I am Mexicano and I'm a Texas Mexican. But if I was born in this country . . . I can draw from all over the world for my work. What I'm contributing . . . is really American literature."[22] Hinojosa insists on situating Chicano culture within America, but his is an America that extends across the borders of the United States to Mexico and beyond.[23] Indeed, his comment suggests that being a writer of American literature means espousing a planetary sensibility that is open to influences from a multitude of regions and cultures. Informed by such cosmopolitan convictions, Hinojosa's novels are firmly rooted in a local community that spans the U.S.-Mexico border, where "going Mexican" is a fact of everyday life, rather than a sign of irreparable decline.

Hinojosa uses the detective novel, among other literary forms, to articulate a mode of American counternationalism that privileges local, binational social formations over state-sanctioned versions of national identity. His chosen mode is the police procedural, which is ideally suited to his concern with community and regional belonging because it emphasizes collaboration and teamwork within the confines of institutions rather than the alienated individualism of the private eye.[24] The move away from the hard-boiled hero reflects an evolution in the scope and nature of illegal activity portrayed by the detective novel. Crimes like terrorism and drug and arms trafficking must be combated with highly specialized technologies and teams of professionals that make the private eye seem like an anachronism. Even when focused on an individual detective, police procedural explores the way partnership and institutional hierarchies can both constrain and enable the task of problem solving. When an investigation crosses national borders, it introduces an added complication, the willingness and capacity of various state agencies to cooperate with one another. The transnational investigation is encumbered by additional layers of bureaucracy, which are precisely what makes borders so attractive to criminal networks seeking to exploit the cracks between different national institutions.[25] Authors of ethnic American detective fiction imagine that the protagonist who has grown up negotiating between different cultural and linguistic traditions is uniquely suited to the challenges of such cross-border investigation.

Hinojosa's two detective novels, *Partners in Crime* (1985) and *Ask a Policeman* (1998), are set in the fictional Belken County, a community that straddles the international border. The local population retains a deep sense of regional history, exemplified by the Mexican judge who quips that the protagonist's surname "Buenrostro" is a sign of the detective's kinship with "one of our illustrious Santa Anna's lost children."[26] His allusion to the infamous Mexican general responsible for losing Texas to U.S. forces in 1848 suggests that history endures in daily interactions among border dwellers. Hinojosa's descriptive style reinforces this historical sensibility by linking current cross-border relations to the past. One telling passage uses background detail to depict the complex ties between the two sides of the border: "The old neighborhood across from the fort, dating back to the 1850s, was now a crowded block of cheap stores and fast-food places catering mostly to the Mexican nationals who crossed the bridge daily. Many came to shop and spend American dollars, and more came to earn their dollars as maids, store clerks, gardeners, painters, carpenters, janitors, and still others to serve as pick-up day laborers paid for work done on the spot" (AP, 32). The mid-nineteenth-century fort is an architectural landmark that identifies the adjacent neighborhood by recalling a prior moment when the border was a zone of military contestation. What was once the site of armed conflict has become a commercial district where businesses owned by U.S. citizens are supported by Mexicans working at low-wage jobs on the U.S. side of the border. Their presence attests to the unequal but interdependent relationship between the two economies, which continue to bear traces of past hostilities and uneasy compromises.

Hinojosa creates a protagonist who is a border dweller ideally equipped to combat transnational crime. Rafael Buenrostro is a Chicano and senior member of his local homicide unit whose close partnership with the Anglo Cully Donovan is a model of interethnic collaboration. Their success in combating the clandestine networks that thrive along the U.S.-Mexican border zone comes from their deep familiarity with local culture, their sense of when it is appropriate to bend the rules, and their willingness to cooperate with Mexican law enforcement agencies. Interpersonal relationships that extend across the lines of racial and national identity are crucial to the smooth functioning of the Belken County Homicide Squad, where Buenrostro and Donovan are old friends as well as coworkers. When a case requires U.S. and Mexican colleagues to work together, they gather at the Lone Star restaurant for a night that "was business, and it was visiting as well; a fine, old valley custom, on both banks of the River. Newcomers chafed, but they either succumbed to the habit or they didn't succeed."[27] As this gathering suggests, borderlanders have their own jokes, rituals, and codes, which have more to do with membership in a regional community than with race or native language, since most are bilingual. They are suspicious of outsiders, or "fuereños" (PC, 117), who must submit to local custom in order to secure the necessary cooperation of regional authorities.[28]

Partners in Crime and *Ask a Policeman* explore the tensions between local and national solutions to the problem of cross-border crime. As some sociologists have recognized, border communities' distance from seats of federal power often means that they are hostile to centralized government.[29] Local transnational organizations often seek strategies for subverting national legislation that they see as out of touch with the daily realities of life in a binational region. Thus when Jehu Malacara of the Klail City First National Bank learns that tellers have been bribed to stay quiet about illegal transactions, he realizes that it is "an obvious Treasury violation" but he also struggles over the appropriate action to take because he knows them personally and is "a borderer, first and last. And, as most borderers throughout the world, he had little confidence in central authority" (PC, 116). One of the ongoing conflicts in Hinojosa's novels concerns border management, an issue that pits Buenrostro and Donovan, who seek nonmilitary solutions to crime in the region, against the bellicose district attorney Chip Valencia, who welcomes federal proposals for increased military presence in the area. While Valencia lobbies to line the border with tanks, the detectives demonstrate their commitment to nonviolence by going unarmed into the final showdown with Mexican crime boss José Antonio Gómez. Their decision is affirmed when Gómez is brought down through the combined efforts of Mexican and Anglo detectives, his only injury a self-inflicted gunshot wound. Such scenarios suggest that the best way to eradicate transnational crime is close collaboration between local law enforcement officers on both sides of the border.

Although he depicts a region plagued by a violent underground economy, Hinojosa refuses the stereotype of Mexican immorality so common in hardboiled detective fiction. Crime thrives on the border not because of Mexicans but because of dysfunctional policies that have made clandestine activities so profitable: in the course of thirty years, for example, the activities of a local crime ring have evolved from pimping to transporting heroine, fueled by the demands of U.S. consumers who remain undeterred by efforts to police the international border. The criminals are ultimately thwarted through teamwork by U.S. and Mexican agencies, each attuned to local communities and respectful of one another. Hinojosa is virtually unique among Hispanic authors in his depiction of local law enforcement officers as modest, hardworking, and resourceful.[30] In an interview he claims that he sought to avoid the figure of "the crooked cop," which he saw as a cliché of leftist writing.[31] His Anglo, Chicano, and Mexican detectives are true heroes in a community endangered by both the drug trade and security measures coming from national capitals of Washington, D.C. or Mexico City.

Hinojosa explains that he turned to the detective novel as a means of bringing visibility to the rising violence that the transnational drug trade had introduced into his community. *Partners in Crime* and *Ask a Policeman* are the most plot-driven, linear contributions to his Klail City series, which is known for its fragmentary, impressionistic narrative style. The turn to realism allows Hinojosa to address social issues more directly, but also to imagine solutions that affirm his longing for binational community. If the transnational criminal represents a corrosive form of globalization, his protagonists introduce an alternative that combines respect for local institutions with an awareness of the region's ties to the world. Even if their skillful detective work cannot fully eradicate the problem of transnational crime, it does prove the necessity of collaboration, the importance of historical perspective, and the borderlander's enduring ties to place.

THE INDEPENDENT EYE OF THE MEXICAN NEOPOLICIACO

At the same time that Hinojosa was beginning his Klail City cycle, the Mexican *neopoliciaco* was coming into its own. Whereas the Anglo-American detective novel flourished in the first half of the twentieth century, critics generally agree that noteworthy examples of the genre did not begin to appear in Mexico until much later. As Braham explains, "[U]ntil the 1970s the field of Latin American detective fiction was both limited and derivative. Through simulation or parody, authors engaged the marginal status and formulaic nature of detective narrative to dramatize Latin America's peripheral position with respect to modern Western culture."[32] Things changed with the arrival of Paco Ignacio Taibo II, the most well known and prolific Mexican detective novelist of his generation. Taibo writes in a subgenre known as the *neopoliciaco*, which is inspired by Anglo-American hard-boiled crime writing. Whereas Hinojosa's novels employ the police procedural to affirm the values of teamwork and institutional authority, the *neopoliciaco* favors the lone detective who must work independently, since the worst criminals are often officers of the law. As a character in Taibo's *Some Clouds* remarks, "[T]he police are behind something like 79 percent of the serious crime in Mexico City."[33]

When Taibo began writing crime fiction in the 1970s, he inserted himself into a market created after World War II, when cheaply produced Spanish-language detective novels enjoyed a broad readership among the Mexican public. Detective fiction in translation, which had been popular with Latin American readers since the nineteenth century, reached its apogee in the 1930s and 1940s, inspiring a host of Mexican imitators to take advantage of a ready market in the 1950s.[34] More recent Mexican detective novelists such as Taibo, Jorge Ibargüengoitia, Carmen Boullosa, and, more recently, Gabriel Trujillo Muñoz reject these Hispanic predecessors as formulaic and derivative ("a generation of parodists and imitators," in the words of Taibo).[35] Instead their models are American writers like Chandler, Dashiell Hammett, and Chester Himes. Contemporary Latin American authors admire the hard-boiled novelists for their proletarian values and their ability to address a popular readership while maintaining a commitment to literary style. Widely read and deeply familiar with the genre, authors of the *neopoliciaco* allude frequently and knowingly to their Anglo-American precursors.

The Mexican *neopoliciaco* is the product of a generation that came of political age in the late 1960s. The October 1968 massacre of student protestors in the Plaza de las Tres Culturas galvanized a generation of intellectuals, some of whom turned to the detective novel as a means of social critique, making its leftist sentiments explicit in a way that would have been unimaginable to their Anglo-American precursors.[36] The decision to embrace a degraded form of popular literature was itself seen as a political act, a reaction against the difficult, experimental fiction of the boom generation. The impact of the events of 1968 is evident in the *neopoliciaco*'s disdain for the state and official institutions, its depiction of a chaotic, wild Mexico City, and skepticism about the possibilities of justice. Even though the detective is often unable to solve the crimes he investigates, the narrative of investigation becomes a means of speculating on the intellectual's role within a national and global society. When these novels are set at Mexico's northern border, they articulate an alternative vision of *mexicanidad* that counters both official versions of Mexican nationalism and the pressures of Americanization coming from the north.

The *neopoliciaco* depicts Mexico as a place of near anarchic corruption, where a dysfunctional state apparatus has given free reign to criminals, while ignoring the needs of ordinary citizens. These novels reflect the widespread public skepticism about official authorities that has arisen in Latin American nations unsettled by decades of short-lived and unreliable government regimes. The detective's most hated antagonists are not individuals but institutions, including the U.S. and Mexican governments, which both perpetrate and condone acts of lawless violence. Often the United States is seen as responsible for amplifying Mexico's problems by pressuring it toward rapid modernization; imposing contradictory immigration and trade policies; and infecting Mexicans with its crass, consumerist mentality. In a context where crime almost invariably involves the state, it is crucial that the investigator be a private eye who obeys no authority other than his own moral code. This figure, who has come to seem outdated to many U.S. detective writers, is taken up by authors of the Mexican *neopoliciaco* as the fitting embodiment of the David-and-Goliath struggle that pits the people against crime syndicates, police, and the state. His temperament and style are cut from the hard-boiled mold, although Taibo's protagonist, Hector Belascoarán Shayne, underscores his leftist politics by rejecting the label "private" investigator in favor of "independent."

Taibo's work is published by major international presses, translated into many languages, and has a large readership among non-Mexican audiences, although it employs highly specific Mexican contexts and uses a local vernacular that Ilan Stavans describes as "replete with malapropisms, offensive insults, and street syntax," which defies translation.[37] The epicenter of Taibo's fictional universe is Mexico City, which he establishes with the kind of thick description that Raymond Chandler lavished on Los Angeles. Like the British Chandler, who claimed California as his adopted home, Taibo is a Spanish immigrant who settled permanently in Mexico City. Just as Chandler's Marlowe is a product of particular California locales and lifestyles, Taibo's detective Belascoarán Shayne is born of an urban, Mexican context, which, for better or worse, is the place where he most belongs. Comparing his setting to Chandler's, Taibo remarked in an interview: "the differences are in the structure of the lone hero, the outsider: a vocation for solitude, a fidelity to friends (in Marlowe's case) and to certain obsessions (in Belascoarán Shayne's case). Raymond Chandler's character moves within rational histories whereas mine is surrounded by a chaotic atmosphere, Kafkaesque and corrupt: Mexico City."[38] As Belascoarán Shayne walks the streets of this massive, chaotic, and decentralized modern metropolis,

> The city opened up to him like a monster, like the fetid entrails of a whale, or the insides of a discarded tin can. In its few hours of sleep, the sleep of a tired man, of a worker worn out by his labor, the city became a character, a subject, signals, and would blow breezes full on strange intentions. The jungle of television antennas was bombarded by wavelengths, messages, commercials. The asphalt, the shop windows, the walls, the cars, the *taco* vendor stalls, the stray dogs all made room for him at the beat of his steps.[39]

In this passage, a dirty, proletarian Mexico acquires the status of a well-developed character. The use of colloquialisms and references to particular Mexican places and histories anchors Taibo's fiction in a very specific urban setting. But because that setting is the vast, cosmopolitan Mexico of the late twentieth century, it is also tied to a global economy and culture.

Like modern Mexico, the name of Taibo's protagonist attests to his cosmopolitan genealogy. The name "Belascoarán" points to the Basque ancestry of Hector's father, who fought with Republican forces during the Spanish Civil War. Hector continues the Basque legacy in his fierce independence and willingness to resort to violence in the pursuit of justice. Association with the Basques, who some believe may have sailed to North America hundreds of years before Columbus, also establishes Hector's belonging in the New World. "Shayne" signals the detective's ties to a modern America in which the United States plays a central role. It pays tribute to the Miami-based detective Michael Shayne, who is the fictional creation of author Brett Halliday. Halliday, in turn, claimed Latin American inspiration by explaining that his detective protagonist was based on a deckhand he met while working on an oil tanker off the coast of Tampico, Mexico.[40] The name Shayne is thus a sign of cultural symbiosis, a reminder of the unacknowledged Mexican origins of much U.S. culture, as well as the reciprocal influence exerted by that culture on contemporary Mexico.

Although their obsessions with Pepsi, female basketball stars, and American literature tie them to the United States, Taibo's protagonists are *chilangos* (inhabitants of Mexico City) who feel profoundly alienated from the northern border, a place that Belascoarán Shayne describes as "*la frontera*, that strange name used to designate a mix of territories branded by the dubious privilege of sucking face with the United States."⁴¹ With such statements, he rejects the kind of cross-border community idealized by an author like Rolando Hinojosa. The transnational crime syndicates that plague contemporary Mexico cannot be combated through the collaboration of national law enforcement agencies, given the extreme corruption of officials on either side. In place of the binational community imagined by Hinojosa, Taibo uses the detective novel to articulate a version of *mexicanidad* that is associated neither with Mexican Americans nor with official modes of nationalism advanced by the Mexican state.

Pancho Villa—heroized for his bold and futile assault on the United States—is an important figure in Taibo's attempt to recover alternative versions of the Mexican past. When a case takes Belascoarán Shayne to Chihuahua in *Frontera Dreams*, he identifies with the civic devotion to Villa, "guardian of the fucked-over who await his triumphant return" (FD, 55). At the museum dedicated to his memory, the detective engages in an act of historical investigation, "a hunt for the unexpected, an attempt to catch a little of the ambiance, a search for General Villa's air of mockery" (FD, 56). A more literal form of historical recovery is the subject of Taibo's "Morán y Pancho," subtitled "(Notas para una novella de canallas y villistas escrita por Dash Hammett y reescrita al paso de los años por Paco Ignacio Taibo II)" (Notes for a novella about scoundrels and Villistas written by Dash Hammett and rewritten some years later by Paco Ignacio Taibo II). The story's protagonist is the hard-boiled novelist Dashiell Hammett, who is investigating, rather than writing about, a murder and finds himself drawn into a search for the missing head of Pancho Villa, "el único general, al que los historiadores de Nueva York insistian en llamar bandolero, que había invadido los Estados Unidos" (the only general, who the historians of New York insist on calling a bandit, who had invaded the United States).⁴² Over the course of his investigation, Hammett repeatedly crosses the U.S.-Mexico border until he finally tracks down the head. Although his quest is successful, the story ends with an ambiguity typical of Taibo since the ultimate fate of the head is left unclear: Hammett may have thrown it into the sea, concealed it in his neighbor's yard, or, most ironically, buried it under a statue of Lincoln "para que los niños norteamericanos rindan homenaje sin saberlo a Pancho Villa" (so that North American children pay unknowing homage to Pancho Villa) (223). Taibo delights in the possibility that the remains of Pancho Villa might sully the memorial to a revered figure in U.S. national consciousness, as well as the idea that Mexico was a formative place in the life and career of one of the United States' foremost authors of detective fiction. This tale of historical recovery also becomes a critique of contemporary Mexico when Hammett's Mexican friend Raul laments that his compatriots no longer deserve the missing head, "aunque me hubiera gustado guardarla para los otros años que vendrán" (although I would have liked to save it for the coming years) (222). The counterhistory of Pancho Villa provides Taibo with an opportunity to recall a moment of bold resistance against the United States, but also to criticize Mexico's failure to live out the promises of the revolution. "If novels were good for something," one of his characters reflects, "it was to tell us what the others were like that we could not be like. It was not, as they thought in the first half of the twentieth century, a means of instruction, which entailed lectures, morals, advice, images to imitate and deny. . . . Even less was it raw material for linguistic experiments. . . . Literature was a resource for the future, the stuff of premonitions: a book of schedules, a real proposed chapter for intervening in real life."[43] Taking seriously the notion of literature as "a resource for the future," Taibo believes in the power of the written word to shore up alternative historical knowledge that might point the way toward a more egalitarian social order. He finds the detective novel, with its broad popular appeal and concern with problems of crime and morality, an ideal form for such an undertaking.

Recently, Taibo has further probed the relationship between literature and political agency in a detective novel written collaboratively with Subcomandante Marcos of the EZLN (Zapatista Army of National Liberation), which was published serially in the Mexican newspaper *La jornada* between December 2004 and February 2005. The partnership between an acclaimed author and the charismatic guerilla leader promises to take the genre in new directions. Widely available via the Internet and contracted to international publishers who will translate the completed narrative into multiple languages, *Muertos incómodos* (The Awkward Dead) is intended to reach a large audience of readers around the world.[44] The finished novel consists of twelve chapters alternately written by its two authors, the sections by Taibo featuring Hector Belascoarán Shayne and the sections by Marcos featuring a Zapatista detective named Elias Contreras (who also happens to be dead). The two investigators meet in Mexico City, where they are tracking a man who is responsible for a wide range of crimes, including participation in the "guerra sucia" against the insurgents in Chiapas; collusion with the Bush government; and plundering the environment for financial gain.

The plot of *Muertos incómodos*, which is thin and often veers into the absurd, frequently digresses into metaphysical speculation (in the chapters penned by Taibo) and political critique (in the Marcos chapters). It is highly topical, remarking on current events such as the videotapes of Osama Bin Laden, the controversial arrival of Wal-Mart in Teotihuacán, and the indictment of Mexico's popular mayor and presidential contender, Manuel López Obrador. It represents a Mexico fully saturated by globalization, which appears in its more positive form in the international band of comrades gathered in Chiapas to participate in the revolution, and, more negatively, in official con-

264 • Rachel Adams

spiracies to decimate the region's natural resources for export and the sinister activities of an ultra-right-wing Mexican group called El Yunque, which has ties to Europe and other parts of Latin America. In many ways, the investigation seems doomed from the outset, given the view articulated in an early chapter written by Marcos that "EL asesino no va a regresar a la escena del crimen, simple y sencillamente porque él es la escena del crimen. EL asesino es el sistema. El sistema sí. Cuando hay un crimen hay que buscar al culpable arriba, no abajo. El MAL is el sistema y los MALOS son quienes están al servicio del sistema" (The assassin will not return to the scene of the crime, simply and sincerely because he is the scene of the crime. The assassin is the system. The system itself. When there is a crime, it is necessary to look above not below. The evil is the system and the evildoers are those who serve the system).[45] At the same time that it cannot hope to defeat "the system," *Muertos incómodos*, much like Taibo's previous work, uses the detective genre as a moral compass and as a means of advocating resistance against wrongdoing, even if justice cannot be served. As one character reminds Contreras, the detective's task is to "[busca] para encontrar al mal y al malo y lo [mira] que reciben su castigo por sus maldades" (seek to find evil and evildoers and see that they receive punishment for their wrongdoing).[46]

Taibo's appropriation of hard-boiled crime writing takes the American detective novel to uncharted territory. Like Hinojosa, his subject is the globalization of crime. However, as he views it, the culprits are not only transnational criminals but law enforcement and politicians. In order to maintain his integrity, the detective must shun all institutional ties. Instead of focusing on a single locality, Taibo situates his critique of the global economy in many locations, from the northern border states to Mexico City to the jungles of Chiapas. And in place of the multicultural cross-border community affirmed by Hinojosa, Taibo imagines solidarity among populations that may be spatially dispersed but share common experiences of oppression. They may travel great distances to defend a cause they believe in or, thanks to the Internet, may communicate instantly with one another. Taibo's investigators cannot hope to bring down the massive networks of corruption they uncover, but they can reveal counterhistories that point out both the ideological investments behind official revisions of history and provide models for action in the future.

Women on the Line: A Case for the Planet

Hinojosa and Taibo provide the detective novel with new characters and geographic locations, while preserving its focus on male bonding and masculine concerns.[47] And despite the fact that both authors allude to actual crimes that have occurred along the U.S.-Mexico border, neither has written of the region's greatest unsolved crime: the missing women of Ciudad Juárez. Since

1993, hundreds of women have been abducted, raped and subjected to other forms of sexual violation, and murdered. Many bodies turn up in the surrounding desert; others are never found. Most of the victims are poor migrants who have moved north to the border to work in the *maquiladora* plants. Women occupy a particularly charged position in the local economy of Ciudad Juárez as they are the primary source of factory labor and are also associated with the city's booming sex industry.[48] In the last eleven years, over three hundred women have been murdered, and 800 more have been reported missing, yet authorities have failed to find a culprit or identify a motivation for the crimes. Often they blame the victims themselves for flaunting their sexuality and being careless about their personal safety. Victims' advocates trace the onset of the crimes to the implementation of NAFTA, arguing that they are an indirect consequence of globalization in the region. The absence of any plausible solution has given rise to numerous popular theories, which attribute the crime to serial killers, satanic cults, organ smugglers, and a trade in "white slavery" or snuff films.[49] Given the magnitude of the case and the abundance of sensational culprits, it is striking that borderlands detective fiction, which so often takes its cue from contemporary events, has paid it so little attention. This silence was broken with the 2005 publication of Alicia Gaspar de Alba's *Desert Blood: The Juárez Murders*, which features a female investigator who probes the gendered dimensions of violence along the U.S.-Mexico border. An author who has worked in many genres, Gaspar de Alba turns to the detective novel as a means of drawing the world's attention to what might seem to be a local crisis. She also uses *Desert Blood* to reflect on the capacity of crime fiction to intervene in the social problems it represents.

With *Desert Blood*, Gaspar de Alba inserts herself into the recently established categories of feminist and Chicano/a detective fiction. Her protagonist, Ivon Villa, is a lesbian who has returned to her birthplace in El Paso in the hope of adopting a child. Like Taibo, Gaspar de Alba invests her character with a proud transnational genealogy. The "daughter of a man who considered himself a great-grandson of the hardheaded Pancho Villa and an Apache woman, . . . she did not bend or break easily" (17). With such bloodlines, Ivon becomes a figure for a binational Chicano community with a long history of rebellion and enduring ties to place. When her teenage sister Irene is abducted, Villa is appalled at the inaction of U.S. and Mexican authorities. She embarks on her own investigation in a desperate effort to save her sister's life. Ultimately, Villa succeeds in rescuing Irene from a perverse crime ring that makes snuff films for sale on the Internet. As she searches for her sister, Villa is confronted by the unsolved cases of the dead and missing women of Ciudad Juárez. By creating parallels between the cases of Irene and the *maquiladora* workers, the novel underscores that all of these crimes are the product of dramatic changes within a community brought into sudden contact with the global economy.

Like both Hinojosa and Taibo, Gaspar de Alba's appropriation of the detective novel invites speculation about her generic choices. Her protagonist is not only an impromptu investigator but an instructor of Chicano/a Studies who is struggling to finish her dissertation. The urgent problem of Irene's disappearance threatens to jeopardize Villa's future as a scholar, since she is facing a looming deadline that must be met or she risks losing her job. The unfinished dissertation is a device that allows the author—herself a scholar of Chicano/a Studies—to weigh the merits of different generic forms. On the one hand, Villa's skills as a researcher are valuable. Her background in cultural studies makes her an effective investigator who "always look[s] for the historical and cultural context of whatever she was researching."[50] Gaspar de Alba's own reliance on scholarly sources is evident in the acknowledgments printed at the end of the novel. On the other, the dead women of Ciudad Juárez make Villa's scholarship seem irrelevant. At the novel's end, Villa realizes that "she ha[s] exactly eight days to finish the last chapter, write a conclusion, print up the whole manuscript, and submit it to her committee" (340). As useful as her academic training may be, she treats her dissertation as an afterthought. By incorporating the problem of an unfinished work of scholarship into *Desert Blood*, Gaspar de Alba can reflect on her decision to write a detective novel, rather than a scholarly book or article. Despite its gravitas, she eschews academic writing in favor of a popular form that long been treated as a degraded mode of literary expression, but has the capacity to reach broad audiences and to encourage their emotional investment in the problems it represents.

Alba draws attention to the many ways that *Desert Blood* breaks with generic convention by calling it an "anti-detective novel." It is true that the story ends neatly with Irene's rescue and the happy reunion of the Villa family. But Ivon is unable to bring the culprits to justice or determine who is behind the murders of the *maquiladora* workers. Ultimately, she rejects the genre's traditional goals when she decides that identifying individual perpetrators is less important than revealing the social and economic dynamics that allow these crimes to continue:

> Pornographers, gang members, serial killers, corrupt police men, foreign nationals with a taste for hurting women, immigration officers protecting the homeland—what did it matter *who* killed them? This wasn't a case of "whodunit," but rather of who was allowing these crimes to happen? Whose interests were being served? Who was covering it up? Who was profiting from the deaths of all these women? (333)

These lingering questions about profit and motivation help to explain why Irene, a middle-class U.S. citizen, comes to a very different fate than the impoverished Mexican women who regularly disappear from the *maquiladoras* and whose relatives lack resources to demand justice. When her own family comes together, Villa thinks of the many Mexican families that have been irreparably broken apart by the murders. The neat resolution of an individual crime is thus unsettled by the novel's insistence that the larger problem it exposes remains unsolved. Using the language of factory production, Ivon realizes that she has uncovered "[a] bilateral assembly line of perpetrators, from the actual agents of the crime to the law enforcement agents on both sides of the border to the agents that made binational immigration policy and trade agreements. . . . This thing implicated everyone. No wonder the crimes had not been solved, nor would they ever be solved until someone with much more power and money than she, with nothing to lose or to gain, brought this conspiracy out into the open" (335). In its portrait of widespread corruption among politicians, corporations, and lawmakers, *Desert Blood* echoes the *neo-policiaco*'s radical leftist sensibilities, as well as its sense of futility about the possibility of eradicating the broad social problems it exposes.

Yet *Desert Blood* is not conceived out of the sensation of powerlessness expressed by its protagonist. Gaspar de Alba frames the writing of her novel as precisely the kind of action that Villa herself feels unable to take. While Ivon believes that the crimes can be solved only by someone with "much more power and money than she," Gaspar de Alba points to the ongoing work of families and grassroots organizations to intervene where established figures of power and authority have failed. Forming alliances across national borders, nongovernmental groups are a line of defense against transnational criminals who operate by exploiting the weaknesses of law enforcement in the region. These organizations, which emerged from public outrage at the indifference and inaction of local officials, have attracted the attention of activists and media outlets in many parts of the world. In her preface, Gaspar de Alba presents *Desert Blood* as a contribution to their efforts. Addressing herself to Anglophone readers, she explains: "It is not my intention in this story to sensationalize the crimes or capitalize on the losses of so many families, but to expose the horrors of this deadly crime wave as broadly as possible to the English-speaking public, and to offer some conjecture, based on research, based on what I know about the place on the map, some plausible explanation for the silence that has surrounded the murders" (vi). Framed in this way, the novel overlaps closely with other forms of media that seek to bring worldwide attention to the problems plaguing Ciudad Juárez. In its alignment with a specific cause, *Desert Blood* differs from the detective novels of Hinojosa and Taibo, which provide a more indirect reflection of current events in the borderlands.

Desert Blood also reflects on the particular role that novels can play in galvanizing public sentiment by exploring how narrative fiction can fill in gaps left by other forms of representation. The novel opens with a short chapter narrated from the viewpoint of an anonymous victim during the final, gruesome moments of her life. As the description of Villa's investigation unfolds, it is interspersed with chapters that follow Irene through the terrifying experience of abduction and sexual abuse. In these episodes, the reader must imagine death from the perspective of the victim rather than the perpetrator or the detective, who surveys the scene of the crime only after it has been committed. By representing the fear and pain suffered by these women, the novel gives voice to the victims and their families. In fiction, the dead can speak out to remind the living of their suffering. Although these crimes are based on actual events, Gaspar de Alba also lends them a metaphoric dimension that underscores the victims' symbolic role in the border economy. Pennies are found inserted into many of the dead bodies that turn up in *Desert Blood*, a detail the author explains in her introduction as an effort "to signify the value of the victims in the corporate machine; the poor brown women who are the main target of these murders, are, in other words, as expendable as pennies in the border economy" (v). The dead women force-fed on a diet of U.S. currency become symbols of a Mexico poisoned by economic reliance on its northern neighbor or, as one character puts it, "just like the maquilas themselves have been shoved down Mexico's throat" (252). This rather obvious metaphor works precisely because of its blunt simplicity; like a political slogan, it compresses a complex situation into an enduring image that surfaces at key moments throughout the narrative.

With *Desert Blood*, Gaspar de Alba brings together elements of the Mexican and Chicano/a detective novel to render one of the worst unsolved crimes in recent North American history in narrative fiction. Although she does not solve the crimes, Villa uncovers a transnational web of corruption that implicates law enforcement, politicians, judges, and reporters in allowing the killings to continue. Behind it she finds the disastrous impact of NAFTA on the fragile social and environmental ecologies of the border region. With writers of the *neopoliciaco*, Gaspar de Alba shares an identification with the powerlessness of the poor and marginal populations of Mexico, a commitment to exposing the underlying social and economic causes of their oppression, and a deep suspicion of politicians and officers of the law. At the same time, *Desert Blood* shares the identitarian concerns of U.S. lesbian and Chicano/a detective fiction. Like many other contemporary ethnic authors, Gaspar de Alba emphasizes her protagonist's identity as a feminist, lesbian, and Chicana, implicitly underscoring her difference from the classic Anglo-American detective. As she traverses the border during the course of her investigation, Ivon also maps tangled bonds of cultural filiation that extend back over many generations. Her story expresses a longing for cross-border connections that is closer to the U.S. Chicano tradition than the Mexican. Adopting elements of both U.S. ethnic and Mexican crime writing, Gaspar de Alba uses the detective novel to address a real crime that has so far defied novelization. It is a crime that brings violence against women to the forefront, highlighting both the troubled sexual politics of border communities and the gender dynamics of the crime writing tradition.

Contemporary crime writers like Hinojosa, Taibo, and Gaspar de Alba are opening a new chapter in the history of American detective fiction, one that cannot be adequately understood without crossing the borders of language, culture, and nation. On the one hand, their work presents a devastating picture of the impact of globalization on the U.S.-Mexico border. Rapid development, the displacement of populations, and the erosion of economic boundaries under NAFTA have introduced high rates of violent crime to the region. Heightened concerns about illegal immigration and national security have brought greater attention to these problems, while doing little to address their underlying causes. The diffuse organization of transnational criminal networks makes the prospect of justice elusive so that, more often than not, confrontations between detectives and criminals end without resolution. The globalization of crime changes the detective's relationship to his (and more recently, her) community. Whereas once the investigator set out to restore social order, this goal is elusive in communities whose populations are dispersed or migratory and where there is little consensus about shared beliefs and values. But globalization has also meant the dispersal of the detective novel itself, as it has been appropriated into a range of cultural and linguistic contexts across North America and around the world. When it enters these new contexts, detective fiction does not fall prey to the homogeneity and standardization so often associated with the globalization of culture. Instead its recognizable formulas have been adapted to address the concerns and traditions of regions that are defined through their membership in broader continental, and planetary, communities. The borderlands, which were once at the edge of the detective novel's imagined geography, have become a meeting ground for some of its most innovative practitioners, who are reimagining the genre's capacity to resonate beyond the printed page and to speak to audiences far beyond the local settings it represents.

Read together, these works can provide a case study in the regional adaptation of a popular form. But my analysis is also intended to serve as a model for approaching the borderlands between other nations and cultures within North America and abroad. This model relies on the continent as an analytic unit whose elastic borders extend outward to the American hemisphere and beyond. Within North America, border literatures attest to the particular burden of geographical proximity to the United States, which can be simultaneously a source of inspiration, a longed-for destination, and a tyrannical hegemon that threatens the economic and political sovereignty of its closest neighbors. For border communities, a history of violence and loss remains alive in conflicts over resources and social values. But as we have seen, the border is also the site of regenerative counterhistories, which underscore the contingencies of current geopolitical formations by imagining alternatives to national community. These become visible only through a geographic frame that encompasses Mexico as well as the United States, and that might be productively expanded to include Canada as well. A wide-angle view of the continent exposes the paradoxes of North American cultural forms that illuminate the tenacity of borders of all kinds, while defying them in deft and surprising acts of crossing.

NOTES

1. Raymond Chandler, *The Long Goodbye* (New York: Vintage Crime, 1992); Michael Connelly, *The Black Ice* (New York: Warner Books, 1993).

2. Chandler, *The Long Goodbye*, 37.

3. *The Wall around the West: State Borders and Immigration Controls in North America and Europe*, ed. Peter Andreas and Timothy Snyder (Lanham, Md.: Rowman and Littlefield, 2000); Lawrence A. Herzog, *Where North Meets South: Cities, Space, and Politics on the U.S.-Mexico Border* (Austin: University of Texas Press, 1990); David E. Lorey, *The U.S.-Mexican Border in the Twentieth Century: A History of Economic and Social Transformation* (Wilmington, Del.: Scholarly Resources, Inc., 1999); Oscar J. Martínez, *Border People: Life and Society in the U.S.-Mexico Borderlands* (Tucson: University of Arizona Press, 1994); Claudia Sadowski-Smith, ed., *Globalization on the Line: Culture, Capital, and Citizenship at U.S. Borders* (New York: Palgrave, 2002).

4. Peter Andreas, "Redrawing the Line: Borders and Security in the Twenty-first Century," *International Security* 28, no. 2 (2003): 78–111, 83–91.

5. Ibid., 78.

6. Bartosz H. Stanislawksi and Margaret G. Hermann, "Transnational Organized Crime, Terrorism, and WMD," discussion paper for the Conference on Non-State Actors, Terrorism, and Weapons of Mass Destruction, Center for International Development and Conflict Management (CIDCM), University of Maryland, October 15, 2004.

7. Ibid., 2.

8. The table of contents of a collection like *The Post-Colonial Detective* illustrates the genre's international diversity.

9. Giles Blunt, *Forty Words for Sorrow* (New York: Berkeley Books, 2002).

10. In "Continental Ops: Crossing Borders in North American Crime Narrative," I compare crime writing from the U.S.-Canadian and U.S.-Mexican borderlands (*Foreign Relations: Remapping the Cultures of North America* [forthcoming, University of Chicago Press]).

11. On Chicano/a detective fiction, see Claire Fox, "Left Sensationalists at the Transnational Crime Scene: Recent Detective Fiction from the U.S.-Mexico Border Region," in *World Bank Literature*, ed. Amitava Kumar (Minneapolis: University of Minnesota Press, 2003), 184–200; and Ralph Rodriguez, "Cultural Memory and Chicanidad: Detecting History, Past and Present, in Lucha Corpi's Gloria Damasco Series," *Contemporary Literature* 43, no. 1 (Spring 2002): 138–70.

12. Walter Mignolo, *Local Histories/Global Designs: Coloniality, Subaltern Knowledges, and Border Thinking* (Princeton: Princeton University Press, 2000), 11.

13. Martin W. Lewis and Kären E. Wigen, *The Myth of the Continents: A Critique of Metageography* (Berkeley: University of California Press, 1997).

14. Although there are a number of programs in North American studies, especially in Europe, these typically focus on the United States with the explicit goal of enabling students to compete in the global marketplace.

15. Naomi Klein, "The Rise of the Fortress Continent," *Nation*, February 3, 2003, 10.

16. Dashiell Hammett, "The Golden Horseshoe," in *The Continental Op* (New York: Random House, 1974).

17. Chandler, *The Long Goodbye*, 370.

18. Ibid., 377.

19. James M. Cain, *Three by Cain* (New York: Vintage, 1989), 7.

20. Leroy L. Panek, "Post-war American Police Fiction," in *The Cambridge Companion to Crime Fiction*, ed. Martin Priestman (Cambridge: Cambridge University Press, 2003), 159.

21. Karen Tei Yamashita, *Tropic of Orange* (St. Paul, Minn.: Coffee House Press, 1997), 246.

22. "The Boss I Work for Dialogue: Leslie Marmon Silko and Rolando Hinojosa" (1987), in *Conversations with Leslie Marmon Silko*, ed. Ellen L. Arnold (Jackson: University of Mississippi Press, 2000), 94.

23. For example, see Elizabeth Espadas, "Bridging the Gap: Rolando Hinojosa's Writings in Their Latin American Dimension." MACLAS *Latin American Essays* 1 (1987): 7–15.

24. Panek, "Post-war American Police Fiction." See also the introduction to *Criminal Proceedings: The Contemporary American Crime Novel*, ed. Peter Messent (Chicago: Pluto Press, 1997); and Robert P. Winston and Nancy Mellerski, *The Public Eye: Ideology and the Police Procedural* (London: Macmillan, 1992).

25. On the contemporary crime novel, see Hans Bertens and Theo D'haen, *Contemporary American Crime Fiction* (New York: Palgrave, 2001); *Sleuthing Ethnicity: The Detective in Multiethnic Crime Fiction*, ed. Dorothea Fischer-Hornung and Monica Mueller (Madison, N.J.: Fairleigh Dickinson University Press, 2003); *Multicultural Detective Fiction: Murder from the "Other Side,"* ed. Adrienne Johnson Gosselin (New York: Garland Publishers, 1999); Kathleen Gregory Klein, ed., *Diversity and Detective Fiction* (Bowling Green, Ohio: Bowling Green State University Popular Press, 1999); Klein, *The Woman Detective: Gender and Genre* (Urbana: University of Illinois Press, 1988); *Criminal Proceedings*, ed. Messent; Richard B. Schwartz, *Nice and Noir: Contemporary American Crime Fiction* (Columbia: University of Missouri Press, 2002); *Detective Agency: Women Rewriting the Hard-Boiled Tradition*, ed. Priscilla Walton and Manina Jones (Berkeley: University of California Press, 1999).

26. Rolando Hinojosa, *Ask a Policeman* (Houston: Arte Público Press, 1998) 140. All subsequent references cited parenthetically in the text.

27. Rolando Hinojosa, *Partners in Crime* (Houston: Arte Público Press, 1985) 173. All subsequent references cited parenthetically in the text.

28. As Hinojosa remarks of his own borderlander identity, "I was born on the Texas-Tamaulipas border, not far from where the Rio Grande flows into the Gulf of Mexico and not far from the last two engagements of the Civil War. The territory was surveyed by the Spanish army and settled by Spanish subjects in the 1850s, and the people who settled there had a sure sense of identity. That self-confidence remains, and the

Valleyites, with all their good and bad points, have one reply when asked where they hail from: 'I'm from the Valley.' They name no town unless pressed to do so." Rolando Hinojosa-Smith, "Commentary," *World Literature Today* 3–4 (Summer 2001): 64–72.

29. Martínez, *Border People*, 23–24.

30. For example, Rudolfo Anaya and Lucha Corpi, two other well-known authors of Chicano/a detective fiction, favor the private investigator who subverts the police and other official authorities, working directly with individual clients.

31. Danilo H. Figueredo, "Ask A Mystery Writer: A Conversation with Rolando Hinojosa," *MultiCultural Review*, September 1999, 27.

32. Persephone Braham, *Crimes against the State, Crimes against Persons: Detective Fiction in Cuba and Mexico* (Minneapolis: University of Minnesota Press, 2004), ix.

33. Paco Ignacio Taibo II, *Some Clouds*, trans. William I. Neuman (Scottsdale, Ariz.: Poisoned Pen Press, 2002), 73.

34. Braham, *Crimes Against the State*, and Ilan Stavans, *Antiheroes: Mexico and Its Detective Novel*, trans. Jesse H. Lytle and Jennifer A. Mattson (Madison, N.J.: Fairleigh Dickinson University Press, 1997).

35. Cited in Stavans, *Antiheroes*, 146.

36. Braham, *Crimes against the State*, xiii.

37. Stavans, *Antiheroes*, 111.

38. Cited in Stavans, *Antiheroes*, 145.

39. Cited in Jorge Hernández Martín, "Paco Ignacio Taibo II: Post-colonialism and the Detective Story in Mexico," in *The Post-colonial Detective*, ed. Ed Christian (New York: Palgrave, 2001), 168.

40. Stavans, *Antiheroes*, 109. For the story of Halliday's encounter, see http://www.mikeshayne.com/htmike.html (accessed June 6, 2005).

41. Paco Ignacio Taibo II, *Frontera Dreams*, trans. Bill Verner (El Paso, Tex.: Cinco Puntos Press, 2002), 106. All subsequent references cited parenthetically in text.

42. Paco Ignacio Taibo II, "Morán y Pancho," in *El juego de la intriga*, ed. Martín Casariego (Madrid: Espasa Calpe, 1997), 200. All subsequent references cited parenthetically in the text. Translations of "Morán y Pancho" are my own.

43. Paco Ignacio Taibo II, *Leonardo's Bicycle*, trans. Martin Michael Roberts (New York: Warner Books, 1995), 273.

44. Richard Boudreaux, "Mexico's Rebel with a Cause and a Knack for Prose," *Los Angeles Times*, December 26, 2004, A3; James C. McKinley, "Solution to a Stalled Revolution: Write a Mystery Novel," *New York Times*, December 13, 2004, A4; Luis Hernandez Navarro, "Cosas del Pasado," *La jornada*, January 18, 2005; Jo Tuckman, "Subcomandante Marcos Pens New Twist to Zapatista Struggle," *Guardian*, December 20, 2004, 11.

45. Subcomandante Insurgente Marcos, *Muertos incomodos*, *La jornada*, December 19, 2004, 6. My translation.

46. Subcomandante Insurgente Marcos, *Muertos incomodos*, *La jornada*, January 30, 2005, 8. My translation.

47. In "Left Sensationalists at the Transnational Crime Scene," Claire Fox notes the gendering of borderlands detective fiction, as well as its neglect of the crimes against women taking place in Ciudad Juárez.

48. Melissa Wright, "From Protests to Politics: Sex Work, Women's Worth, and Ciudad Juárez Modernity," *Annals of the Association of American Geographers* 94, no. 2 (2004): 369–86.

49. John Burnett, "Chasing the Ghouls," *Columbia Journalism Review*, March 2004, 12; Alma Guillermoprieto, "A Hundred Women: Why Has a Decade-Long String of Murders Gone Unsolved," *New Yorker*, September 29, 2003, 83; Chris Kraul, "Frustration Grows Over Killings," *Los Angeles Times*, February 1, 2005, A3.

50. Alicia Gaspar de Alba, *Desert Blood: The Juárez Murders* (Houston: Arte Público, 2005), 118. All subsequent references cited parenthetically in the text.

CHAPTER 11

African, Caribbean, American: Black English as Creole Tongue

Wai Chee Dimock

Is AFRICAN-AMERICAN LITERATURE NATIONAL, or it is diasporic? Just how important is the first half of that hyphenated word? Does "African" reside solely in the pigment of the skin, or is it more active than that, more tenacious, working its way into ritual and music, into the very words one uses and the grammar that strings together those words? Is there a research program embedded in the word "African," and if so, how does it square with the geography and chronology of the United States?

The "practice of diaspora" is emerging as a pivotal question in African-American literature.[1] In this essay I explore it as a linguistic force—articulated in the vernacular rather in formal speech, and bearing witness to the planetary circuit of tongues, the mixing of syntax and phonemes across continents. It is this planetary circuit that makes African-American literature an exemplary paradigm, not only for mapping the broad circumference of literature, but also for tracing the lineaments of a new human science, a creole anthropology, with intercontinental pathways threaded into nonstandard speech.

NATIONAL HUMAN SCIENCE

Since the diasporic has not been always accepted, it is worth recalling an earlier form of human science, more rigidly bounded, based on the analytic adequacy of the nation. According to this model, the "African-American" is no more than a *subset* of the "American." A bilateral entity turns out to be unilateral after all: two continents add up to one. "African," on this view, is dead on arrival; only a visual marker remains. Had it not been for their physical appearance, African-Americans would have vanished without a trace into the melting pot. They have no backward extension that might impede that process, nothing prior to the Middle Passage carried over as a lasting tie. Their hyphenated state is skin deep: it makes no intellectual demands upon us, it never changes the temporal and spatial coordinates of the United States.

This was the premise of many sociologists and anthropologists writing in the early twentieth century. R. E. Park spoke for a consensus when he wrote:

"My own impression is that the amount of African tradition which the Negro brought to the United States was very small. In fact, there is every reason to believe, it seems to me, that the Negro, when he landed in the United States, left behind him almost everything but his dark complexion and his tropical temperament."[2] E. Franklin Frazier turned this impression into a programmatic statement: "Probably never before in history has a people been so nearly completely stripped of its social heritage as the Negroes who were brought to America. . . . [O]f the habits and customs as well as the hopes and fears that characterized the life of their forebears in Africa, nothing remains."[3]

ABIDING TRACES

Linguists were the first to cast doubt on this presumed "nothingness" of the African past. Traces *do* endure, they argue, to be found (not surprisingly) in language, a medium intertwined with human history and bearing witness to its long life through the evolution and migration of words. In a paper presented at the annual Modern Language Association meeting in 1938, entitled "Western African Survivals in the Vocabulary of Gullah," Lorenzo Dow Turner from Fisk University offered an extensive catalog of such words, making survival rather than erasure the key term in the movement of languages from Africa to America. Subsequently expanded into his groundbreaking book *Africanisms in the Gullah Dialect* (1949), this emphasis on survival opens up a new way to think about input from the past, the routes it travels, the housing it receives on the way, and the scale on which all of these are to be investigated. The planet emerges here as a single unit of analysis, for these etymology-trailing words suggest that the world is "rhizomatic" (to take a word from Gilles Deleuze and Felix Guattari[4]), with many levels of grafting and mixing, generating linguistic kinships across vast distances and across the Western/non-Western divide. For the first time, it is possible to think of the black vernacular as a *creole* form, of tangled parentage and laterally reproduced, a significant departure from standard English.

Lorenzo Turner focuses on Gullah, a dialect spoken by the predominantly black populations on the Sea Islands off the coasts of Georgia and South Carolina. He argues that the ties between these regions and Africa were vital and dynamic well into the second half of the nineteenth century, a contention borne out by subsequent studies.[5] Slaves were brought to the Sea Islands throughout the eighteenth century; a conservative estimate gives the number at 100,000. This direct importation was officially banned by the Slave Trade Act of 1808, but an illegal traffic persisted. As late as 1858, the slave ship *Wanderer* brought approximately 420 slaves to the Georgia coast.[6]

This continual traffic meant that the influx of African languages continued well into the mid-nineteenth century. And, even after it came to an end, residual (and increasingly creolized) forms of these languages continued to flourish in areas with predominantly black populations, as on the Sea Islands. According to Turner, "Africanisms" can be detected in all aspects of the spoken tongue. In its phonology and, above all, in its vocabulary—in its personal names, it forms of abbreviation and forms of colloquialism—Gullah bears witness to a genesis not strictly Indo-European. Languages from the West Coast of Africa—Wolof, Malinke, Mandinka, Bambara, Fula, Mende, Vai, Twi, Fante, Ga, Ewe, Fon, Yoruba, Bini, Hausa, Ibo, Ibibio, Efik, Kongo, Umbundu, Kimbundu—all left documentable traces.[7] Two-thirds of *Africanisms in the Gullah Dialect* (188 pages) comprise a list of words derived from these West African tongues.

Lorenzo Turner, writing as a linguist, understandably focuses on language as primary evidence. The anthropologist Melville J. Herskovits, writing around the same time, proposes a larger domain of inquiry. The survival of Africanisms becomes a general paradigm for studying every aspect of culture: not just the spoken tongue but also material objects, secular and religious practices, and the mental universes that underwrite their operations. All of these, according to Herskovits—in effect the sum total of African-American life—can be adequately studied only when the adjective "African" is given as much weight as the adjective "American." What is called for, in short, is not only a prehistory but also something like a "pregeography." These take Americanists far beyond the borders of the United States, to archives encompassing the entire hemisphere: "firsthand field study of New World Negroes in Dutch Guinea, in Trinidad," as well as in "countries of South America."[8] This two-Americas approach would, in turn, benefit from research done on the other side of the Atlantic: "in Nigeria, the Gold Coast, and more especially in Dahomey [where] it has been possible to study at first hand the important ancestral civilizations."[9]

CREOLIZATION

This is what it means to take both continents seriously. The backward extension of the temporal axis extends the spatial axis as well, generating an enlarged kinship network, a "family," though not in the traditional sense. This family is born not of the nearness of blood but of an alchemical overcoming of distance; it multiplies not by linear descent but by the circuitousness of shipping routes. Kinship is anything but transparent here. It is oblique, centrifugal, laterally extended, taking the form of arcs, loops, curves of various sorts: complex paths of temporal and spatial displacement. Nonadjacency is the unexpected ground for kinship. Cross-fertilizing takes place when far-flung arcs meet at distant points.

Since this is the case, since it is these far-flung arcs that integrate the globe, that turn distant populations into distant cousins, we might want to rethink the meaning of "ancestry" itself. Rather than being land based, patrilineal, and clannish, it is here oceanic, flotational, a large-scale and largely exogenous process of "drifting." The dynamics between the global and the local play out in such a way as to make the genetic ground itself a "nested" formation, for the local here is not purely indigenous, but a "cradling" of the global within one particular site: a sequence of diffusion, osmosis, and readaptation.[10] Ancestry here has less to do with origins than with processes. Transmutation rather than transmission is its lifeblood.

Borrowing a term from linguists, we might speak of this maritime genesis as a *creolizing* process, taking the term to describe the dynamics and consequences of cultural contact, and taking it to designate, furthermore, a primary (rather than incidental) order of phenomena. Robert Hall, in his classic study *Pidgin and Creole Languages* (1966), distinguishes between two "contact languages," two hybrid forms born of the meeting between linguistic groups. A *pidgin* arises when the grammar and vocabulary of a natural language are drastically reduced to facilitate communication; it is a pared-down language, minimalist in its functions, used sporadically and superficially, mostly for the purposes of trade. It expressive capability is therefore limited, not adequate to the needs of any speech community, a mother tongue to no one on earth. A *creole*, on the other hand (from the Portuguese *crioulo* and the Spanish *criollo*, "native," subsequently morphing into the French *creole*), comes into being when a pidgin evolves into an autonomous tongue, with a fully developed grammar and an ample lexicon to match. As the mother tongue for an entire speech community, it is "native" in every sense.[11]

Putting pidgins and creoles at center stage, Hall argues that these two can no longer be dismissed as crude, debased, or marginal. "[D]espite their humble social status," he says, they "must be given their rightful standing as the equals of other languages."[12] A study of these "corrupt" languages has major implications for the discipline of linguistics, for while the birth of most languages took place in the primordial past, forever unrecoverable, pidgins and creoles are recent developments, with data readily available. They are the testing ground for any genetic account of language, any theory that purports to explain how and why human beings came to speak the way they do. Furthermore, since at least two languages come into play in the making of a creole, with one serving as the "lexifier"—the host language supplying the bulk of the words in use—the question inevitably arises as to the fate of the other tongue. That one, though gradually phased out and supplanted, would nonetheless seem to have left traces of itself. Where do these traces persist? In what manner and on which level of the linguistic structure? Do they make up a "substratum" lurking beneath the surface features of the host language? Hall summarizes the debate:

One of the major problems under discussion in linguistics, for over a century, has been that of the nature and extent of substratum influence. The problem is substantially this: is it possible that a given language, when it is abandoned by its speakers in favor of a new language (as when speakers of Celtic abandoned that language for Latin in Roman Gaul) can leave traces in the new language? If the answer is affirmative, three further questions arise: (1) In what aspects of linguistic structure can substratum influence be manifest? (2) By what mechanisms are substratum features carried over into the language that replaces the earlier substratum, as Latin replaced Gaulish? (3) In what cases should we ascribe a given linguistic change to the effects of a presumed substratum? That a language can preserve traces, often numerous traces, of a previously spoken substratum in its vocabulary, is now admitted by everyone: for example, French *alouette* "lark" < Celtic *alauda*; Spanish *vega* "flat lowland" < Iberian *baika*. Concerning other levels of linguistic structure, however, there has been extensive debate. Some linguists are disposed to admit the possibility of substratum on all levels—phonological, morphological, and syntactic as well as lexical; others deny it completely.[13]

Though Hall is specifically interested in the creolization of African tongues in the New World, it soon becomes clear that "creolization" is a paradigm that touches on virtually all languages, in all historical periods. The relations between Latin and Gaulish, between French and Celtic, between Spanish and Iberian all come under this rubric. It is nothing less than the central paradigm in linguistics. It demonstrates in no uncertain terms that a history of languages is a history of global migrating, adapting, recombining. Whether or not they admit to it, most languages are creoles. They have a durational existence— and a traceable path—largely because of this long-standing, ongoing, and never-ending synthesis. The enfolding of a Wolof or a Fon "substratum" through standard English and into the black vernacular is analogous to the enfolding of a Celtic substratum through Latin and into French; the enfolding of an Iberian substratum through Latin and into Spanish; and (most salient example of all), the enfolding of an Anglo-Saxon substratum through Latin and French and into modern English. These European and non-European languages are kin not because they stem from the same origins but because each of them went through an analogous process of extension and transformation: an uprooting, a meandering, followed by reentry and relexification, a dialectic of drift and cradling.

LINGUA FRANCA

The whole of linguistics can be studied under this rubric. The recent work on creolization is thus a belated tribute to the German scholar Hugo Schuchardt (1842–1927), most prescient of linguists, the first of international stature to put pidgins and creoles at the center of linguistics. Writing in the 1880s, Schuchardt brought with him knowledge of three language groups: Indo-European (in which he was trained); Hamitic (a group of African languages comprising ancient Egyptian as well as several tongues still extant, such as Berber and Cushitic, in turn related to Semitic languages such as Arabic); and Finno-Ugric (such as Hungarian).[14] Out of this knowledge of languages spoken on four continents, Schuchardt was able to single out pidgins and creoles as key players in linguistics. These were "slave languages," he pointed out. As the speech of the unfree, those who had an imperfect command of words as of their own bodies, these were humble concoctions indeed. Still, they must be linked to a larger class of phenomena, namely, the *lingua franca*, for they shared with the latter an involuntary genesis: "Necessity is the sculptor of such languages, which we therefore term 'necessity languages.'"[15]

By "necessity," Schuchardt had in mind the need of the slave owners to communicate with their slaves, who often had only a rudimentary knowledge of English. He had in mind as well the linguistic gulf among the slaves themselves. Due to the multitude of tongues in Africa (prevalent in even small areas, such as Western Nigeria, from which most of the slaves were taken), those from the same vicinities often could not converse. Some lingua franca was needed, some slave *koine*, in order to convey even the most basic information. This language, hastily cobbled together, was in this case compounded of European and African languages. But Schuchardt cautioned against seeing these as necessary ingredients, for, as the very name *lingua franca* suggests, this improvised tongue was initially the product of a different linguistic environment; it was medieval and Mediterranean before it was modern and Atlantic. It first came into being as a mix of Indo-European and Arabic languages, and there is no reason why its future incarnations should not involve still other ingredients:

> Lingua Franca is the communicative language formed of a Romance lexicon that arose in the Middle Ages between Romans and Arabs and subsequently Turks. . . . The Arabs termed the language of the Europeans with whom they came into contact the language of the Franks, *lisan al-farandz* (al-afrandz), or Frankish, as the Romans were called. . . . [W]e ought not therefore seek the essence of a creole in a connection between European lexicon and African or Asiatic grammar; it would be just as incorrect to say that Lingua Franca is Romance with Arabic or Turkish grammar. As speech mixture always presupposes bilingualism, then it will more readily occur and further extend itself the further bilingualism is extended—that is, by broader contact between two speech communities, intimate connection between two peoples.[16]

Rather than seeing the creole form as the descendent of specific languages, Schuchardt sees it instead as a structural property of bilingualism itself: a bilingualism that, he hoped, would spread across the planet, becoming the general condition of cultural contact, the basic requirement of an educated person.[17]

Anticipating in reverse the current talk about the "clash of civilizations,"[18] Schuchardt sees instead a merging of civilizations, an expanding web of words, populating the world with linguistic first and second cousins. Just to cite one example, "[F]or ghost (i.e. departed soul, spectre, spook), we have Sranan Black English *djombi*, Trinidadian Creole French *zombi*, Santhomian Creole Dutch *ziumbi-kawai*, 'ghost horse', cf. Oldendorp (1777:117), from Mbundu (Angola) *nzumbi*, 'the peaceful spirit of a departed soul', cf. Congolese *zumbi* 'luck-bearing fetish'; Jamaican Creole *duppe*, from *dobbo* in Ewe, according to Oldenburg (1777:336), 'evil, disease-producing spirits'."[19] Linguistic cross-fertilization is the ground of the world's oneness. These loops and clumps of words—sometimes parallel, sometimes not, but always interconnected in their mediating form—suggest that a "family" is not just a metaphor.

PRIMACY OF SYNTAX

What does it mean to have membership in such a family? What are the stakes in thinking of American dialects as creole tongues, and restoring them as such: to a linguistic continuum stretching across the Mediterranean, across the Atlantic? What difference does it make to think of black English, in particular, as being dotted by clumps of African languages? And, if its seemingly ungrammatical features are indeed traceable to such diasporic loops, how would that affect its pragmatic status: as legal and political instrument, educational vehicle, and medium for creative expression?

Robert Hall ends *Pidgin and Creole Languages* with a plea on behalf of such vernaculars. Focusing on Haiti, he expresses the hope that one day "Creole would be admitted on parity with French in the formal activities of the government, in Parliament, in newspapers, in the law courts . . . [and] in education."[20] The same argument for parity could, of course, be made on behalf of nonstandard speech in the United States. Should black English be seen as an ungrammatical deviation from standard English, or should it be recognized as a *coherent* departure, a law-abiding phenomenon unto itself, with a grammar of its own, and a claim to political, cultural, and educational legitimacy? In a series of influential talks and essays published in the late 1960s and early 1970s, William A. Stewart made a forceful case for the latter. "It is pedagogically important," he said, "to know whether or not the majority of American Negroes make up one or more cohesive sociolinguistic speech communities and, if so, what the specific nature of these communities is."[21] Does black English have the autonomy of a linguistic subset? If so, what underwrites that autonomy: the geographical clustering of the black population, the effect of socioeconomic class, or some cognitive attribute of ethnicity?

Comparative work is needed to address these questions—a four-prong analysis, according to Stewart. In order to determine the degree of integrity of black English, it must be examined not only against standard English but also against two other vernacular forms: on the one hand, nonstandard white dialects, and on the other hand, creole tongues elsewhere in the world with clearly established ties to Africa. This four-prong analysis will not be easy. Where does the fundamental kinship (or fundamental difference) lie, on which evidentiary register, which level of the linguistic structure? Is the primary evidence to be found in the lexicon, the system of words; in the phonology, the system of sounds; in the morphology, the derivational and inflectional rules governing nouns, verbs, and pronouns; or in the syntax, the grammatical structure of the sentence? Stewart summarizes the difficulty:

> One further reason why both language teachers and dialectologists have failed to appreciate the extent to which non-standard Negro dialects may differ from non-standard white dialects (even in the Deep South) may simply be that such differences now remain mostly in syntax (i.e. grammatical patterns and categories) rather than in vocabulary or lexico-phonology (i.e. word forms), and are thus not normally uncovered by the word-comparison techniques which dialectologists and non-linguists rely on so heavily.[22]

Written in 1968, this cautionary note came at the heels of a major upheaval in modern linguistics, one that transformed the very aims and procedures of the discipline. Spearheaded by Noam Chomsky's *Syntactic Structures* (1956) and *Aspects of the Theory of Syntax* (1965), this new linguistics sets aside its traditional emphasis on taxonomy, on the cataloguing of phonetic or lexical phenomena, and turns instead to a study of deep structure, a subterranean "generative grammar." This grammar, lying beneath the surface features of words, manifests itself as a set of syntactical rules, a logic that defines the relations among categories of words, making it possible for words from the same category to be substituted for one another. The number of sentences generated is infinite. Every human being can make up such sentences, and every human population has an endless supply of them. Chomsky thus puts syntax at the center of human cognition. According to him, it is syntax that allows the human mind to use words at all; it is syntax that is universal to our species.

Armed with this insight, Stewart comes up with an analytic paradigm that, while clearly indebted to Chomsky, also parts company with him in important ways. Setting aside Chomsky's ambitious use of the generative grammar to establish the *identity* of syntax in all languages, he tries to prove only the *kinship* among languages that are not obviously connected. As with Chomsky, the logical relation among categories of words is key. This is the analytic focus. And this in turn points to an evidentiary domain that is buried rather than in plain view, an object of deduction rather than an object of cataloguing. Stewart thus focuses not on the "lexico-phonology"—the words and sounds residing on the surface—but on the underlying logic that gives rise to the structure of the sentence. It is on this linguistic level that he conducts his four-prong analysis, comparing four versions of a simple conjunctive sentence: in standard English (STE), in southern white nonstandard basilect (WNS), in Negro nonstandard basilect (NNS), and in Gullah Basilect (GUL):

> **STE**: We were eating—and drinking, too.
> **WNS**: We was eatin'—an' drinkin', too.
> **NNS**: We was eatin'—an' we drinkin', too.
> **GUL**: We bin duh nyam—en' we duh drink, too.

If one were to look simply at the individual words, NNS (Negro nonstandard English) would seem to be virtually identical to WNS (white nonstandard English). These individual words do not tell the full story, however, for the syntax, the underlying logic of the sentence, points to a very different set of relations, not discernible simply by cataloguing words or simply by looking at the surface data. It is worth quoting Stewart at length:

> [A] comparison of the sentence structure of these dialects shows a somewhat differ-ent kind of relationship. In the foregoing equivalent sentence, this is evident in the treatment of the subject pronoun and the tense-marking auxiliary (or copula). For, although STE, WNS, NNS, and GUL can all repeat the subject pronoun and auxil-iary in a conjunctive clause (e.g. STE "We were eating—and we were drinking, too"), this is not generally done in any of them. Instead, one or both will usually be omitted (provided, of course, that the subject and temporal referents remain the same). But in terms of what they omit, these dialects split along lines which are different from those indicated by word-form similarities and differences. Both STE and WNS normally omit both the subject and the auxiliary in a conjunctive clause, although the tense-marking auxiliary must be present if the subject is not omitted. But NNS, like GUL, often repeats the subject pronoun in a conjunctive clause while omitting the auxiliary—even when this indicates past tense. . . .
>
> If, in such features as the omission of a redundant auxiliary (while retaining the redundant subject pronoun) Gullah and other non-standard Negro dialects part company with standard English and non-standard white dialects (of both America and Great Britain), they do have counterparts in a number of pidgin and creole forms of English, which, though used far from the shores of the United States and in widely separated places, are all the legacy of the African slave trade. To illustrate how much these forms of English resemble Gullah and other non-standard Negro dialects with respect to auxiliary omission, the same equivalent sentences are given in Jamaican Creole (JMC); Sranan, the creole English of Surinam in South America (SRA); and West African Pidgin English (WAP):

> **JMC**: We ben a nyam—an' we a drink, too.
> **SRA**: We ben de nyang—en' we de dringie, too.
> **WAP**: We bin de eat—an' we de dring, too.

In addition to the grammatical correspondences, the word-form similarities of these languages with Gullah will be apparent.[23]

West Africa, South America, the Caribbean, North America: this is what it takes to contextualize black English, for this American dialect has distant cousins on distant shores. Analyzed through them, it regains its grammaticalness, its membership in a law-abiding family, for its seemingly aberrant syntax is in fact the norm in many languages, lexified as a creole continuum by Portuguese, Spanish, Dutch, French, as well as English. This continuum requires a world atlas to become legible. It urges upon us a research program of equal breadth.

What would the humanities look like if we were to embrace this research program, taking seriously the extension and duration of that word, *human*? Nation-based models would have to be modified. No longer a given, they would have to be tested by an empiricism committed to data gathering, and not deciding, ahead of time, that all the necessary data can be found within the borders of one jurisdiction. If such an empiricism were to prevail, a broad-based study of the world's languages would become our first order of business. Any history of the English language, in particular, must take into account the full spectrum of pidgin and creole forms. This is the circumference as well for Americanists. For, as with black English, it is worth making the effort, even when we are dealing with what appears to be a local phenomenon, to go beyond the evidence supplied by a single nation, beyond a methodology that isolates a part and fancies it to be the whole.

Deleted Copula and Negative Concord

A linguistics based on syntax demands the whole, and tentatively offers it in the form of a deep structure, a cognitive foundation that can be predicated of every human being on the globe. "Globalism" of this sort is sufficiently at odds with current models to be worth exploring. Its local implications, meanwhile, are also explosive. For if syntax is the underlying logic of the sentence, if it marks the crossover point between cognitive function and linguistic usage, it seems reasonable to assume (and Chomsky has made it his central contention) that it is the same in *all* languages. Standard English does not have a monopoly here. Nonstandard dialects have sentences that are equally grammatical, and equally well formed. How, then, can we justify our usual view of these dialects as illiterate, a sign of educational (and perhaps even cognitive) deficit, to be corrected wherever they appear? For Stewart, this is a benighted view. Black English, he argues, deviates from standard English not because it has no grammar but because it has a prior history, bearing the "structural traces of a creole predecessor."[24] Acknowledging this creole predecessor restores the dialect to its rightful place. It changes the protocol of education itself:

For the teacher, this means that such "Negro" patterns as the "zero copula," the "zero possessive," or "undifferentiated pronouns" should not be ascribed to greater carelessness, laziness or stupidity on the part of Negroes, but rather should be treated as what they really are—language patterns which have been in existence for generations and which their present users have acquired, from parent and peer, through a perfectly normal kind of language-learning process.[25]

Does black English have a grammar of its own? Are its nonstandard features equally logical, but logical by a different route and a different set of rules? Can it claim cognitive parity with standard English, not to say political, artistic, and pedagogic legitimacy?

This is the challenge taken up by William Labov in his now classic study *Language in the Inner City* (1972).[26] A veteran researcher in the field, funded in 1965 by the Office of Education in light of pedagogic failures in the New York City schools, Labov and his team conducted a series of taped sessions in south-central Harlem with teenage gangs—the Jets, the Cobras, and the Thunderbirds—to explore the nature of the language they spoke. The book tackles some explosive issues ("Is the Black English Vernacular a Separate System?" and "The Logic of Nonstandard English"), but there are highly technical chapters as well, devoted to the "Contraction, Deletion, and Inherent Variability of the English Copula" and "Negative Attraction and Negative Accord."

These chapters (difficult for humanists) are not just cerebral exercises. For the technicality here is entirely in the spirit of Chomsky, arguing for the grammaticalness of all spoken tongues. This is not so easily done. How does one go about proving that the following is a grammatical sentence: "He a friend"? This is a classic example of the deleted copula. The word "is" is deleted here, the present tense of the auxiliary *be*. A sentence without a verb, it seems a clear violation of a cardinal rule of English grammar.

Labov shows, however, that there are other rules at work, nonstandard rules, but rules nonetheless, demonstrable and formalizable. For it turns out that there are constraints on the *deletion* of the auxiliary *be*, constraints that are parallel, furthermore, to the constraints on the *contraction* of the auxiliary in standard English. In standard English, one cannot contract the auxiliary when it occupies the final position of the sentence: one cannot say, "He's as nice as he says he's." So too, in black English, one cannot delete the auxiliary when it occupies the final position of the sentence: one cannot say, "He's as nice as he says he." These two sets of constraints are parallel, each dictated by the word order of the sentence. They are further parallel, in that the permissibility (or not) of the deletion and contraction seems to have to do with how the sentence *sounds*: each represents a phonological contribution to a syntactic rule. It is this complex, multiplane correlation that suggests that the black vernacular is just as law-abiding as standard English. The grammar of one, while different in its surface features, is commensurate with the other in its deep structure, in the logic governing what is allowed and what is not, sharing with the other the same probability distribution of its formal variables.[27]

The rigors of syntax prove a democratic point. So too does an empirical knowledge of languages outside the Indo-European family. Labov notes in passing that the deleted copula in black English bespeaks no cognitive deficit, for "there are many languages of the world which do not have a present copula and which conjoin subject and predicate complement without a verb. Russian, Hungarian, and Arabic may be foreign, but they are not by that same token illogical."[28]

Empiricism of this sort—with a planetary database—also helps to vindicate black English on another front: the seeming illogicality of its "negative concord." Negative concord refers to the duplication of the negative in more than one syntactical position, as in the following: "It ain't no cat can't get in no coop."[29] Is this as grammatical as standard English? Labov's answer is emphatically yes. He writes: "The naive view is that the nonstandard dialects simply have too many negatives. Historically-minded linguists and dialectologists point out that multiple negation is the traditional pattern and that our standard form is a rule imposed on English by grammarians in the 18th century."[30] He goes on:

> The Anglo-Saxon authors of the Peterborough Chronicle were surely not illogical when they wrote *For ne woeren nan martyrs swa pined alse he woeron*, literally, "For never weren't no martyrs so tortured as these were." The "logical" forms of current standard English are simply the accepted conventions of our present-day formal style. Russian, Spanish, French, and Hungarian show the same negative concord as nonstandard English, and they are surely not illogical in this.[31]

"Globalizing" the syntactic form of black English, Labov restores it to a kinship network, and to cognitive legitimacy. This is exactly the sort of work that Chomsky hopes syntax would do, that changes our understanding of the human species even as it changes the discipline of linguistics.[32] Steven Pinker, in his mainstream (and best-selling) *The Language Instinct* (1995), fully endorses this position.[33] Citing a sentence spoken by Larry, the toughest of the Jets ("In order for *that* to happen, you know it ain't no black God that's doin' that bullshit"),[34] Pinker writes: "Larry's speech uses the full inventory of grammatical paraphernalia that computer scientists struggle unsuccessfully to duplicate (relative clauses, complement structures, clause subordination, and so on), not to mention some fairly sophisticated theological argumentation."[35] He ends up repeating Labov's central point: "The great majority of sentences were grammatical, especially in casual speech, with higher percentage of grammatical sentences in working-class speech than in middle-class speech. The highest percentage of ungrammatical sentences was found in the proceedings of learned academic conferences."[36]

NONVERBAL DATA

Universal grammaticalness is about as far as one can go in ontologizing democracy. Literary critics (along with legislators, educators, editors, and just about everyone else) have yet to catch up with its implications. But we have to stop and ask as well: is grammar the single most important trait about our species? Can syntactical relations serve as the protocol for all possible relations we might have: to ourselves, to others, to the myriad objects of the world? And, when it comes to the centuries-old legacies from Africa, does language keep a complete record, giving us all the evidence we need, or are there data to be found elsewhere? In short, is the survival of "Africanisms" first and foremost a linguistic phenomenon, or is the story better told through other records, *nonverbal* records? And how do the claims of the nonverbal affect the claims we make on behalf of literature?

These questions obviously cannot be answered with any degree of finality. But they can be tentatively pursued—on two fronts. First, among neuroscientists and cognitive scientists, the competing claims of the verbal and the nonverbal are now hotly debated issues. Most would probably still line up on the "verbal" side. The language-based paradigm, put forward by Chomsky, remains (in modified forms) the central paradigm for the field's leading figures: Daniel Dennett, Jerry Fodor, Gerald Edelman.[37] Even the "computational" model of the mind, seeing it as syntactical "software" driving semantic processes, seems an austere extension of Chomsky's syntactic theory.[38] The privileged relation of language to thought is in no imminent danger of collapse. Still, there has been a significant shift, a reorienting of the discipline as a whole, with a growing number of practitioners leaving behind their traditional focus and embracing an entirely new one. *Cognition* is no longer the sole player, the sole determinant of consciousness, and the unfailing ally for language. *Emotion* has entered the field as a new, undertheorized, and potentially more interesting research topic, with as yet untested implications.

Antonio Damasio has been pivotal here. Beginning with *Descartes's Error* (1994), and continuing with *The Feeling of What Happens* (1999), and, most recently, *Looking for Spinoza* (2002), he makes a series of linked arguments challenging the primacy of thought in the workings of the human brain.[39] Cognition, Damasio argues, represents a higher-level neural activity, and is therefore not fundamental to our core consciousness, not the defining mark of what it means to be "human." Descartes's famous dictum, "I think therefore I am," is wrong for that reason: it has gotten things exactly backward, taking a secondary phenomenon as the determining ground. For Damasio, *being* necessarily comes before *thinking*. This priority is both evolutionary, in terms of the survival history of the species, and physiological, in terms of the neural biochemistry of the human brain. On neither count does thought have priority. This radical observation changes the ground rules of the verbal/nonverbal debate. For if it turns out that human beings are emotional beings first and foremost, if cognition is something of an afterthought, that would seem to make language an afterthought as well. The close alignment of these two dislodges one along with the other. Damasio removes both of them from our core consciousness. We first register objects in a "nonlanguage form," he argues, for our core consciousness rests on a mental substrate at once precognitive and prelinguistic: a "*nonverbal, imaged* narrative"[40] that serves as the neurophysiological ground for our powerful emotions.

This challenge from neuroscientists is not likely to go away soon. Meanwhile, on another front, and in the context of a largely unrelated discipline, a parallel challenge is being voiced, most pointedly by the French linguist Robert Chaudenson. In a series of books beginning with *Les créoles français* (1979), and culminating in *Des îles, des hommes, des langues* (1992), revised in collaboration with Salikoko Mufwene as *Creolization of Language and Culture* (2001), Chaudenson casts doubt on the adequacy of verbal evidence as historical evidence, especially when it comes to the survival of African cultures. Language is not the most reliable witness, he argues, for its power of endurance (and therefore power of testimony) is weak under oppressive conditions. The large number of African languages, their mutual unintelligibility to one another, coupled with the active efforts of slave owners to stamp them out, means that English soon dominated the field as a much needed lingua franca. This lingua franca owed little to the languages of the slaves, for none had broad currency, and none had the demographic muscle to survive. Language was the line of maximum pressure from the slave owners, and the line of minimum resistance from the slaves. Chaudenson thus returns to the earlier thesis about the eradication of African tongues—but with a difference. For him, the nonsurvival of *languages* does not mean the nonsurvival of African cultures as a whole. Quite the contrary. He cites with approval the scene in Alex Haley's television series, *Roots*, when the hero, trying to talk to the other slaves but finding no common tongue, improvised on a medium other than language: "only by drumming together on the planks of the ship can they express their common revolt."[41] The slaves survived, and something else survived with them, but in a nonlanguage form. *That* is the database we ought to be consulting; scholars who limit themselves to text-based archives are looking in the wrong place. Chaudenson writes:

> It is easy to see that the elements that have survived in material culture and music owe this survival largely to their non-verbal character. Thus it is strange that for decades some scholars have obstinately sought to identify in creoles traces of direct and positive transfers from the languages of the slaves, which are so obviously absent. Simple and rapid observation of material culture would have provided much more evidence of this non-European inheritance.[42]

Chaudenson's polemics should probably be taken with a grain of salt, but his general point remains. The cross-fertilization of cultures takes many forms, leaving behind many records, language being only one of them, and often not the primary one. Words, in and of themselves, never tell the full story. It is a small part of a much larger domain of evidence—something like the "creolization of cultural systems"—under which rubric Chaudenson discusses music, cuisine, folk medicine and magic, and oral literature.

Language, in short, is a subset rather than an autonomous set when it comes to evidence. Literary critics—as much as linguists—must come to terms with this. A combination of the verbal and the nonverbal might turn out to be the best strategy at once to enlarge the circumference of literature and to highlight its local inflections.[43] The methodology of Melville Herskovits has much to tell us.[44] And, since the 1940s, a rich body of material has sprung up, assembled by musicologists, anthropologists, and art historians, linking the Americas to Africa across a range of expressive media, and providing an invaluable frame for text-based records.[45] I am thinking of the WPA oral histories, for instance *Drums and Shadows* (1940), put together by the Savannah Unit of the Federal Writers' Project, with this subtitle: *Survival Studies among the Georgia Coastal Negroes*. The verbal testimonies assembled here are preceded by images of material objects—masks, wooden figures, carved sticks, baskets—unmistakably stamped with the influence of Africa and reminding us that nonstandard English might be seen as a parallel development.[46] I am thinking also of the art history of Robert Farris Thompson, dedicated to "art in motion" and celebrating a "black Atlantic visual tradition" as a supreme instance of this migrating art, bringing Africa to the Americas, with especially strong input from "Yoruba, Kongo Dahomean, Mande, and Ejagham."[47] And I am thinking, above all, of the musicology of Alan Lomax, a meticulous, monumental labor, assembling a massive archive to prove a point, namely, that "black African nonverbal performance traditions had survived intact in African America, and had shaped all its distinctive rhythmic art, during both the colonial and postcolonial periods."[48]

Traveling tirelessly, and using a computerized model called cantometrics, Lomax records singing performances from every part of the world, "2500-plus songs from 233 cultures."[49] This database allows him to tabulate a list of "frequent musical behaviors," including melodic contour, melodic form, melodic range, phrase length, interval width, and so on. That tabulation, in turn, yields some striking patterns, some clustering of these musical behaviors, with one proving especially common. Spread across several continents, it typically includes these features: percussive rhythm; the predominance of one-phrase melodies (the litany form); overlapping call and response; choral integration or part-singing; polyrhythmic ("hot") accompaniments; and offbeat phrasing of melodic accents.[50] African-American music clearly belongs in this company. Lomax writes:

Figure 11.1. Carved masks and wooden chains, *Drums and Shadows*.

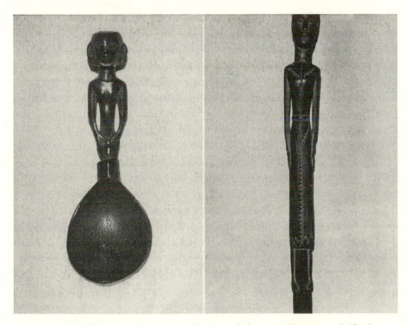

Figure 11.2. Spoon and stick with carved figures; *Drums and Shadows* is produced by the Savannah Unit, Georgia Writers' Project, Work Projects Administration, with photographs by Muriel and Malcolm Bell, Jr. (Athens: Univ. of Georgia Press, 1940).

[T]he main traditions of Afro-American song, especially the old-time congrega-
tional spiritual—are derived from the main African song style model. European song
style did influence the African tradition in regard to melodic form and, of course,
textual content. In most other respects Afro-American song has hewed to the main
dynamic line of the principal African tradition. . . . This tradition is perhaps the
most stable and the most ancient, and, in many ways, the most highly developed of
the musical families of mankind.[51]

LITERARY ECOLOGIES

Students of language can only bow their heads in light of such evidence.
When it comes to documenting the life of the species—in its duration and
variety—nonverbal records win hands down. A strictly language-based archive is incomplete at best, and misleading at worst. Art historians, musicologists, and students of material culture simply have more robust data at their
disposal.

What are the implications of all of this for literary studies? I would like to
think of it as an entry point rather than a closed door. For to think of language
as not self-contained is to multiply its lines of filiation exponentially. It is to
reorient the field in some fundamental way, giving increasing emphasis to that
zone of interaction where nonverbal input combines with the verbal "lexifier"
to generate a more complex geometry. Literature, in this sense, is a creole
formation not only in the commingling of tongues, but equally in the commingling of expressive media. This is one way in which it differs from linguistics
proper. To test one against the other, and to take note of the divergence of
the two, is to have a clearer sense of the peculiar ontology of literature, under-
scored by linguistics as a foil, by what it is as well as what it is not. The two do
overlap: literature, like linguistics, works (for the most part) with grammatical
sentences, sentences that are law abiding, that demonstrate the cognitive
wherewithal of their authors through their syntactical rules. These rules, however, do not even begin to tell us what is compelling about these sentences.
Literature is both syntax and more than syntax, both a collection of grammatical sentences and something not necessarily inferable from that grammar.

It would be interesting to think more about this discrepancy, and to make
a claim for literature on this basis. The literary text, I suggest, is a linguistic
entity whose modes of access to the world are nonetheless not strictly language
based. Its kinship network is broader than a set of grammatical rules; its input
map is also broader. We can think of it as an "ecology," perhaps, a multiplane
environment, allowing for aggregation and interaction on many different levels, presided over by no single law.[52] Syntax, for that reason, is no longer
the foundation here, no longer the rule-giving and logic-bearing substrate (as
linguists urge), but part of a less determinate landscape, sometimes no more

than a mere lexical entry. These lines, from Derek Walcott's "A Tropical Bestiary," serve as well as any to demonstrate this difference:

> The sea crab's cunning, halting, awkward grace
> is the syntactical envy of my hand.[53]

The sentence is crystal clear as far as its grammar goes. This clarity is belied, however, by that strange phrase, "syntactical envy of my hand." The word "syntactical" is here a cipher, inserted into the poem's semantic field, and subject to ambient inflections and qualifications. In this case, an entire landscape, an entire map of the world, seems to have sprung up around it. This map first takes it to the vicinity of an emotion, envy. That emotion, in turn, is vested in a body part, the hand. And the hand, in turn, is stretched outward, gesturing toward a nonhuman creature, a sea crab, whose "cunning, halting, awkward grace" apparently answers to a human desire, a human aspiration.

Walcott's sentence is literally an ecology, in more senses than one. The human and the nonhuman are gathered together here; scripts made with words and scripts not made with words are also gathered together. This sort of ecology is infinitely vital but not foundationally verbal, for its common ground is traced not on the platform of human language, but on a very different sort of platform, a bodily register much more "primitive," which is to say, much more elemental. Creatures on this planet are all united on this platform. This is where Walcott would like to put himself. Here and elsewhere, he speaks of his chosen medium as a material medium, less cerebral than manual: "language made with our hands."[54] It is the physicality of the hand that puts words on paper, and that looks enviously upon the sea crab, whose physicality produces a sinuous form of "writing" that the hand can only dream of, having only stiff and angular words at its disposal. The pairing of these two, the sea crab and the human hand, points to a world in which the somatic register of the body is the lowest and therefore most trustworthy common denominator. Derek Walcott is one with Antonio Damasio on this point. Our cognitive apparatus *is* an afterthought within the ecology of the planet. Human language must cede its primacy to the script made by other species in the plenitude of their nonverbal lives.

AFRICAN RHYTHM

It is not altogether accidental that it is Derek Walcott, a poet from St. Lucia, who should make such an eloquent plea on behalf of wordless eloquence. The nonverbal has always been central to African-American poetics in general, and to Caribbean poetics in particular. Within this poetics, language and nonlanguage are not antithetical, but complementary, part of the same continuum. This is the single most important legacy of the diasporic: a synthesis of the verbal and the nonverbal, giving rise to a switchable medium on both sides of the Atlantic. Kofi Agawu, in his important study *African Rhythm*, points to just this synthesis in Ewe music. Agawa notes "the absence of a single word for 'rhythm' in Ewe." The "semantic fields of the word are broadly distributed rather than lodged in one place," so that, while the Ewe word *vugbe* literally means "drum language" (vu = drum, gbe = language), the word can come to mean rhythm in any number of contexts.[55] Rhythm is multidimensional; it is the common thread running through music, dance, language. It enlists the physicality of the body as the unifying ground for an entire range of expressive forms, from the unscripted pace of everyday gestures to the choreographed motions of dance, from the erratic phrasing of the spoken word to the formal notations of vocal and instrumental music. J. H. Kwabena Nketia, in his study of African vocal music, also notes that "African traditions deliberately treat songs as though they were speech utterances. . . . The Yoruba, for example, exploit the overlapping elements of speech and music in their four major chants: the *rara*, *iwe*, *ifa*, and *ijala*."[56] This synthesis of language and nonlanguage extends even to percussive instruments. Akan drumming, for instance, often has a verbal basis. The drumming patterns are, literally, musical restatements of strings of words, thanks to the practice of musicians who invoke the pitch-tone configuration of words in their musical phrasing, and the practice of poets who use onomatopoetic syllables to create an aural pattern analogous to the pitch contour and rhythm of the drum.[57] This verbal/nonverbal synthesis is enhanced by the fact that "almost every one of the languages spoken south of the Saraha is tonal, using pitch distinctions to differentiate words."[58]

This, then, is the most enduring input from Africa. In the United States, it is most evident in the musical languages of blues and jazz, languages marked by the same "vocalizing" of musical instruments and the same "instrumentalizing" of the human voice through such techniques as whooping and octave-jumping.[59] These musical languages, in turn, underwrite an entire aesthetics, informing every aspect of African-American expression. Houston Baker refers to it as a "blues matrix": "a womb, a network, a fossil-bearing rock, a rocky trace of a gemstone's removal, a principal metal in an alloy, a mat or plate for reproducing print or phonograph records."[60] Sherley Anne Williams speaks of "the blues roots of contemporary Afro-American poetry."[61] Edward Kamau Brathwaite points to a Caribbean genre he calls the "jazz novel,"[62] a fusing of words and music that he also dramatizes in a poem fittingly titled "The Making of the Drum":

> vowels of reed-
> lips, pebbles
> of consonants,
> underground dark
> of the continent.

You dumb *adom* wood
will be bent,
will be solemnly bent, belly
rounded with fire, wound-
ed with tools

that will shape you.
You will bleed,
cedar dark,
when we cut you;
speak, when we touch you.[63]

The sound of the drum enacts, on a percussive register, the "bleeding" of the *adom* wood; and the human voice enacts, on a linguistic register, the reedlike and pebbleslike sounds of the nonhuman world. These phenomena are kindred and interlocking. African-American poetics enlarges upon that kinship, and creates an ecology out of it, a meshing of language and more than language. This poetics is by no means limited to just one group of authors. Wilson Harris (in tribute to Faulkner) speaks of literature in general as an endeavor that goes "beyond given verbal convention into non-verbal arts of the imagination in the womb of cultural space, as though an *unstructured force* arbitrates or mediates between articulate or verbal signs and silent or eclipsed voices of nemesis in folk religions, whose masks or sculptures subsist."[64] Unlike linguistics, literature taps into a preverbal layer of consciousness; it has input from expressive media that do not rely on words. Its multiple tonal planes stem from this fact, open to different levels of switching, and carrying a semantic surcharge as pure grammar does not.

Limbo Dance

Wilson Harris himself has put forward a theory of the *limbo* dance as a metaphor for the multiplane ecology of literature. In the limbo, "the dancer moves under a bar which is gradually lowered until a mere slit of space, it seems, remains through which with spread-eagled limbs he passes like a spider. *Limbo* was born, it is said, on the slave ships of the Middle Passage. There was so little space that the slaves contorted themselves into human spiders."[65] But Harris argues that the limbo is not simply a measure of oppression. It is, quite literally, a *countermeasure*, defying measurement, for at work here

is the curious dislocation of a chain of miles reflected in the dance so that a retrace of the Middle Passage from Africa to the Americas and the West Indies is not to be equated with a uniform sum. . . . For *limbo* (one cannot emphasize this too much) is not the total recall of an African past, since that African past in terms of tribal sovereignty or sovereignties was modified or traumatically eclipsed with the Middle

Passage and with generations of change that followed. *Limbo* was rather the rena-
scence of a new corpus of sensibility that could translate and accommodate African
and other legacies within a new architecture of culture.[66]

According to Harris, the bodily contortions of the slaves transform the very
metric of space. The latitudes and longitudes of any locale cease to be a numerical given, and its distance to any other locale ceases to be a "uniform sum."
Quantification breaks down. The map of the world varies with the intensity
of connection, and with the nature of the kinship being traced. Africa is,
ordinarily speaking, thousands of miles from the Americas. But, on a certain
emotional register, these thousands of miles can contract to zero.

I can think of no better way to theorize the ecology of literature: a set of
coordinates sometimes taking in the whole world and sometimes tightening
to a knot, sometimes finding adequate housing in the domain of language and
sometimes haunted by what is beyond. Americanists have much to learn from
this Caribbean poetics. The fact that Wilson Harris is not a familiar name to
many of us only underscores the need to extend our circumference at just this
point. African-American literature is infinitely richer when it is seen not as
nation-based, self-contained within the United States, but as a diasporic formation, a literature of the two Americas with arcs reaching back to Africa.
And American literature is infinitely richer when it takes its cue from this
extended corpus, embracing a map of the world that commingles languages
and cultures, just as it commingles word and sound, the verbal and the nonverbal. Such a map is, in some sense, the underside of linguistics, its penumbra,
that shadowy region not reducible to our cognitive apparatus, not predicated
on its logic and not necessarily observing its grammar.

Nonstandard Cartography

Gloria Naylor's *Mama Day* gives us a map of the world mind-boggling in just
that way:

> Willow Springs ain't in no state. Georgia and South Carolina done tried, though—
> been trying since right after the Civil War to prove that Willow Springs belong to
> one or the other of them. . . . So who it belong to? It belongs to us . . . who at one
> time all belonged to Bascombe Wade. And when they tried to trace him and how
> he got it, found out he wasn't even American. Was Norway-born or something, and
> the land had been sitting in his family over there in Europe since it got explored
> and claimed by the Vikings—imagine that. So thanks to the conjuring of Sapphira
> Wade we got it from Norway or theres about, and if taxes owed, it's owed to them.
> But ain't no Vikings or anybody else from over in Europe come to us with the
> foolishness that them folks out of Columbia and Atlanta come with—we was being
> un-American.[67]

Nonstandard English, nonstandard cartography. Naylor is right: there is indeed something "un-American" about African-American literature, for the weight of the hyphen is such as to produce just the sort of spatial contortion that Wilson Harris speaks of, the twisting of the United States from a "uniform sum," a fixed measurement, into a much less recognizable shape. Like Willow Springs, *Mama Day* is stateless. It does not belong to Georgia, South Carolina, or North America; it cannot be found on any official map. This statelessness seems to come from the ecology of literature itself: the shades of Africa are summoned, as well as the shades of Europe, and all for the benefit of something that cannot be called logic. The novel opens with a slave girl, Sapphira, flying back to Africa. It goes on to chronicle the mysterious illness of its female protagonist, victimized apparently by a conjure woman who, in turn, is punished by another conjure woman still more powerful, a "Miss Miranda." Descended from *The Tempest* and sixteenth-century England, this Miranda is responsible now for yet another warping of space and time: "when she's tied up the twentieth century, she'll take a little peep into the other side."[68]

Distances vary with human ties. That is why, in Paule Marshall's *Praisesong for the Widow*, the Sea Islands legend of Ibo Landing is still a compelling legend after hundreds of years. As told by Aunt Cuney, the Ibos were able to transport themselves across the Atlantic in a peculiar fashion. Having been brought to America, and "sizing up the place real good," they just turned and walked back into the ocean: "Now you wouldna thought they'd of got very far seeing as it was water they was walking on. Besides they had all that iron on 'em. Iron on they ankles and they wrists and fastened 'round they necks like a dog collar. 'Nuff iron to sink an army. And chains hooking up the iron. But chains didn't stop those Ibos none. Neither iron."[69]

From a logical point of view, that of the laws of physics, or that of standard cartography, the story makes no sense. But logic is not all, it seems, for the story does make sense—make sense on the plane of human emotions—for this is how water would have behaved, how physical distance would have behaved, if their operations had been governed by human desire, by the needs and impulses of the body. It speaks to the scope of literature that it is able to find housing for these needs and impulses, a dimension of reality oblique to what dismisses them and makes fun of them. If literature is an ecology, as I have tried to argue, a gathering of the cognitive and precognitive, language and more than language, its landscape would seem to be vitally layered, made up of alternate geographies, alternate histories, bearing a more and more tangential relation to the national map, with its flatly numerical coordinates. Human emotions operate on a different register: their pathways are elusive, their arcs stream across the Atlantic. Deviation from standard English is only the first of those arcs. There are others, binding the Americas to Africa, and stretched to their outermost limits by their historical freight.

That freight in some sense defines the hyphen in African-American literature: a hyphen anything but straightforward, and anything but a secure plank of passage. Unlike their ancestors, the descendants of the Ibos do not walk across the Atlantic. They are as un-African as they are un-American. At the end of *Praisesong for the Widow,* when the names of the African nations are called out, only a few old people answer. Ancestry of this sort will not suffice, for the force of diaspora resides, in fact, not in the maintenance of tribal names, but in the nesting of them in a new creole medium: globalized, to be sure, permeated by world history, but also grittily local in its below-the-threshold existence. Here, that creole existence takes the form of an African-Caribbean dance, nothing fancy, only a sturdy beating of feet on the ground, thrilling on a somatic rather than linguistic register: "Even when the Big Drum reached its height in a tumult of voices, drums and the ringing iron, . . . her feet held to the restrained glide-and-stamp, the rhythmic trudge, the Carriacou Tramp, the shuffle designed to stay the course of history."[70] It is this rhythm of tramping and trudging, a rhythm born of centuries and continents, that threads a deep kinship through us:

> And for the first time since she was a girl, she felt the threads, that myriad of shiny, silken, brightly colored threads (like the kind used in embroidery) which were thin to the point of invisibility and yet as strong as the ropes at Coney Island. Looking on outside the Church in Tatem, standing waiting for the *Robert Fulton* on the crowded pier at 125th Street, she used to feel them streaming out of everyone there to enter her, making her part of what seemed a far-reaching, wide-ranging confraternity.[71]

NOTES

1. This development is best exemplified by Brent Edwards's important work, *The Practice of Diaspora* (Cambridge: Harvard University Press, 2003). While Edwards is especially interested in the transatlantic commingling of labor movements, the Anglophone and the Francophone, in this chapter I concentrate on the transatlantic commingling of languages. It is important to recognize that for some African-American authors (Ralph Ellison, for instance), diaspora is probably not the most vital issue.

2. R. E. Park, "The Conflict and Fusion of Cultures with Special Reference to the Negro," *Journal of Negro History* 4 (1919): 116.

3. E. F. Frazier, *The Negro Family in the United States* (Chicago: University of Chicago Press, 1939), 21.

4. Gilles Deleuze and Felix Guattari, *On the Line,* trans. John Johnston (New York: Semiotext(e), 1983), 1–68.

5. See, for instance, Philip D. Curtin, *The Atlantic Slave Trade* (Madison: University of Wisconsin Press, 1969); James Rawley, *Transatlantic Slave Trade* (New York: Norton, 1981).

6. Patricia Jones-Jackson, *When Roots Die: Endangered Traditions on the Sea Islands* (Athens: University of Georgia Press, 1987), 9.

7. Lorenzo Dow Turner, *Africanisms in The Gullah Dialect* (Chicago: University of Chicago Press, 1949), 2. Turner's work has been affirmed and extended in several recent collections. See, for instance, *The African Heritage of American English*, ed. Joseph E. Holloway and Winifred K. Vass (Bloomington: Indiana University Press, 1993); and *The Crucible of Carolina: Essays in the Development of Gullah Language and Culture*, ed. Michael Montgomery (Athens: University of Georgia Press, 1994). There have also been challenges to Turner, a debate collected in *Africanisms in Afro-American Language Varieties*, ed. Salikoko S. Mufwene (Athens: University of Georgia Press, 1993).

8. Melville J. Herskovits, *The Myth of the Negro Past* (New York: Harper Brothers, 1941), 6.

9. Ibid., 6–7.

10. For a detailed discussion of the analytic vocabulary of "nesting" and "cradling," see my introduction to this volume, "Planet and America: Set and Subset."

11. Robert A. Hall, *Pidgin and Creole Languages* (Ithaca: Cornell University Press, 1966).

12. Ibid., xi.

13. Ibid., 107–8.

14. T. L. Markey, "Editor's Note," to Hugo Schuchart's *The Ethnography of Variation: Selected Writings on Pidgins and Creoles*, ed. and trans. T. L. Markey (Ann Arbor, Mich.: Karoma, 1979), xxi.

15. Hugo Schuchart, "On Lingua Franca," in *Ethnography of Variation*, 26–47, quotation from 27. The essay is also collected in *Pidgin and Creole Languages: Selected Essays by Hugo Schuchardt*, trans. Glenn G. Gilbert (London: Cambridge University Press, 1980), 65–88.

16. Schuchart, "On Lingua Franca," 26, 32, 27–28.

17. For a contemporary plea in this spirit, see Doris Sommer, *Bilingual Aesthetics: A New Sentimental Education* (Durham, N.C.: Duke University Press, 2004).

18. I am thinking, of course, of Samuel Huntington.

19. Schuchardt, "Saramaccan," in *Ethnography of Variation*, 75–76.

20. Hall, *Pidgin and Creole Languages*, 141.

21. William A. Stewart, "Observations (1966) on the Problems of Defining Negro Dialect," postscript to remarks made in April 1966 at the Conference on the Language Component in the Training of Teachers of English and Reading, held in Washington, D.C., by the Center for Applied Linguistics and the National Council of Teachers of English, reprinted in *Perspectives on Black English*, ed. J. Dillard (The Hague: Mouton, 1975), 57–64, quotation from 63.

22. William A. Stewart, "Continuity and Change in American Negro Dialects," *The Florida FL Reporter*, vol. 6, no.1 (Spring 1968), 3–4, 14–16, 18, reprinted in *Perspectives on Black English*, 233–47, quotation from 243.

23. Ibid., 244–45.

24. Ibid., 234.

25. Ibid., 234.

26. William Labov, *Language in the Inner City: Studies in the Black English Vernacular* (Philadelphia: University of Pennsylvania Press, 1972).

27. This is a crude summary of Labov's complex argument in "Contraction, Deletion, and Inherent Variability of the English Copula," in *Language in the Inner City*, 65–129. For an illuminating discussion of Labov in the context of Mark Twain, see Jonathan Arac, *"Huckleberry Finn" as Idol and Target: The Functions of Criticism in Our Time* (Madison: University of Wisconsin Press, 1997), esp. 203–6.

28. Labov, *Language in the Inner City*, 68.

29. Ibid., 130.

30. Ibid., 131.

31. Ibid., 226.

32. For a good account of Chomsky's impact on linguistics, see Howard Gardner, *The Mind's New Science: A History of the Cognitive Revolution* (New York: Basic Books, 1985).

33. Steven Pinker, *The Language Instinct: How the Mind Creates Language* (New York: HarperPerennial, 1995).

34. Labov, *Language in the Inner City*, 217; Pinker, *The Language Instinct*, 31.

35. Pinker, *The Language Instinct*, 31.

36. Labov, *Language in the Inner City*, 222; Pinker, *The Language Instinct*, 31.

37. See for instance, Daniel Dennett, *Consciousness Explained* (Boston: Little, Brown, 1991); Jerry Fodor, *The Language of Thought* (Cambridge: Harvard University Press, 1975); Gerald Edelman, *Bright Air, Brilliant Fire: On the Matter of the Mind* (New York: Basic Books, 1992).

38. Ned Block, "The Mind as the Software of the Brain," in *An Invitation to Cognitive Science*, 4 vols., 2nd ed. (Cambridge: MIT Press, 1995), 3:377–426.

39. Antonio R. Damasio, *Descartes' Error: Emotion, Reason, and the Human Brain* (New York: Avon Books, 1994); Damasio, *The Feeling of What Happens* (New York: Harcourt Brace, 1999); Damasio, *Looking for Spinoza: Joy, Sorrow, and the Feeling Brain* (Orlando, Fla.: Harcourt, 2003).

40. Damasio, *The Feeling of What Happens*, 186.

41. Robert Chaudenson, *Creolization of Language and Culture*, rev. in collaboration with Salikoko S. Mufwene, trans. Sheri Pargman et al. (London: Routledge, 2001), 79.

42. Ibid., 309–10.

43. The essays by David Palumbo-Liu and Susan Stanford Friedman in this volume are exemplary.

44. Herskovits devotes almost half of *Myth of the Negro Past* to two long chapters, "Africanisms in Secular Life" and "Africanisms in Religious Life," discussing at length West African influences on family structure and magical rituals.

45. Aside from the three mentioned below, I would like to acknowledge the following: *African Roots/American Cultures: Africa in the Creation of the Americas*, ed. Sheila S. Walker (London: Rowman and Littlefield, 2001); *Africanisms in American Culture*, ed. Joseph E. Holloway (Bloomington: Indiana University Press, 1990); Grey Gundaker, *Signs of Diaspora, Diaspora of Signs* (New York: Oxford University Press, 1998); Frederick Kaufman and John P. Guckin, *The African Roots of Jazz* (New York: Alfred Publishing Co., 1979); Betty M. Kuyk, *African Voices in the African American Heritage* (Bloomington: Indiana University Press, 2003); Sterling Stuckey, *Slave Culture* (New York: Oxford University Press, 1987), esp. 3–97; John Vlach, *By the Work of Their Hands* (Ann Arbor: University of Michigan Press, 1991).

46. *Drums and Shadows: Survival Studies among the Georgia Coastal Negroes*, by the Savannah Unit, Georgia Writers' Project, Work Projects Administration (Athens: University of Georgia Press, 1940).

47. Robert Farris Thompson, *Flash of the Spirit: African and Afro-American Art and Philosophy* (New York: Random House, 1983), xiv. For related arguments, see also Thompson, *Africa, Art in Motion* (Berkeley: University of California Press, 1974).

48. Alan Lomax, *The Land Where Blues Began* (New York: Pantheon Books, 1993), xiii. Other scholars support this conclusion. See, for instance, Portia K. Maultsy, "Africanisms in African-American Music," in Holloway, *Africanisms in American Culture*, 185–210; Olly Wilson, "'It Don' Mean a Thing If It Ain't Got That Swing': The Relation between African and African-American Music," in Walker, *African Roots/ American Cultures*, 153–68.

49. Alan Lomax, "The Homogeneity of African-Afro-American Musical Style," in *Afro-American Anthropology: Contemporary Perspectives*, ed. Norman E. Whitten Jr. and John F. Szwed (New York: Free Press, 1970), 181–201, quotation from 181.

50. Ibid., 189.

51. Ibid., 199–200.

52. I am inspired here by Ernst Mayr's discussion of the difference between biology and physics. The latter is governed by the "law of physics," which can predict outcomes with great precision given a determinate input. In biology, however, there are no comparable "laws of biology," since the multiple levels of aggregation and interaction make outcomes highly unpredictable. See Mayr, *Toward a New Philosophy of Biology* (Cambridge: Harvard University Press, 1988), 18–19.

53. Derek Walcott, "A Tropical Bestiary," in *The Castaway and Other Poems* (London: Jonathan Cape, 1965), 21.

54. The phrase is from the poem "The phrases of a patois rooted in this clay hillside," from Walcott, *The Bounty* (New York: Farrar, Straus, Giroux, 1997), 38.

55. Kofi Agawu, *African Rhythm: A Northern Ewe Perspective* (Cambridge: Cambridge University Press, 1995), 6.

56. J. H. Kwabena Nketia, *The Music of Africa* (New York: Norton, 1974).

57. J. H. Kwabena Nketia, *Drumming in Akan Communities in Ghana* (London: Thomas Nelson and Sons, 1963), 32–50.

58. Jack Berry, "Language Systems and Literature," in *The African Experience*, ed. John Paden and Edward Soja (Evanston, Ill.: Northwestern University Press, 1970), 87.

59. Paul Oliver, Tony Russell, Robert M. M. Dixon, John Godrich, and Howard Rye, *Yonder Come the Blues: The Evolution of a Genre* (Cambridge: Cambridge University Press, 2001), 1–12, 90–105; Robert Palmer, *Deep Blues* (New York: Viking, 1981), 1–47.

60. Houston Baker, *Blues, Ideology, and Afro-American Literature: A Vernacular Theory* (Chicago: University of Chicago Press, 1984), 3. Baker's point is amply substantiated by an impressive collection of essays, *The Jazz Cadence of American Culture*, ed. Robert G. O'Meally (New York: Columbia University Press, 1998), which extends the discussion from blues to jazz.

61. Sherley Anne Williams, "The Blues Roots of Contemporary Afro-American Poetry," in *Afro-American Literature*, ed. Dexter Fisher and Robert B. Stepto (New York: Modern Language Association, 1978), 72–87.

62. Edward Kamau Brathwaite, "Jazz and the West Indian Novel," in *Roots* (Ann Arbor: University of Michigan Press, 1993), 55–110.

63. Edward Brathwaite, "The Making of the Drum," in *Masks* (London: Oxford University Press, 1968), 7–10, quotation fron 8.

64. Wilson Harris, introduction to *The Womb of Space: The Cross-Cultural Imagination* (Westport, Conn.: Greenwood Press, 1983), xv–xx, quotation from xix. Italics in original.

65. Wilson Harris, "History, Fable and Myth in the Caribbean and Guianas," in *Explorations* (Mundelstrup, Denmark: Dangaroo Press, 1981), 20–42.

66. Ibid., 25, 26–27.

67. Gloria Naylor, *Mama Day* (New York: Vintage, 1989), 5.

68. Ibid., 312.

69. Paule Marshall, *Praisesong for the Widow* (New York: Dutton, 1983), 38–39.

70. Marshall, *Praisesong for the Widow*, 250.

71. Ibid., 249.

Index